NEW HOMELESS AND OLD

*Community
and the
Skid Row Hotel*

Conflicts in Urban and Regional Development
a series edited by John Logan and Todd Swanstrom

NEW HOMELESS AND OLD

Community and the Skid Row Hotel

Charles Hoch
and
Robert A. Slayton

TEMPLE UNIVERSITY PRESS
Philadelphia

Temple University Press, Philadelphia 19122
Copyright © 1989 by Temple University. All rights reserved
Published 1989
Printed in the United States of America

The paper used in this publication meets the minimum
requirements of American National Standard for Information
Sciences—Permanence of Paper for Printed Library Materials,
ANSI Z39.48-1984

Library of Congress
Library of Congress Cataloging-in-Publication Data

Hoch, Charles, 1948–
New homeless and old: community and the skid row hotel / Charles
Hoch and Robert A. Slayton.
p.   cm. — (Conflicts in urban and regional development)
Bibliography: p.
Includes index.
ISBN 0-87722-600-8 (alk. paper)
1. Urban poor—United States.   2. Single-room occupancy hotels—
United States.   3. Homelessness—United States.   I. Slayton,
Robert A.   II. Title.   III. Series.
HV4045.H63 1989
362.5′0973—dc19   88-21669
                                                                CIP

For Susan Stall
and Rita Slayton

CONTENTS

ACKNOWLEDGMENTS

Work on this book began as part of practical efforts to protect and provide low-rent housing for the homeless in Chicago. A study of SRO hotels, funded by the Chicago Community Trust and conducted jointly by the Jewish Council on Urban Affairs (JCUA) and the Community Emergency Shelter Organization (CESO), offered evidence of the value of hotel living for the single poor. We found the results convincing and used these insights as a point of departure for the preparation of this book.

Diane Spicer (CESO) coordinated and implemented the research on SRO hotels with the energetic assistance of Joni Levin Saffrin (JCUA) and the thoughtful guidance of Alan Goldberg (JCUA) and Susan Walker (CESO). The excellent interviewing by Irene Gooden and Sheila Ellsberg, under the careful direction of Karen Corrigan of the Survey Research Lab at the University of Illinois, ensured valid survey results. Scott Geron of the Taylor Institute provided crucial assistance in data management. In addition, the Chicago Urban League and its president, James W. Compton, provided critical financial and staff support for this project.

NEW HOMELESS AND OLD

Community
and the
Skid Row Hotel

1 Introduction

Descriptions of the homeless in the 1980s usually depict vulnerable people enduring undeserved deprivation. Research studies and policy reports contrast the demographic characteristics of the "new" homeless with the "old" homeless on Skid Row, using human interest stories to spotlight the special vulnerabilities that make today's homeless individuals deserving subjects for our sympathy and care.

This perception of the homeless as a new social problem gained popularity among reporters and analysts documenting the effects of the 1981–82 economic recession. The human interest stories they told were not only descriptive accounts of personal suffering but included speculations about the responsibility of others. In other words, homelessness was presented not as an individual problem with bad social consequences, but as a social problem that overwhelms individuals.

The story of Jerry Peterson, for example, blames his homeless condition on the effects of economic dislocation and unfair competition rather than flaws in moral character. Jerry Peterson did not reject the work ethic; he was simply unsuccessful in a competitive world.

> Seven years ago, Peterson owned a carpet cleaning business and had just bought a house in Streamwood [a Chicago suburb] for $54,900. He started cleaning carpets in 1975 to supplement his income as a police officer in Rolling Meadows, a job he worked for nearly ten years after leaving the U.S. Army in the mid 1960s. When business boomed, he quit the police force and started Tri-R-Carpet, a company that worked for apartment complexes and other large customers.
>
> "We had more business than we could handle," he recalls. "I was making about $30,000. Then a couple of big companies moved in and wiped us out."
>
> Peterson found himself too old to return to the police force, so he took on part-time work as a private security officer that turned into full-time work when Tri-R-Carpet went under in 1978. Guarding shopping malls, hospitals and race tracks is unskilled labor that doesn't pay much, so that even when he was able to fit two full-time positions into his schedule, he still fell farther and farther behind on mortgage and utility payments and other bills he, his wife and four children were generating.
>
> The family lost their house in 1981 and began to live a nomadic, Dickensian existence in the northwest suburbs, frequently cooking on camping stoves when the gas was turned off and seldom having a telephone. They filed

for bankruptcy in the spring of 1982, and since then have found it impossible to buy anything on credit.

Unable to make sufficient income for an apartment large enough for the entire family, the family split up. The mother took the two youngest children to live with their oldest married daughter in Florida. Another daughter moved in with friends to finish high school in Hoffman Estates. Jerry moved into a tiny basement apartment in a house owned by a cousin.[1]

Besides stories of class slippage, reporters have also told tragic stories of how the vulnerable poor struggle to survive in the face of economic decline. These accounts emphasize the limitations of poor education, the disadvantages of poverty, and other characteristics of the homeless that frustrate individual efforts to make ends meet. Unlike the "old" homeless on Skid Row who allegedly rejected the work ethic and other social responsibilities, the "new" homeless act responsibly but are overcome by a combination of their own vulnerabilities and changing circumstances. The most moving reports are those describing the suffering of single mothers and their children, like the story of Odetta:

Cloaked in quiet dignity, "Odetta," a black woman in her early thirties, softly recounted her odyssey to the women's shelter. Once she had lived with her two children, now seven and two years old, in a small apartment in East Baltimore. About six months ago, word came that her mother had fallen ill and was not expected to live.

As often happens in families, the responsibility for caring for the mother fell to her daughter, so Odetta dutifully packed up her children and journeyed to Detroit to be by her mother's side. The older woman survived and the family judged it best to return to Baltimore, bringing the mother with them. In that way Odetta could resume her former life as well as care for her mother. However, the mother's illness and the travel expenses consumed the family's slender resources, and Odetta found herself having no place to stay in Baltimore. . . .

Odetta said over and over again she never thought anything like this could happen to her: she had always provided a home for her children and had believed they were safe from the harsher realities of life. But she had really been afraid when she could find no place to stay, crying, "How could I sleep on the streets with those children?" [2]

Another change is that even when the subject's profile matches that of the "old" homeless on Skid Row, the contemporary version offers tales of hope and dignity rather than despair and degradation. For example, William Breaky and Pamela Fischer write about their encounter with a drunk in just this fashion.

We met "Freddy" in Fells Point, sitting on a bench with two other seemingly drunken men. He talked with us freely about his alcoholism and his life on the streets. He told us about a hiding-hole where he spends the night, but would not tell us its location. As we talked with him further about his past and his future, he asked if we would help him. We expressed some interest in directing him to help and discussed several possibilities. He wanted us to give him a ride to the hospital and as we talked, one of his companions jumped to his feet and joined in the conversation. It was his contention that there is no help for the Skid Row alcoholic and that all our treatment methods are futile. As we walked away, his voice rang in our ears. "Can you really help him? Is there anything you can do to help him?" [3]

The alcoholic, the addict, the mentally ill, the poor single mother, and the structurally unemployed, in stories like these, testify to a common social ill, the "new" and growing privation of homelessness. The stories evoke compassion, arouse a sense of moral outrage, and identify many reasons for homelessness tied to the particular vulnerabilities of different groups of people. The "new" homeless now appear deserving, but the causes of their condition appear extremely complex. The interventions are correspondingly complex, as various professionals, paraprofessionals and advocates propose specialized care for two-parent families, single mothers with children, mentally ill individuals, runaway youths, battered women, and the physically handicapped. Appropriate professional skills and organizational services are matched with the need of a segment of the homeless. This need becomes the social problem which these specialized caretakers can satisfy. And as the needs of various groups of homeless increasingly justify specialized treatment, those treating the homeless soon perceive this need as the reason for homelessness itself.

We believe the popular conception of the "new" homeless needs to be drastically modified if we are to avoid manufacture of a false social problem and the danger of reinstitutionalization. This does not mean we intend to blame the homeless for their predicament, as some conservative critics have done. On the contrary, we find the suffering endured by the homeless to be undeserved, but not for the sorts of reasons offered in the popular human interest stories. The problem with these stories is that they focus public attention on *individual* vulnerabilities rather than the *institutional* roots of homelessness.

Public service providers and professional caretakers have thereby unwittingly promoted a politics of compassion in their efforts to secure the development and expansion of specialized shelters and services for the homeless. While expressing genuine regret in building what are little more than modernized versions of the old lodging-house dormitory, the caretakers make pragmatic appeals for beds and services from local philanthropic organizations and municipalities. These efforts are not only rapidly expanding the number of these dormitories for the poor but are legitimizing their institutional value as a solution to the problem of homelessness. Paradoxically, what at the turn of the century represented the worst housing accommodations to both residents and reformers alike in the 1980s have become an allegedly necessary if unattractive solution to the problem of homelessness.

The most forward-thinking have proposed plans for "transitional" housing that would provide long-term shelter for the homeless who show promising signs of improvement. The intent is to help the previously homeless get "back on their feet" by providing a secure living environment managed by professional staff. This policy of care, while valuable for treating the illness and disorientation of the homeless, mistakes these conditions as causes. The professional training of the caretakers in social pathology, mental illness, and the culture of poverty sometimes keeps them from seeing the urban community of the single working poor as a community with benefits for its members. As a result, the homeless become the latest in a series of needy groups whose social significance is defined by caretaking institutions outside the control of the urban poor themselves. The result of this policy very likely could be another institutionalized population like the one in public housing.

Stories and reports that treat the moral worth and dignity of homeless individuals as if this were a new development mislead the public. Our research, which includes both historical scholarship and recent survey analysis, demonstrates that the homeless, both past and present, are capable of creating coherent and complex social communities. In addition, the highest social priority in these communities was, and continues to be, personal autonomy. In other words, the "new" homeless are really no more deserving than the "old" homeless, if individual dignity and moral character are the standards of distinction. The contemporary homeless are not more deserving than their Skid Row predecessors, but simply the unfortunate latecomers to a homeless condition previously thought to have been solved with the physical destruction of Skid Row.

Furthermore, the "new" homeless do not, as a kind of afflicted population or group, represent a unique or even an uncommon social problem. The "new" homeless endure the same economic difficulties as the "old" homeless and have the same class origins. Both come mainly from the ranks of the urban poor. The differences in demographic characteristics and vulnerabilities between the two reflect differences mainly in the composition and afflictions of the urban poor. For instance, the "new" homeless are more likely to be younger and single mothers with children because the contemporary urban poor are now disproportionately composed of younger, single mothers with children. The poor have always been more vulnerable.

The number of poor people in the United States increased rapidly throughout the 1970s and peaked during the 1981–82 recession. Although the proportion of households below poverty has declined slightly since that time, compelling evidence indicates that income among the poor has also declined. This means that while some of the poor have benefited from the economic recovery of the mid-1980's, others are experiencing greater privation. Most of these people are concentrated in the inner city.

Besides the economic uncertainty imposed by lower income, the urban poor have also had to confront the declining availability of low-rent housing. In particular, the single poor lack access to the affordable single room occupancy (SRO) hotels formerly concentrated in Skid Row communities where the single poor had found ways to make ends meet. We argue that the primary reason for the unexpected rise in the number of homeless people and their persistent dependence has more to do with the nearly wholesale destruction of the SRO hotels during the past thirty years than either the changing social composition or personal vulnerabilities of the urban poor. Furthermore, we contend that the implementation of public policies to solve an earlier social problem, Skid Row itself, laid the foundations for today's urban homeless problem. Using historical argument, we recast the conception of the "new" homeless as members of the urban single poor who have lost access to the community institutions that enabled the urban homeless in earlier generations to maintain their autonomy and avoid dependence on the formal caretaking system. Urban renewal destroyed not only cheap housing but a unique form of housing, the SRO hotel, that contributed significantly (if inadequately) to the maintenance of social community among the poor residents on Skid Row.

Unless existing urban development policies are changed to discourage the destruction of low-rent housing and encourage its provision, the number of homeless will continue to grow, producing social costs much greater than the costs policy makers, developers, caretakers, and other professionals presently project. Allowing present urban redevelopment practices (including both abandonment and gentrification) to continue unchecked will not only intensify the spatial and economic displacement of the working poor, but in so doing, increase the number of dependent homeless people requiring public assistance. We question, for example, how much the tax benefits of speculative land developments offset the social costs of providing for those who are displaced. But even more important in the long run is the impact the destruction of low-rent housing will have on the economic viability of the downtown. The rapid growth of postindustrial cities like Chicago, New York, and Los Angeles has already begun to change the urban economy by drastically increasing the demand for both low-wage and high-wage service-sector employees. Yet, at the same time, the efforts of local growth coalitions to capture the value of land speculation downtown is destroying the housing for low-wage service workers. The prospects of labor shortages due to expensive commuting and housing costs are likely, and already exist in some areas.

Thus, the contemporary homeless are not a new kind of social group, but members of the single working poor victimized by urban policies that encourage the destruction of SROs and other types of low-income housing, changes in the national economy that increase unemployment and underemployment among the independent poor, and welfare policies that undermine the social autonomy of the dependent poor. A politics of compassion that identifies the vulnerabilities of the homeless as the cause of their predicament too easily overlooks the social and economic history of the urban working poor and their struggle for affordable shelter. Although the homeless do suffer a disproportionate number of the social and physical vulnerabilities that might afflict us all, their poverty combined with the loss of affordable SRO housing accounts for their homelessness. This book tells the story of the homeless in Chicago in order to uncover the roots of contemporary homelessness and what should be done to put an end to it.

Organization of the Book

The book uses the case of Chicago to tell the story of the changing relationship between the SRO hotels and the single urban poor between 1870 and the present. For a century Chicago has been an important center for transient laborers with thousands of cheap hotel rooms to house them. A substantial, if greatly diminished, portion of this housing stock remains to this day.

In chapters 2 through 6 we reconstruct the history of the SRO hotel in Chicago from the wealth of archival material and early studies of Chicago's homeless. By conducting a case study in depth, we provide a fuller, more complete understanding of the SRO hotel, the role it played in housing the single poor, and the policy context in which it operated. We argue that Skid Row hotels provided the single poor with a form of shelter that provided not only an affordable and private place to sleep but also a location accessible to a range of urban services and activities necessary to make the life of a single person of limited means secure and sociable. The layout of the SRO hotel was suited to those who desired personal privacy but had limited means.

As we studied the historical record, we focused on the relationship between the SRO hotel and the social community of the urban single poor. Instead of presuming that residents of the SRO hotels or the hotels themselves presented a social problem, we assumed that the hotels offered a solution to the individual shelter problems of the urban single poor. The evidence of autonomy and community we uncover provides a powerful antidote to the simplistic, negative stereotype of Skid Row that gained legitimacy from the reports of Skid Row offered by journalists and researchers. Our complaint is that the social and economic viability of the SRO hotel as a community institution serving the urban single poor has been obscured by interest and emphasis on Skid Row pathology and by attempts to gain sympathy for today's homeless population.

We analyze the contemporary condition of the SRO hotels in Chicago in chapters 7 and 8, not only laying to rest the stereotypical misconceptions of the hotel residents but analyzing the social and economic contributions the SRO hotels make to the personal security and autonomy of the single poor who live in them. The misperception of the hotels as breeding grounds for social disease continues to legitimize public policies designed to remove and replace the hotels. In chapter 9, we explore the effects of these policies in the 1970s and 1980s, arguing that the loss of SRO hotels was more the result of public initiative and subsidy than of the economic pressure of the urban land market.

In the last three chapters we take up the social problem of the "new" homeless and possible remedies. Chapter 10 includes a review of the policy debates surrounding the definition of the "new" homeless. Despite the intensity of the disagreements among proponents of greater social control, expanded entitlements, or compassionate care, we contend that compassion has become the most popular justification for the provision of shelters and other caretaking facilities, which have become the primary de facto policy response to the increasing number of homeless people. Unfortunately, as we point out in chapter 11, this growing shelter care system suffers from serious limitations that threaten to increase the permanent dependence of the homeless.

We conclude in chapter 12 that the policies for coping with the homeless should not focus on the homeless people, but the institutions and actors who benefit directly and indirectly from their predicament. This means concentrating on changing public policies that encourage the destruction of affordable housing, especially SRO hotels, and instituting policies that foster preservation rehabilitation and even new construction instead. We do not argue for a return to Skid Row, but rather that those interested in solving the homeless problem recognize that the working poor still manage to maintain autonomy and community in settings like SRO hotels.

2 A New Kind of Housing: Middle-Class Transients and the Industrial City

The industrialization of the United States in the late nineteenth and early twentieth centuries was largely a private-sector affair. There was limited governmental input into policy decisions as to what kinds of industries would be formed or what kinds of cities would be built, especially before the Progressive Era of reform. Businessmen decided not only the type of product their factory would produce but also where the plants would be located, and the type of transportation a metropolis provided to get workers to their jobs. These decisions had enormous impact not only on profit and loss but also on cities and their neighborhoods. Thus, many of the institutional aspects of community life in U.S. cities were a direct result of private decisions and needs.

The pattern holds true particularly of housing policy for the employed and unemployed transient, both middle and working class. First, these populations were a direct product of the creation or expansion of industries, and their labor needs. In the cities, for example, the service industries exploded, as department stores and offices became major employers of middle-class women and men. At the same time, the conquest of a continent via railroads, mines, industries, and farms meant that a pool of transient labor had to be available for work anywhere in the country.

The home base for all these toilers at intermittent jobs, whether middle or working class, was the urban metropolis. It was here that the middle class found a burgeoning downtown employment market and that the transient working class had facilities for shelter, food, recreation, and companionship. This kind of market, these facilities, were present in the entire range of U.S. cities, from smaller regional centers like Omaha to world capitals like New York.

The social response of these cities to migrants was also dominated by the private sector. New forms of housing arose, reflecting not only the transient working conditions imposed by the marketplace but the low wages as well. Furthermore, these buildings—the rooming houses and the lodging houses, the cage hotels and dorms and flops—were designed, constructed, and purchased almost exclusively by speculators and private developers. Similarly, services like meals and entertainment shifted from group activity to a more open, individualistic approach.

The dominance of the private sector does not mean that other sectors did not deal with the issue. Local government provided shelter in a variety of ways, from the police station flop to the municipal lodging house. In addition, the not-for-profit sector established charitable hotels and missions to try to meet the needs of the poor. But these efforts, though important, were clearly secondary. The primary response to housing needs, the one used by most members of the transient population, was created by the private sector. Far more middle-class singles lived in rooming houses than at all the YMCAs and YWCAs put together, just as most workers stayed in cage hotels, not missions.

The great irony, however, was that the public policy debate over housing for the transient poor—the homeless and near homeless—was and still is solely based on comparisons of these three sectors: private, government, and not-for-profit. Unrecognized and uncredited (a situation that still exists) was another system of social prioritization, management of resources, and provision of services, the one devised and implemented by residents themselves. These individuals had a firm set of values that valued personal autonomy and privacy, and they made shelter choices that reflected this. The alternative they created, despite its absence from formal policy debates, was both realistic and humane in its approach. We will examine it closely in an attempt to raise it to equal status in both past and present policy discussions, and ultimately will argue for it as the basis for an alternative policy to current programs.

We begin this chapter by explaining the relationship between industrialization and migration and the resulting change in shelter needs. Next, we explore the impact these changes had on cities, particularly Chicago. We conclude this chapter by detailing exactly how this process worked itself out in the case of one population, the transient middle class.

Industrialization and Migration

The Industrial Revolution produced massive mobility in the American populace. Large numbers of people moved from farmstead to city, seeking employment in the new, burgeoning industrial sector. Millions more came from abroad to swell the work force, filling the need for laborers as well as for skilled operatives. In cities this influx resulted in an unprecedented turnover of population. Stephen Thernstrom, for example, has documented how Boston's population changed almost entirely each decade from 1880 to 1920, as most of the citizenry left every ten years, to be replaced by an entirely new group of residents.[1]

Turnover was also evident in factories. Of course, the dirtier and more dangerous the work, the lower the wages, the less likely any employee would stay. In the Chicago stockyards, for example, the worst jobs were in the fertilizer plants because the odor was horrendous, even for an industry known for its foul smells. In one week during November 1900, for example, one shop hired 126 men, but by Saturday all but 6 had quit. One student of hobo history has argued that "the average East Coast manufacturing center [at the turn of the century] had a turnover of more than half the local unskilled labor force every decade."[2]

Chicago was at the center of this industrial change. Its growth was a product of the massive industrialization of the United States in the late nineteenth and early twentieth centuries. As industry grew, the city expanded from 298,877 people living on 35 square miles in 1870 to 1,698,575 on 190 square miles in 1900. By 1930 the population had doubled again.[3]

The city became, as historian Kenneth Allsop put it, "the greatest labor exchange of any city in the United States," supplying regular as well as seasonal and casual labor to an entire region of the country. One 1914 study demonstrated that there were nearly 50 million people within one night's railroad trip of Chicago, approximately half the population of the continental United States at the time. The report explained how Chicago's labor pool fed an area extending west to Omaha, east to Pittsburgh, north to Minneapolis, and south to Nashville. Forty railroads radiated out from the city, America's railroad axis, and there were 3,000 miles of track within the municipal limits. Because of its role as the national transportation hub, as many as 500,000 workers without permanent homes regularly flowed in and out of the Windy City. It was common, for example, to see large gangs of railroad workers, called "gandy dancers" (because of the shuffling back-and-forth movement they made while working on the tracks), shipped as far as 400 and even 1,000 miles to work on distant railroad projects. As late as 1922 the city still had more than 200 private employment agencies that placed a quarter-million men annually, in addition to the constant hiring going on at factory gates all over town. Chicago's "Main Stem" along West Madison Street continued to be the foremost gathering place of hoboes in the country, prompting one tramp to comment that he felt better in Chicago than "anywhere else in the world."[4]

The soaring growth in the transient working population of the city created a sudden and drastic need for inexpensive housing, a crisis exacerbated by the Great Fire of 1871. Housing decisions, therefore, rose out of the business context, a set of institutional, demographic, and economic opportunities (and constraints) that formed the matrix in which developers and landlords made investments in housing. But these decisions also helped determine the type of living quarters, the life-environment of a multitude of workers, across the United States and in the Windy City. Thus, whether the migrant to Chicago was an educated young lady from a small midwestern town looking for work as a secretary, the son of a peasant farmer in Slovakia seeking employment in the steel mills, or a migrant laborer pausing on the Main Stem SRO district between jobs, she or he needed a place to live. With the swelling population, the existing housing stock was insufficient to meet the need; new forms, new buildings, had to be created to deal with the problem.

The SRO hotel was designed as a way to maximize density and provide for the minimal needs of these migrants, most of whom came as single individuals. In some ways, however, the term "single room occupancy hotel" is a misnomer, a current term to describe current conditions. Developers, speculators, and landlords created these buildings to house poor, transient middle- and working-class single persons (and even some families) at the lowest cost. Some units occupied more than one room, and in some cases one large room was a kind of mass dwelling unto itself, as in workers' dormitories where multiple beds were lined up against the wall. In some cases there were few of the services we normally associate with "hotel style" living and none of the amenities, although most provided at least some of these facilities. Yet, all these buildings housed one kind of resident—poor, transient working people—who moved back and forth within a self-defined poverty scale seeking dignity and autonomy. This population is central to the concept of the single-room facility as it is used in this study.

Because our definition of an SRO is based on clientele, as well as the physical characteristics of the housing and the type of services rendered, we have included a wide variety of buildings and arrangements. All of these fit the criteria of industrial America's new minimal housing, designed to serve the city's most recent additions.

These buildings were also part of a unique type of downtown community. SRO districts retained the urban environment of the older walking city, where all kinds of buildings and activities—industrial, commercial, residential, entertainment, and recreational—existed within the same limited area, thus emphasizing the diversity traditionally associated with cities. This downtown location, however, was also dictated by economics; it provided access to offices and stores for the middle class, and to transportation hubs for the transient workers.

By the first decade of the twentieth century three major transient districts had emerged in Chicago. The largest of these was on the West Side, in the area between the Chicago River and Halsted Street, and Randolph to Harrison streets. Lodging houses were more common in this section, but there were also plenty of rooms available. The second district was on the North Side, from the Chicago River north to Division Street (later to North Avenue), from Rush Street on the east to Wells Street on the west. As noted earlier, rooming houses were more common in this area. The third section was on the South Side of the city, from Sixteenth to Thirty-Third streets, from Prairie Avenue to Clark Street. This included parts of the black belt, so an entirely different set of conditions prevailed.[5]

SRO districts were typical of industrial cities; they existed in just about every urban center. These neighborhoods, their distinctive housing stock, and the historical and current policy issues they created were common to the urban experience in the United States, not unique to Chicago.

The Boarding House

SRO hotels were generally associated with the working class. Although many of these buildings were dedicated to shelter at low rentals for this group, workers were not the only clients of the SRO. The middle class also had its own type of SRO housing, with a separate district, a distinct building type, and a particular social arrangement, which though unique in some ways, in others mirrored the priorities of all SRO residents. By studying this group, therefore, we make use of an initial example of SRO life, enabling us to explore basic assumptions about the link between housing and social structure.

Before the industrial boom of the late nineteenth and early twentieth centuries, the standard quarters for middle-class single people, especially those in town temporarily, was the boarding house. According to the terms of this arrangement, a tenant would receive not only the use of a room but meals as well. All boarders in the house would assemble in the dining room at set times and break bread together, a critical element of boarding-house life.

Boarding was considered a humane system, providing for conversation both during and after meals, as well as the development of friendships. As depicted in the idealized vision of the boarding house, the parlor could be used for a friendly game of cards, or to receive visitors. Summer found the boarders gathered on the porch or the front steps; in winter they might play cards. In general, the arrangements were likened more to a family than to an impersonal apartment complex; as one writer put it, boarding houses had "something of the home element."[6]

The people who stayed at these boarding houses were generally middle class, with occupations such as clerk, secretary, and salesman. Eventually these individuals began to turn to the rooming house as their housing of choice, dooming the boarding house as an urban housing form. There were three primary reasons for this shift.

First, the boarding house could not handle the massive numbers of young middle-class men and women who flocked to the city to take positions in offices, retail stores, and other service industries. Boarding-house facilities were limited and difficult to establish; the housekeeper had to be willing not only to maintain the premises but to provide meals and other services as well. The rapidly increasing demand for housing, a result of private-sector labor needs, produced facilities that were more basic: they provided shelter and nothing else. In addition, the system of furnished rooms asked little of tenants in regard to capital expenditure: neither furniture nor security deposit was required. This was a critical factor, given the limited wage scale.

Second, the reality of life in a boarding house was also far different than that portrayed by nostalgic reformers. Meals were often monotonous, and their quality depended on the culinary skills of the landlady. Boarders had to be on time for meals or else miss them; payment, however, was in advance, so the boarder paid for all meals, whether he or she ate them or not.

Even worse, landladies often had little respect for boarders' privacy or well-being. An article entitled "Landladies I Have Known," for example (written by "The Bachelor Maid"), told how "all the comforts of home" referred to "the following delights: a close watch on your coming and going, confidential and fluent revelations as to the most intimate miseries of your landlady's existence . . . paucity of towels . . . slim lunches." One particular landlady "had as one of her strong points the motherly interests with which she kept tab on the movements of her lodgers . . . it was unappreciative and nasty of me to feel irritated when my breakfast greeting was 'Somebody's gas burned mighty late last night,' or 'I woke up at a quarter to one, and everybody had come in but Miss ———— .' " Other landladies included "the one who appropriated . . . hairpins, and abstracted . . . new hats from their boxes and gowns from their hangers, when we were out, in order to copy them . . . the one who posted the notice 'Two hot baths ONLY allowed per week'; and the one who regularly opened all letters and packages which came for me to see if she could not find proof that I was being made love to by a married man." [7]

In other words, boarding houses failed to provide autonomy and privacy. These were major goals of the new urban middle class, and especially of young people moving to the city in search of excitement and opportunity. The last thing they wanted was the rigid social control the boarding house represented. Middle-class migrants wanted the freedom to eat when, where, and what they wanted, and to answer to no one but themselves. As one critic put it, discussing the shift to restaurant meals, "the *café* accords with the free spirit of the times." One of the leading commentators on rooming houses at the turn of the century described this as the main difference between the two facilities: "The boarder eats and sleeps in the same place. The . . . 'roomer' sleeps in one place and 'takes his meals out.' " As a result, he stated with finality, "The lodger (or roomer) is not a boarder." By rejecting the boarding house, therefore, middle-class singles were already establishing social priorities. Even within a limited market for shelter, they rejected a supervised environment in favor of one that permitted greater autonomy and privacy. [8]

The Rooming House

For the middle class the alternative to the boarding house was the rooming house. The number of rooming houses in Chicago grew tremendously

TABLE 2-1

Boarding and Rooming Houses in Chicago, 1885–1915

YEAR	BOARDING HOUSES	ROOMING HOUSES
1885	742	492
1890	928	572
1895	875	988
1900	689	1,156
1905	451	1,483
1910	333	2,390
1915	230	2,424

Sources: *Chicago City Directory*, 1885–1915.

after 1900, while boarding houses became almost extinct. According to the *Chicago City Directory*, in 1885 there were 742 boarding houses and 492 rooming houses. In 1893 the number of furnished rooms overtook the number of boarding houses; and by 1915 the number of boarding houses had dropped to 230, whereas the number of rooming houses had increased dramatically, to 2,424 (see table 2-1). In addition, by the late 1920s the Illinois Lodging House Register listed 1,139 rooming and lodging houses on the near North Side alone, housing 23,007 people in rooms. This figure includes lodging houses (a different type of building entirely, which housed poor workers), as well as rooming houses. The housing in the district was largely rooming houses, however, so the drop-off is not as great as it would have been in other, similar transient districts. Still, fewer than six boarding houses were found in the area. In addition, when ninety blocks from this district were selected for closer examination by researchers from the University of Chicago, they found that 71 percent of all homes took in roomers. Another indication of the magnitude of this business was the scope of the Chicago Rooming House Association, which held lavish annual banquets and wrote of "this gigantic enterprise of furnishing accommodations and service to hundreds of thousands in Chicago . . . capital and energy . . . have reached such magnitudinous heights that combinations have been resorted to." [9]

This trend toward rooming houses was particularly prevalent among Chicago women. In 1880, 77 percent of the single women who rented rooms in commercial lodgings were boarders; by 1910 their proportion had dropped to 32 percent. Another indication was the shift away from boarding with private families; between 1880 and 1910 the proportion of single women who chose this housing alternative dropped from 92 percent to 52 percent. [10]

This change was typical of industrial cities at the turn of the century. By 1895 in Boston, for example, 83 percent of the households listed as living in boarding or rooming facilities were actually in rooming houses. In San Francisco boarding houses made up 40 percent of the commercial housing listed in the city directory in 1875, less than 10 percent in 1900, less than 1 percent in 1910.[11]

Rooming-house districts were areas that had once been fashionably middle class but that had gone out of style, with a resulting drop in the value of real estate. They were, therefore, the direct result of speculation in land and the resulting change in land prices. In Chicago the near North Side, which became the rooming-house district, was originally considered a stylish area because of its proximity to the downtown business, commercial, and entertainment districts. The 1893 World's Fair, however, led to the development of Hyde Park and the South Side lakeshore, and many middle-class Chicagoans moved to this new section. The extension of the elevated railways to the most distant north and south regions of the city meant that these suburban-like districts also began to attract residents. In addition, the creation of cable-car lines along Clark and Wells streets in 1885 led to a building boom in Lincoln Park, which drew population away from an older residential neighborhood. All this activity damaged the housing market on the near North Side, which enabled speculators to buy buildings at a cheap price, subdivide the apartments into rooms, then sell at a profit.[12]

The houses themselves were usually adaptations of large private residences, or even mansions. They were generally about twenty-five to forty years old, and three to four stories high. Landlords divided a single flat into two or three smaller apartments; the usual practice was to turn each of the rooms into a separate furnished room, linked by newly formed corridors, so that a typical boarding house had sixteen or eighteen rooms. In mansions the parlor or sitting room alone could become three or four small furnished rooms, some without windows, although many had their own fireplaces. Bathroom facilities were usually minimal, often only on the second floor. Rooming houses were also made out of tenements, which became "apartment hotels" with as many as one hundred furnished rooms. Developers also created rooming houses out of formerly lavish hotels; the Virginia and the Metropole, for example, fashionable family hotels of the 1880s, were considered third-rank rooming houses by the 1920s.[13]

Such changes meant that the development of an SRO district was the result of a multitude of small, private investment decisions. The historian Sam Bass Warner, Jr., wrote that "the physical forms of American cities, their lots, houses, factories, and streets have been the outcome of a real estate market of profit seeking builders, land speculators, and investors." James Borchert, studying alley life in Washington, D.C., similarly concluded that low-income housing during this period was "the result of many individual decisions by landowners, builders and others . . . the potential for profit, and the efforts to realize it, profoundly affected the nature and character of the . . . communities that developed." In other words, in the nation's capital, as in the Windy City, housing and the social environment were shaped by economic decisions based on a changing labor force.[14]

Managers of rooming houses were almost always single women in their middle years, usually a widow or someone who had never married. In the vast majority of cases where a man held title to the property, however, the male was owner in name only; his wife or daughter actually ran the rooming house. This was considered one way to use female skills to bring in extra income. By 1900, 92 percent of the rooming-house keepers in Chicago were women, a situation typical of cities like New York, Philadelphia, and Saint Louis. In Boston, for example, 94 percent of the rooming-house keepers were women; of these, 51 percent were over forty-five years of age, 7 percent were over sixty-five. About half were native born. Only a quarter were married, while 49 percent were widowed, 4 percent were divorced, and 23 percent were listed as "single," a category presumably referring to women with no marital experience of any kind. Most of these women turned to managing rooming houses as a way of earning a living, but some were former roomers themselves who had decided to strike out on their own in entrepreneurial fashion, gaining economic power and social autonomy.[15]

These buildings were advertised as potent money makers. The October 1926 issue of *The Rooming House and Hotel Guide*, for example, listed ads for buildings that could be rented by prospective managers. One building that rented for $100 a month was claimed to have an income of $275, plus use of two rooms by the landlord. Another rented for $500 but had an income of $1,350 a month.[16]

The reality was far different. Unscrupulous real estate brokers would fill a building with "straw roomers" for a week or two before the signing of a new lease with a landlady to disguise the fact that rooms were often vacant, the result of seasonal business fluctuations. Such conditions forced tenants to abandon their bid for independence and instead to return home, turn to charity or to prostitution, or else join the ranks of the homeless. This situation was particularly common during the summer, when a large proportion of Chicago's (and the country's) furnished rooms were empty, usually because of unemployment. Thus, even for the single middle-class citizen, there could be movement in and out of poverty, and between differing levels of shelter.[17]

Empty rooms were not the only plague of the rooming-house landlady. Plumbing often went bad, the result of overuse by a far larger population than the system was ever designed for. Furniture was often sold at high prices by "installment sharks" and quickly fell apart.[18]

The landladies developed several responses to these problems. Every economy possible was practiced, which lead to frequent harassment of roomers to minimize their use of hot water and other utilities. Repairs were avoided whenever possible, so blight and decay set in. Every room, including the parlor, was used to house paying tenants, so there was no public area to receive guests. Since this resulted in women bringing gentleman callers up to their rooms, it was considered an invitation to immorality.[19]

Most important of all, landladies had to do everything they could to fill the rooms. Even some not-for-profit rooming houses found they could not maintain their budgets with the standard vacancy rates. As a result, many landladies accepted any tenant that showed up, regardless of circumstances, and closed their eyes to infractions of middle-class morality. One Chicago landlady, when asked how many married couples lived in her building, replied, "I don't know—I don't ask. I want to rent my rooms." Similarly, a colleague of hers in Boston told a researcher, "It is best not to know too much about your lodgers." Thus, the social environment of the rooming house was also influenced by economic factors.[20]

The Roomer and Housing

The people who stayed in rooms were Protestant and native born. In the North Side district 52 percent of the roomers were single men, 10 percent single women, and 38 percent couples living together "without benefit of clergy." The men were usually white-collar workers; females predominantly held white and pink-collar jobs. One 1889 study by the U.S. commissioner of labor on working women living in not-for-profit rooming houses found that 24 percent were in domestic service, 13 percent were in secretarial and clerical positions, 11 percent were saleswomen (in retail stores), and 10 percent were students. According to a later, 1906 survey of Boston's roomers, 14 percent of the men were professionals and 46 percent were in commerce, usually in sales positions. Many of the rest worked in offices as clerks, accountants, bookkeepers, or secretaries. These were part of the new urban work force: by 1900 over 110,000 city women in the United States worked in offices and 65,000 in stores; in Chicago 21 percent of all wage-earning women lived as roomers or boarders, a figure representing 22,000 individuals. Rooming or boarding was particularly common among blacks (49 percent) and native-born whites of native-born parents (37 percent). Figures were lower for foreign-born whites (24 percent) and native-born whites of foreign parents (only 13 percent). Housing tenure, for both men and women, was brief; in one survey of 117 registrations, 59 percent had lived in their current residence for under one year. Similarly, an observer claimed that the entire population of the North Side rooming-house district "changed every four months." [21]

These women, and their male companions, found rooms through several established ways. One was to check the ads in the papers. Another was to walk the streets of the rooming-house districts and look for a card in the window that said "Room For Rent." Such searches were exhausting; the telephone was far from common, so roomers had to walk the streets, dragging their luggage, in search of accommodations. The absence of decent street lighting and the common practice of rooming houses to have house numbers that were barely discernible meant that a night-time search was particularly daunting. These problems were often unavoidable, however, for those arriving in the city after dark.[22]

The facilities these women and men found were meager, and often laced with troubles. Rates were from three to fifteen dollars a week, with most rooms between six and ten dollars (one of the elements that differentiated middle-class rooming houses from working-class lodging houses, besides higher rates, was that in the former rent was paid by the week, whereas in the latter it was usually paid one night at a time). Landladies frequently preferred to rent to men instead of women because men were considered to be less troublesome. In particular, men were less likely to break rules prohibiting cooking and doing laundry in the rooms, and they used less hot water. The small rooms offered few comforts, typically a gas burner for heating water or doing some light cooking, a bed, and a chair, with perhaps a nightstand and a dresser or closet. One social worker claimed that many Chicago women called home "a place where we can unpack our trunk, anchor our electric iron and hang our other blouse over the chair." Bathrooms were shared; one survey found that 26 percent of the bathrooms in rooming houses in the South Side district were used by more than six persons, a situation that existed in 41 percent of the cases in the North Side district and 52 percent of those on the West Side. Only 2 percent of the rooms in all these districts had private baths, though 42 percent had their own toilets. In Boston hot water was not provided during the summer, and it was reported that the communal bathroom often looked like "a general store-room for dirty linen, brooms and other household utensils." Such minimal facilities, however, were dictated by the intermittent employment and low wages of tenants.[23]

Morality versus Independence

The morality of rooming-house life was a great concern to Progressive Era reformers. Writers like Harvey Zorbaugh in Chicago and Albert Wolfe in Boston told tales of desperate loneliness, noting how children were the best neighbors but that this was a childless world. Cramped up in garrets, young women (and men) lived lives of morbid aloneness. Walter Krumwilde, a Lutheran writer, told the story of a "frowzy child in the street" approached by a "philanthropic lady." The woman asked, "Where is your home?" The child replied, "Hain't got no home." "Poor thing," she asked, "what do you do?" The child's answer: "I board." Krumwilde went on to describe "the modern rooming . . . house system," which was "spreading its web like a spider, stretching out its arms like an octopus to catch the unwary, sleeping soul." He claimed that anyone living in a rooming house was "to be pitied and prayed for," and that in rebuttal the church should "constantly hold up 'the divine dignity and sacredness of the Christian home life.' "[24]

But it was not just religious writers who held this position. Even as sensitive a social observer as Albert Wolfe could claim, "When a young man and a young woman are thrown together in illicit relations by the very force and circumstances of the [rooming house] environment, and . . . the girl becomes a suicide or the boy a murderer, the [rooming] house must be responsible for social dissolution." Joanne Meyerowitz quotes a working-class woman who lived with her parents because "if a girl didn't live at home, we thought she was bad"; a Chicago waitress also hesitated to move into a rooming house because "I was afraid on account of what people would say about a girl living alone."[25]

More recent analysis by historians, especially women, has challenged these concepts. These writers argue that females chose rooming houses over boarding houses for exactly those reasons that reformers condemned. If, as one survey showed, 49 percent—almost half—of all rooming houses allowed men up to rooms (an unheard-of practice in boarding houses), this was the preference of the women tenants. They went to these rooms for the privacy and the freedom they offered and by so doing doomed the boarding system as well. As Meyerowitz, whose work we draw on here, has so aptly put it, "Many women disliked the protection that reformers insisted they needed."[26]

Her conclusion is corroborated by the statements of women (and men) at the turn of the century. Harriet Faye, for example, writing in the March 1899 issue of *Municipal Affairs*, argued that although one effect of women's taking rooms was that it made them "more independent and freer to refuse proposals of marriage," she was not sure if this was "an advantage or disadvantage. . . . Would not conditions be improved were women more independent? Are not the forces leading to an early acceptance of matrimonial offers already too strong?" Similarly, a young man wrote in the May 7, 1904, issue of the *Living Age* that "the truth is . . . almost every man is at heart an early Franciscan. . . . He wants to get away from everything, to leave behind . . . his social liabilities." If some girls chose to live in places like the Franklin Square House in Boston, where the doors were locked at 11:00 P.M., after which the night watchman had to be summoned with a doorbell, others totally rejected that kind of existence. When one writer asked a group of working girls about guidelines for running not-for-profit rooming houses, one of them said, "there should be no rules at all, any more than in any decent hotel." When another pointed out that she lived in a building where everyone had to be in by 10:30 every night and that the house was full, the first speaker replied, "that only shows how much a good [rooming house] is needed, when girls will put up with such restrictions to have a decent home." [27]

This was all part of what Gunther Barth has called the "atmosphere of expanding personal freedom and individual opportunity" in turn-of-the-century cities, which "severed the old ties of men and women with the countryside." He noted that although "any big city has inspired visions of the free life," the "American modern city . . . actually generated a novel degree of personal freedom that allowed greater numbers of people to live as individuals more fully than before." [28]

Thus, women chose to leave the farm and come to the freer environment of the city to, in Meyerowitz's words, "escape the restrictions routinely imposed upon daughters in the family economy," or, as Barth put it, "to get away from the doldrums of household and farm chores." [29]

There were many reasons why women came to the city to live alone, but most had to do with gains in personal freedom and autonomy. An Italian woman in Chicago moved out when her father "would not allow her to go out evenings into the street." Another woman came to the Windy City from Michigan when, after staying out late on a date, she was whipped by her stepfather, who "accused me of wanting to do things which I'd not even thought of doing up to that time." Other children ran away when parents demanded that they turn over all their wages.[30]

The preference for rooming houses, therefore, reflected and in turn was a response to social and cultural shifts, such as an increasing desire for privacy. Young newcomers to the city were not interested in a family life or a boarding-house experience where, as one woman wrote, "the family from whom I rented a room were inquisitive and prying . . . they investigated my room during my absence." Instead, as Meyerowitz accurately points out, "wage-earning women and men . . . preferred contractual tenant relations over the more personal imitations of family." They also found that, as Paul Groth has stated, "as long as one paid one's bills in a hotel (or rooming house), one's personal life was virtually unfiltered by the sorts of social contracts and tacit supervision of the group life found in most households." [31]

One other attraction of the rooming house was its relatively open sexuality. The reformers were, in fact, correct that there was greater sexual freedom in the rooming-house districts, but this was sought after by many young women, rather than being a lure that dragged them to their moral doom. As noted, many rooming houses permitted guests in rooms, and this did occasionally lead to casual liaisons, but with the full consent of both parties. In addition, some women, faced with a shopgirl's meager wages, found that the only way to afford the entertainment offered in abundance by the city was to trade their favors for dates. Women were also influenced by their surroundings; the North Side rooming-house district was in the middle of the cabaret section of the city, with its numerous houses of prostitution. Women living in the area were used to seeing a free-and-easy sexuality and may have considered such events as prostitutes picking up johns as common occurrences. In addition, this was the area with the highest concentration of male and female homosexuals, so residents were exposed to alternative concepts of sexuality. All of this led to the fact that, as Albert Wolfe put it, "the tendency of [rooming-house life] is to postpone marriage and the intention to marry"; many couples also found that by sharing rent and a small space, two could "live as cheaply as one," as the old phrase stated.[32]

One of the other ironies of sexuality and the rooming-house district was that some women sought out the city and the rooming-house area as a refuge from small-town immorality and narrow-mindedness. Contrary to reformers' glowing images, small towns had their own share of depravity. Women who had been raped or seduced often sought out the anonymity of the city to deliver a socially unacceptable or unwanted child, or to start a new life.[33]

The independence of urban life was also facilitated by the network of services. No SRO district could survive for long without the plethora of small shops that served the needs of roomers, needs that were very different from those of a family with its division of labor. Boston's rooming-house district, for example, included 87 cafes, 65 basement dining rooms, 41 saloons, 24 liquor stores, 27 drug stores, 112 pool rooms, 78 laundries, and 70 tailor shops. Of particular importance was the cheap restaurant, which was a key element of independence, especially when compared with meals in the boarding house. Women and men clearly preferred to eat where and what and when they chose, and to make their own decisions regarding company and privacy.[34]

This is not to say that rooming-house life was all rosy. Young men and women lived a life on the verge of poverty and were often forced to desert the city as a result of layoffs. Wages were low, and women who traded favors for entertainment were often lonely and desperate. When Albert Wolfe wrote of the isolation of the roomer, of "the absence of all semblance of home ties, of companionship and friendship," there was considerable truth in his description. One boarding-house keeper, describing a familiar feeling for anyone who has ever lived alone in a big city, explained that "the metropolis is the loneliest place . . . because, while there are thousands of people all around you, you never get acquainted with more than a few of them."[35]

The point is not whether there was poverty and loneliness in the rooming houses. Rather, it is that these districts offered a new and unprecedented degree of personal freedom and control of one's own destiny, and that thousands of individuals sought this out. Furthermore, such freedom was in contravention to social standards that frowned on such behavior, espe-cially among women. The rooming house was an SRO, not only in its facilities but in the fact that it granted inexpensive living conditions to a group of middle-class single working people seeking autonomy. Middle-class transients chose rooming houses, despite the minimal facilities and the loneliness, because they could come and go as they pleased, and determine for themselves the conditions of their lives.

Blacks

One way to verify the accuracy of this description of the social priorities and organization of the rooming house is to compare it with other examples. These are usually sought out in other locales and metropolises, but in Chicago (and other cities as well), another alternative was close at hand. Since the turn of the century Chicago has been rigorously segregated on the basis of skin color; the black belt was, and remains, a city within a city, physically contiguous but in every other way apart. By examining SRO housing for blacks, therefore, we can draw comparisons with a group that had similar characteristics of place and occupation and class but that lived a separate existence because of a system based on race.

The experience of black middle-class transients, though in some ways similar to that of whites, was shaped by the racism of American society. From the turn of the century through the first two decades, Chicago experienced a rapid growth in its black population. In 1900 there were 30,150 blacks in Chicago, making up 1.9 percent of the population. By 1920 there were 109,458 black residents, 4.1 percent of the population. Blacks, like their lighter-skinned counterparts, went looking for rooms. There were descriptions in the black belt of "hundreds of unattached men and women . . . on the streets as late as one or two o'clock in the morning, seeking rooms shortly after their arrival in Chicago." In 1920 the Indiana Street Y, one other alternative for the recent immigrant, reported that 142 black females had made use of their shelter facilities temporarily.[36]

But, as a general rule, these searches yielded meager results. Squeezed into a narrow, packed black belt, Afro-Americans were forced to take whatever facilities they could. There was no space for a separate rooming district, so rooming houses sprang up all over, intermixed with single-family homes and institutions of vice. This mixing was one of the plagues of the black community; whites, especially police, saw it as a large vice district unto itself, and consequently the authorities used the black belt as a dumping ground for unsavory characters. Gambling houses, brothels, drug dens, and other similar places were thus interspersed with housing for a law-abiding population, undercutting attempts at maintaining order.

Blacks were forced to take the smallest apartments and squeeze the greatest number of family members into them. One study of families living in rooming houses found that more than 88 percent of black families on the South Side lived in just one room. This compared with only 58 percent of

TABLE 2-2

Proportion of Rooming House Apartments Occupied by Families,
by Size of Apartment, District, and Race

NUMBER OF ROOMS	SOUTH SIDE (Black)	SOUTH SIDE (White)	WEST SIDE (White)	NORTH SIDE (White)
1	88%	44%	58%	46%
2	10	41	30	41
3	1	10	12	12
4	1	5	0	1
Totals	100%	100%	100%	100%

Source: Evelyn Wilson, *Chicago Families in Furnished Rooms* (Ph.D. dissertation, University of Chicago, 1929), pp. 43–47.

white families on the West Side SRO district, 46 percent of white families on the North Side, and 44 percent of white families in their part of the South Side district (see table 2-2). Families were defined as households with at least two members. Of those black families living in one room, 53 percent had more than four members, 30 percent had more than five. Black transient workers also eschewed the lodging-house districts; at the turn of the century only 4 percent of these residents were black. This pattern was also similar to the experiences of the black community in Philadelphia, where 35 percent of the families studied by W. E. B. Du Bois lived in only one room, and 54 percent lived in three rooms or less.[37]

These small rooms were known as "kitchenettes," and like the rooming houses, they were the result of business decisions by landlords. St. Clair Drake and Horace Cayton, authors of *Black Metropolis*, told how six-room apartments in the black belt renting for $50 *a month* could be separated into six kitchenettes, each renting at $8 *a week*. Subdivided, the same space would now generate revenue of $192 a month.[38]

The overcrowded conditions also produced a communal atmosphere. A woman would style the hair of a neighbor in exchange for use of pots and pans in the floor's only kitchen. Milk was traded for bread, since there was little money, and bartering involved commodities, services, and utensils.[39]

One acute problem for black residents of rooming houses was that services for white transients were frequently closed to blacks. Ida Wells-Barnett complained that not only the Salvation Army but the YMCA and the YWCA excluded blacks. In 1926 the superintendent of the Chicago Women's Shelter told social workers that the institution "could not care for colored cases" and that her experience in these situations had been "unsatisfactory." In one "large northern city" a black woman was excluded from dressmaking classes at the YWCA. The teacher conducting preliminary interviews had taken this action, claiming that it was association policy that no blacks were allowed into any of its activities. The young woman's protests led to a search of records, however, which showed that no such policy existed. In consequence, the general secretary, after consulting with a black social worker, suggested setting up separate classes for whites and blacks. When the original candidate was presented with this idea, however, she declared that she would not register for any classes at the Y, and especially refused to participate in a Jim Crow setup. In addition, she asked that her application for Y membership be withdrawn.[40]

Black Chicagoans in SROs faced a set of conditions different from and yet similar to whites. Their experiences in the job and housing markets, and in community institutions, was shaped by the virulent racism of white society. On the other hand, they also sought the right to run their own lives and whenever possible, to fight racism as it imposed on their community.

Conclusions

Between 1880 and 1920 the cities of the United States underwent massive transitions, caused in large part by changing economic conditions and by the needs of the private sector. These changes included massive growth, both in terms of land space and of population, as well as the constant migration of transient workers.

Many of these people came from middle-class backgrounds and were seeking work in the service industries. They also wanted to experience the metropolis, to participate in the world of bright lights. Their opportunities to explore and enjoy the new urban environment, however, were severely constrained by chronic unemployment and low wages.

To house these individuals, private developers and speculators invested in a form of minimal shelter, the rooming house. These buildings were easily produced, and their units were rented at cheap rates. Facilities were meager: a small room and a few pieces of furniture.

Reformers presented the public policy debate over these buildings in terms of morality. Rooming houses represented free-market anarchy, where the cash nexus negated community ties and fostered immorality. The reformers' alternative was the charitable, paternalistic hotel, where rules imposed a communal situation and limited personal freedom.

The residents of all these buildings, however, saw a third alternative. Their top priority was autonomy, the ability to come and go as one pleased, to run one's own life off the job. To implement this choice, they ignored boarding facilities and moved instead to rooming houses, avoiding charitable institutions whenever possible. Clearly, although they may have *re-*

sented the poor physical conditions the private sector provided, they absolutely *rejected* the constraints imposed by authoritarian forms of shelter.

Their preference, therefore, was for decent facilities, but where each individual could decide how his or her own life should proceed, and where communal issues were decided by the building's residents. This approach, combining adequate physical conditions with personal autonomy and local democratic control, represented then, and still does, an effective and enlightened policy alternative, where neither material needs nor dignity and independence are slighted. It was devised and practiced whenever possible by the participants in the urban/industrial structure, rather than by its primary leaders—private businessmen—or its secondary ones—the social reformers. As a result, this approach never became a recognized policy alternative, despite its efficacy in meeting the real needs of the population.

3 The Lodging House: Shelter for the Working Class

In the United States the Industrial Revolution created not only a transient middle class but a transient working class as well, which labored at projects all across the nation, building railroads, cutting forests, providing the skill and muscle to subdue a continent's resources.

Their world, like that of the middle class, was dominated by the private sector. Businessmen decided what kinds of jobs would be available, where, and at what pay scale. Developers also created a range of shelter alternatives for single workers, with variations based on level of physical comfort and degree of privacy. These SRO facilities for the working class were generally referred to as "lodging houses," a designation that we use as well.

Private business was not the only institution that provided shelter for the single transient worker, just the most common one. Municipal government opened at various times, and with various motives, the police station, the city hall, and the municipal lodging house. Similarly, not-for-profit organizations launched many projects to deal with the housing needs of transient workers. Philanthropists built elaborate hotels, with superior facilities and paternalistic regulations. A more common approach was the mission, where the price for services was feigned religiosity and conversion.

As with the middle class, these seemed the three policy alternatives regarding the housing of single working-class transients: private sector, government, and not-for-profit organizations. Their relative merits were and are debated, each being granted strengths and weaknesses, although it is clear that the private sector was dominant in terms of the numbers housed.

But again, as was true for the middle class, another alternative existed for the working class. Single workers developed an elaborate social system that not only created a minutely detailed hierarchy but also established clear priorities regarding shelter, based on personal autonomy. This system enabled them, despite rigid economic control by the private sector and social control by the public and not-for-profit sectors, to exercise freedom of choice in selecting their accommodations, as they balanced financial and social considerations. The world these men and women created, and the values they adhered to and practiced, carry valuable lessons for a successful shelter policy for single working-class Americans.

The Main Stem

The lodging house was a basic form of shelter, designed to meet the needs of a traveling population of laborers. When these men and women came to Chicago, either to stay for a while or just to pass through, there were four lodging areas they could choose from. Each of these was referred to as a "stem," off of the central downtown district of the city, the Loop. The entertainment stem was on South State Street, where a hobo or tramp could find vaudeville and burlesque houses, dance halls, peep shows, and houses of prostitution. The jungle stem or outdoor flop stem was in Grant Park, along Lake Michigan, adjacent to the Art Institute, Field Museum, and Illinois Central tracks. In warm weather men would sleep on the verdant lawns of the city's cultural institutions, or else berth and make their toilet along the lakefront. There was also the intellectual stem on North Clark Street and around Bughouse Square, where orators held forth, and where the cafeterias featured a more elevated level of conversation.[1]

The most important was the "Main Stem"—West Madison Street, between Halsted Street and the Chicago River, and for several blocks north and south—the primary lodging house and service district for homeless and nearly homeless men and women in Chicago (see map 3-1). This was the destination for hobo, tramp, and bum, and it had its counterparts in most of the industrial cities of the country: the Bowery in New York, Pratt Street in Baltimore, Twelfth Street in Kansas City, South Main Street in Los Angeles, Third Street in San Francisco, Scollay Square in Boston, and Skid Road in Seattle. In New York, for example, two-thirds of the city's licensed lodging houses at the turn of the century were located in the Bowery, where three-quarters of the buildings in that community catered to homeless and nearly homeless working men. Chicago's Main Stem, however, was considered the national capital of Hobohemia. An old hobo tune explained that "if you want to do me a favor / When I lay down and die / Plant my bones by the Main Stem / so I can hear the trains go by."[2]

The Main Stem and its counterparts were urban neighborhoods. Madison Street resembled the ethnic cluster so common in Chicago, but residency in it was rooted in one's approach to travel and work, rather than in one's ethnicity or national heritage. Unemployed men were all over the area, sitting outside, talking in groups, clustering around the notices posted in the day-labor agencies. The area was also the center of all the services that kept Hobohemia going: the cheap restaurants, saloons, secondhand clothing shops, pawnbrokers, bookstores, tobacco shops, and missions.

Here, too, the exception was blacks: they were not permitted in this

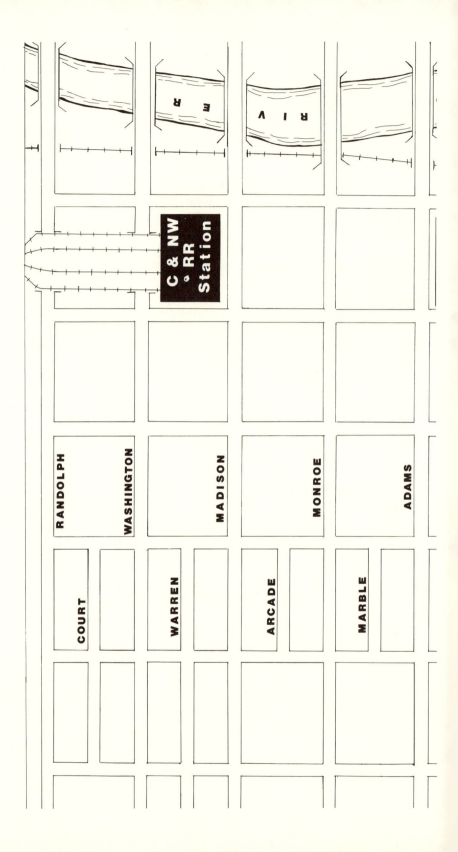

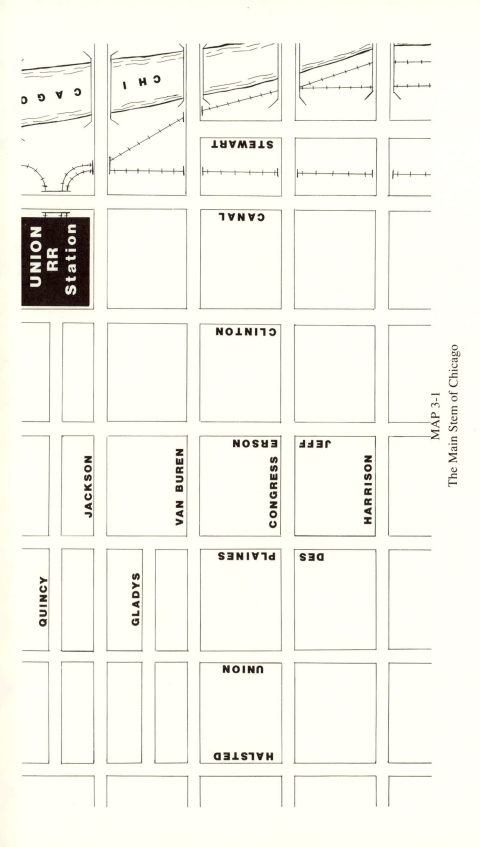

MAP 3-1

The Main Stem of Chicago

area and had to develop their own version of the Main Stem, similar in conditions but segregated by race. None of the lodging houses in the white district would rent space to them, regardless of whether these facilities were private or charitable enterprises; even the worst excluded blacks. This was typical of other cities as well: in New York the manager of the not-for-profit Mills Hotel told a group of Chicago businessmen, "We will not admit colored men, not because we have any prejudice against the colored laborer, but because the hotel is managed upon a business principle, and we cannot afford to do anything which would interfere with its business." In San Francisco a black carpenter interviewed in 1925 said that he was barred from every form of lodging house, even the most expensive ones.[3]

In Chicago blacks developed their own lodging-house district on South State Street, originally between Twenty-second and Thirtieth streets. Later, the district expanded south and east to the area around Forty-seventh Street and South Parkway, now Martin Luther King Jr. Drive. This area was a natural center for SROs: not only was it at the core of the segregated black metropolis, it was close to two of the leading employers of black workers (the railroads and the meat packers). The area had good transportation links to both these industries, as well as to a third, the steel mills on the far South Side. As a result, the section around that intersection still houses one of the largest concentrations of SROs in the city.

At this time the proportion of blacks in the homeless population was quite small, in contrast to the current situation. In Philadelphia, for example, between 1891 and 1896 only 4 percent of the lodgers at police facilities were black, and only 9 percent of the arrests for vagrancy between 1887 and 1896 involved persons of color.[4]

Blacks also created their own sense of community, in part based on the freedom to come and go without interference from a racist white society. In this sense Chicago's black SRO district resembled poor black communities everywhere. All of these groups maximized their use of public space, because private space was so limited, and enjoyed a closeness based in large part on the hardships of race. James Borchert, writing of alley life in Washington, D.C., explained how "space could not be defined by any physical barrier; it belonged to everyone." He also quoted one elderly black gentleman who argued, "Of course, I lives here because of cheap rent but if I had lots of money I wouldn't want to move." The reason for this opinion was that "I knows where I'm at here in the alley. All the folks is colored and I don't have to watch stepping on a white man's toes." Blacks also created their own facilities for persons without shelter, such as Philadelphia's Home for the Homeless, which in 1896 took in ninety women and dispensed almost 4,800 meals to male lodgers and others just passing through.[5]

All the SRO districts, including the black one, spawned and were in turn dependent on a vast network of service institutions. Aside from the labor bureaus and SRO facilities, the two most basic services were those providing drink and food. Every transient district was honeycombed with taverns of every sort, which were centers for companionship and entertainment. When they bought alcoholic beverages, men also availed themselves of the free lunch available at many of these places. Saloons advertised the meals they served, and some claimed "the best free lunch in the city." But there was also a wide variety of cheap restaurants to serve the needs of this poor, transient population. Chili parlors, chop suey joints, hash houses, tea rooms, soft drink parlors, cafeterias, and "white-tile" restaurants were all available to feed the lodging-house tenant. Prices were kept appropriately low, a meal going for ten or fifteen cents. This could include sausage and mashed potatoes, liver and onions, hamburger roast, or steak and fried potatoes, which the novelist James M. Cain described as "the hungry man's dream of heaven." The importance of this population to the growth of the budding restaurant business was confirmed by the fact that, as early as 1880, a third of the restaurants listed in the San Francisco city directory were in its Main Stem district. In addition, these places supported the independent life-style that roomers and lodgers sought.[6]

There was also a multitude of shops. Secondhand stores, resale shops, cigar stores, turkish baths, and taxi stands were all standard features of these districts. There were trunk shops and commercial storage facilities that catered to migrant laborers. Bookstores and newsstands were important, for, as the sociologist Nels Anderson noted, "the homeless man is an extensive reader. This was especially true of the transients, the tramp and the hobo." Particularly well known was the Hobo Bookstore on West Madison Street. Four barber colleges were located on the Main Stem, and men could get their locks shorn for free, provided they were willing to submit to the efforts of students in training.[7]

Pawnshops were especially important. For the single poor man or woman living in a city, the pawnshop served the same function that child labor served for the poor family: it was a way to increase the household's cash flow. Some hoboes made a habit of always carrying a gold watch or ring that they could use to raise a few dollars in an emergency. Many pawned their clothes, and overcoats were frequently used for this purpose. According to an 1899 study by the Department of Labor, the most common item pawned in Chicago was clothing, followed by gold watches. Clothing, as might be expected, was the poor man's pawn: the average loan per pawn was only $1.73, compared with an overall average for all items of $5.08 (see table 3-1). The use of pawn loans as a way of temporarily increasing income to tide one over, or to pay for something special, was also indicated by the daily distribution of pawnshop loans; most took place on Saturday or Monday, at the start or close of the weekend spending period. By 1921 there were still as many as sixty-two pawnshops on the Main Stem.[8]

There was also the host of institutions that hoboes, tramps, and bums cre-

TABLE 3-1

Pawnshop Loans in Chicago for One Month, 1898

ARTICLE	NUMBER OF LOANS	AVERAGE LOAN
Gold watch	5,160	$7.80
Silver watch	2,980	$1.77
Ring	4,822	$7.08
Jewelry	2,276	$11.35
Clothing	6,543	$1.73
Musical instrument	356	$2.16
Firearm	596	$2.06
Miscellaneous	1,724	$3.14
Total	24,457	$5.08

Source: W. R. Patterson, "Pawnbroking in Europe and the United States," Bulletin of the Department of Labor 21 (March 1899): 274.

ated for themselves. These included the Hobo College, a school established by transients, for transients; "Mother" Greenstein's Restaurant, where the penniless could dine free of charge—monetary, moral, or religious; plus Bughouse Square, Chicago's oratorical answer to London's Hyde Park.[9]

It was these facilities, along with the cheap entertainment—movies, dance halls, cabarets, burlesque halls, and houses of prostitution—that enabled the residents of the rooming-house and lodging-house districts to survive. They created a community, a place where men could interact, take care of their business needs, and find camaraderie and friendship. It was these features that made the Main Stem a real home for its residents, as well as a desirable destination for traveling workers from all over the country. Without these amenities and services, the districts would have disappeared more quickly than any urban renewal process could have accomplished.

The Immigration Fallacy

Lodging houses were associated with the immigrant industrial laborer, an assumption that must be carefully analyzed. It was indeed true that conditions in the American factory system created a large body of transient workers; several studies of Chicago's packing industry, for example, showed that only half of all laborers were employed for a full year, and that the number of employees at slack time could be as little as 51 percent of the peak work force.[10]

For immigrant workers, there were two patterns of finding shelter. A large proportion came to the United States, and to Chicago, with instructions to seek out a friend, relative, or, more often, a neighbor from the same village in the Old Country. This contact would get them a job and a place to stay. More often than not, the form of shelter arranged was a room with a family, a pattern that produced the widespread practice of boarding that occurred in industrial neighborhoods in Chicago and other cities.

The second pattern, however, involved the millions of immigrants who came to Chicago and other American cities without references, merely seeking employment. These workers took lodging in the downtown area, then fanned out throughout the city looking for work. The downtown site provided them the advantages of contact with the local transportation hub, the Loop, and its connecting elevated trains. These included cheap and convenient shelter and services and proximity to the day-labor agencies that dotted the lodging-house districts, thus providing a means for making ends meet till a regular job could be found.

A worker's stay at these downtown domiciles, however, was brief. Within a relatively short period one of two decisions was made. If a man found a steady job and became part of a circle of work-related colleagues, he would move into their community, probably boarding with a family at first. Thus, he entered the cycle of housing and community activity that eventually led to membership in the social order. If, on the other hand, the worker did not find employment, he eventually left to try his luck in another city, continuing the process until the right opportunity came along.

The accuracy of this analysis is borne out by statistics developed at the turn of the century. An 1894 report, for example, showed that the foreign-born residents of a Chicago slum were much more likely to be boarders than lodgers, when compared with the native-born population of the area. The study showed that although 59 percent of the foreign-born males preferred boarding to lodging, this was true for only 17 percent of the native-born men. A 1906 study of lodging-house residents in Chicago showed that 65 percent were native-born men, a much higher percentage than in the overall city population. As late as 1921 Nels Anderson found that 85 percent of the hoboes he interviewed were native born; of the other 15 percent, more than a third had already become naturalized citizens. Anderson claimed that other studies further demonstrated that 60 percent to 90 percent of tramps and hoboes were native born, and that the vast majority of the foreign born came from the British Isles, especially England, with very little representation from the countries of the "new immigration." He was thus prompted to write that "the tramp is an American product," and he compared him to that quintessential American, the cowboy. All this evidence supports the theory that immigrants usually came with references and, if they had none, tried to join a community as soon as possible (see table 3-2).[11]

Additional evidence came from a survey of men living in the municipal lodging house: 33 percent had been in the city less than five days, and

TABLE 3-2

Demographic Profile of
1,000 Chicago Homeless Men,
1900–1903

CHARACTERISTIC	%
NATIVITY	
American	62.5
German	9.2
English	6.6
Irish	6.1
Canadian	2.5
Scandinavian	2.4
Other	7.4
Unknown	3.3
AGE	
10–14	1.9
15–19	9.8
20–24	12.9
25–29	10.4
30–39	20.0
40–49	18.5
50–59	11.8
60–69	8.5
70 and over	4.9
Unknown	1.5
CONJUGAL STATUS	
Single	74.0
Married	7.8
Widowed	11.6
Divorced	1.5
Separated	4.9
Unknown	0.2
EDUCATION	
Illiterate	5.2
Common school	87.2
College	5.1
Unknown	2.5

CHARACTERISTIC	%
OCCUPATIONAL STATUS	
Professional	6.2
Business	3.3
Clerical and sales	11.4
Skilled	21.3
Partly skilled	10.9
Unskilled	33.4
Miscellaneous	0.7
No work record	6.8
Unknown	6.0

Source: Alice Solenberger, *1000 Homeless Men* (New York, 1911), pp. 20, 135.

another 25 percent had been there from five days to a month. Overall, 58 percent had been in the city for a month or less, verifying that many workers sought permanent residences as soon as possible, or else moved on. These reports and others stated that many of the residents of lodging houses were unskilled laborers in such industries as railroads and steel, or in agriculture. The better class of workers—skilled railroad men, waiters, teamsters—were more likely to take space in a rooming house or even an apartment hotel.[12]

This pattern was true in other cities as well. Kenneth Kusmer found that 60 percent of the vagrants in Philadelphia were native born. In 1906 in New York, 60 percent of the adult male residents of the municipal lodging house were also native-born Americans.[13]

The Social Hierarchy of Hoboes, Tramps, and Bums

The group that, more than any other, made up the lodging-house tenantry was transient workers. This was actually a diverse conglomerate, with many different categories, including hoboes, tramps, and bums. Among these subgroups there were very different attitudes toward work and toward society. Hoboes, for example, worked steadily and believed in the virtues of hard labor. They differed from the stable middle class primarily in the terms of their employment: although they were continuously employed, their jobs were of short duration and scattered across the continent. Others, such as tramps, also traveled but felt that work was something to be avoided if possible. Bums were the stationary element; they included segments that both favored and disdained labor. All of these groups, however, looked on unemployment as an occasional, inevitable, and manageable state of affairs. Consequently, one thing these men and women had in common were limited financial resources and the need for inexpensive housing and other services.

These workers shared certain characteristics (see table 3-2). Most of them were unmarried and had never been married. As noted, they were generally native born, and the majority of the foreign born came from the British Isles or from Canada (historian John Schneider has pointed out that most personal nicknames were regional or urban, rather than ethnic, another reflection of the relative homogeneity and lack of ethnic tension among this population). The majority were in their middle years; only 12 percent were under twenty, and less than a quarter of these were under sixteen. Drinking was also much less prevalent than imagined; in one Chicago study 197 of the 1,000 men studied had drinking or drug problems, and "in only 16 instances (1.6%) was their health so seriously affected that their physical condition, as well as the habit itself, handicapped them in matters of employment." [14]

There were also relatively few blacks in the group. A number of studies in various cities, all conducted around the turn of the century, showed that whites generally made up more than 90 percent of the homeless population. There are several explanations for these figures. One is that migrant blacks faced stiff discrimination: work camps, bunkhouses, lodging houses, and recreational facilities were all strictly segregated on the basis of race. Also, much of the economy of the homeless and nearly homeless was based on handouts—of shelter, clothing, and, most especially, food—and handouts were much less likely to be offered when the recipient's skin was black. Thus, although the hoboes developed their own social organization separate from the middle or stable working class, they adopted the values and patterns of racial discrimination of mainstream America. [15]

The major differentiation among residents of the Main Stem, besides race, concerned their traveling habits. Workers were first divided into those who were mobile and those who were stationary. The former enjoyed higher status among the residents of the Main Stem because they at least enjoyed the freedom of travel, with all the new experiences that this brought. Autonomy, the ability to control one's movements and to come and go freely, was important to these men and women. While this mirrored the classic American virtues of individualism and freedom, it simultaneously created fears, among the middle class, that they were a rootless, wandering group without social ties. These fears would eventually help shape the government's response to this population, as well as to the buildings and communities it lived in.

Thus, at the top of the heap in Chicago's and other cities' Main Stems (the SRO districts), was the hobo, who was a migratory worker. One writer referred to him as "the shock-trooper of the American expansion." Unlike his more recent counterpart, the migrant worker of the late twentieth century who works almost exclusively at unskilled agricultural jobs, the hobo labored at the wide variety of skilled and unskilled tasks that were part of the taming of the North American continent. Some of these were agricultural, especially before full-scale implementation of mechanized farm equipment. The term "hobo" is itself supposed to come from the American West, a derivative of the term "hoe-boy," that is, the men who did harvesting with hoes. Many hoboes, therefore, followed the planting seasons, picking fruit, beets, potatoes, and other produce. In addition, they brought in basic grain crops that were later harvested by large machines, wheat, for example, in the early days of the gigantic bonanza farms.[16]

But hoboes worked at a variety of other jobs as well. Hoboes laid the rails for most of the train networks of the country, dug ditches, and cut through forests. These traveling workers tunneled through mountains, dug ravines, and built bridges. They also worked extensively in the construction and fishing industries (especially salmon fishing on the West Coast and oyster fishing on the East Coast).

The kinds of work they did implied that some of the hoboes were skilled laborers, often with training and education. Alice Solenberger found, for example, in her study (the foremost of its kind) of 1,000 homeless men in Chicago that over 21 percent were in the skilled trades, almost 11 percent were in the partly skilled trades, 11 percent were clerical workers, and 6 percent were professionals (see table 3-2). Hoboes were also supposed to be relatively intelligent. When Northwestern University students administered the Alpha intelligence tests (used by the U.S. Army to screen recruits during World War I) to attendees of the Hobo College, the hoboes scored higher than seniors at the university.[17]

The hoboes' diverse employment resulted in a colorful vocabulary of occupational descriptions. Besides the "gandy dancers" there were "skinners" (someone who drove horses or mules), "muckers" or "shovels stiffs" (manual laborers on construction jobs), "rust eaters" (track layers who dealt with steel sections), and "splinter-bellies" (men who did rough carpentry or bridge work).[18]

The most important aspect of a hobo's life, besides travel, was his occupation and the fact that he was constantly working. As one social scientist put it, "the main thing to remember is that the hobo did work, would work and often worked hard. . . . There is no need for any stigma of pauperism to be placed on the typical hobo." For the hobo there was, however, no steady employment at the same job for any length of time. He was strictly a migrant, using the boxcar as his Pullman. Although the hobo shared the American belief in hard work, his sporadic routine and the scattered geographic pattern of his labor distanced him from his middle- and working-class counterparts. The distance made him the focus of fear and suspicion, as well as occasional romanticization.[19]

The hobo's existence was tied to the city; his work and travel were in distinctly urban patterns. As the historian Eric Monkkonen has pointed out, hoboes "used cities as the hubs of their information networks," traveling from a city to a job on a farm, then back to the city for rest and recreation, then out to another farm or to a forest or to a fishing or mining community. Sometimes they worked as skilled or unskilled labor in shops or factories. Monkkonen has described this overall pattern as "urbancentric" and contrasted it to today's migrant laborers, who never connect with city centers in the course of following the harvests. As Monkkonen pointed out, in the world of the hobo and tramp "simple, obvious factors like the trains and cities accounted for far more than did wanderlust or regional culture." This also explains why Chicago, the nation's foremost railroad town, became a center for hoboes.[20]

Most of the hobo's work, however, depended on good weather, so he developed a seasonal life-style, with some of the time devoted to leisure. During the winter the hobo settled in somewhere to pass the cold months. Interestingly, most of these places were in the colder, northern parts of the country. The hoboes chose the northern cities because of their fully developed "hobohemias" that provided the full range of services hoboes needed, including restaurants, shops, entertainment, day-labor agencies that provided the opportunity to pick up a few extra dollars, companionship of other "knights of the road," and, especially, inexpensive lodgings. Anderson said that the Main Stem of Chicago and other cities served as "a winter resort for many of those seasonal workers whose schedule is relatively fixed and habitudinal." Hoboes usually came with a nest egg to tide them through the winter and were prepared to do a little extra work, like cutting ice in Lake Michigan, if they needed help making it through till spring. Those who came without money either worked regularly at odd jobs or else descended to the category of bums, a totally different group to be discussed shortly. This meant, therefore, that the hobo's lodging house, like the middle-class rooming house, was often vacant in the summer, ironically because of full employment rather than unemployment.[21]

The hoboes' social and cultural life also reflected the close link between economic and cultural autonomy. Industry needed large numbers of transient workers; the resulting mass made possible not only communities but a hierarchical social structure. Economic needs, therefore, fostered a set of values and an organized society to implement them. At the same time, the seasonal nature of hoboes' work prevented the development of families or permanent ties.

Economic factors also affected spatial relationships and the development of housing policy. Hoboes came to the city because it enabled them to fulfill physical and social needs without establishing permanent relationships. They had the freedom to move in and out as they pleased, a critical element if they were to respond to the job market. This freedom, however, also had the effect of prompting middle-class fears of a group with no obligations to the majority's social structure and values. The fears would eventually manifest themselves in public efforts to control this population and minimize what was perceived as a disruptive influence.

Below the hobo came the tramp, a different species altogether. St. John Tucker, one-time president of the Hobo College, said that the difference between the hobo and the tramp was that the former was a migratory worker but the latter was a migratory nonworker. Ben Reitman, one of the founders of the Hobo College, explained in a more poetic fashion that "the hobo works and wanders" while "the tramp dreams and wanders." Whereas hoboes were seen as traveling workers who dressed appropriately, tramps were more likely to be dirty or slovenly because of their unwillingness to earn a decent living. Tramps enjoyed traveling around the country; one tramp, for example, collected post office cancellations as a hobby. Whenever he came to a new town, he went to the local post office and asked postal workers to stamp his book in the same way that the postage on letters are cancelled. Tramps were also considered specialists in "getting by." Many were expert beggars; others came up with elaborate schemes to gain an income. One tramp used to go into small-town newspaper offices dressed as a typical migrant, then spin elaborate tales of adventures on the road ("he has been pursued by bloodhounds in the South . . . he is the only man who has beat his way on the Pikes Peak railroad"). He then would offer to sell the paper a brief story on his exploits. Most tramps were not usually drunkards but, rather, "easy-going" individuals who lived "from hand to mouth." [22]

The tramp's resistance to honest labor, however, meant that he was the object of the hobo's scorn. The categories for different kinds of tramps were generally negative, revealing a public image of at best a predator, at worst a fool. A "jungle buzzard," for example, was a tramp who hung around a jungle camp and begged from hoboes. A "road yegg" was a bandit who hijacked hoboes and stole from them; a "fagin" or "jocker" was a middle-aged or elderly tramp who trained young runaway boys (called "road kids") to beg or steal in return for protection. A homosexual relationship was usually involved as well. In addition, there were "ring tails" (silly, ignorant tramps) and "fuzzy tails" (wise-guy, smart-aleck tramps).

The next category involved men who did not travel. The stationary worker (and nonworker) was known as a "bum." Like the transients, who were separated into "hoboes" and "tramps," there were different ranks within this category, marking differences between those who worked and those who did not, as well as other characteristics.

Stationary men made use of the same primary distinctions as their peripatetic counterparts. The most important distinctions among bums was whether they worked or not, and the kind of work they engaged in. At the top of the heap, the elite of bums, was the "home guard" (some writers felt that the home guard were sufficiently employed to merit a separate category from "bum"). Members of the home guard were stationary casual laborers; because they did not travel, they lived in the same city, usually on the same Main Stem, all their lives. Many of the home guard were former hoboes who had settled down. Work was unskilled and casual, and usually performed by the day or even hour. Most were in the service trades; one might be for example, a dishwasher in a Loop restaurant, porter in a hotel, or janitor in a downtown office building. Pool halls and saloons had occasional odd jobs as well. Some members of the home guard even worked as clerks in lodging houses.

Members of the home guard arrived on the Main Stem by one of two routes. In many cases they could not make it in the more established working-class districts. This was usually because of economic reasons (unemployment due to layoffs or physical disabilities), social reasons (alcoholism or other sociopathic behavior), or, as was most common, a combination of the two (for example, when a newly arrived worker was laid off before he had joined a local social structure with support mechanisms). Other members of the home guard were hoboes or tramps who could no longer roam, because of age or infirmity or some other condition. Some of these also became beggars and other, lower classes of bum. Among the home guard, however, the work ethic was still relatively strong, evidenced by Anderson's comment, "Petty as these jobs are and little as they pay, men not only take but seek them." [23]

The main point, therefore, is that, regardless of which route one followed in becoming one of the home guard, membership was based to a large degree on economic failure. Many of the stationary residents of the Main Stem or Skid Row, even at the turn of the century, were there because of problems encountered in the job market, rather than because of their own social pathologies.

The next social rank down, after the home guard, was that of beggar. According to Alice Solenberger, beggars were usually of middle age: few men below the age of twenty or over the age of fifty-nine begged. More than half of the beggars she studied were born in the United States, and another 21 percent came from the British Isles. Most had a grade school education, but 6 percent were "college men." [24]

Even among beggars, there were categories. The street beggar, for example, approached strangers on the boulevards of cities like Chicago and New York, pleading for alms. Josiah Flynt argued that "the street-beggar is . . . the cleverest all-round vagabond in the world. . . . [He] knows more about human nature than any other . . . and can read its weak points with surprising ease." One New York beggar, for example, chose Fifth

Avenue as his turf, and women as his special clients. He claimed that he could tell immediately, just by looking in their eyes, whether or not to "tackle" them. When a likely target appeared, he would adjust his story and voice accordingly, deciding when to whine or grovel, when to talk straight, and when to make a woman laugh. This was considered the best trick of all, because a laughing person is probably in the right mood to make a donation.[25]

Some street beggars depended on more than their wits. There were those who sold their skill, like the "mush fakers," beggars who had learned, while in a penal institution, to repair umbrellas. Other sold particular items; peddlers such as "timbers" sold pencils, a "wangy" sold shoe laces, and "wires" sold articles made from stolen telegraph wires.[26]

More common, however, were the beggars who claimed any of a variety of afflictions. They beseeched the pity of all passersby, crying out for a little dose of mercy. Among the established types were the "flopper," who sprawled on the sidewalk in crowded business thoroughfares; the "stiffy," who simulated paralysis; and the "dummy," who pretended to be deaf and dumb. There were distinctions between a "straight crip" (someone who was actually crippled) and a "phoney crip" (someone who was faking a deformity, or whose problem was self-inflicted). Willard Motley, author of *Let No Man Write My Epitaph*, portrayed a character named "Weepy" because he had "such a good line." In addition, there were nine different terms to describe the variety of bodily losses possible as a result of railway accidents. These included "peg," the loss of one or both feet; "wingy," the loss of one or both arms; "mitts," the loss of one or both hands; "blinky," the loss of one or both eyes; and "halfy," the loss of both legs below the knee.[27]

Pitches like these were not used just in the street, however. There was also the house beggar, who went door to door with his affliction, and the office beggar, or "sticker," who worked the downtown offices. The latter was considered the more difficult occupation, since the office beggar dealt almost exclusively with men, who were much more likely to argue about a story than women were.[28]

Despite the horrible deformities denoted by terms like "blinky" or "halfy," these men were still not considered the bottom of the rung among bums. Below them were the drug addicts ("hop heads" or "junkies"), "mission stiffs" and "grafters." Mission stiffs faked conversions in return for bed and board; grafters exploited charitable organizations. Both groups were considered by other beggars to be hypocrites, and beneath contempt.

Below that there was the "two cent dosser" ("doss" refers to sleep); a "two cent dosser" spent two cents a night on lodging. These men did a little begging, then went to saloons where, for two pennies, they could get a stale beer and the right to sleep in chairs, benches, or on the floor.[29]

At the very bottom of the heap was the "tomato can vag" (for "vagrant"). These men needed no income at all to survive. They lived in boxes, cellars, and doorways; they picked the refuse of restaurants, in alleys, and from tomato cans for food. The alcoholic beverages they consumed were usually the stale remains in empty beer kegs left outside saloons. Most of these were old men who had been hoboes or tramps in their younger days.[30]

This detailed description of the lexicon of the impoverished, starting with hoboes and ending with tomato can vags, has several purposes. First, it shows what a strong social organization these men and women created. Like African tribes that maintained minute status differentiations based on ancestry and familial relationships, the homeless and nearly homeless of the United States' industrial age created fine distinctions that defined status. Nicknames provided information as well, explaining the owner's mode of work, travel, or begging, to the smallest detail. This kind of organization implies that, despite the fact that these peoples' lives were supposedly totally at the mercy of economic forces, they were still able to claim some autonomy, defining the ranks and orders of their own society to a remarkable level. As one writer explained, "There is a strict class or caste system among the various migratory and homeless types. The hobo is proud of his status and looks down upon the tramp and bum. Both the hobo and the tramp snub the bottle bum, jungle buzzard, etc." This is a remarkable statement, given that he is describing people who traditionally had been written off as the epitome of social disorganization.[31]

This social structure has policy implications as well. Service providers and academics have portrayed the homeless and nearly homeless as "disorganized" and "disaffiliated." These terms indicated that in the minds of these others the group was not only leaderless but incapable of understanding or creating solutions to its own problems. Instead, the belief was, caretakers would have to be provided from outside before any advances among the client population would be possible. The minute social organization established by hoboes and tramps and bums, however, belies the need for caretakers and suggests instead that since leaders and priorities have already been established, campaigns for empowerment and self-determination would be very successful.

It is also clear that they created a cultural framework that, even as it adopted the individualism of the dominant culture, did so without its rural, conservative, and predominantly middle-class outlook. Consequently, the common public perception of the hobo, tramp, and bum, then and now, emphasized social disorder, chaos, and the threat to community, an attitude communicated by the labeling of these people as moral deviants with character defects. Some politicians and social reformers were quick to apply these judgments, but the successful social and cultural organization of life in Hobohemia indicated that they may have been wrong.

The other reason for detailing the lexicon is to note its strong relationship to economic factors. These men and women were far from being slaves of the industrial system, but much of their life was defined by whether or not they could or would find work, the kind of work they did, and what happened to them on the job. As noted earlier, the emergence of homelessness, and the hobo, tramp, and bum, were directly related to the rise of the industrial economy and its deprivations. Even Solenberger, who still placed much of the blame for homelessness on the individual's moral character, observed that "previous to the Civil War, the word 'tramp' did not appear upon the statute books of any state in the union. Today nearly all recognize his existence and endeavor to cope with the problem he presents." Other writers have also noted how the number of homeless and nearly homeless workers skyrocketed after the depressions of 1873 and 1893; how, as historian Kenneth Kusmer has noted, "for many workers, employment was sporadic regardless of the general health of the economy"; that, according to Solenberger, the "most potent . . . among the industrial causes of vagrancy . . . is the seasonal and irregular character of employment in a good many trades and occupations"; and that often, as the U.S. government reported, "irregularity of employment is due to a deliberate policy of employers to lessen the chance of organized movement." [32]

Thus, homeless and nearly homeless workers were usually on the Main Stem because of economic conditions, not because of defects in their moral character. Joseph Kirkland was wrong, for example, when he supported the views of a Pacific Garden Mission volunteer whom he interviewed for his article in the July 1892 *Scribner's* magazine, "Among the Poor of Chicago." The missionary was asked where one could find "the poverty that springs from misfortune rather than drink." The "pregnant answer" came "impulsively": "There is none. You might find one or two others in five hundred, but it is drink in the case of all the rest." This notion— that moral imperfections (particularly alcoholism) was the primary cause of residency on the Main Stem or Skid Row—has controlled social welfare work for a century and continues in effect today.[33]

As the homeless workers' lexicon demonstrates, however, the assumption was not true in most cases. This is not to say that alcoholism, thievery, and other socially deviant tendencies did not exist on the Main Stem, but rather that they were not nearly as important as much of the subsequent literature, both popular and academic, implied. The hoboes, tramps, and bums knew that most of the reason for their condition was economic, and the terms they made up reflected that. They told numerous stories that reflected their reality. *McClure's* magazine, for example, ran an article in 1908 entitled "A Bunk-House and Some Bunk-House Men" that described the experiences of Edward Dowling, "a gentleman" who had soldiered in India. Later, he had worked at ranching, until an accident deprived him of the use of an eye, so he spent all he had trying to preserve his sight. Homeless and penniless, he wound up living in one of New York's lodging-house districts, eking out a living by repairing umbrellas (that is, as a mush-faker). Similarly, a lecturer at the Hobo College spoke on "Why a Man in Rags Cannot Get a Job," complaining that although he was a skilled clerical laborer, "When my clothes are all worn out, my collar is dirty, my hat is crushed, I know better than to even go around the retail houses looking for work." Another speaker, a one-armed peddler with lung trouble, was unable to find work, and he slept in barns, wagons, and boxcars. Charitable institutions, he felt, "did nothing but make men feel ashamed." He demanded, "Whose fault is it that I am not working? I want to work!" Even Samuel Wilson, author of the critical tract *Chicago and Its Cess-Pools of Infamy*, wrote that "many deserving persons are classed among the tramps . . . [they] gladly accept any work offered them, and escape from their wretched companionship as soon as they are able to do so." [34]

As Nels Anderson so aptly summed up, "In each of these cases arrival in Hobohemia had been preceded by a different series of events (defeats and disappointments)." Most of the homeless and nearly homeless had failed to make it in the industrial economic system, but their ability to create a complex social order, despite these adverse objective conditions, suggests that their talents and character were at times formidable. Many of the burdens depicted in their descriptions ("wingy", etc.) were not of their own making; by creating a self-defined social structure, however, they found a way to gain respect for their work habits as well as their social and cultural accomplishments. [35]

Lodging Houses

The conditions and values of the homeless and nearly homeless were best expressed by their housing. Shelter was built and run on the basis of economic decisions of supply and demand resulting from changes in the work force. But hoboes and tramps and bums had their own ideas about what kind of world they wanted to live in, and they found that their choice of housing was one of the best ways to achieve that goal. The range of SRO facilities known as lodging houses, therefore, was more than a matter of housing; it represented a way to translate a life view into the practical reality of day-to-day existence.

Lodging houses, SROs for the working rather than for the middle class, actually existed in each of the three major SRO districts mentioned in the last chapter; by the turn of the century there were 200 lodging houses in Chicago. The term generally applied to cheap, transient facilities that rented by the night or by the week, rather than by the week or month, as was the case with rooming houses. Tenants were usually men only. Other than these features, however, the term "lodging house" was used to refer to a wide variety of working-class housing that ranged widely both in price and especially in quality. As Jacob Riis noted, "There is a wider gap between the 'hotel'—they are all hotels—that charges a quarter and the one that furnishes a bed for a dime than between the bridal suite and the every-day hall bedroom of the ordinary hostelry." An analysis of the different types of lodging houses and, therefore, of the choices available to the homeless and nearly homeless provides an understanding not only of their housing conditions, but of the means by which they made decisions regarding shelter, and ultimately, their lives.[36]

There were several types of lodging houses for working men and women. The best of these were the workingmen hotels that catered to skilled mechanics and craftsmen. Rooms in these buildings cost more, up to a dollar a night, and were in far better condition than those in any of the other kinds of lodging houses. The Mohawk, for example, charged forty to seventy cents a night, and the residents wore collars and creased trousers. Stationery and desks were provided as a service of the hotel. Some elderly, single, middle-class men also preferred these facilities because of their affordability, the services they offered, the lack of care they required (compared with an apartment), and their proximity to services like restaurants and entertainment. Many of these buildings were converted apartment buildings; others were hotels built expressly for this purpose. Some are still in use and comprise a significant part of the current Chicago SRO stock.[37]

The next step down—a big one—was the cubicle or "cage" hotel, which rented for fifteen to twenty-five cents a night. Owners divided warehouses or other open indoor spaces (usually in light industrial buildings) into small rooms by running huge lengths of wood or corrugated iron along the floor, then subdividing the space with cross pieces. The height of the walls varied; some were nine to fourteen feet high, while in some rooms the ceilings came down so low that, according to Riis, they were "just large enough to . . . allow the man room to pull off his clothes." Average floor space per cubicle was 5 by 7 feet. Each room was provided with a 2½-by-6-foot iron bed with wire springs, a mattress (often of straw), bedding, and quilt, occasionally a locker and almost always a chair, with a fifteen-watt bulb dangling overhead. As many as two hundred such rooms could exist on a single floor of a building that could go as high as six or seven stories.[38]

One reason these places were known as "cages" was that the walls always stopped one to three feet short of the ceiling and floor, and the gaps were then fitted with wire mesh. This arrangement provided for ventilation but also permitted noise, vermin, liquid, and semi-liquid matter to pass freely between rooms. The writer Josiah Flynt told how he left a wakeup call for 7:00 A.M. at the front office in one cage hotel and found that his request was "distinctly obeyed." At 6:30 A.M. he was awakened by "a man poking me in the ribs with a long stick leveled at me from over the partition wall" (Flynt clearly was getting deluxe service: after the hotel worker had prodded him, he added the warning, "Eh bloke, time to get up"). The wire barrier also prevented theft; before the mesh was used, thieves would crawl over the walls and grab clothing. Later, however, wily crooks learned that they could take strong wire and bend the end into a hook, then reach through the wire netting and steal clothing outright or hold it close to the mesh and rifle through the pockets. Veteran lodgers tried to foil these devices by folding their clothes and storing them in the locker or under the chair.[39]

Conditions in these cubicles were dismal. Only the rooms on the end had a window, so floors with as many as two hundred rooms might have only four with any ventilation. Unlike the city of Minneapolis, which required that ventilation be maintained "beyond the control of lodgers," Chicago permitted lodgers to decide their own conditions. If it was a cold day, the lodgers on the end would naturally try to warm themselves by shutting the windows, cutting off even this meager flow of air, so that "there is often absolutely no ventilation." This did little to provide more heat, however: hotels were found where one stove heated ninety-four rooms, and one hotel had a single stove for 172 lodgers. In another building there were two entire floors without any source of heat, and in another three floors were unheated. The city's provision for 400 cubic feet of air per tenant was infrequently complied with and, according to one report, was "a farce." In addition, as Lawrence Vieller, the famous New York housing reformer, pointed out, "Far more important than the mere *amount* of air space are the kind and quality of the air, the frequency of its renewal, the possibility of its movement within the room." The cage hotels, obviously, had little circulation. As a result, Nels Anderson observed, "the smells accumulate from day to day so that the guest on entering a room is greeted by a variety of odors to which each of his predecessors has contributed."[40]

Mattresses and bedding were also distressed. Boston, New York, and Minneapolis all had laws requiring that mattresses in lodging houses had to be encased in waterproof material, although this law was not always followed scrupulously. No such law existed in Chicago, so, according to one social researcher, "the condition of mattresses in some of the houses is better imagined than described." Men preferred comforters that were thick and warm to ordinary blankets, but the former were impossible to clean. Sheets were changed usually once a week but sometimes every two weeks. In some places they never washed the linen at all, instead leaving it on the beds till the sheets literally wore out. Under any circumstances, however, the transiency of lodgers meant that men frequently slept in dirty sheets and blankets that had been used by numerous others before them, an invitation to disease. Many of the blankets and sheets had vermin, and, according to Josiah Flynt, "there was a bad odor about everything." Pillows were made of feathers, with a greasy case, and, as one investigator claimed, "were often as heavy as lead and harder than the mattresses."[41]

Toilet facilities were dismal, as were those for cleaning. Whereas New York required one toilet for every fifteen beds, the average in unregulated Chicago was one for every forty beds. One hotel, however, had two toilets for 172 men, and another had six toilets for 300 men. These were generally filthy and odorous. Boston required that bathroom floors be made of concrete, marble, or some other waterproof material, but in Chicago many were constructed of wood, which retained smells as well as germs. Many of the toilet rooms had no outside ventilation, but opened onto sleeping rooms or halls. Few of the doors for these rooms fit snugly, and some of the rooms had no door at all. In many cases doors were fastened into an open position so that their slamming would not disturb the sleep of other lodgers. Use of disinfectant was rare, and towels were either on a roller or in common use. There was often only one drinking cup per floor. Many of the lodging houses had no hot water, and there were few wash basins. Minneapolis and New York required one basin for every ten beds, but in Chicago the average was one for every twenty-eight beds. One hotel had five bowls for 200 lodgers, another six bowls for 300 lodgers. Similarly, New York law stipulated one bathtub for every twenty-five beds, or one shower for every forty beds. Chicago, however, had an average of one bathing facility for every 116 beds. Even worse, most of these facilities were tubs, which most men wisely shunned for fear of contagion. The fact that there were only twenty-four showers in fifty hotels housing 8,500 men was appropriately cited as "one good reason why the lodging house habitue is generally dirty." [42]

Disease was naturally a problem in these dank quarters. Vermin and skin diseases were easily communicated, as were respiratory illnesses. One lodging house that sheltered 200 men each night had seventeen deaths from tuberculosis in one year. In nine lodging-house blocks (five on the white South Side, four on the West Side) there were 123 tuberculosis deaths in a single year, compared with a total of 951 patients who were admitted to the Tuberculosis Institute during that same time, representing a city with over 2 million population. According to the March 11, 1913, weekly bulletin of the Chicago Department of Health, the percentage of tuberculosis cases in "semi-suburban parts of Chicago" was 174.2 per 100,000 persons. The rate in the lodging-house district was 729 per 100,000, roughly four times as high. It is not surprising, therefore, that some of the cheap lodging houses in New York were referred to as "morgues." [43]

Fire was also a danger since corridors and cubicles were constructed of cheap wood. Even central corridors were narrow and dark, and many hallways took false turns or were blind alleys. In one lodging house on the South Side that sheltered one thousand men a night, a house employee acting as guide to researchers had to take a candle with him, and twice on a single floor he went down blind alleys thinking they were direct routes. Large posts often obstructed passageways, forming gaps of only 20 inches for men to pass. Some of the aisles leading to fire escapes were only 30 inches wide and were blocked by stoves that were red hot in winter. [44]

Still another danger was crime. Lodging (as well as rooming house) sections were known for the presence of "jackrollers," felons who would grab drunks and "roll" them, that is, accost them and steal their money. Those who had already passed out were even handier targets, because they would offer only the most minimal resistance.[45]

The next step down from the cages was the dormitory-style lodging house, which rented a bed for ten or fifteen cents a night. A large industrial building would be set up as a massive sleeping chamber and general service pavilion. The downstairs would be rented out to stores and/or saloons, and, in some places, space would be set aside as a reading room or assembly hall. Bathrooms were also on this floor. Upstairs the walls were lined with beds in one of two fashions. One method was to place cots in rows, sometimes with a locker at the foot of the bed. According to Illinois law, there had to be two feet of open space on each side of the bed, but this was never obeyed. One study found as many as six beds crushed together in a row; dozens of others were only a few inches apart; and in no instance was the full two feet permitted. The other way was to set up a series of bunk beds along the walls. These could be made of metal, with quilts instead of mattresses; of wooden shelves three feet wide built out of the walls and stacked three high; or, most commonly, from canvas. This material could be stretched between posts, or else one side could be fastened to the wall, the other to a series of floor-to-ceiling posts, so that four such bunks were fit into each row. Jacob Riis claimed that this was "not the most secure perch in the world. Uneasy sleepers roll off at intervals, but they have not far to fall to the next tier of bunks." From 50 to 200 workers could be squeezed into a single room using either of these methods, although they generally paid more for a cot (especially one with a locker) and less for a bunk.[46]

In none of these situations, however, was there privacy of any kind whatsoever. Although in a few ways the dorm had better facilities—ventilation, for example, was better than in the cage hotel because of the large, uninterrupted spaces—it was still a wide-open dwelling where each man's presence imposed on all the others. Stephen Crane described this environment in a story appropriately entitled "An Experiment in Misery": "there . . . came to his nostrils strange and unspeakable odors that assailed him like malignant diseases with wings. They seemed to be from human bodies closely packed in dens; . . . the fumes from a thousand bygone debauches; the expression of a thousand present miseries . . . and all through the room could be seen the tawny hues of naked flesh, limbs thrust into the darkness, projecting beyond the cots. . . . For the most part they were statuesque, carven, dead." Riis told how "I have stood in such a lodging-room more than once, and I listened to the snoring of the sleepers like the regular strokes of an engine, and the slow creaking of the beams under their restless weight, imagined myself on shipboard and experienced the very real nausea of sea-sickness. The one thing that did not favor the deception was the air; its character could not be mistaken."[47]

If one could not afford the dormitory lodging house, there were other alternatives even worse. For two cents or a nickel a man could stay in a flophouse. All he received for his money was a few square feet of space on a floor inside a room with walls—in other words, literally the right to flop down and go to sleep out of the elements, nothing else. For bedding and blankets the lodger supplied his own newspapers, or else used his coat for a pillow and overcoat as a cover. This kind of place was more likely to be operating in the winter than in the summer, because so many migrants took shelter during that season and then ran short of cash. At times the flops got so crowded that men were placed right next to each other in rows along the floor, so that if one rolled over he hit his neighbor. This arrangement again created dense, difficult situations. Nels Anderson told of a night spent in the most famous flophouse in Chicago, "Hogan's," describing how there was no need for using one's shoes as pillows in this establishment, since "a planking along the wall affords a resting place for weary heads." The atmosphere was demonstrated by his tale that, when a man ran to the toilet to vomit, "a wag called to him, 'heave it up.' " Anderson also encountered Hogan's legendary vermin (a tramp once said that "Hogan may be dead but the bugs that were in business with him are still on the job"). He asked a fellow lodger if the bugs bothered much and was told that they were better organized than the German army. That night he "felt something on my hand. I crushed it . . . I lay down to try and sleep again. A second attack brought me suddenly to my feet." Eventually, another lodger stomped out, cursing the bugs and claiming that he knew of an engine room that provided more amenable sleeping quarters. Since someone else had "weakened first," Anderson felt vindicated and left.[48]

As Anderson's fellow lodger noted, there were still alternatives to the flophouse for those short of cash. Saloons, for example, also known as "barrel-houses" or "stale beer dives," permitted patrons who had purchased a mug of beer either to flop or, in some cases, to sleep all night in their chair, or on a table or in an old beer barrel. A night's lodgings, therefore, was attained for the several pennies' cost of a beer (the desperation of these circumstances is indicated by the fact that most bars in factory districts demanded the purchase of two beers, not one, before one could be eligible for the free lunch). Other places permitted patrons to sleep in sheltered hallways for three cents. The absolute rock bottom of these places, however, were facilities that, for a penny, merely permitted callers to hang on a series of ropes stretched across the room. In one description of this system, bars in New Orleans stretched ropes across the room so that men could lean on them while sleeping. Riis also described a method whereby clotheslines were strung in pairs, and sleepers hung by their armpits. Wake-up was by "a labor saving device . . . in the morning the boss woke them up by simply untying the line at one end and letting go with its load." This was probably the only form of shelter that made the flop look good.[49]

And, of course, below that were the truly homeless, men and women who could afford neither cage nor flop nor ropes. In warm weather they would sleep outside: in Grant Park on the Jungle Stem, on park benches, in vacant lots, in hallways or doorways or alleys. In cold weather they sought out all-night facilities like restaurants, the stale beer dives, or, later, movie theaters, or they remained out in the cold in the same places they stayed in during the summer.[50]

These different ranks and levels of lodging houses have several meanings. First, it is clear that the homeless and nearly homeless had alternatives, choices that could be made among various types of housing. In many cases the choice was made for the individual, in a sense, by economic conditions. Housing was a fluid and uncertain situation; eventually most of this population used all the alternatives—cages, flops, dorms, and the streets—at one time or another. When this law did not apply, when a very minimal amount of discretionary income was available, the hobo or tramp or bum was a free agent. And whenever this was the case, the housing of choice was the cage hotel. This was true even when alternatives with roughly similar levels of depravity, like the dorm, were available at a considerably cheaper price, a formidable factor for those living in a state of relative poverty. The difference in price, for example, between a fifteen-cent dorm bed and a twenty-five-cent cage hotel room, represented an increase of 66 percent. The modern equivalent would be an increase from $150 to $250 for rental of a room.

The reason for the success of the cage hotels, aside from the fact that they filled the desperate need for housing, was that they provided other advantages: privacy and freedom. Every room had its own lock and key, and the resident could come and go as he pleased. Researchers noted how important this was to the men, and how this was the critical ingredient in the success of the cage hotels. As Solenberger, no fan of the cages, explained, "Each man sleeps alone in a tiny room, the door of which he may lock when he enters, and this fact alone accounts for their greater favor." The popularity of cage hotels did not stem from any great improvement in the physical setting (which was marginal at best), but rather in the qualitative benefits of a private room.[51]

Like their middle-class counterparts in the rooming houses, working class men in the lodging houses were demonstrating that independence was a critical aspect of their world view. Their choice squared as well with their notion of how the world should be run: the hobo's and tramp's itinerant lifestyle, the bum's occasional income, all spoke to a world view that stressed freedom. If, as one historian has claimed for these men, "travel signified their freedom to control their own time," then the door to the cubicle did the same. It should not be surprising, therefore, that despite all the horrors of the cage, as many as 40,000 to 60,000 men stayed in such places every night in Chicago at the turn of the century, and during depressions or winters this figure could go up to 80,000. The Chicago pattern is not atypical. Estimates of the number of beds in New York's Bowery lodging houses, as well as those in other cities, ran in the tens of thousands.[52]

These values carry enormous implications for present-day policy. The key social priorities of the homeless and nearly homeless were (and remain) independence and autonomy, and they chose their housing to advance these goals. We can reasonably expect, therefore, that they will continue to gravitate toward housing solutions that permit these values to flourish (such as decent SRO housing) and reject programs that discourage individual freedom (such as large, open shelter facilities, which are throwbacks to the older SRO dormitories).

Working- and middle-class single people also shared a cosmopolitan outlook in their selection of housing. Both groups sought a small private space in the center of a complex and diverse public space. The freedom and autonomy of urban life required on the one hand a secure and private place to sleep and store one's possessions, and on the other a dense public space to obtain work, food, and other merchandise, recreation and social interaction.

These types of lodging houses, therefore, from the workingmen's hotels to the tavern bench, represented the range of shelter provided by the private sector for the transient working man. Their variety reflected the fluid and often desperate economic circumstances of the clientele. But these individuals' choice of the cage hotel also demonstrated the importance of autonomy in the world view of single working-class people, and hence its potential importance for the development of an effective shelter policy for this population.

Social Control and the Government's Housing Alternatives

The worst forms of the lodging house were the housing choices provided by the private sector for the homeless. These were not the only alternatives, however, for people without the means to purchase even the most dismal form of shelter. The city, for example, also maintained various facilities for this population. These facilities represented a second, alternative housing policy.

Municipal efforts to provide shelter were originally carried out on an ad hoc basis, without careful thought or planning. William Stead, author of *If Christ Came to Chicago*, claimed that the "great sleeping place of the tramp" was, in fact, City Hall. Each night, at the turn of the century, the doors to the combined City Hall and Municipal Court House were opened to those who needed a floor to sleep on. On a winter's night, as many as 1,000 to 2,000 individuals availed themselves of these facilities. The first to arrive chose the stairs, each one taking a step as his individual berth. Later arrivals spread out on the floors; and when that area was filled so that only narrow aisles remained, some men chose to spend the night standing up in the warm corridors, instead of fighting the cold. Only the ground floor was available for such use; tramps were not permitted in the City Council or in any of the offices. Eventually the city installed wire doors on the stair-wells to maintain this separation.[53]

Studies of the people who slept on the City Hall floor verified that they were unemployed workers. One survey showed that only 2 percent worked for less than a dollar a day, the lowest wage scale, and most earned from one to three dollars a day. Fifty-nine percent were native-born Americans, and of the foreign born, the most numerous were German, Irish, and Scotch, respectively. Most of the men were aged twenty to forty-five. The largest single employment category was common laborer (33 percent), and most of the rest were in services rather than industrial trades.[54]

The most common municipal arrangement, however, at the turn of the century was to use the police station as a shelter for the homeless. This was a standard urban practice in cities across America. Eric Monkkonen, in *The Police in Urban America*, reported that "during very bad depression years or harsh winters, the number of overnight lodgings provided by a police department exceeded all annual arrests." By 1890 the police stations in New York were providing 150,000 lodgings a year, and eight years later the comparable figure for Chicago was 139,578. Here, too, the population was mostly the working poor: the police officer in charge of the Harrison Street police station in Chicago claimed that bums were a minority among lodgers, and that most were instead "hard-working men, eager to find work." [55]

Police stations were primitive facilities, and few of the tenants stayed long. Men and women went there only for shelter and usually received nothing else (some juvenile delinquents preferred staying in the police station, however, because it guaranteed an alibi. As one young man put it, "If you sleep in the station and anything is pulled off in the town, they ain't got anything on you"). The floors were usually cold, bare stone, although some police stations (especially in New York and Boston) had soft wood floors that were occasionally white-washed for cleanliness. An open gutter at the rear provided the only toilet facility. Tuberculosis, venereal disease, and especially lice were common problems.[56]

Notwithstanding these horrors, this arrangement was a remarkably popular one, for several reasons. In some cases the police acted in a humane fashion, providing meals (coffee and a roll) for lodgers. In most cities the police station was the only free housing available for the homeless; they were the first municipal shelters. Monkkonen estimates that "between 10% and 20% of the U.S. population in the late nineteenth century came from families of which one member had experienced the hospitality of a police station." As a result, such "lodging . . . was something experienced or understood by many if not all poor Americans." [57]

By the turn of the century reformers began to launch attacks on the police station lodging house. They argued against its filth and dismal conditions, but also complained because the police employed no means test whatsoever; officers were occasionally caring and gave personalized service; the police department should deal strictly with law enforcement matters, not those of social service; and only trained social workers should deal with these problems.

As a result of these attacks, the police station ceased to provide lodgings, and this function was taken up by an institution usually called the "municipal lodging house." Chicago's version began service in 1901 when the City Homes Association, a reform organization interested in slum clearance, raised $5,000, rented and equipped a building, and opened the facility on December 21. The city was not able to take over for another two years, when the municipal lodging house became an operation of the Chicago Police Department; the City Council voted a $10,000 appropriation that year. In 1908 responsibility for the facility was transferred to the Department of Health, and in 1917 to the Department of Public Welfare.[58]

The population of the city's facility was a familiar one. According to a survey of residents performed by the Department of Public Welfare in 1925, the most common characteristic shared by the men was unemployment. Sixty-five percent were native born, and less than 1 percent were black (four out of five hundred). This was considerably less than the percentage of blacks in the city as a whole, which was 4.1 percent at the time.[59]

A night spent at the municipal lodging house was in many ways a difficult one. After registering, men had to give their life story and if caught in a lie were sent to the police for incarceration as criminals. There were two meals, breakfast and supper, often only a cup of coffee and rolls. Each client was given a physical examination and then fumigated, while his clothes were taken away to receive the same treatment. Ben Reitman, the hobo doctor, spent a night at the lodging house disguised as a vagrant and woke up choking on the sulphur fumigant. After that he slept on a cot or iron bed. No one was permitted to stay for more than four nights in a row.[60]

From the beginning municipal lodging houses faced criticisms, some of them familiar today. Politicians and reformers in many cities complained that the lodging house took in nonresidents (clearly this had the makings of an oxymoron: it has yet to be discovered how a homeless person can have a place of residence) and calculated the cost of these foreign paupers. In 1918 Chicago closed its municipal lodging house on the grounds of diminished need because of wartime prosperity. It did not, however, reopen the building until 1923, despite the harsh winters of 1920–21 and 1921–22.[61]

The most controversial aspect of the municipal lodging house was the means test. This was basic labor, originally working on garbage disposal or general alley cleanup. The labor was not supposed to be good for body or soul, let alone any kind of training for outside employment. Rather, it was a test, designed to separate out the sincere unemployed workman from the lazy parasite. Reformers believed that the former would not be bothered by such demands, whereas the latter would turn away rather than work. In 1905 the first work test was imposed: one day of labor for every three days of lodging. After 1908, however, the number of lodgers still rose, so additional measures were taken. Distinction was made between first-time and repeat clients. Everything was done that encouraged the former "to secure work and impressed upon him the seriousness of the situation." By 1914 these measures included forcing him to sleep on the floor and, if he idled on the work detail, eliminating the one meal of the day that included meat.[62]

Notwithstanding these changes, the number of lodgers increased from 78,392 in 1913 to 462,361 in 1914. In response, the city opened the municipal wood yard in 1915, where residents of the lodging house had to spend two hours a day sawing wood. This was considered to be, according to the *Bulletin of the Department of Public Welfare*, a "progressive policy." In the month of March 1916, alone, 7,046 men worked in the yard, and eventually clients sawed 3,000 cords of wood, "much of it hard oak and maple, and the rest of it pine and cedar." In 1924 the means test and wood yard were abandoned, on the grounds that "substitution of an employment office, effective cooperation with other charitable and correctional agencies" represented better solutions.[63]

The real effect of the municipal lodging house and the wood yard was not only the punitive one but also a decrease in the number of lodgers housed by local government, and thus the amount spent on this service. In this regard the municipal lodging house had a mixed success. In 1901, the year the lodging house opened, police stations provided 92,951 lodgings. A year later the lodging house provided 11,097 lodgings and police stations gave another 5,740. Thus, as historian Thomas Philpott has pointed out, "the lodging house *reduced* the amount of municipal service to homeless men by 82 percent." The following year the number of lodgings dropped even further, to 5,562. By 1904 the superintendent of the municipal lodging house recommended that the police refuse to furnish lodgings except in extremely cold weather or only after 10:00 P.M. in emergencies. But even work tests could not deal with the recession of 1907–1908, and the number of lodgings had risen to over 100,000 by the latter date. As noted, the number jumped quickly after that, with the Department of Public Welfare reporting 488,218 lodgings for the 1914–15 season. That year, however, the wood yard was instituted: in 1915–16 lodgings fell to 44,866, a drop of 91 percent; the number of meals served went from 824,789 to 86,612, an 89 percent decline.[64]

Municipal housing facilities, therefore, underwent shifts in both form and emphasis between 1880 and 1920. Originally an informal system designed to provide protection from the elements and little else, shelter provision eventually became formalized and elaborate. By the time the municipal lodging house opened, a major policy alternative had been created by government. This system provided lodgings that were often superior to their more prolific counterparts in the private sector. They were operated, however, on the basic premise that residents' moral character was inferior. Measures of social control, such as the wood yard, had to be utilized to guard against what officials perceived as an opportunity for parasites and deviants to take advantage of government. The homeless and nearly homeless, of course, avoided any facility that devised policy and procedures on this basis.

Charitable Hotels and Religious Missions: The Not-for-Profit Sector

Besides the array of different kinds of private-sector, for-profit lodging houses and the municipal facilities, there were various efforts by not-for-profit groups. At the top of the scale were the Mills Hotels. In 1897 philanthropist D. O. Mills opened the first of several of his Mills Hotels in New York, to show that decent workingmen's houses could be provided at a reasonable cost. This facility had more than 1,500 rooms and provided a clean bed in a private room, clean bathrooms with showers, and free pajamas and slippers, along with an inexpensive restaurant on the premises. The Mills Hotel was considered a model program, and rightfully so, but it took a Chicago observer to note its limitations: it was priced to exclude the less affluent workingman and catered solely to those who were better off. A commentator in the *Chicago Tribune* reported, "The day I inspected the Mills Hotel I did not see a poor looking individual, but, in fact, a middle or medium class." He went on to say that a "Mills Hotel in Chicago will not be a blessing to the poor" because of its high rates. The city's leading citizens took their cue, and although a Mills Hotel was established in 1900, the primary response to homelessness was to create the municipal lodging house instead.[65]

There were other charitable efforts priced for the poorer workingman. In 1916 the Young Men's Christian Association opened a nineteen-story building with 1,821 rooms at Harrison Street and Wabash Avenue, in the South Loop. The Rufus G. Dawes Hotel was built by Charles Dawes, one-time controller of the currency of the United States, in memory of his son Rufus (who drowned at age twenty-one). Facilities included 100 private rooms at ten cents a night and 200 beds in open, dormitory-like areas for five cents. A meal of soup, coffee, and doughnuts in the restaurant cost only five cents, easily competitive with the chili parlors along Madison Street. Although many workmen used this facility when nothing else was available, Anderson claimed that it was not popular, "like all paternalistic, quasi-charitable institutions."[66]

One alternative to these facilities was the missions. The Salvation Army began operations in New York in 1891 and added forty-four more missions within the next decade. In Chicago the army ran dormitory hotels that housed 1,142 men a night, offering them, for the dime rental, lodging, coffee, and rolls in the morning, and a religious service. Army facilities in a few cities, however, required a spell in the wood yard in return for food and shelter. The Chicago Christian Industrial League also provided work, food, and shelter to hundreds of men, fighting against the conditions in "Satan's strongholds." The league went throughout middle-class Chicago collecting old goods and newspapers, which were turned into usable commodities in their workshops. This arrangement not only provided the income for the charity, it also gave the men employment.[67]

Other missions provided a variety of environments and services. The Pacific Garden Mission, still in existence, had the distinction of carrying out the original conversion of a former baseball player named Billy Sunday, who went on to an illustrious career as a revivalist minister. Over the door hung a lantern with the description "Strangers Welcome," and the walls were covered with scripture texts and homilies like "God is Love." This mission, like all the others, offered a modest meal and place to sleep in return for attendance at a religious meeting or sermon. Some also distributed old clothes; overcoats were especially sought after in the winter, and were referred to as "bennies" (for benefits). One problem with many of the missions, including the Pacific Garden, was that the men were not permitted to flop on the floor and instead had to spend the night sitting in chairs, dozing off intermittently. One unemployed worker, who spent three nights sleeping in the mission and four days looking for a job, complained that "when you're on your feet all day and cannot get a lay-out at night, your legs swell almost to the knee. You become lame and cannot even go hunting the job no one seems able to find."[68]

These places were used extensively because of the pressing need but were not favored by transient men because of the heavy tariff in religious conversion they required. Even the Salvation Army was criticized by one sociologist on the grounds that the army was primarily a religious group seeking converts, rather than a nondenominational charitable organization. The argument was that the army "is as much of a denomination as the Baptists or Methodists or Presbyterians or any other Protestant sect. It is not doing Good Samaritan work solely and purely from the love of such work, but as a part of its plan to build up a powerful denomination in the United States."[69]

The missions, thus, were seen as places of last resort that did some good by handing out food and shelter but extracted in return a tariff of hypocrisy. A leading mission in Boston, for example, threw out a "steady man" who refused to testify, but allowed the man who was "gloriously saved" to have free room and board, regardless of the honesty or dishonesty of his confession. One turn-of-the-century article on beggars argued that missions had "less human interest than the lodging houses without the religious taint. . . . In them, dexterity with pious cant is at a premium." Among the residents of the Main Stem, the worst type of bum was considered to be the "mission stiff" who feigned conversion to get a place to sleep or a meal. A tramp ballad told how "In my heart was pallor / An' in my heart was shame / An' so forgive me Jesus / Fer mockin' of thy name." As one writer put it, "the relationship between Skid Row men and the missions . . . always has been the opposite of mutual respect. One has to sing for one's supper." [70]

It is important to point out, as well, that the hoboes, tramps, and bums were right when they claimed that the missions had more on their agendas than religious activity. Recent research indicates that missions served a variety of social functions that had little or nothing to do with their stated purpose. James Rooney, for example, argued that missions actually made a living by failing at their stated goals. The purpose of the missions, ostensibly, was to convert the Main Stem and all its residents to a Christian way of life; as Frank Beck, a minister, put it: "Conversion is the alpha and omega of a mission's . . . activities."

Yet, in this work the missions failed dismally. Their efforts to convert the population, however, helped them to gain funding and provide employment opportunities for religious workers, since as long as there was a Main Stem, the missions would remain in business. Total conversion, on the other hand, would have shut them down. This focus also had a negative effect on their relationship with clients, who had to be presented as the dregs of society, and bitterly resented it. Nevertheless, such a depiction was necessary to justify the work of the mission. The homeless and nearly homeless also recognized that their poverty-ridden existence was crucial to the mission's survival, since, as Beck explained, "bums are the best patrons of rescue missions." They were also just about the only ones. [71]

The other very real function of the missions was to uphold a system of *private*-sector provision of social needs. In many cases missions gave clients, instead of a meal and a cot, "chits" good for a meal at a local cafeteria or for a night at a cage or flop, or else just enough money to afford these facilities. Eventually, this would become a widespread practice, as missions saw their purpose more and more as service providers. But with limited funds, they found that the easiest and cheapest way to do this was to pay others, via the clients and their "bed-tickets," to perform this service. The result, however, was that the missions became responsible for keeping many of the cages in business long after they would otherwise have lost favor and become no longer profitable. The missions put into place, and maintained, an alternative system of providing basic social service by subsidizing some of the worst aspects of the private sector. The fact that this alternative function could dominate the work of a mission is demonstrated by the figures for one Main Stem mission along Madison Street. During the year ending September 1921, 56,718 men visited the mission, and nearly 29,000 meals were served. At the same time, 4,145 tickets were issued entitling the holder to a night's sleep at a flop or a cage, but only 4,016 conversions occurred.[72]

The support of the missions is one of the reasons, also, that cages lasted longer in cities like Chicago than in other cities; whenever there is artificial subsidy of a type of building, it stays in existence long after the private market would have eliminated it. Subsidies become particularly important in the more recent period, when we compare the effect of city support for SROs, as exists in New York, for example, with a free market, the situation in Chicago.

The not-for-profit sector, a third policy alternative, mirrored municipal government both in its benefits and drawbacks. The originators and operators of these facilities were often caring individuals who sincerely wanted to help the poor. Some of their buildings, especially the charitable hotels, were a large step above the private sector's cage hotels and worse.

The not-for-profit operations, however, also required some kind of payment. Charity services asked clients to act subservient before paternalistic overseers. Missions put a premium on religious conversion, real or faked. These informal stipulations were unacceptable to a population whose chief priority was personal autonomy, so the not-for-profit alternative was rejected whenever possible.

Conclusions

The private sector dominated the lives of the transient working class, as well as their choice of housing. Status evaluations as well as social descriptions were based on a man's work pattern and its effect on his body. Hoboes, tramps, and bums took this situation, however, and used it to create a multilayered social order that enabled them to gain dignity and prestige for their skills and employment history.

Shelter alternatives were also dominated by the private sector. Landlords created the cages and dorms and flops, depending on the amount of capital they chose to sink into a building and the type of clientele they wanted.

Government and charities also attempted to care for the needs of this population. They added another dimension, however, to shelter policy: morality. Their depiction of the homeless and nearly homeless as men and women of poor character meant that some form of control mechanism, such as the wood yard or conversion, had to be included. As a result people avoided these facilities whenever possible.

Thus, the hierarchy of shelter alternatives available to the homeless and nearly homeless was primarily a reflection of their uncertain economic condition. The variety of types and prices of accommodation (see table 3-3) meant that men and women in all stages of the employment cycle

TABLE 3-3

Types and Costs of Shelter for the Transient Worker

	PAYMENT	
SECTOR AND TYPE	Cash	In-kind
PRIVATE		
Workingman's hotel	$.50–1.00	None
Cage hotel	$.15–.25	None
Dormitory	$.10–.15	None
Flop, beer hall, etc.	$.01–.05	None
PUBLIC		
Municipal lodging house	Free	Day labor
Police station	Free	None
City hall	Free	None
NOT-FOR-PROFIT		
Charitable hotel	$.05–1.00	Paternalism
Mission	Free–$.10	Religious conversion

could find housing of one sort or another. In addition, this hierarchy also reflected the social and financial fluidity of this population. Given enough time without work, the recently employed hobo in the cage hotel could become the beggar seeking handouts, surviving nightly in flops or taverns.

This hierarchy demonstrates, however, that the social value of shelter was based on the degree of privacy and autonomy it offered, a value reflected in price as well. Privacy was the key factor that made cages more appealing than dorms, and the importance of self-respect accounted for the opprobrium attached to municipal shelters as well as to charitable hotels and missions.

An alternative housing policy was thus carved out by SRO residents. Despite poverty and constant efforts at control by outsiders, this population created an intricate social hierarchy and a system of values, then made shelter decisions on this basis. The structure they created reflected their economic circumstances, but also their belief in autonomy and self-worth. These values were ignored by all the other sectors, however, as dominance in housing policy began to shift in the 1920s.

4 Scientific Welfare: The Rise of the Public Sector in Housing

In the 1920s the dominant force in SRO housing policy began to shift from the private to the public sector, a movement that culminated during the Depression of the 1930s. This meant that an entirely different set of assumptions was used to determine policy and the programs that would implement it. Part of the reason for this change was the decline in the need of the private sector for transient workers. By this time the continent had been conquered by rails and farms and factories, most of the railroad track used in the twentieth century had been laid, and the agricultural sector was increasingly mechanized. Large business operations now harvested natural resources on a regular basis, rather than in sporadic attempts to roll back the wilderness. Many of the jobs held by transient workers were eliminated, reducing this population and causing the Main Stem and its companions across the country to decline. At the same time, the private sector was also losing interest in low-income housing. Building codes and other reforms made it no longer profitable to build tenements and other types of shelter for the poor, including lodging houses.

While the impact of the private sector on the working-class transient and his housing was waning, government was becoming a major force in the setting of housing policy. Its involvement was the result of powerful new, scientific ideas and tools developed by reformers to deal with social issues. These gave greater credibility to the solutions devised by social scientists. At the same time, however, reformers continued to use moral arguments to justify their programs, in part because of their own beliefs, in part because of the need to win over politicians and the general public.

Influenced by researchers at schools like the University of Chicago, public officials began to devise a very different approach to SROs and their tenants. Basing their analysis on the theory of human ecology, professors and administrators viewed the SRO district as a social deviation because it combined functions like housing and work and recreation rather than segregating them into different districts, a concept eventually codified into zoning laws. Thus, policy was increasingly aimed at transforming residents and eliminating their housing, in contrast to the tendency of the private sector to use housing as one more way to exploit the residents.

This change was completed during the Depression decade. The economic crisis forced government to take over the provision of basic needs, such as work and food. In the case of housing for single workers, the Depression cemented the doctrine that this was best handled by government and by trained public administrators, institutionalizing their dominance over SRO policy. It also produced the concept of separating "good" and "bad" transients on the basis of factors such as family ties and employment history, then developing different policies for each group. This decision had an enormous impact on policy, not only regarding transients but the homeless as well. These are the policies that are followed today. We must understand their origin and nature, therefore, before we can assess and revise current policy initiatives.

The Decline of the Main Stem

In the 1920s the private sector began to lose interest in, and dominance over, transient workers and their housing, largely a result of a shift in economic conditions and a change in the labor force. The frontier was gone, and with its demise went the need for a large seasonal migrant labor force. Most of the forests had been cut down, and the rest were lumber farms, harvested by stable crews. Similarly, western mining became a steady operation, with resident populations around the mines. The bonanza wheat farms were totally mechanized and no longer required streams of workers at harvest time. Roads, rails, bridges, water, and sewer systems were all built and the systems rationalized, so that there was no longer any need for a mobile work force. By 1923 Nels Anderson felt that he was witnessing the "last days of . . . the 'slave market,' " the day-labor agencies along West Madison Street. Kenneth Allsop noted how "the bum may soon go the way of the stage driver and the Mississippi pilot." [1]

The population and institutions of the Main Stem were greatly affected. Fewer men came in search of work that did not exist, a pattern reinforced by the introduction of the car to American society. The 1920s saw the rise of the "flivver bums," laborers who managed to buy a car of some sort and used it to travel from job to job. Theirs was the ultimate form of freedom for workers on the move, since they were no longer dependent on the railroad. However, they were no longer drawn to railroad centers, like Chicago, after finishing a job. Increasingly, the Main Stem became a place inhabited by the home guard only, men who stayed in one place and did casual labor. By 1925 the majority of residents in Milwaukee's district, for example, fit this category. As a result of this change, the population was aging; in 1930,

10 percent of the residents of the Bowery were over sixty, 28 percent over fifty. Lodging houses, faced with the decline in population, began to shut down (Minneapolis lost 30 percent of its lodging houses between 1915 and 1920). In addition, Prohibition augmented the process because it shut down the saloons that frequently provided hotels' profit margins.[2]

Another key reason for the shrinking number of SRO-type units, however, was that the construction of low-income housing was no longer profitable. Although it is generally recognized today that building new housing for the poor is impossible without subsidy, historians like Kenneth Jackson have argued that this has been true since the 1920s. Jackson claimed that "by the second decade of the twentieth century . . . entrepreneurs were shunning the low income housing market, and most private investors displayed little interest in the field."[3]

The lower profits were a by-product of housing regulation, which, by raising housing standards, increased the production cost; developers could no longer get an acceptable return (in the form of rents) to justify the capital investment. Thus, housing reform had contradictory effects: it improved the quality of housing for the poor while reducing its availability. Anthony Jackson, who analyzed the history of tenement housing in New York, explained how: "The grade of dwelling that private enterprise had supplied for the use of nineteenth century immigrants had been rejected by the rising standards of housing reform, which had served the community rather than the poor by preventing private enterprise from reaching down to this level."[4]

The Rising Role of Government in Housing

While the hold of the private sector on housing was loosening, the strength of government was growing, partly because of the power of scientific methodology. One of the most significant aspects of the Progressive Era was the rise of science as arbiter of public policy regarding human behavior and the social environment. All aspects of these subjects came under the scrutiny of scientific researchers. In business, for example, Frederick Taylor's concepts of scientific engineering redefined the worker's role within the company as well as his relationship to management. Later, in the 1920s, Elton Mayo's experiments at the Western Electric plant further refined these concepts as a way of tying workers to their jobs.

Public administration and social work were also transformed by the adoption of new, scientific practices. Powerful methodologies and tools, like the case study approach and statistical analysis, were developed. Institutions of higher learning like the University of Chicago started undergraduate programs in these areas, as well as opening the School of Social Service Administration (SSA). By supplying a means of certification based on these concepts and procedures, the universities guaranteed that this new system of providing social service would dominate the field.

The government's predominance in social service did not mean that morality was eliminated. If anything, it played a larger role in discussions of government policy than it had in those of the private sector. In the debate over rooming houses, for example, morality was a major concern for reformers like Harvey Zorbaugh, who sought to influence social work professionals and civic leaders, rather than the business community.

There were two reasons for the moral aspect of reform policy formulation. One was the background of the participants: a large part of their motivation stemmed from ethical and religious impulses. The Reverend Washington Gladden's *Social Gospel*, for example, a plea for Protestants to become socially involved in the issues of the day, was a major inspirational text for the reform movement. Similarly, in 1912 at the Progressive Party convention, a moment that many historians believe marks the height of the Progressive Era, delegates clasped hands and sang "Onward Christian Soldiers." Their religious orientation meant that reformers would be spurred by some of humanity's noblest concepts of decency and charity, but it also ensured that moral issues would play a major role in the supposed "scientific" development of policy.

The other reason welfare officials included a moral element was the political controls they had to contend with. Unlike entrepreneurs, who could implement concepts and programs as they chose, public administrators did not control the government's decision-making apparatus. Instead, policy was decided by the mayor and by the City Council, each with a separate political agenda. These officials were in turn responsive to public opinion and to influentials like the newspapers. In sum, welfare administrators functioned within a democratic society, with power vested in the citizenry and its representatives. As a consequence, scientific arguments were rarely sufficient unto themselves, and additional support from politicians and the public had to be obtained via moral explanations that rallied emotions as well as logic.

Reform and the University of Chicago Connection

The reform movement was given added strength by concepts devised and advocated by sociologists at the University of Chicago. These men and women did more than just devise theories, however; they were also active in the political struggle to transform ideas into policies. Thus academics took the lead in *defining* the reform agenda, as opposed to carrying out its implementation, which was handled by government bureaucracies. Like other Progressives, they believed in progress, which could be achieved only by conscious human effort. Furthermore, as Steven Diner explained, progress was "measured by the extent to which individuals in a society worked toward a common goal." [5]

This common goal was determined by science. A scientific public policy involved, first, the collection of data on specific problems such as housing, infant mortality, and the like. Using this evidence, experts such as professors could devise programs for the common good. Their solutions would be unlike those demanded by special interests, who ignored the needs of society to advance selfish goals. Political bosses and corrupt businessmen were standard examples of these "special interests." [6]

At the forefront of this movement was the University of Chicago, and especially its sociology department. Faculty at the University of Chicago did not believe that their ideas should operate in a vacuum. By the twentieth century, the image of the academic had shifted from that of a somewhat eccentric monk-like figure to a man of the world who sought prestige and success, the latter in part defined by his ability to influence the events of the day. Merle Curti has referred to this change as "the secularization of scholarship." [7]

Such an attitude was fostered at the University of Chicago. William Rainey Harper, its founder and first president, believed that institutions of higher learning should be "a potent factor in public life." He not only encouraged professors to get involved in social issues but even pressed other civic leaders to make use of his faculty's talents. Once, for example, he wrote a newspaper editor concerning a statistics professor's interest in "municipal affairs" and on another occasion responded to an inquiry by stating that members of the sociology department should be looked to "in deciding how to furnish relief for Chicago's unemployed citizens." [8]

Harper's philosophy was taken to heart by the sociology department. Its founder was Albion Small. A former Baptist minister, in the 1890s Small helped found the Civic Federation of Chicago. In the classroom he pushed students to engage in field work rather than empty theorizing, and he proposed that they view Chicago as an object of research. Similarly, Professor Charles Henderson, another Baptist minister turned social scientist, worked extensively with welfare agencies on matters such as labor problems and the "dependent, defective and delinquent classes." Henderson wrote, "The scholar's duty is to aid in forming a judicial public opinion, as distinguished from the public opinion of a class and its special pleaders." Other members of the department followed Henderson's advice: according to Steven Diner, between 1892 and 1919, 73 percent of all sociology professors at the university for five years or more became involved in local reform movements. Later, in the twenties, Robert Park and Ernest Burgess, founders of the human ecology school of analysis, continued in this vein; they viewed Chicago as the department's private research laboratory. [9]

There were both direct and indirect ways that academics could control or influence policy. Of the former, the most powerful was to devise or control programs or agencies, or to sit on the boards that directed or advised them. The City Club's housing committee, for example, was chaired by Professor James Tufts. Under his direction the committee helped revise the state and the municipal housing codes. Another example was the city of Chicago's Department of Public Welfare, which resulted from an ordinance drawn up by Professor Charles Merriam. One of the department's first actions was to create an advisory board, which included Albion Small and Grace Abbott, a founder of SSA. Similarly, the not-for-profit sector called on academics for support. After the Depression of 1893, when the Civic Federation acted to centralize nongovernmental relief in the Bureau of Charities, Albion Small (a federation founder) and Charles Henderson were among the leaders. In 1912 Henderson became president of the bureau's successor, the United Charities.[10]

Another way professors could influence the design and implementation of policy was by conducting or assisting with research that formed the basis of new legislation. James Tufts's housing studies influenced the housing code revisions, and Robert Park, Ernest Burgess, Charles Merriam, and Sophonisba Breckenridge (another SSA founder) were all frequently consulted by the commission investigating the 1919 race riot.[11]

Professors also influenced policy by helping form an interlocking network of welfare reformers and public administrators which, according to Steven Diner, "enabled upper strata reformers . . . to unite and press their demands on a variety of fronts." Thus, "professors in Chicago were a force to be reckoned with because they united effectively with other groups." [12]

There were many different connections. Diner found that more than half of the city's reformers lived in one of two areas, either a stretch of the South Side that included Hyde Park (and the university), or the Gold Coast on the north side of the city. In addition, 67 percent of the men were members of the City Club and 33 percent were members of the Union League Club. Similarly, 76 percent of the women belonged to the Women's City Club, and 48 percent belonged to the Chicago Women's Club.[13]

Reformers, including academics, were often thrown together in the course of their work. Alice Solenberger, who wrote *One Thousand Homeless Men*, the leading study of Chicago working-class transients at the turn of the century, conducted her research while running the Central District of the Chicago Bureau of Charities. Both Albion Small and Charles Henderson, as noted earlier, had played major roles in the founding and operations of this agency. Another University of Chicago professor active in housing reform was George Vincent, dean of faculties, arts, literature and science, who held a Ph.D. in sociology. He was a member of the first executive committee of the City Homes Association, which was the leading housing reform organization in Chicago at the turn of the century. Similarly, Anita

McCormick Blaine, one of the city's leading social benefactors, was close friends with the university's John Dewey and sat on the executive committee of the Bureau of Charities (to which she was a major donor).[14]

Connections like these meant that the professors could get their ideas advocated and implemented through a variety of channels. By broaching a new concept at any of a number of functions, they made sure that society's leaders would hear and consider their ideas. Thus, because academics were so intimately tied into this network, it was common for their concepts to eventually be developed into policy and programs, even when the authors were not directly credited. This was one of the most important types of influence that academics possessed.

The other important source of power for academics derived from their influence over the individuals who implemented these programs. One aspect of the Progressive Era reform movements was the drive for professionalization. In a number of fields, of which law and medicine are the best known, practitioners began to create and define professional status for themselves, by establishing entrance requirements and schools to teach these, by setting standards, and by forming trade organizations. Professionalization had the effect of placing the expert as arbiter of most intellectual endeavors, as well as guaranteeing that the professoriate would control the form and shape of the emerging disciplines.[15]

The drive for professionalization was an active force in Chicago's social work community. Emerging professionals sought to eliminate, or at least control, the vast numbers of volunteers that conducted most welfare activity. Caseworkers argued, legitimately, that their training separated them from the well-meaning but uninformed amateur. In particular, professionals prided themselves on their ability to create a scientific data base and to then successfully interpret this evidence and design effective programs to deal with any problem.[16] Social workers, therefore, needed specialized training, a key element, because it was precisely what set them apart from the nonspecialist. Thus, the university played a critical role in achieving the goal of professionalization.

Discussions of special training for social workers came as early as 1893, when Anna Dawes read a paper on this subject at the Columbian Exposition. In 1903 a group of reformers founded the Institute of Social Science as part of the Extension Division at the University of Chicago. Four years later the institute received a grant to organize a research division, which was headed by Julia Lathrop. She in turn recruited two brilliant young economists, both of them with doctorates from the University of Chicago and a marked interest in public policy and welfare reform issues. The two, who quickly rose to leadership of Chicago's social work community, were Edith Abbott and Sophonisba Breckenridge. In 1908 the institute became the Chicago School of Civics and Philanthropy and declared its independence from the university. Nevertheless, classes were still taught by university-affiliated reformers such as Charles Henderson. As the school gained a national reputation for leadership in the field, the university responded and in 1920 reincorporated the program as the School of Social Service Administration. In 1924 Abbott became dean.[17]

By controlling the social work curriculum, academics were able to do more than define the nature of the discipline. First, they established themselves as the definitive experts, who would be consulted in the formulation of policy by both the not-for-profit sector and by government. Julia Lathrop, for example, the first head of the Children's Bureau in Washington, was succeeded by Grace Abbott, Edith's sister. Throughout the twenties and into the Depression this federal agency not only financed a great deal of SSA's research, it served as a conduit for political influence in the national government.[18]

Second, this leadership expanded the network academics could use to transform theory into program. Roy Lubove wrote that "if social work could claim any distinctive function in an atomized urban society with serious problems of group communication and mass deprivation, it was not individual therapy but liaison between groups and the stimulation of social legislation and institutional change." [19]

Finally, and most important, reformers implemented many of their ideas by training generations of students in their theories. These individuals went on to become the administrators and caseworkers who designed and ran Chicago's social service system. They carried out, in the most practical way, the ideas that academics had introduced in the classroom.[20]

Housing Reform in Chicago

Initial efforts by government to control policy centered on the establishment of a building code, and its extension to cover SROs. This, a typical pattern in Progressive Era municipal reform, originated in New York City, with its European levels of density. New York was also home to the nation's best known early housing reformers, Jacob Riis and Lawrence Veiller; the latter is regarded as the father of the modern building code. Other cities soon followed New York's example. A Boston reformer advocated that "there should not be in any city uninspected lodging houses where the criminal and diseased may congregate." Similarly, as late as 1901 a Chicagoan could bemoan the fact that his city had "no intelligible, well-planned building and sanitary code." [21]

Despite the last comment, housing reform in Chicago actually started in the late nineteenth century. In 1874 the City Council passed a tenement house ordinance, which was strengthened in 1879 and 1880. Enforcement was placed in the hands of the Health Department, which had authority to check on such conditions as lighting, ventilation, and heating. The first inquiries into conditions in SROs were made in 1893, when the city hosted the Columbian Exposition and hordes of visitors came to the city, most of them staying in hotels. That year civic groups conducted an inspection of lodging and tenement houses.[22]

Their work did not precipitate immediate action. Not until 1897 did reformers join together in regular meetings to talk about housing reform in Chicago. Even then, it took two years till, in 1899, the City Homes Association was founded to work for a stronger and more efficient municipal system for regulating buildings. In December 1902 a building code was passed, which defined provisions for protection against fire, for sufficient light and air, for sanitary regulation, and for enforcement.[23]

There was no question that the reformers wanted to extend these rules to cover the rooming and lodging houses, and with great justification. In 1899 the Bureau of Associated Charities appointed a special committee to look into the problem of the homeless and their lodging. Their recommendations included the closing of police stations as free lodging houses and the arrest of all "professional wanderers." The lead sentence in the *Chicago Tribune* story announcing their findings accurately reported that the bureau "is determined to drive tramps and beggars out of Chicago."[24]

But this was easier said than done. As late as 1915 the city Board of Health exercised little or no control over lodging houses, while the state Board of Health, which was mandated by state law to have "supervision of all lodging houses," exercised minimal authority. Although a few of the worst places were shut down, the board was hampered by an inadequate staff of inspectors and by a body of vague and indefinite laws that gave little mandate to a vigilant inspector. The vagueness was a by-product of several Chicago conditions, including a strong real estate lobby that blocked any kind of housing regulation, and the support given lodging houses by politicians, who hired the city's drifting population to swell the rolls at election time.[25]

Human Ecology and Zoning

By the 1920s housing policy in Chicago began to be affected by a theory developed at the University of Chicago sociology department: human ecology. According to this concept, the natural growth of cities resulted in the creation of separate sectors having different purposes. Robert Park of the University of Chicago wrote of "natural areas," "each with its natural function." He felt that "as the community grows there is . . . a process of differentiation and segregation." These thoughts were echoed by his colleague, Ernest Burgess: "As a city grows its structure becomes more complex, its areas more specialized." But Burgess also believed that the process created a "natural" division into social classes, thus implying that any community where they were intermixed was inherently primitive and "disorganized." Thus, the theory of human ecology provided a detailed explanation for the changes in Chicago's physical and social geography in the twentieth century. By so doing, however, it fitted the concept of spatial segregation into a framework of evolution, thereby implying an inevitable and inexorable social force.[26]

These theories held sway not only among academic sociologists, but also among the welfare policy initiators and administrators whom they influenced. The sociologists had "proved" that hotel life was an anachronism that only slowed the natural growth of cities. The roomer or lodger lived downtown, rather than in an area set aside as residential, which harkened back to the early days of the walking city. Yet, reformers and social scientists believed that one of their greatest triumphs was the ability to recognize that the city was divided into different regions. According to this concept, certain areas of the city should be reserved for industrial use, others for commerce, recreation, entertainment, housing, and so forth. Most citizens had to travel to different sections of the city, depending on the activity he or she wished to pursue.

SRO residents, however, lived, worked, and shopped downtown, carrying on a life-style closer to that of the first urban dwellers in the walking city. Even in a city neighborhood, shops were located on a main street or crossroads, surrounded by secondary streets with housing. But the SRO was on the main street, and residents could go next door to shop, get a drink, or see a show. This total immersion in the city, a characteristic of hotels in general, was anathema to reformers who fought to control the growing metropolis by dividing it into different zones.

Thus, in the view of reformers, SRO living failed to provide the proper division between public and private life. SRO residents, for example, experienced social interaction that was casual and marked by few controls. The walls of a cage hotel, for example, through which a resident could hear a dozen different conversations, enforced these conditions. Social activity for the middle class, on the other hand, was both organized and formal. Similarly, Victorian culture dictated that middle-class order be based on the protection and elevation of the private sphere from the hurly-burly of the public realm. It was believed that since the SRO was so intimately a part of the downtown environment, roomers and lodgers lacked respectability and character; they were dangerous because they were tainted by the chaos of urban public life.

One of the great ironies of housing reform, therefore, was that its leaders rejected SROs and tried to destroy them, in part because they linked them to an immoral and dangerous public world, rather than to the self-contained order of private, middle-class residences. In fact, however, by choosing cages over dorms and flops, the near homeless were demonstrating that not only did they share middle-class notions of privacy but that they were willing to make even greater sacrifices than their more affluent cousins were to achieve this. It was one thing to purchase privacy when one has

considerable disposable income; it was still another when the choice of a
more expensive shelter, simply one with a door, was made at the expense
of food, clothing, or other basics. For the homeless and nearly homeless,
the quest for privacy was limited by poverty, not, as claimed, by cultural
values.

It should be noted, however, that privacy had somewhat different meanings for the SRO resident than for the middle-class citizen. To the former,
privacy meant freedom, individual social control, the right to determine
how and why and when one came and went. To the latter, privacy was
based on the acceptance of limits, of participation in a system of group
controls imposed by institutions such as family and community.

But worries about social segregation were only part of the reason behind
the attack launched by reformers on SROs. The concerns of the human
ecology school played on and legitimized the other moral qualms professors, reformers, and their supporters had always harbored toward the
transient population and its housing. At the turn of the century, according to
Roger Bruns, journalists reported that "the tramp had no more rights than
'the sow that wallows in the gutter . . . he is no more to be consulted, in his
wishes or his will . . . than if he were a bullock in a corral.' " Civic leaders
felt that these men were social outsiders without social controls. In addition, by depicting these men as exceptions whose life-style was unamerican,
apologists for the business community could use them as convenient explanations for labor unrest and other social problems, while claiming that the
system was not flawed. Other writers proclaimed that "the American tramp
is a pariah," and noted "the popular recognition of his aversion to work,
his contempt of veracity, his predilection for beer, and his horror of water
both for interior and exterior use"; the *Chicago Tribune* even suggested that
the solution to the tramp problem would be to lace handouts of food with
strychnine. Chicago sociologists added to this depiction by reporting that
the highest rate of mental illness of any local community existed in the
central business district, which included some SROs. Next highest was an
adjacent SRO area, and third highest was the North Side rooming-house
district. All of the top ten were in SRO or slum districts. This data, offered
without qualification, helped legitimize the negative images of SROs and
their population.[27]

The buildings that housed these individuals were also rejected by reformers. Mrs. Charles Russell Lowell, the New York reform leader, was
not content with attacking lodging houses because "they are vicious and
demoralizing," but went further and drew "indictment against them all,
good and bad, and against all inexpensive provision for homeless men,
on the . . . ground that they attract the incompetent to the city." Another
range of charges, legitimate ones, stemmed from the horror of conditions
in cages, dorms, flops, and other troubled housing facilities. Though much
of this kind of criticism was both warranted and necessary, reformers failed

to examine the options available to homeless and nearly homeless men and women.

The core of the reformers' attack on the SRO, however, was a moral one, rooted in the fact that it did not fit Victorian middle-class concepts for home, family, and community. One problem with the SRO, for example, was that it fostered casual relationships. At no point were there the close ties of blood or marriage; these were replaced by chance meetings in a lobby or a cafeteria. In addition, most services were performed on a cash basis only, rather than utilizing the division of labor within the family. Thus, even small acts, like getting laundry done, pushed the roomer or lodger further away from the ties that normally bound one to the hearth.

These arguments ignored the fact that kinship ties and those of marriage were often replaced in SROs with ties based on acquaintanceship and the sharing of resources. Instead of being bound by the inherited duties of the family unit or the acquired ones stemming from marriage or parentage, hoboes, tramps, and bums responded to the chosen obligations of friendship.

Nevertheless, the early emphasis of reformers and administrators on the pathology or deviance of the transient and homeless populations set a precedent for public policy on this issue. Because it was generally accepted that transients and homeless were deviant or sick, they were considered dependents eligible to become wards of the state.

The moral concerns and particularly the spatial issues stemming from the theory of human ecology were most clearly dealt with by the development of zoning codes, a German import. New York was the first major city to pass a zoning ordinance, in 1916. Within a decade, 591 cities in the United States had similar codes. Zoning became a leading weapon in the battle for housing reform, as well as in efforts to achieve what historian Sam Bass Warner, Jr., has called the "segregation of industrial, commercial and residential land" that "became the hallmark of the metropolis." Originally designed to keep residential sections separate from potentially harmful industrial activities, zoning regulations began to serve other, unofficial functions. The most important of these was to rationalize land investment and thereby help maintain central area real estate values. Zoning also institutionalized residential class segregation, or, as Kenneth Jackson noted, "zoning was a device to keep poor people . . . out of affluent areas." This signified a critical shift in policy toward SROs, in that regulation was now focusing primarily on the Main Stem as a fixed, dangerous section, rather than on a mobile population. As a consequence, policies would be geared toward changing the physical nature of the area rather than reforming individuals. This approach, carried through at first by zoning and later by policies like urban renewal, was so complete that by 1945 critics like Catherine Bauer were writing, "For the past generation practically every effort in the field of city planning . . . has been pushing us toward enormous

one-class . . . developments as completely separated from one another and
from work places as possible." She also noted that the classism inherent in
these theories represented a "confusion of order with feudalism."[28]

The Great Depression:
The Shift to the Public Sector Consummated

The Great Depression of the 1930s consummated the shift of dominance
in housing policy from the private sector to the public sector. This move
was part of a larger change in the American approach to social problems,
namely, a general agreement that government was now responsible for the
welfare of the citizenry. As a result, government and university-trained
experts now dictated housing policies.

The Depression created massive unemployment as well as dislocation,
with millions of people moving around the country looking for work. Many
of these individuals came through Chicago, the nation's railway hub and a
traditional center for those seeking jobs. Local government and charitable
organizations responded to their housing needs by opening shelters. An
indication of the extent of the housing problem was the number of lodgings
provided in Chicago by various agencies between October 1, 1930, and
September 30, 1931: more than 1 million, an unprecedented figure. In the
next twelve-month period, however, it went to 3.25 million. The peak did
not come till 1933–34, when a total of 4,288,356 lodgings were provided
in Chicago. This pattern was typical of industrial cities. In New York the
number of persons registering with the city's municipal lodging facilities
rose from 158,677 in 1929 to 2,230,086 in 1933, or from a daily average
of 434 to 6,110.[29]

The Depression had varying impacts on the homeless and nearly homeless and their shelter facilities. There was virtually no new construction of
SROs during this period or after, so almost all existing buildings predate
the 1930s. Many levels of government used SROs as shelters, so while
inspections increased and facilities improved, some of the worst buildings
might have closed down because of proper enforcement of the building and
health codes.[30]

At the start of the Depression, prior to the New Deal, the majority of
local efforts to deal with shelter problems were in the hands of not-for-
profit agencies. A gubernatorial-appointed Commission on Unemployment
and Relief recommended the creation of a Clearing House for Unemployed
Men and raised private funds to this end. The Clearing House opened in
November 1931 and assigned men to emergency shelters run by the Salvation Army, the Chicago Urban League, the Christian Industrial League,
and the city's Department of Public Welfare. It also allocated funds to these
agencies in proportion to number of meals and lodgings provided.[31]

These shelters, and the public and private facilities that followed them, had to deal with a new population unlike the traditional inhabitants of the Main Stem. The economic distress of the Depression created new groups of the homeless, each with an unprecedented number of members. There were much higher proportions of single women and, especially, families. This latter usually traveled as complete units; 91 percent of the families served by federal programs were intact, with all members present, and almost all had both male and female heads of household. The men were usually employable, and the reason for traveling was economic distress. By 1935, for example, the Federal Transient Service provided shelter to 293,716 households, and it was estimated that 2 million workers crossed state lines each year in search of jobs.[32]

There were also a great many single men without housing (the federal shelter program alone housed an average of 200,000 men), but this population was very different from that of hobo, tramp, and bum. The homeless and nearly homeless were now increasingly men who had never had to undergo this kind of poverty before and did not know how to deal with it. As one study pointed out, hoboes were now "outnumbered ten to one by novices of the road."[33]

This new group had, on the whole, different characteristics than its predecessors. Probably the only trait the two groups shared was economic difficulty: over 75 percent of the migrants in federal shelters were looking for employment. Other than that, however, they had little in common. The new group was older; an average of forty-five years, an age that is normally considered prime or even post prime for workers. The ethnicity of the group also came closer to matching that of the city's population as a whole, with the foreign born now comprising 50 percent of the group. Poles, an ethnic group that had many representatives in the mill communities of the city but few on the Main Stem, numbered 18.4 percent of the clients of the Clearing House. Occupational breakdown was also different: according to one study only 13 percent of the adult male migrants had been employed in the service sector, whereas 37 percent had worked for industrial firms. A further breakdown of occupational status is listed in table 4-1. Another indication of the change was that 70 percent of the men had been on the road less than a year, according to a study by the Chicago Relief Administration. Their experience was considerably different from the long-term, mobile work patterns of the hobo and tramp.[34]

Note, however, that, according to this data, there were more white-collar workers than bums. Even the government commented on this difference; in explaining that some of their shelters were on the Main Stem, the Illinois Emergency Relief Commission remarked, "This should not, of course, be taken to indicate that individuals cared for by the shelters are of the hobo type. An increasing proportion of the men have come from the productive classes."[35]

TABLE 4-1

The Occupational Status of Men in Shelters, 1935

CATEGORY	PERCENTAGE
Bum	5
Home guard casual laborer	15
Migratory laborer	20
Steady unskilled laborer	33
Skilled laborer	20
White-collar worker	7
Total	100

Source: Edwin Sutherland and Harvey Locke, *Twenty Thousand Homeless Men* (Chicago, 1936), pp. 50–62.

The introduction of this new population of displaced workers was not, however, in the long run the biggest change that the Depression brought to the Main Stem. Within a decade these men would be gone, off to jobs created by wartime and postwar prosperity. Of infinitely greater consequence was the change in government policy. The New Deal was a turning point in United States history in that it established the principle that government must look out for and maintain the welfare of the citizenry. This change guaranteed that government policy, rather than decisions by private businessmen and women, would now have the greatest impact on the fate of the Main Stem.

At first the *immediate, direct* impact of the federal government on the homeless and nearly homeless was limited. In 1933 Congress passed the Federal Emergency Relief Act, and in September the Federal Transient Bureau was created under the auspices of the Federal Emergency Relief Administration (FERA). The bureau defined as transient anyone who had been in a state less than a year, and it agreed to pick up all costs for shelters and meals, or to establish tent camps along the road. By October 1934 all states but one (Vermont) were participating in the program.[36]

Within two years, however, by 1935, the Federal Transient Bureau was shut down, and the relief function was transferred to the Works Progress Administration (WPA). The result was a significant curtailing of the federal effort on behalf of transient workers. WPA projects and local programs all had stiff residency requirements that could not be met by people who were moving around the country in search of employment. In addition, federal programs in many cities, including Chicago, were taken over by the local political structure, so that a relationship to precinct captain or ward organization was a prerequisite to benefits. Nels Anderson told how "migrant unemployed have little chance of getting assigned to project employment. . . . Cases of migrants who are assigned to WPA employment are so rare as to be conspicuous." [37]

The transient program, furthermore, had never been a popular one, in large part, as one observer noted, "because migrants are not popular." In this regard, therefore, the federal government's policies reflected attitudes held by the larger society. Throughout this period and later, national policy toward the homeless generally ignored the needs of the single unattached person. While low-income housing for families was assisted by loans, then later built outright by federal grant, no facilities for single people (other than the elderly) were constructed. If anything, federal bulldozers destroyed SROs. [38]

The city's role in housing transients was larger than that of the federal government, but not dominant. Most of the city's effort went to subsidizing existing cage hotels by paying for room and board for indigents. The clientele of these places were the usual Main Stem residents—hoboes, tramps, home guard, and bums. Meals provided by the city were dismal, and the typical problems associated with the cages were ever present, including lice, dirt, and lack of safety features for fire or other emergencies. [39]

Far and away the most important level of government in dealing with this problem was the state. On February 5, 1932, the Illinois Emergency Relief Commission (IERC) was established; this agency took charge of all relief service in the state and in Cook County. At its height the commission had a yearly budget of $130 million and employed more than 10,000 people. Shortly after the founding of the IERC, the Service Bureau for Men, a branch organization, began operation and took over all the various facilities run for homeless men. [40]

These agencies maintained the traditional ties to the reform movement and, especially, to the University of Chicago. One of the commissioners was Neal Jacoby, an assistant professor of finance at the university. A specialist in state and local finance, Jacoby also contributed to a volume published by the University of Chicago Press under the auspices of the Social Science Research Commission, which included sociologists like Louis Wirth. By 1939 Jacoby was acting chairman of the IERC. In addition, Frank Glick was associate executive secretary. Glick, the former director of the School of Social Work at the University of Nebraska, was a close friend of Edith Abbott of SSA. Professor A. Wayne McMillan also was in charge of the 1932 U.S. Children's Bureau investigation of boy transiency, and he wrote the subsequent report. These connections indicate that there were several different channels for academic ideas from the University of Chicago to be incorporated into policies for the homeless, in the IERC as well as nationally. [41]

In addition, academics influenced the IERC by placing their students in various social work positions. By 1934, 60 percent of the county supervisors had spent at least one quarter in a school of social work or the equivalent in supervised experience, and 78 percent of case aides had at least some college training. Almost half of the members of this group were college graduates.[42]

By 1934 the IERC's local representative for single homeless men, the Service Bureau, ran nineteen shelters, most of which were located in the vicinity of the Main Stem. A variety of types of buildings were taken over, including seven factories, five abandoned schools, the shell of the old Criminal Court building, an abandoned fire station, a former school dormitory, and four cage hotels. As many as 15,000 men stayed in these facilities.[43]

The two basic services provided by the state were food and shelter. The former was minimal in amount and taste, and institutional in quality: some shelters fed more than 3,000 men, residents and others, at a single meal. Nutritionally the meals were not much; at one shelter breakfast consisted of black coffee, oatmeal with sweetened milk (which was half water), bread, eight stewed prunes, and no sugar. No lunch was served, and dinner was beef or liver stew, with bread. Some shelters provided sandwiches for lunch; others went days without serving any meat at all. Sugar was almost never provided, and fresh food was about as rare. Sometimes bugs or worms were found in the food, and rotten fish, meat, and vegetables were not uncommon. The researcher masquerading as a client who had to deal with sour green oranges was probably seeing the better side of shelter life.[44]

This quality of food was about what might be expected, given an average cost per meal of two and one-half to three cents. It was, according to David Scheyer of the *Nation*, "a starvation diet." Scheyer felt that this regimen served several functions as well, besides cutting costs. One was that it made life in the shelter so bad that no one would prefer not to work, "an imaginary danger conditioning most shelter supervision and supervisors." In addition, it kept the clients in "a dull, bewildered mood, inactive and unprotesting."[45]

Shelter facilities were just as bad. Abandoned factories, schools, and the like were turned into dormitories, and there were also some cage hotels in the program. One shelter, for example, provided clients with a steel bed, two sheets, and a pillow; another used army cots and blankets, with twenty-five beds to a room. Lice and bugs were ever present, as in the classic days on the Main Stem. Also unchanged was the occasional misfit or sociopath who made evenings hell for the rest of the men. A researcher told how, during a night in one of the dormitories, while some men expectorated onto newspapers spread on the floor, one resident spit all over the researcher's coat and trousers. Another man coughed so long and loud that he woke all the other tenants of the room, one of whom yelled out, "For God's sake, shut up or get to hell out of here." The power of suggestion seemed to take effect, since the man coughed only twice more and was silent.[46]

Other services were provided as well, with mixed effect. All clothes had to be fumigated. Though eventually this was done with smoke and hot air, originally sulphur fumes were passed through the clothing. Not only did this make the garments smell terrible, it faded colors and disintegrated fibers so that clothes fell apart. Toilet facilities were grimy and overcrowded. When basins became stopped up, they filled with dirty water; on one occasion a man had a severe nosebleed and the water was "a dirty red" color. On the other hand, showers and soap were available, as well as tubs and other laundry facilities. This squalor was not atypical. One New York shelter had 1,724 beds in one enormous room, a situation described as "like nothing else under the sun, perhaps a scene from Dante."[47]

The shelters did little to provide meaningful activities. During the day residents had to leave and walk the streets, or go to the "bull-pen," a large open room in the basement where men could pass the time, but with little or nothing to do. Classes were provided, but most of the men were too dispirited to go to them. Handicrafts were dropped in 1935, after an efficiency expert ordered all rugs, materials for rugs, tools, and equipment for handicrafts be burned, on the grounds that this work was useless and an inappropriate expense for the government. One of the best facilities was the one in the Newberry Library, where residents had access to books, paper, and pencils. A sign on the wall, however, read, "Write to mother today, now!"[48]

One aspect of the shelter system was its blatant classism. Certain shelters were set aside for homeless white-collar workers. These places were "much higher in service and institutional standards than the regular shelters . . . [and] were designed to present a residential club atmosphere." In addition, white-collar men were excused from all work requirements when these were mandated by the shelters.[49]

The shelter system created or institutionalized a number of basic precepts regarding care for transients and the homeless. The most important, of course, was that care would become primarily a function of government. Consequently, policy would now be set by politicians and professional administrators, who would also be in charge of running programs. Another concept that the Depression created, and embedded in our culture, was a separation between the "good" and the "bad" homeless, a difference based on moral concepts. The "good" homeless were the "new" homeless, families and individuals who were thrown out of work by the Depression. These people had good character and moral values but were temporarily dispossessed by a national calamity. One sociologist spoke of the changes that "made it impossible for men who had previously supported themselves to continue to do so." A study by the Chicago Relief Commission reported, "These men have definite purposes and sensible reasons for moving." Similarly, the executive vice-chairman of the Cincinnati Community Chest explained how "among the transients of the depression are people of excellent social history, work record and general background." Even Harry Hopkins, head of the federal relief programs, argued frequently that transients were not hoboes, tramps, or bums, but rather honest working men.[50]

Their opposites were the transients of the Main Stem. According to popular culture, these individuals were lazy, shiftless, and avoided work (and cleanliness) as much as possible. Begging was their favorite and primary source of income. Their character and morality were negligible, and pathological conditions, especially alcoholism, were common among them.

Explicit comparisons were made on the basis of these moral judgments. "Hobohemians," claimed one sociologist, "adjust more easily to shelter food, regimentation, and other external conditions than do non-Hobohemians. Hobohemians were habituated to a poor and coarse diet and feel at home in flophouses." They also allegedly responded better to the lack of work in the shelters, which already fit with their life-style, whereas this absence of productive labor was much harsher on the newer residents of the shelter community.

Such a dichotomy was also a highly political one. It elevated the status of the large numbers of recently impoverished citizens by establishing a group that was below, and morally inferior, to them. In addition, it was a handy defense against outside attacks. The IERC was constantly under pressure by the legislature and the press. There was a belief among many civic leaders that the unemployed did not want to work and were taking advantage of the government. Relief allocations, they argued, should be so meager as to force clients to look for jobs. Although newspapers reported on unemployment in a fairly straightforward way in the early years of the Depression, many responded to New Deal programs with disdain. The *Chicago Tribune*, for example, published an editorial, "The Right To Alms," that concluded: "The recipients of unemployment relief are objects of charity . . . money has been given not because the victims have any right to it but because the community has a heart." The *Chicago American*, a Hearst paper, preferred to cover scandals, carrying headlines like "Vilest Kind of Racket Exposed in Operation of Government Relief," or such comments as, "Rather than risk the stigma that might ensue to the lofty profession of social workers, thievery, swindling, forgery and plundering have been allowed to go on on a wholesale scale, unchecked and unhampered." [51]

These attacks meant that programs were often a compromise between what welfare administrators wanted and what politicians, responsive to the press and to pressure groups, were willing to provide. They forced reformers to resort to simple moral appeals in order to gain support for their programs. Thus, a Chicago Relief Administration study of homeless men took pains to point out that the typical client was native born, white, "fairly well-educated," healthy, and with a work history. These men have "had little public assistance and are looking for work, not relief." The difference between this group and its predecessor was also made explicit: "Their problem is one of unemployment recently begun, not rehabilitation." [52]

The problem was that the dichotomy was a false one. The hoboes, tramps, and bums that lived on the Main Stem were not, by and large, any more morally degenerate than any other part of the city's population. They were, however, poor and transient, and had been so for a lot longer than anybody else in the country. They had also developed a community life that, though ably serving their own needs, seemed to be in marked contrast to that of middle-class society. Even that perception, however, was a victory of style over substance, since many of the Main Stem's highest social priorities—privacy, for example—were similar or identical to those of the middle class. In reality, not only were there few differences between the "new" and the "old" homeless—the "good" and the "bad"—there were similarities that were far more important. Above all else, both groups were the products of economic forces beyond their control. Poverty, not morality, was their defining characteristic; both the "old" and the "new" homeless were plagued by a common, overwhelming problem, an inability to command the resources necessary to purchase shelter in the marketplace.

Such differentiation, however, was not new to the Depression. It stemmed from earlier concepts defined by reformers, that the traditional resident of the Main Stem was a social deviant and therefore should become a client of government social service programs. The New Deal, however, by institutionalizing government as the dominant force in addressing social problems, embedded this notion at the heart of the public-sector approach to the problem of housing single poor persons and transients.

Thus, despite the fact that both groups struggled with poverty, this dichotomy became an accepted part of the national culture. As a consequence, the government's policy toward the homeless and nearly homeless, as adopted during the Depression and continued to the present, was inherently short-sighted. If the focus was limited to the "new," or good, homeless, then reform efforts had to stop when this group was housed. Thus, as the economy rebounded in the 1940s, homelessness was no longer a major national issue. In the meantime, however, the core population, still needing help to deal with the ramifications of economic distress, was relatively neglected, a situation that was the logical outcome of a policy that dealt primarily with only one, very temporary aspect of the problem. This meant that government policy did not deal effectively with homelessness, and cannot do so until it dispenses with moral categories and recognizes the practical and economic roots and solutions of this problem.

Equally enduring was the method government devised to deal with homelessness. The shelter system was not only dismal, it also removed from poor single men one of their few freedoms, the independence of movement and of life in Hobohemia, the ability to control the direction of their lives. The sociologists Sutherland and Locke called this process "shelterization," the adjustment to the totally controlled environment in the shelters, which another writer simply called "getting into a rut." [53]

Several characteristics of the shelter system fostered this process. One was the intense regimentation and control that prevailed in this setting. Conditions in the shelters seem to be those of a prison, not a place to house homeless men: "Their whole life is regulated for them; they are told when and where to sleep, are awakened at the same time day in and day out, are told how much, or better how little, to eat, and where and when and what should be eaten. . . . Everything is a matter of routine; and to make certain that the men do not even have to use their minds to remember these prescribed duties, they are bulletined all over the building." Such conditioning was enforced from the very start of the shelter experience. When a man entered, mainly seeking food and housing, he was immediately subjected to intensive questioning about his past, data that was unnecessary and never used for any constructive purposes, to help him get a job or even to construct a statistical profile of residents. Everything else involved taking orders and waiting in line, for food, for soap, for toilets, or for anything else. Shelters also isolated the men; they were no longer part of a community like the Main Stem. Thus, they were removed from the one society that tried to provide the goods and services that met the needs, psychological and social as well as material, of the homeless and nearly homeless. Finally, by not providing any kind of hope or progress toward work or any other goal, the shelters gave men nothing to look forward to. One day in the shelter was the same as any other: "In the morning the gloom and despair of the shelters seem to be in the men's bones." The impersonality of this situation was further heightened by the stipulation that all clients had to be attended to by a caseworker, but there were far too few of these personnel, so each was overloaded and meetings became perfunctory and annoying.[54]

The effect on the men was predictable. They became despondent and often child-like, dominated by authority, going through the motions of life. One resident said that there should be no fear of communists' organizing the men in the shelters because "There's no life in these shelters. . . . They wouldn't fight nothin' in here." [55]

The greatest irony of the situation was that another way of doing things existed and had for some time. The priorities established earlier by the transient population—autonomy and privacy—remained valid in the thirties. Thus, although the sociologists were correct when they noted that the residents of Hobohemia were used to slimmer diets, the more observant among them understood that "it is one thing for a man to go to the Penny Cafeteria on Madison, choose stew and macaroni, and go to a corner and eat his meal, and quite another to line up and have a stew and macaroni thrown on his plate, be herded to a table, and be unable to choose his table companions." The hoboes, tramps, and bums had spent decades developing a system for getting by with little money or housing, but with lots of control over one's own destiny. Therefore, not surprisingly, they managed to avoid the shelters and hang onto their cubicles, their white-tile cafeterias, and their independence. As noted above, most of those who went into the shelters and were destroyed were newcomers, not the traditional denizens of the Main Stem. To reiterate the figures in table 4-1, the shelters had a higher proportion of skilled laborers than home guard, more unskilled laborers than hoboes (migratory laborers), and more white-collar workers than bums. In addition, 70 percent of the men had been on the road less than a year. Thus, the Main Stem, viewed as a social, cultural, and economic environment, went relatively untouched by the Depression, since poverty had long been a familiar way of life to its residents. The shelter, however, stood apart, an alien entity, because it rejected the social priorities of autonomy and privacy.[56]

Thus, the experts were wrong when they argued that "there was no radical difference between living in a commercial flophouse and a government shelter" and that the ability of men to support themselves, and their attitudes toward independence, "vary directly with the level of the occupation." If anything, this last statement was correct, but the order was the inverse of the one intended. It was the residents of the SRO, "the commercial flophouse," that could have taught the newcomers how to survive and remain socially and spiritually intact, if they had been given half the chance.[57]

This alternative, of democratic community self-control and government cooperation, was available but rarely used. In South Chicago, in the Calumet Harbor district, a group of unemployed sailors decided they did not like conditions in the local shelter. When they complained to the manager, he threatened to call the police. Instead, the seamen went to the offices of the relief commission and staged a sit-in. They won control of the shelter and began to operate it, using federal monies. The shift in authority was indicated by the fact that "any case worker who goes near it must be prepared to answer rather than ask questions."

This kind of approach, however, was never applied on a wide scale. The reporter who wrote up this story for the *Nation* felt that "this is part of the solution to the flop-house problem but an isolated part and likely to remain so. Men who have spent a year, two years in the bull pen will never discover it." They remained, instead, "relatively helpless recipients of relief." Given the negative image of the Main Stem, so bad that its residents were classified as worse than other transient, homeless people, this outcome was predictable, if unfortunate.[58]

Finally, the other legacy of the Depression was the concept of using federal funds for locally sponsored demolition of undesirable buildings. The practice would culminate in the urban renewal programs, but as of 1935 federal monies were available only for the demolition of structurally defective buildings. According to Judith Trolander, the availability of such funding "spurred" reformers to increase building code enforcement so as to gain the maximum allocation and hence destruction. This policy of eliminating low-income housing without replacing it was a familiar one for housing reformers. The difference after the New Deal was that federal law and cash would now provide the muscle for implementing this approach.[59]

Conclusions

The New Deal programs of the 1930s completed a process begun in the previous decade and before. During the 1920s dominance in housing policy began to shift away from the private sector and toward government. As a result, a different set of rules and players would dictate how society provided housing for single transients, as well as how it dealt with their most common form of housing, the SRO.

There were many reasons for the transition. The most important was a change in the nation's economy. As the frontier withered, the need for a traveling labor force disappeared. It was during the 1920s that Jacob Coxey, the general who had led the march of the dispossessed in 1893, walked through the Main Stem with Nels Anderson and remarked, "The old timers will not be here much longer." [60]

At the same time, the private sector was also losing interest in providing low-income housing. Housing regulation had the beneficial effect of making housing safer and better, but it also meant that landlords could no longer profit from the construction of tenements. As a result, they stopped building them and let others worry about how much housing was available for the poor.

The definition of the policy issue had also changed. Before the 1920s the focus had been on the population, its deviancy, and particularly on its mobility and threat to the established order. Reformers designed programs, based on this analysis, that tried to adjust the character of their clients by such punitive measures as requiring work in the municipal wood yard. As the number of hoboes, tramps, and bums declined, however, and as they became more settled, the emphasis began to shift to a spatial definition of the problem, although questions of deviancy remained. Reformers thus began to form solutions that dealt with the physical aspect of the Main Stem, including its residential structures.

Simultaneous with these changes, the power of the public sector was on the rise, fueled by the development of new scientific techniques like the case study and statistical analysis, which enabled reformers to base their conclusions on objective facts rather than blind prejudice. Notwithstanding this approach, civic leaders could not escape questions of morality, partly because their religious backgrounds sparked much of their belief in change, and partly because they needed to dramatize issues in order to win public and legislative support.

Support for reform also came from the academy, and particularly the University of Chicago. Sociologists at this institution argued a theory of human ecology, whereby the city was divided into natural areas on the basis of function. According to this theory, SRO districts were an anachronism, a throwback to the early, walking city where all activities took place within a confined circle that was dictated by the distance a person could walk. Such districts were now considered dangerous anachronisms that failed to separate public and private lives.

Such arguments were not taught in a vacuum. The university atmosphere encouraged scholars to become involved in the political life of the city. Academics sat on committees and pressured civic leaders to implement their theories. Most important of all, they inculcated their ideas into generations of students who went on to staff the budding social service apparatus. Slowly the ideas of the academics were turned into the reality of legislation and program. Housing reform started with a building code and eventually grew into zoning ordinances that institutionalized the segregation inherent in the theory of human ecology.

These changes were completed during the New Deal, when the government assumed responsibility for the welfare of its citizens. Combined with the abdication of the private sector from concern for housing the poor, government involvement meant that low-income housing policy, including that for transient singles and for the homeless, would now come from the City Council, from the state house, and from Washington.

The implications for the future were mixed. Though greater resources might be available, the politics of the New Deal taught the country that there was a difference between the "good" and the "bad" homeless, the former a family with children, the latter a single male. This false dichotomy, which ignored the common economic origin of homelessness, meant that ongoing shelter problems would be ignored once the immediate crisis was over. In addition, the government designed a form of housing—the shelter —that robbed men of dignity. Not surprisingly, the residents of the Main Stem, who prized autonomy and privacy, shunned these facilities whenever possible. Unfortunately, no one asked their advice when the system was established, or even what they thought was important and useful about their housing. Another ominous trend was that the New Deal supported the shift in problem definition, from the population to the physical structures of the Main Stem, by incorporating traditional reform solutions that got rid of housing for the poor without providing replacements. For the first time, federal funds were being used to shape the physical environment of the SRO districts via demolition.

Thus, the New Deal institutionalized a shift that had roots sunk many years before. As Steven Diner said, "For several decades before the depression of the 1930's . . . professors, social workers, and philanthropists, steadily constructed a foundation for large-scale government intervention in people's lives to guarantee minimum standards of social and economic well being." By so doing, they assumed responsibility for a shelter policy in which the private sector was no longer interested. Government and reform leaders, generally with the best of intentions, would go about correcting many of the worst mistakes of the past, while proceeding to implement many new ones as well.[61]

5 Skid Row: Poverty Versus Pathology

After the end of World War II the Main Stem continued its metamorphosis to Skid Row. This process, as Anderson and others had noted, began as early as the 1920s, when the demand for migrant unskilled labor began to dry up. But after the war the pace accelerated tremendously. Buoyed by wage increases won by industrial unions, workers more than ever settled into steady jobs and traditional neighborhoods, thus depleting the clientele for the lodging houses. Similarly, the rooming-house districts disappeared, as middle-class individuals married at an earlier age and moved to the suburbs. Women particularly followed this pattern, as society increasingly frowned on the notion of the female with a career.

Skid Row was in some ways different and in many ways quite similar to the Main Stem. It was, for example, much smaller and the population older, the result of national trends that left just a few service workers and old men surviving on pensions in the SRO districts. Most of the workers provided unskilled labor in the service industries that kept the downtown section—the Loop—running properly. This work was sporadic and ill paid. Thus, as in earlier days, men stayed on West Madison Street because it was all that they could afford. Statistics on tenure, however, showed that residents were much less likely to be transients than permanent residents.

Nevertheless, Skid Row became associated, more than anything else, with alcoholism. The general image of the area was that just about every resident was deep in the bottle. However, every scientific investigation, whether in Chicago or elsewhere, showed that alcoholics, though proportionately a larger group than in any other section of the city, still formed a small minority of the Skid Row population. One of the main purposes of this study, therefore, is to redress the balance of research by focusing on the working men that made up the bulk of the residents of the SRO districts.

For these men, autonomy and privacy were key priorities, as had been true for their predecessors. They demonstrated their priorities in their choice of housing; they sought workingmen's hotels when they could afford them. Otherwise, the cage hotels still existed, with the same horrid conditions, but with the door that could be used to close off the rest of the world.

Following the changes in policy that were completed during the Great Depression, the institution most affecting these men's lives was government. Although the city spent considerable sums of money on welfare provisions (including chits for a night's lodgings, which enabled the cages to stay in business), its primary means of intervention was the police. In the past, the function of the police had been shifted from social control to the pursuit of criminals. Police in the Skid Row period, however, were used to define the boundaries of Skid Row and hence protect surrounding areas, and to maintain modest levels of middle-class decorum within the neighborhood by conducting frequent and repeated arrests.

The greatest impact, however, came under the urban renewal program, designed to clear slums and provide better, alternative housing. Unfortunately, slum clearance enjoyed tremendous success but the provision of alternative housing saw modest gains, at best. Academics, however, enjoyed the funding that urban renewal provided for the study of Skid Row, but this led them to a sole concentration on alcoholism, to the exclusion of other analytical interpretations. In the end, however, all their theories were rendered moot, as the Chicago Department of Urban Renewal bulldozed most of the SRO districts anyway, and provided little in the way of replacement housing.

The postwar period is particularly important, therefore, because it shows that, even in a period of decline, the SRO district still provided, in however meager a way, for the needs of the working man on the lower end of the scale. These individuals, rather than the alcoholics that government programs and social science researchers focused on, are the subject of this chapter, along with the various ideas and institutions that controlled their environment.

From Main Stem to Skid Row

The post–World War II period saw the end of the Main Stem, which was replaced by Skid Row. Skid Row was, in reality, only a slightly different kind of community, but in the minds of both the public and the academic community, it was a very different and more deviant place than the Main Stem had ever been.

The term "Skid Row" originated in Seattle, where it referred to the street used by Henry Yesler, a local lumberman, to roll or skid logs to his sawmill on the waterfront. Lining the street were cheap hotels, taverns, restaurants, brothels, and other services catering to lumberjacks. By the 1920s, however, "Skid Road," as it was originally called, primarily housed poor, unemployed ex-loggers as well as short-term workers in the city's service industries. In time, the name of the area was shortened to "Skid Row," and it was applied as a pejorative, generic term. Skid Row designated, in any American city, a place where drunks were both concentrated and highly visible. There was also the implication of downward mobility (being on the "skids"), as well as a constrained physical, economic, and social environment (a "row").[1]

Skid Row replaced the Main Stem for a number of economic and demographic reasons. As noted in the preceding chapter, by the 1920s the demand for migrant industrial workers had declined considerably, so there were far fewer hoboes and tramps in cities. In the decades following World War II these trends were accelerated. Unskilled nonfarm labor as a percentage of all employed workers declined from 12.5 in 1900 to 9.4 in 1940 to 4.8 in 1960. In industries that had traditionally given jobs to unattached men, the drop was even greater. The relative proportion of workers in logging declined by 50 percent between 1900 and 1960, and in metals, mining, and quarrying the figure was more than 80 percent. Even in agriculture, the proportion of the labor force employed in this sector went from 38 percent in 1900 to 19 percent in 1940 to 6.6 percent in 1960. Thus, the more an SRO section depended on nonskilled laborers as the core of its population, the greater the rate of decline. The downward slide was confirmed by the sociologist Barrett Lee, who, using regression analysis, found that communities "with labor-oriented occupational structures were more likely to undergo rapid decline than were areas with smaller proportions of [unskilled workers]."[2]

This shift was further accelerated by wartime employment, and then afterward, by the reigning prosperity that lasted through to the Vietnam War period. These generally favorable economic times were coupled with an increased standard of living for the American worker. The new prosperity was the result of higher wages, a product of the rise of industrial unions as an accepted, viable institution in American society, and the advances they gained for many workers. Consequently, the American working class gained a stability and security that it had never enjoyed before. World War II veterans also benefited from a package of social welfare programs such as the GI Bill that ran the gamut from education to medical assistance.[3]

These changes caused the SRO districts either to disappear or to shrink considerably. The rooming-house section clustered around North Clark Street was changed radically. It no longer provided shelter to single men and women fresh to the city; instead, it housed a stable population of working-class families. One reason was that the role of women had changed. As Betty Friedan noted in *The Feminine Mystique*, the image of the independent working woman, so prevalent in the 1930s and early 1940s, was replaced by one of the woman as housewife. When a woman did take employment, it was to supplement her husband's income rather than to pursue a career, and she did so within the context of marriage and family, rather than of a single person's life-style.

The rooming-house district thus became a stable working-class neighborhood, with more families. One study of this district, conducted in the late 1940s, found a wealth of social organizations binding residents. The popu-

lation had changed, from middle-class transient workers fresh to the city
to a steady group of working-class people engaged in service industries,
repair work, and various skilled trades. These people lived in an autonomous world, similar to all the other working-class family neighborhoods in
the city; they had few contacts with either the urban underclass below them
or with the middle and upper classes. Within their own domain there was a
sense of dignity and security. One local restaurant, for example, took care
of "regulars" by saving favorite foods for them, receiving their mail and
phone calls, and offering credit or even free meals. A regular who got a
food package from relatives or came across some long-neglected favorite
item in a store could have it prepared at the restaurant. This kind of attention flattered them and offered ego satisfaction, as well as the security of
a guaranteed welcome at a neighborhood institution. Thus, although the
population changed, the critical role of community places remained the
same.[4]

One other aspect of the North Side district that did not change was its
attraction to the offbeat and unorthodox. This section was known to house
most of Chicago's bohemians, as well as its red-light district. With its
cabarets and dance halls, the area was the primary entertainment section,
not only for transients but for the whole city. It hosted characters such as
Casey with the Cleats. Casey had ambitions to be a dancer but was deterred
by a physical ailment; he could not move his legs, up or down, backward
or forward, more than two inches at a time. But Casey wanted to perform.
Accordingly, he covered the soles of his shoes with cleats, so that he shot
off a storm of sparks as he walked, always in time to the little song he sang
to himself. The district was also the home of Loudspeaker, "a mammoth,
inarticulate Swede." After consuming his third or fourth bottle of beer,
Loudspeaker would begin to deliver long, loud lectures on his favorite
topic, "the geopolitical patterns of war."[5]

Aside from its characters, the North Side rooming district traditionally
had more than its share of vice. Pawnbrokers and fences flourished here,
and prostitution was rampant. A missionary worker told how, "on all the
cross streets . . . one can see soliciting going on almost any time of night."
About 1915 Mayor Carter Harrison II was walking up Clark Street between
Division Street and North Avenue when a prostitute grabbed his lapels and
said something to the effect of "Come on upstairs, honey, I'll show you a
good time." A major clean-up followed, but like all reform efforts of this
kind, it was short lived. A decade later one of a pair of investigators from
the University of Chicago persuaded a bellboy at a local hotel to "get him a
wife" by tipping the lad fifty cents. The woman he supplied in turn went out
and brought in another prostitute for the intrepid researcher's companion,
thus "giving clear evidence of the nature of the place."[6]

This atmosphere continued well into the sixties. At the start of that
decade, the near North Side was considered a steady area of working-class

TABLE 5-1

The Population of SRO Districts in Chicago, 1958

DISTRICT	N	%
Madison Street	7,525	63.1
South State Street	2,910	24.4
North Clark Street	691	5.8
Uptown	370	3.1
Jails, hospitals	430	3.6
Totals	11,926	100.0

Source: Donald Bogue, *Skid Row in American Cities* (Chicago, 1963), p. 82.

TABLE 5-2

Services in Chicago SRO Districts, 1972

DISTRICT	HOTELS	EMPLOYMENT AGENCIES	MISSIONS
Madison Street	20	21	25
South State Street	9	2	1
North Clark Street	5	2	2
Uptown	2	11	1

Source: William McSheehy, *Skid Row* (Cambridge, 1979), p. 14.

families, intersected by the bright-light attractions of major arteries like Clark Street. Little was left of the rooming houses. Within ten to fifteen years, however, even low-income family housing would begin to disappear, as the area underwent massive gentrification.

The remaining SRO districts, dominated by the lodging house, were the converted Main Stem along West Madison Street (far and away the largest), South State Street, a small group of lodging houses adjacent to the old rooming-house section on North Clark Street (still the Bohemian and red-light district of Chicago), and an area on the mid-North Side of the city, around Wilson Avenue and Broadway (see tables 5-1 and 5-2). All of these sections were collectively referred to, and investigated by academics, social workers, and journalists, as Skid Row.[7]

There were several major differences between Skid Row and its prede-

TABLE 5-3

The Shrinking Population of Main Stem—Skid Row

YEAR	POPULATION
1907	60,000
1923	30,000
1958	12,000

Sources: 1907—Alice Solenberger, *One Thousand Homeless Men* (New York, 1911), p. 9; 1923—Nels Anderson, *The Hobo* (Chicago, 1923), p. 13; 1958—Donald Bogue, *Skid Row in American Cities* (Chicago, 1963), p. 82.

cessor, the Main Stem. The most important was that it was much smaller. As shown in table 5-3, the population was only a fraction of what it was in the heyday of the hobo, tramp, and bum. The population had also changed considerably. As the number of working persons in the area diminished, the proportion of residents with social and personal problems rose, although the concentration was never as great as sociologists and journalists suggested. A fuller discussion of this issue is found below. The smaller population, however, meant that the number of service facilities also dropped (see table 5-4). In particular, the number of employment agencies went down precipitously, and the number of vacant lots went up.

It is important to note that the changes were primarily the result of the national trends mentioned above; a similar decline occurred in the SRO districts of many other cities in the United States. On the Bowery in New York City, for example, there was a 49 percent decline in population between 1949 and 1963. Whereas in 1935 the city's municipal lodging house provided 19,000 lodgings a day, in 1944 it provided only 550 a day. According to one study of twenty-eight cities conducted by Howard Bahr and Theodore Caplow, officials in twenty-four believed that the population of their Skid Row district was decreasing, in three cities that their section was stable, and in only one city (Tacoma) was there a sense that the population was on the rise.[8]

It is clear from this data that by the 1950s "Skid Row" was seen as a general American phenomenon. As Donald Bogue, author of *Skid Row in American Cities*, the first and most comprehensive of the Skid Row studies of this period, noted: "Almost every American city of 500,000 or more has a Skid Row neighborhood. Tendencies toward such a development are present in most (and possibly nearly all) cities having 175,000 or more residents."[9]

TABLE 5-4

Facilities Along West Madison Street, 1923 and 1964

FACILITY	1923	1964
Taverns	6	7
Restaurants	6	3
Barber colleges	4	2
Employment agencies	10	1
Clothing stores	5	3
Hotels	8	9
Cigar stores	1	0
Drug stores	1	0
Fortune tellers	1	1
Grocery stores	0	1
Cleaners	0	1
Funeral homes	0	1
Empty lots	1	8
Key shops	0	1
Parking lots	0	2

Source: Ronald Vander Kooi, "Skid Rowers: Their Alienation and Involvement in Community and Society" (Ph.D. dissertation, Michigan State University, 1966), p. 33.

A general stereotypical image of Skid Row was nationally accepted. This was overwhelmingly a negative one. Gone was the figure of the transient working man—the hobo or the "knight of the road," the tramp—his community memorialized only by phrases like "stemming," referring to the way of life on West Madison Street. Skid Row was now a section of the city where cheap rooming houses, missions, street bums, and alcoholics were concentrated, where only the very dregs of society lived. The population was viewed as being not only poor but pathological, helpless before the ravages of character weakness, particularly drunkenness. The accuracy of this depiction, however, needs to be examined.[10]

The Population of Skid Row

The shrinkage of Chicago's and other cities' SRO districts came about because of changes in the national economy. After World War II there was little call for mobile workers, other than in agriculture. Even in this sector, however, employment figures were greatly reduced from their height at the turn of the century. In addition, the American industrial worker's wages reached all-time highs, and working conditions were improved as well, the results of work by industrial unions as well as the postwar prosperity. More workers than ever enjoyed economic security, which in turn led to social stability.

Thus, the mobile roaming groups—hoboes and tramps—were eliminated from the occupational hierarchy of this country. What was left in the SRO districts were the stationary individuals, generally labeled bums. But as noted in chapter 3, this designation covered an extremely diverse population.

The residents of Skid Row ranged, therefore, from the elite of bums, the home guard, down to homeless alcoholics and beggars. Most of them, however, were in the former category—stationary, occasional workers. Many of these were former hoboes and tramps who had settled down because of age, disability, lack of available jobs, or some other circumstance.

We argue, therefore, that Skid Row was far closer to the Main Stem than to the alcoholics' graveyard described by journalists and academics. Though it is true that drinking problems were far more common here than among the general population, it is also accurate to state that the majority of residents were poor working people, and that their most common characteristic was poverty, not pathology.

There are several ways to test this thesis, using available data. One is to look at figures on employment. The employment record of these men showed them to be a somewhat more steady group than the stereotypical image of the bum would suggest, but still considerably less stable than the average Chicago worker. According to Bogue, 73 percent of the men were in the work force; of these, 47 percent were gainfully employed and the other 26 percent were looking for work. Another 16 percent were disabled or elderly and hence unable to work. Among workers, 35 percent had worked more than fifty weeks in the past year, and 52 percent had worked forty weeks or more. Only about 40 percent of the men had held only one job within this period, however, and 16 percent worked at spot jobs of a day or so duration. The employment figures thus denote that this was an independent population able to maintain economic autonomy.[11]

The work these people did was almost all in the private sector. Government workers and self-employed individuals combined made up less than 3 percent of the population. Although almost 8 percent had jobs as craftsmen, 9 percent worked as clerical workers, and 14 percent were operatives, the majority did not fare nearly as well. Thirty-four percent worked in the service industries, especially in restaurants, and 31 percent also classified as unskilled laborers (see tables 5-5 and 5-6). Common jobs were dishwasher, waiter, or short-order cook in restaurants; porter or janitor in restaurants, bars, or offices; freight handler; industrial laborer; hospital and nursing home laborer; many worked in resorts throughout the area. Ac-

TABLE 5-5

Skid Row Occupational Structure, 1958

OCCUPATION	%
White collar workers	9.2
Craftsmen	7.2
Operatives	13.7
Services	33.6
Laborers, farm	0
Laborers, unskilled	30.6
No information	5.7
Total	100.0

Source: Donald Bogue, *Skid Row in American Cities* (Chicago, 1963), p. 176.

TABLE 5-6

Skid Row Employment, by Industry, 1958

INDUSTRY	%
Agriculture	3.2
Construction	5.7
Manufacturing	15.7
Transportation, railroad	16.4
Transportation, other	3.6
Wholesale and retail	6.8
Restaurants	20.4
Business services	4.4
Personal services	6.5
Entertainment	5.9
Religious, welfare	5.0
Industry not reported	6.4
Total	100.0

Source: Donald Bogue, *Skid Row in American Cities* (Chicago, 1963), p. 177.

cording to studies by Wallace and by Blumberg, Shipley, and Barsky, these
jobs were standard in New York's Bowery and Philadelphia's Skid Row as
well. These positions were not generally covered by union contracts, so pay
scales were poor.[12]

Of all the men, 85 percent made less than $2,500 a year; only 41 percent
of the entire Chicago labor forced earned this little. Only 15 percent of
Skid Row's workers made $2,500 to $5,000 a year, levels reached by 47
percent of all Chicagoans on the job. Less than 1 percent of Skid Row
residents made over $5,000, whereas 13 percent of the workers in the entire
city earned this much or more. On the last job worked before the survey,
59 percent earned one dollar an hour or less. An indication that minimal
wages were not unique to Chicago's Skid Row came from Bogue's analysis
of forty-one cities, which found that whereas 49 percent of the Skid Row
residents in these cities earned less than $1,500 a year, only 27 percent of
the population of these places earned that little.[13]

It is also important to note that almost 47 percent of all the men on
Skid Row were pensioners, drawing funds from public assistance, Social
Security, and military and railroad pensions. This fact partly explains the
poverty. At the time Bogue conducted his survey, the ceiling for the state's
Old Age Assistance and Disability Assistance was $80 a month; there were
few locations other than Skid Row where a man could survive on that
amount. Though no exact figures exist on pensioners' income, Bogue found
that of those with moderate or severe handicaps (a group whose income
most likely derives from outside sources), only 32.3 percent made more
than $1,500 a year, compared with 44 percent of all men on Skid Row in
Chicago. Thus, a woman living on Skid Row in 1955, asked by Sara Harris
why she chose that community, replied simply, "Where else am I going to
live on forty-five dollars a month?" When Harris asked a man if he liked
living on Skid Row, he told her, "What else is there . . . like, schmike, it
don't mean a thing. I got to do what I got to do." [14]

Another indication that the Skid Row population was primarily made up
of poor, unskilled, but steady working men, many of them former hoboes
and tramps who had settled down and joined the home guard, comes from
figures on tenure. The usual depiction of the Skid Row resident was that he
was a homeless vagrant, transitory and without roots. According to Bogue
and others, this impression was false. Fewer than 10 percent of the men
had been on Skid Row for less than a month, 55 percent had resided there
for a year or more, and 10 percent had been on Skid Row for ten years or
more. Census data were even more positive; according to these, 68 percent
of the men had stayed in the same apartment for at least two years. Bogue
found that 71 percent of the men had not moved within the past year. This
figure was confirmed by Ronald Vander Kooi in a separate survey; Vander
Kooi found that 81 percent of the men had not moved in the past year and
that only 10 percent had lived on Skid Row for less than a year, whereas 73

percent had lived there for four years or more. As the survey researchers explained it, "Contrary to popular belief, skid row is composed primarily of non-transient persons . . . [it consists] of long-term residents who do not move around very much." Similarly, the New York researchers Bahr and Caplow admitted, "Fewer of them [Skid Row residents] were transients than had been supposed." [15]

Data on age also reinforces the image of the Skid Rower as an older working man, the last remainders of the hobo and tramp populations. Willard Motley, for example, describing the last remnants of hobo culture and wisdom along Skid Row, told how waitresses' tips got "thinner" in the late fall, since "her customers like herself had to plan for winter." Bogue found that the median age of Skid Row residents was forty-nine years, with the modal period forty-five to sixty-four years, compared with twenty to forty-four years for the city as a whole. Vander Kooi found, in his survey, that the median age was fifty-two years, whereas Howard Bain, in an earlier study, discovered that the median age of one hundred 1948 Veterans Relief Service clients from Skid Row was fifty-four years. Again, this was true of other cities as well: in 1930 a census of Bowery lodging-house residents found that 75 percent were under fifty years of age; by 1966 approximately the same proportion were over fifty. Similarly, in 1940 one-third of Minneapolis' Skid Row population was over fifty, but by 1958 this figure had gone up to half. Motley described these old men as they appeared in Jefferson Park, just off West Madison Street: how they "leaned over the benches in their age . . . bundled in their coats [they] picked at the leaves with their canes, or stabbed them through, cruely, in a sort of revenge or distaste. Their old bodies, stooped, leaned toward the ground as if it would claim them." [16]

Other demographic characteristics also remained at levels similar to those of the Main Stem. Like its predecessor, Skid Row was overwhelmingly male (96 percent) and single (97 percent). In addition, there were still few immigrants, a fact that should not be surprising, given that restrictions had been placed on immigration since the 1920s. The vast majority (85 percent) of the population was native born, and most residents came from northern European backgrounds. Bain found that, of 100 Veterans Relief Service clients living on Skid Row, 59 percent were of British or Irish extraction, and another 18 percent had German ancestry.[17]

Another way Skid Row remained identical to the Main Stem was in its racism. Although the number of blacks had grown somewhat (by 13 percent between 1940 and 1950), racism and segregation were undiminished. Thus, although approximately 1,100 blacks lived in the various SRO districts (9 percent of the total population), they were concentrated in the South State Street section, where two-thirds lived; most of the other third resided on West Madison Street. Even this, however, masked the true extent of segregation and racial hatred. Hotels were either all-white or all-black, with only the missions permitting an integrated population. Whites held virulent racist attitudes and moved rather than live in the same building with blacks. In 1950 the Mission Hotel on West Madison became the first hotel in the district to accept blacks; whites moved out and it quickly became segregated. A Skid Row resident told Howard Bain, "They're all right in their place but I don't want 'em sleeping next to me." Bogue found that 80 percent of the white residents expressed active dislike of blacks, and Vander Kooi and Bain found a generally high level of prejudice, including a belief that most jackrollers were black. Similar patterns were also found in Philadelphia, where racial discrimination was found on the streets, in parks, housing, food, drinking, employment, and public assistance facilities; and on the Bowery in New York.[18]

Alcoholism

If there was one characteristic that the public associated with Skid Row more than anything else, it was drinking. This was the section where alcoholics concentrated. Thus, this single feature was both the major difference between the old and new versions of the SRO district, as well as the most important defining characteristic, and the one that was most publicized.

The reality was that, although the rate of alcoholism was much higher than for the city as a whole, the vast majority of residents were not addicted to liquor. Only 17 percent of the men in Bogue's survey were confirmed alcoholics. Alcoholics and heavy drinkers together accounted for 43 percent of the population. Fifteen percent did not touch alcohol at all, and nondrinkers combined with light drinkers made up 43 percent. The rest were considered moderate drinkers. A more detailed analysis showed that more than half (55 percent) of the men on public assistance were teetotalers or light drinkers. Younger men tended to be heavier drinkers; older men were more likely to be light drinkers or teetotalers. Heavy drinkers were most prominent among those who were unemployed or spot job workers, or those who were employed in the service industries. Foreign-born men and blacks were less likely to be alcoholics, whereas native-born white men of native-born parents had the highest rate of problems: 43 percent were either heavy drinkers or alcoholics.[19]

Thus, the majority of men on Skid Row were working men, not alcoholics. Another reason that this fact was overlooked was because many researchers lacked familiarity with working-class social patterns. Like other working men, particularly those who are single, most of this population did go to bars and did drink, but in moderation and as a social activity. This pattern was common in all of Chicago's workers' neighborhoods, and it was recreated by most of the Skid Row population. Sara Harris, author of *Skid Row, U.S.A.*, for example, called bars "bloody buckets" but noted that they were "the nearest approach to social clubs" the neighborhood had, and that "even the . . . Rowers who are not heavy drinkers come to bloody buckets to meet their friends." When Vander Kooi asked his interviewees how much alcohol they had consumed the day before, 59 percent said "None" and 22 percent told of a moderate consumption, such as a few glasses of beer, one or two glasses of wine, or a single shot of liquor.[20]

The point here is not to deny that there was a high rate of alcoholism on Skid Row, but rather to acknowledge that most of the residents were working men and acting according to standard social patterns. Howard Bahr, one of the early writers on Skid Row, while citing the high rate of alcoholism, recognized that "most skid row men are not problem drinkers, and they are not on skid row because of their drinking." Bogue wrote that "there seem to be two types of Skid Rows, whose populations are intermingled: (a) The Skid Row of the unattached man with low income who drinks moderately if at all, and (b) the Skid Row of the chronic alcoholic, the jackroller, the lazy beggar, and the derelict in an advanced stage of mental or physical deterioration." We are not trying to deny that the latter category exists, nor the need for analysis and treatment programs to deal with its members. In the past, however, these individuals have been the sole focus of study, despite the fact that they were always a minority of the Skid Row population. Our intention is to readjust that balance, to examine the social structure and priorities of the majority.[21]

Skid Row Social Structure

Skid Row residents lived in what Vander Kooi called "a viable community in which many social activities and attitudes similar to those found in all communities are sustained." This society provided such standard advantages as close personal friends. According to one study, a friend was most likely to be another person living on Skid Row (15 percent), a working man not on Skid Row (18 percent), a Skid Row businessman or professional worker (15 percent), or a family member (30 percent). Sharing was common, with the panhandler and the donor frequently reversing roles, depending on the fortunes of the day. Bogue found that 68 percent of the residents "almost never felt hopeless," and that only 10 percent felt hopeless "most of the time."[22]

Reliance on friends was true even for heavy drinkers and alcoholics. The aristocrats of these categories belonged to drinking groups that shared money and drinks, providing friends and a guarantee that members "need never live in loneliness." One Skid Row alcoholic from a middle-class background spoke about the time he had the d.t.'s and pneumonia at the same time. He noted that his wife loved him, "but I don't think she would have had the stomach to see me through that illness." Instead, his drinking

companions put him up in an SRO and "took turns nursing me. . . . Nobody
in the world would have done that for me. Not my wife or my children or
any of my so-called friends." [23]

A key priority of Skid Row society was independence and personal autonomy, similar to the world of the Main Stem. In a remarkable study of a
Skid Row district in 1964, Pat Nash, examining the Bowery for the New
York Department of Welfare, found that the most common phrases used by
residents to describe their life-style and environment were positive ones, in
particular that "no one bothers me" and that each person is "free to come
and go." Nash explained how "freedom to 'come and go' in a lodging
house might be interpreted as no one noticing or caring how many times
during the course of a day a person might enter or leave." This was not
however, the meaning as defined by Skid Row residents. To them, the stress
was not on the absence of personal ties, but on the acceptance by all of
freedom of action by the individual. Nash stated how "no explanations or
apologies are needed" for any conduct that did not abuse others and contrasted this to the rooming house, where "relations with the landlady are
likely to be much more personal." Nash also found that the men were "extremely proud . . . and have well developed egos," an observation verified
by James Spradley in his study of Seattle's Skid Row. Spradley found that
men who had been arrested and held in the drunk tank over the weekend
were particularly upset about their appearance when appearing before the
judge. One complained, "You're not washed, hair not combed, look like a
tramp in rumpled clothes," and another felt that "you look like a bum after
a couple of days in the drunk tank." Spradley felt that "one man summed up
the deepest feelings for most when he said that the worst thing was simply
'the degradation.' " [24]

At times this attitude of independence bordered on defiance. Willard
Motley, in *Knock on Any Door*, told what happened when a tour bus
went down West Madison Street and local residents heard the microphone-
enhanced voice of the guide describe the area in deprecatory tones. A
"skimpy tramp" yelled into the taverns "Here they come!" and "the men
on the sidewalk all turned toward the bus. The drunks on the stools, the
half-drunks at the tables all turned toward the street. . . . All the men,
in chorus pruned their lips and gave the rubberneck bus the razzberry—
loudly, raucously." Similarly, when Sara Harris told a female Skid Row
resident to pursue government support more aggressively, the woman rejected the advice angrily, telling her interviewer, "This girl's got plenty of
pride. Anyone don't think so can drop dead. You too, sister." [25]

Of course, this desire for independence had little opportunity to surface
and was often not apparent, most often, of course, because the residents'
limited incomes allowed few choices. Vander Kooi noted, for example,
that contrary to the image that Skid Row residents were wasteful spenders
indulging in binges, most were very careful with money, since "they have

TABLE 5-7

Housing on Skid Row, 1958

TYPE	POPULATION	%
Cage hotel[a]		
Large (over 300 units)	4,624	38.8
Medium (200–300 units)	1,779	14.9
Small (under 200 units)	1,635	13.7
Workingmen's hotel	1,677	14.1
Mission	975	8.2
Rooming house	806	6.8
Hospital, jail	320	2.7
Homeless	110	0.9
Totals	11,926	100.0

Source: Donald Bogue, *Skid Row in American Cities* (Chicago, 1963), p. 84.
[a]The total population in cage hotels was 8,038, for an overall percentage of 67.4.

little with which to be wasteful." One of the few ways, however, that they could exercise freedom and establish priorities and act on them was in their choice of housing, making it a crucial focus of analysis.[26]

Housing

In many ways neither the type of housing nor residents' priorities had changed since the days of the Main Stem. The most common form of housing was still the cage hotel. Bogue found that 67 percent of his interviewees lived in cubicle hotels, 39 percent in large cubicle hotels of 300 units or more. Only 14 percent lived in "hotels with rooms" (the elite workingmen's hotels), and 8 percent lived in missions. Another 0.9 percent "slept out," in the same pattern as today's homeless. The dormitory hotel and the flop had disappeared altogether (see table 5-7).[27]

As in the past, conditions in the cage hotels were miserable. More than two-thirds of the hotels did not have sufficient plumbing facilities to meet the requirements of Chicago's building code, which required one toilet and one shower for every twenty residents. More than 90 percent of the large cubicle hotels could not meet this standard. Eighty-three percent of these buildings had two or more building code violations, and all of them had a similar number of fire code violations. One group of thirty-two structures had between ten and fourteen building and fire code violations each.[28]

The rooms were the small dark spaces they had always been, with little light or ventilation, but many odors and vermin. The size, about 5 by 7 feet, was unchanged, as were the sparse furnishings. As in the days of the Main Stem, there were many uninvited guests; one tenant argued that his room was "the home of more cockroaches, mice and rats than you can imagine." When he took a shower, "the scum on the floor was so slippery I thought I would slip and bust my head. Finally by hanging onto the side I got myself clean." Similar conditions were reported in other cities, including New York and Philadelphia.[29]

It should also be noted that one reason some of the more shabby hotels managed to stay in business was that welfare and social service agencies still sent clients to Skid Row as an affordable means of providing shelter. Not only missions but also the Chicago Department of Welfare handed out chits for shelter and housing that could be honored only at Skid Row institutions. The chits were a major source of income: in one month of 1958 alone, public agencies provided almost 110,000 nights' lodgings, and charities dispensed another 31,000. In addition, hospitals with black outpatients and charity patients also sent these clients to Skid Row. As in the past, this was a double-edged policy. On the one hand, it enabled buildings that should have been closed down to stay in business. At the same time, however, it kept intact for later groups units of low-income housing that might otherwise have been torn down.[30]

The reasons why men chose to live in each kind of housing available on Skid Row resembled those of their predecessors on the Main Stem. Lodging in a cage hotel was cheap, only one to three dollars a night, depending on the quality. For someone employed at minimal wages, or on a pension, this was about all that could be afforded.

There was still a great deal of personal freedom. The vast majority (76 percent) of men found their domiciles on their own, without assistance from charities or government. The residents of Skid Row had a clear idea of what kind of shelter they preferred, if given a choice that was not limited by poverty. Bogue found that, when they were asked to choose some kind of housing, 92 percent of his respondents picked either single rooms or "light housekeeping apartments." But almost all of those who chose the room with cooking facilities insisted on sole occupancy, leading the sociologist to conclude that "the vast majority of homeless men want either to live in a single room or to live in a room where they can cook" (see table 5-8). It appears that privacy and autonomy remained critical priorities, a factor further demonstrated by an analysis of vacancy rates: the large cubicle hotels had a 26 percent vacancy rate, the medium sized had a rate of 16 percent, and the small cubicle hotels and workingmen's hotels had a rate of only 8 percent.[31]

TABLE 5-8

Housing Preferences of Men on Skid Row

TYPE	%
Single rooms	49
Apartment alone	35
Apartment shared	6
Open dormitory	5
Cubicle	1
Single family home	1
No response	3
Total	100

Source: Donald Bogue, *Skid Row in American Cities* (Chicago, 1963), p. 447.

Missions and Other Service Institutions

As in the past, the relationship between the mission and the Skid Row resident was a strained one. Some missions took in the truly homeless and, in exchange for room and board, put them to work full time repairing furniture for resale or some other work that brought revenue to the charity. Thus, the supposed beneficiaries of charity were, in truth, merely the exploited. In addition, mission workers saw few of the subtleties of the area: the fiftieth-anniversary report of the Chicago Christian Industrial League, for example, published in 1959, contained the revelation that 70 percent of the residents of Skid Row were "alcohol addicts," a figure disputed by every scientific survey and study. Of course, the men returned these attitudes in kind, calling the mission workers "hallelujahs," telling interviewers to "stay out of the missions. There's nothing lower on this earth than a mission stiff," or that "I'd rather be in the jungle than these missions. They're nerve-racking." In Philadelphia, when a team of researchers led by Leonard Blumberg asked the men what form of aid they would prefer, 41 percent suggested that jobs be made available, but only 8 percent suggested that more or better missions should be provided.[32]

Another critical institution to the men of Skid Row and, like the mission, one that had both benefits and drawbacks was the employment agency. This kind of firm provided work but did so in an extremely exploitative manner. Few, if any, of the jobs held by Skid Row men were covered by union contracts, so there were few safeguards. Deductions for fees, taxes, and transportation could go as high as one-half to one-third of the amount paid by the employer, leaving the worker with about the equivalent of one dollar an hour or less.[33]

Among recreational institutions on Skid Row, the most important was the tavern. As in any other working-class neighborhood, bars served as social centers. Vander Kooi noted, for example, that the "rate of interaction was very high. Almost no one was observed sitting and drinking in complete isolation." A great deal of information and many services were also exchanged or performed: passing along job information, inquiring after absent friends, leaving messages for others, arranging for loans, holding money for safe keeping, and ordering goods. For a few, the bar was still a place to sleep in an emergency.[34]

In addition to the bars, Skid Row depended on various service facilities. Lunch rooms provided more than sustenance, functioning as places to meet or to rest. Willard Motley described how "men sat at the table with their legs stretched out over the floor and their elbows on the table, making a rest for their chins." One place, the Nickel Plate, "was tables with old faces under hats and coffee cups coming up to mouths with spoons still in them and held still by worn thumbs. The Nickel Plate was coffee at three cents a cup, squint eyes bent close to day old newspapers." Poverty also forced many residents to sell blood to the blood banks; in New York it was estimated that as much as 10 percent of the 300,000 pints of blood used annually came from the Bowery. In addition, some of the men used commercial banks: one Minneapolis bank claimed that one-third of its 4,000 savings accounts came from Skid Row, as well as smaller numbers of safety deposit boxes and checking accounts.[35]

Skid Row Programs and Policies

Although some aspects of life on Skid Row, such as the conditions in the cage hotels, were determined by private businessmen, the most important impact on the neighborhood was wielded by the various branches of government. As noted in the preceding chapter, this was the direct result of a fundamental change caused by the Great Depression, that government now held primary responsibility for the welfare of the citizenry.

Public responsibility was carried out in various ways. The Chicago Department of Welfare provided hundreds of thousands of chits for lodging and meals, at an estimated cost of almost $250,000 a month. At Cook County Hospital a continual load of about 150 beds was created by Skid Row residents. This cost, when added to the expenses for emergency room work and for the use of a clinic, came to almost $60,000 a month. Another $4,000 a month was spent on the Chicago Alcoholic Treatment Center (all figures are in 1958 dollars).[36]

The most popular of these facilities was the Reading Room maintained by the city in the Madison Street SRO district. Besides television and magazines, there were facilities for bathing and shaving, sewing, dispensing first aid, and doing laundry. Stationary was available for writing letters. Blacks were welcomed, unlike in most of the other Skid Row institutions, and the truly homeless could get their mail sent there.[37]

The government program most commonly encountered by the men of Skid Row, however, was the police. By the 1950s the job of the local police department had done an about-face, returning to an earlier function of social control. In chapter 3 we explained how, at the turn of the century, arrests for vagrancy dropped considerably as the police shifted their mission to dealing with criminal activity rather than with social control and social welfare. The shift was the result of several factors, particularly the rise of social work as a profession. But with government taking on the full obligation for maintaining social well-being, the police were once again required to perform tasks that had less to do with catching criminals than with rehabilitation and keeping the streets free of unseemly individuals.

Consequently, the men of Skid Row were subject to frequent and repetitive arrest. In 1955 the Monroe Street Court, serving Chicago's Skid Row, called 70,000 cases, more than half of which involved repeat offenders of minor violations. Vander Kooi found that 19 percent of the men in his survey had been arrested between 40 and 250 times each, and that from half to two-thirds of all appearances before the bench resulted in immediate release. At the same time, however, the felony arrest record was very low, only 3 percent of the city total in 1947.[38]

The use of police to regulate the social world of Skid Row was a national norm in this period. In Minneapolis, where the police court handled minor offenses such as drunkenness and vagrancy, in one year half of the 12,000 cases came from that city's Skid Row section. On New York's Bowery in 1963 arrests for disorderly conduct and related offenses totaled more than 50,000, approximately one-quarter of *all arrests in the entire city on all counts*. Across the continent, in Los Angeles, one-fifth of the persons arrested for drunkenness were responsible for two-thirds of all arrests for that offense.[39]

The purpose of such enforcement was apparent to all, including the officers involved. John Schneider, in a paper entitled "The Police on Skid Row," pointed out that the job of the patrolman was primarily to maintain "the spatial order by seeing that the accepted boundaries of Skid Row were maintained." This was done by confining the men to their specific neighborhood and prohibiting spillover into middle-class sections. Much to the same purpose was the enforcement of a level of public decorum whenever a Skid Row man left this area. In addition, Schneider noted that there was a general attempt, usually at moderate levels unless a local campaign was underway, to sweep Skid Row itself. Although such law enforcement often resulted in arrests that were beneficial to the population (when jackrollers were taken in, for example, or men too drunk to take care of themselves), some was simply harassment of the population.[40]

In this way governmental policy was enforcing not only the law but social and cultural rules as well. Drinking in American society is permitted, for example, but it is restricted to certain times and places in middle-class environments. Drinking by the poor, or in public or in working-class bars, was the subject of suspicion and regulation. Even transgression of these rules, however, was shaped by poverty; drunk drivers are usually let off with a fine, whereas Skid Row men who drank in public but had little available cash were arrested repeatedly and frequently jailed. In Detroit, therefore, the plainclothes officers assigned to Skid Row referred to themselves as "ragpickers," and a journalist described their job as keeping "depravity . . . from becoming too assertively public." Police also took out their frustrations on prisoners; Willard Motley claimed, for example, that turnkeys used to take a pail of water and throw it "in between the bars on . . . drunks who wouldn't keep quiet."[41]

Conclusions

In many ways Skid Row was different from the Main Stem. It was smaller, older, marred by more pathologies. But in fundamental ways the two neighborhoods were alike. In different eras, both performed the same function, the provision of low-cost housing and services for working men on the bottom of the social scale. The vast majority of the population was in fact neither alcoholic nor pathological, but simply poor, either because of the wages they were able to command or because of the pension allowed for their age or disability. When most of them drank (although many did not), it was in the same context as any other working man who walked into a neighborhood bar for relaxation and camaraderie.

This is not to state that there was not a high incidence of alcoholism, nor that programs should not have been devised to deal with this problem. Merely, it is to readjust the balance, by focusing on the larger group in the population rather than the smaller.

6 Skid Row: Social Theory and Physical Destruction

The Skid Row stereotype, despite its inaccuracy, was widely accepted and utilized. It formed the basis for much of the analysis conducted by social scientists during the 1950s and 1960s, as well as justification for the most important government programs that impacted Skid Row. As a result of the negative image, as well as pressure from local growth coalitions, all the public programs aimed at the elimination of the Skid Row district rather than at fostering its survival and improvement. Not surprisingly, the programs were remarkably successful.

The roots of the popular Skid Row stereotype today can be traced back in part to studies of the Skid Row homeless conducted by two kinds of social scientists during this same period: the social problem analysts and the social order analysts. On the one hand, the *social problem* analysts presumed that Skid Row homeless were a social problem requiring attention and treatment and used survey research to study Skid Row residents. On the other were the *social order* analysts interested in describing and explaining the integrity of Skid Row social life. They believed that the norms of survey researchers and their funders presupposed that Skid Row homeless were disaffiliated and so overlooked the social community of the homeless Skid Row residents.

The social problem analysts wanted to understand the scope and nature of deviant characteristics and behaviors among Skid Row residents. They were willing to accept a clear hierarchy of values and so used survey questionnaires administered by outsiders to randomly selected residents of Skid Row as a means of assessing the characteristics, experience, and meaning of the disaffiliated homeless who lived there. The social problem analysts asked about health conditions, drinking, social relationships, employment, and other social characteristics in order to measure the size and intensity of residents' problems and needs. The studies were usually sponsored and funded by philanthropic organizations, local redevelopment agencies, or federal agencies committed to rehabilitating alcoholics. Predictably, the surveys did find a disproportionate share of alcoholism, physical illness,

107

serious disabilities, social isolation, and other problems among Skid Row residents as compared with the population citywide. The survey reports em-' phasized the disaffiliation, dependence, and passivity of the Skid Row residents, which justified a variety of public assistance programs from alcoholic rehabilitation to employment training. Additionally, the reports usually included negative evaluations of Skid Row lodging houses, missions, and SRO hotels, calling for their wholesale destruction.[1]

The social order analysts were interested in basic theoretical questions about the possibility of social bonds among what the reformers presumed were disaffiliated homeless. They combined open-ended interviews with the participant observer method. Purposely withholding judgment on the marginality of the homeless, these social analysts temporarily entered the world of the homeless as observers, searching for social meaning. Unwilling to accept the preconceptions of the survey researchers, these participant observers utilized a pluralistic approach that emphasized the centrality and autonomy of individual action as the source of social meaning.[2]

Fascinated with the vitality of social life among the marginal and allegedly disaffiliated homeless, these analysts in their search for community were quick to fault those who would label the homeless as deviants or anomic, arguing instead that the homeless on Skid Row possessed a rich subculture among themselves. The social order analysts usually lived among the residents of Skid Row in order to learn the rules and conventions Skid Row men used to give order to their social lives. The studies conducted by these analysts did not lend themselves to wholesale programs of social rehabilitation or urban renewal. Rather, the results offered documentation of successful social adaptations created by the poor residents to overcome the disadvantages of poverty and physical or mental disabilities.

Despite the community life on Skid Row, the problem of social marginality for the homeless remained. The participant observations, when written into stories about individual homeless, provided convincing portrayals of social actors making choices and enduring the consequences. But focusing exclusively on interpersonal relations in small group settings tended to evoke an ambiguous response from the public: compassion for those homeless unfairly burdened with the consequences of severely limited choices and contempt for the homeless whose imprudent decisions apparently resulted in so much misfortune—a response once again popular in the 1980s with respect to the "new" homeless.

The social order analysts, therefore, believed that the authorities should leave the Skid Row homeless alone. Reacting against the research of those who could justify the meddlesome and all too frequently repressive intervention of social service providers and charity workers, the participant observers hoped the stories they told would undermine the credibility of the reformers' research.[3] Hence, in their work as social scientists, the social order analysts of Skid Row avoided the issue of the moral significance of the homeless. At the minimum they seemed to tell us that the homeless, though marginal, were neither harmful nor diseased.

> Skid row is not just a place nor is it merely a deviant community alienated from the larger society and confined to a recognizable region of the city. Skid row is a subculture in which men live together, not as a simple aggregate, but rather in meaningful relationships which affect the lives of individuals and shape the subculture in which they live.[4]

Within this context, it was logical that the social problem analysts like Bogue, Bahr, and Caplow should focus on the alcoholic residents of Skid Row, even though alcoholics were a minority of the total population. In part, their focus stemmed from both their sociological curiosity about the unusual as well as their moral interest in understanding and treating alcoholic men. Bahr summed up this attitude in his often quoted remark that the Skid Row man was "about as different from *homo sociologus* as it is possible to be while remaining human. For the price of a subway ride, [the researcher] can enter a country where the accepted principles of social interaction do not seem to apply." The exclusive focus on alcoholism also facilitated the policies of Skid Row removal promoted by those seeking urban renewal. If all residents of Skid Row were alcoholics, there was much more justification for removing the victims from a terrible environment, rehabilitating them, and bulldozing the area to make way for new developments.[5] It was not surprising, therefore, that Bogue's grant application defined "the problem and poses the goal for the area—the ultimate elimination of skid row," or that he wrote in his final report that "Skid Row is a major barrier to urban renewal . . . [it] must be regarded as a liability to the community, with no necessary or indispensable economic function." [6]

The social problem analysts' view also followed the general public conception of Skid Row. The *Saturday Evening Post*, for example, described Skid Row as the home of "wretched misfits, the dregs of our society. . . . Skid row . . . is a place of physical and moral infection." Articles in popular magazines like *Collier's* and *Commonweal* also highlighted the alcohol problem on Skid Row. Perhaps most important was a series of lurid articles that ran in the *Chicago Daily News* from August 13 to August 26, 1949. Two reporters, William Mooney and Frederick Bird, were sent to West Madison Street and told to write about what they saw. Their reports ran on the front page for two weeks, with added emphasis in the form of pictures covering the last page of the paper's first section. The series created a shakeup of Skid Row in part because it included the names and addresses of every tavern owner in the area, and it was responsible for a 20,000 increase in circulation for the paper. Howard Bahr reported that these issues were also avidly read by residents of the district. However, this kind of publicity meant that in the public's mind, as one novelist put it, "If the man is not dirty, smelly, unshaven, beat up, and drunk, he can't be from Skid Row." [7]

Regardless of motivation, the concentration by researchers on alcoholism was well-nigh absolute. Donald Bogue, for example, used alcohol consumption as his single dependent variable in every one of the dozens of tables in his study, the most comprehensive of this period (when social service groups and the city published a synopsis of the report, even they could not follow this exclusive concentration on alcoholism and cross tabulated many of the tables for SRO district instead). Even such sympathetic observers as Samuel Wallace could write that "the status of drunk is the essential core of skid row subculture . . . to be completely acculturated in skid row . . . is to be drunk," and Ronald Miller argued that "derelicts . . . epitomize Skid Row."[8]

If everyone who lived on Skid Row was either an alcoholic or, as Bahr referred to them, "disaffiliated," then all the residents were automatically dependent and hence potential clients. Ronald Miller wrote, "If Skid Row means disease, alcoholism and malnutrition—and it does—it may be diminished by . . . social service strategy." Programs were designed, therefore, with the view that the population would be dependent on service providers. Blumberg, Shipley, and Shandler, for example, in describing the kind of shelter facility that should be created, noted that "the institutional arrangements should allow for as much individual autonomy and for as little stigmatizing as possible. Men should be permitted to leave if they wish and they should be welcomed back." The implication here is clearly that staff would control the facility; professional workers would "permit" residents the freedom to come and go as they wished. It is also apparent that it would be staff who would have to "welcome back" the men who had chosen to exercise the option of leaving."[9]

The concentration on alcohol and disaffiliation implied that after adequate treatment and rehabilitation the Skid Row residents could move back into mainstream society. In turn, this would mean that Skid Row could be broken up, since rehabilitated residents would be dispersed throughout the city. Although the desire to ease these men into the urban mainstream was a well-meaning one, it was impossible to accomplish without providing jobs or more substantial economic benefits. Without economic security, however, former Skid Row residents would lack the inexpensive services such as the hotels and restaurants they had used to survive on meager incomes; they would be removed from the downtown environment that had supported their community life-style. In many reports the lack of appreciation for the economic and social community of Skid Row meant that programs at best ignored these institutions and at worst blamed them for contributing to disaffiliation. Bogue's work, for example, called for the destruction of the cubicle hotels in the first year of urban renewal, with the replacement of units to be constructed in years two through five.

Skid Row as a Class Community

Perhaps the most comprehensive analysis of Skid Row undertaken by the social problem theorists was conducted by Howard Bahr in collaboration with Theodore Caplow. Caplow had been a student of the transient single poor since the Depression, and was a notable authority on the subject who had organized a 1958 study of Skid Row in Minneapolis. Bahr and Caplow provided the most well-developed definition of homelessness, which they, along with the other social problem analysts, take to be the most "salient social characteristic" of the men on Skid Row.

> Homelessness is a condition of detachment from society characterized by the absence or attenuation of the affiliative bonds that link settled persons to a network of interconnected social structures. . . . In general, homeless persons are poor, anomic, inert, and irresponsible. They command no resources, enjoy no esteem, and assume no burden of reciprocal obligations. Social action in the usual sense is impossible for them.[10]

Drawing from the sociologist Robert Merton's anomie theory, Bahr and Caplow argued that homelessness is a form of social disaffiliation. "Traditionally, the homeless man has been viewed as unattached, and to describe the homelessness in terms of disaffiliation is not an extreme departure from earlier definitions; but it does extend the phenomenon from the skid row population to all persons characterized by the absence or attenuation of affiliative ties."[11] In order to assess the degree of disaffiliation among the residents of New York's Bowery and Camp LaGuardia (the Skid Row and mens' shelter they were studying), Bahr and Caplow compared the degree of disaffiliation of the Skid Row residents and two control groups: male residents of Park Slope, a working-class neighborhood, and male residents on upper-class Park Avenue. No other study provided such a comparison across class boundaries.

In comparing the three samples, Bahr and Caplow found large differences in the extent of disaffiliation between the residents of the Bowery or Camp LaGuardia and the upper-class men on Park Avenue. However, the differences between Skid Row and shelter residents and the other working-class men in the neighborhood of Park Slope were relatively small. Most striking was the fact that "the respondents with the highest status were more affiliated than the other respondents on every item."[12] In other words, the higher the socioeconomic standing of a respondent, the higher the affiliation score. So great was this correlation that Bahr and Caplow did not include the Park Avenue sample in their analysis of the syndrome of homelessness since there was little likelihood that these upper-class residents would show any signs of homelessness. Thus, in their pursuit of deviance and disaffiliation the analysts overlooked the obvious contribution of class differences to their measures of disaffiliation.

Bahr and Caplow assumed that social affiliation and high social status naturally go together. They did not consider, as we do, that their measures of disaffiliation were actually measures of differences in social class. Hence, later on in their book, when they discovered that many of the factors associated with homelessness in their and other studies of Skid Row were also associated with working-class men in Park Slope, they did not recognize the anomaly this finding created for their own analysis. If the researchers found that disaffiliation leads men to homelessness, then why did the settled working-class men with similarly high levels of disaffiliation not live on Skid Row? Bahr and Caplow never really answered this question except to suggest that disaffiliation is relative, existing among members of all social communities, not just residents of Skid Row. Like other functional explanations, their analysis suffers from a sort of tautological bind— Skid Row men are homeless because they are disaffiliated. To their credit, Bahr and Caplow compared the disaffiliation of different social classes, as well as of different working-class communities. They simply missed part of the significance of their own findings. The major differences between the working-class men on Skid Row and those in the Park Slope neighborhood were economic (Skid Row men had less stable jobs, which left them poorer and more dependent on public assistance), physical (Skid Row men suffered from more physical disabilities and illnesses), and social (Skid Row men reported having a more reckless youth and more marital discord). But the social differences may reflect a desire for autonomy and independence as much as they indicate deviance. Furthermore, comparing single men on Skid Row with family men in a working-class neighborhood will necessarily turn up a greater incidence of marital discord among Skid Row residents since there will be a greater proportion of separated and divorced men on Skid Row than in a neighborhood composed largely of married couples and families. The economic and physical factors also highlight the difference between the independent and dependent members of the urban working class. Ironically, Bahr and Caplow provided important empirical evidence that residents of Skid Row were not a socially distinct class, but members of the working class whose poor employment opportunities, single status, and physical vulnerabilities placed them outside the working-class neighborhood. They even went so far as to admit that "skid row, like any other area of the city, may include affiliated men as well as disaffiliates." [13]

The class analysis of Skid Row residents conducted by the social problem theorists was complemented by the ideas of another group of sociologists who used and developed the ideas of social ecology first developed by Chicago School sociologists in the 1920s and 1930s. In a nutshell, the social ecologists traced the origins of the modern metropolis to natural or "biotic" cycles of economic growth that push upward at the center and outward at the periphery, generating rings of functionally and socially segmented areas. The economic transformation of land use and density was explained using the ecological concepts of invasion, competition, succession, and accommodation. The organic metaphor enabled the ecologists to assume that the economic competition of urban land markets possessed the same basic self-regulating qualities of an ecosystem. They asserted that urban growth, like biological growth, was inevitable, and that such growth contributed to the evolution of modern society, just as the biological processes of growth ultimately contribute to the evolution of living species. Though there have been many critics of social ecology as far back as the 1930s, the ideas remain popular today in the ideology of civic boosterism.[14]

Regardless of the empirical validity of the ideas of the social ecologists about how city neighborhoods change in relation to the central area, the ideas did provide a powerful and useful justification for the elimination of Skid Row. For instance, as the social scientist Mark Gottdiener points out in his critical assessment of the social ecologists, they acknowledged that the zone of transition that formed near downtown (which usually included the SRO hotels and Skid Row) was the result of speculation in a competitive land market that encouraged owners to subdivide dwellings into rooming houses that attracted the transient urban poor.[15] This zone was also at the bottom of the social hierarchy. The social standing of neighborhoods improved as one moved outward to the city's edge. Gottdeiner writes, "Traversing the urban form from the central business district to the periphery, the Chicago School researchers, using official census data, found that the incidence of social pathology decreased while homeownership and nuclear-family status increased. The inner zones, therefore, were discovered to be the areas of much crime, illness, gang warfare, broken homes, and virtually every other social indicator of disorganization." [16]

The ideas of the social ecologists justified the basic assumptions of the proponents of federally funded urban redevelopment programs, who argued that the natural market forces that had once made downtown the central commercial hub of the metropolis simply required some public-sector help to return to its former dominance. Demand for land downtown had not kept pace with the post–World War II economic revival mainly because of the legacy of small parcels and dilapidated buildings that depressed the land market near the central business district. If government were to intervene by clearing the land and assembling large-scale parcels suitable for construction of office and commercial buildings, then the private market would reclaim these areas with new construction. Although land-clearance programs failed to prime the economic pump as expected in most cities, they did wipe out Skid Row hotels and other slum housing in the zones of transition, making way for some new development.

Thus, although the findings of the social problem analysts helped legitimize the destruction of Skid Row and promote a profile of the Skid Row resident as a hapless and disaffiliated derelict, they did accurately describe the growing proportion of dependent poor on Skid Row. The social order analysts, reflecting on their observations and experience, argued that the deviant life-style of Skid Row residents represented a coherent and orderly social world that did not conform to middle-class social values. While the social problem analysts defined the homeless on Skid Row as needy misfits, the social order analysts identified the Skid Row homeless as members of a deviant social community. In either case the ideas undermined the legitimacy of Skid Row as a viable community of urban residents. Emphasis on the deviant and pathological supplied public officials and professional caretakers with powerful justifications for actions that affected all residents of Skid Row, regardless of the actual distribution of addiction and illness. The compassionate could argue that massive rehabilitation efforts were necessary for the good of the vulnerable and dependent residents, and those threatened by Skid Row homeless could justify demolition and dispersal to destroy the source of social and criminal contagion.

Both social problem and social order analysts focused their research exclusively on the social characteristics and organization of Skid Row residents. The analysts acknowledged that the contours of social class channeled the routes followed by the homeless on their journey to Skid Row, but they did not ask how these contours were formed nor who was responsible for their maintenance. We believe they accepted the assumptions of the social ecologists and so simply assumed that changes in the urban ecology and the shifts in the stratification of classes naturally produced the spatial push and social pressure that altered the urban topography to which the Skid Row homeless had to adapt. The very social weakness of the Skid Row homeless encouraged the analysts to ignore the possibility that the social significance of Skid Row life might be more accurately understood as a result of larger institutional forces that in turn created a functioning community of resistance rather than as either a residue of social deviance or a cultural adaptation within an ecological niche of modern urban social life.

We do not believe that the demise of Skid Row and the SRO hotels was the inevitable result of market forces, or that Skid Row residents embodied peculiar social and psychological characteristics that produced deviant and pathological social behavior. In the next section we briefly explore how urban renewal could not succeed if in fact Skid Row residents were not seen as being as pathological as has been believed, or if the economic revival of downtown development were not viewed as being as inevitable as claimed.

Urban Renewal and the Growth Coalitions

The massive suburbanization that accompanied the postwar boom created decentralized metropolitan regions with multiple commercial and administrative centers that housed activities that formerly took place in the central business district. Although this decentralizing trend had been on its way since before the turn of the century, the challenge it posed to the dominance of central cities became a serious political issue when downtown business owners, commercial real estate agents, and city officials witnessed abandonment of downtown office and retail spaces and the devaluation of land values that contributed to the erosion of the city property tax base. The decline of the center not only contradicted ecological theory, more importantly, it threatened the economic investments of the downtown elite.[17]

Throughout the country, businessmen in large cities came together to form what sociologist Harvey Molotch calls growth coalitions. These were primarily privately organized partnerships that collected members from the ranks of local business elites whose economic interests were tied directly or indirectly to downtown property development. Although business dominated, Molotch argues that the organization of the coalition ultimately mobilized the collaboration of participants from frequently antagonistic economic sectors and social classes. For example, corporate executives and labor leaders from the construction trade unions could and did jointly support plans promoting local growth.[18] Robert Dahl's famous defense of pluralism in American urban politics also relied heavily on an analysis of the formation of a growth coalition supporting urban redevelopment plans in New Haven. Dahl documented collaboration among actors from seemingly antagonistic elites and classes as evidence of countervailing political power, not recognizing that he was selecting an issue where common economic interests temporarily outweighed social and political differences. Later revisions of Dahl's original empirical data by G. William Domhoff and his own reevaluation of the influence of economic power led Dahl to conclude that corporate officials enjoyed a disproportionate concentration of political power that enabled them to set the urban redevelopment agenda.[19] Nevertheless, the coalitions have proven successful because they can act in ways that support Dahl's initial theory of pluralist collaboration and so obscure the uneven accumulation of economic benefits up the social hierarchy, as well as the displacement of economic costs upon social strata further down. Ironically, growth coalitions used the public resources and authority of redevelopment agencies to stimulate lagging growth in and near the central business district, while they justified the intervention as a process simply removing the barriers (both social and physical) to natural and inevitable renewal.

Urban renewal was a product of the Housing Act of 1949, which sought to make decent housing available to every American citizen, and which also mandated massive clearance of slums. The measure had tremendous support among big-city mayors because it linked the two concepts—construction of new public housing and demolition of older areas—in a fundamental way. Senator Robert Wagner of New York released in 1948 the result of a questionnaire he had mailed out to government officials. Mayors from seventy-eight cities representing 41 percent of the nation's urban population reported that 1.8 million units of housing were substandard. Ninety percent of the replies indicated that the private sector could not meet the housing needs of low-income persons, and that public housing was the necessary answer. The title of the report, however, was "Slum Clearance." Under the act as passed by the federal government, either through negotiation or via eminent domain, cities could acquire land designated to be cleared. This could be sold, leased, donated, or retained by the local agency of the Urban Renewal Program, whose stated purpose was the elimination and prevention of slums.[20]

Urban redevelopment and renewal efforts fueled with federal funds and armed with the police power of local government concentrated on removing structures from the "zones of transition," which included Skid Row and other working-class neighborhoods sheltering poor families. Skid Rows and slums had proven formidable obstacles to private renewal efforts since they were first targeted for reform at the turn of the century. The spatial concentration of the poor in Skid Row and slums made piecemeal redevelopment a risky undertaking, not only for individual speculators but housing reformers as well. Although no SRO hotel or slum tenement could successfully compete for central location when pitted against the rent revenues generated by construction of a new office tower, the presence nearby of many such hotels or tenements could easily resist the encroachment of new construction. The concentration of low-rent SRO hotels in effect devalued the economic promise of centrally located land. Such a stable land market offered little incentive for new investment, but it did keep property taxes low, which contributed to lower operating costs for SRO hotel owners. Furthermore, residents enjoyed the advantages of a central location without paying the speculators' premium in their rents. When Leonard Blumberg and his colleagues conducted a longitudinal market analysis of rooming houses in the Philadelphia Skid Row, they discovered that its residential buildings remained profitable in the midst of considerable economic decline nearby.[21] SRO housing, even with the high vacancy rates of the 1950s and 1960s, proved a formidable impediment to private redevelopment.

What made the demise of Skid Row housing inevitable in Chicago and other large cities was the policy of wholesale land clearance adopted by redevelopment agencies and supported by the local growth coalitions. The modest revenue of the SRO hotels could not compete against the financial promise of commercial redevelopment plans backed up by the threat of condemnation under the municipal police power of eminent domain. Owners sold their buildings, and thousands of SRO hotel units were destroyed, their tenants displaced and dispersed throughout the city. Although large-scale clearance seldom ushered in the real estate boom its proponents claimed it would, it did succeed in destroying most Skid Row housing. Reporting to Congress in 1964 on the progress of urban renewal projects between 1950 and 1963, William Slayton, the commissioner of the Federal

Urban Renewal Administration of the Housing and Home Finance Agency, proudly claimed success when he explained that more than 1,300 urban renewal projects had been initiated in which 21,970 acres of land had been acquired and 129,000 structures demolished. Most important, he pointed out these efforts resulted in an 427 percent increase in land values after redevelopment projects were initiated or completed.[22]

Urban renewal was a massive program. By March 1961 alone, more than $800 million in new housing had been started, and another $3 billion was in the pipeline. Much of this work came under heavy criticism, for a number of reasons. By 1961, 126,000 units had been eliminated, and only 28,000 new ones were built. There were also serious problems with relocation and affordability: one study of projects in forty-one cities showed that 60 percent of the households forced out merely relocated in other slum areas —in Philadelphia the figure was 70 percent. In Boston a study of families dispossessed by urban renewal found that the median monthly rent went from $41 to $71 after the move. A similar study of black families in Chicago found that the median rent burden rose from 35 percent before relocation to 46 percent afterward. Coupled with this was the most minimal effort on the part of the government to assist in a traumatic process: between 1949 and 1964 only one-half of one percent of all federal expenditures for urban renewal went to relocation of households; if payments were included, the figure went up to 2 percent. Urbanologist Herbert Gans concluded that urban renewal was "a method for eliminating the slums in order to 'renew' the city, rather than a program for properly rehousing slum-dwellers." [23]

The burdens of displacement and neighborhood destruction that wholesale renewal efforts imposed on low-income black and ethnic neighborhoods stimulated spirited and eventually effective resistance by residents and their allies. The overall economic failure of renewal schemes was intensified by protesters who quickly learned about the class composition of the growth coalitions and wasted no time in politicizing what at first had been privately managed public enterprise. Renewal programs were eventually modified in many cities to involve neighborhood leaders in the planning process and to emphasize rehabilitation and housing rather than clearance and commercial development. But, as John Mollenkopf argues, residents seldom gained control over local development decisions or managed to banish the growth politics of the business elite, although they have managed to stop community-crushing renewal and change the political agenda to include the interests of low-income neighborhoods.[24]

Efforts to eliminate the SRO districts in Chicago did not start with urban renewal. In 1926 property owners on the near West Side of Chicago organized the West Central Association to protect their interests. For decades they worked to reform, or eliminate, the area along West Madison Street, to convert it to middle-class occupancy. In 1945 the state legislature in Springfield appropriated $10 million for slum clearance, at least half of which went to Chicago; the City Council passed a $5 million bond issue for the same purpose. When the Chicago Housing Authority (CHA) began operations after World War II, one of its first projects was Dearborn Homes along South State Street, in the heart of the black belt. As a result of eminent domain, in 1946 the authority acquired land that included 158 vacant lots, 9 commercial structures, 6 single family homes, 91 small and large apartment buildings, and 6 shacks that were still being used for shelter. Demolition of these structures produced a loss of 406 units, of which 190 were in the Douglas Hotel, an SRO. By definition, new CHA buildings, which replaced these facilities, did not house single-person households.[25]

The usual procedure of urban renewal was to designate conservation areas in the city, then appoint a community council of nine to fifteen "representative" residents. Assisted by technicians from the federal and local governments, this board would then draw up an antislum, antiblight program for the area.[26]

In SRO districts, however, another aspect of the urban renewal program was utilized. These areas were designated as "redevelopment projects" that did not require any community input at all. (Kay Marrin, coordinator of the Madison-Canal Project, said that she had no rehabilitation staff and there was no conservation committee because "We are a total clearance project. None of the buildings can be saved.") The redevelopment project, instead, involved three steps: designation of an area as slum and blighted, approval of a redevelopment plan, and sale of the land for redevelopment. These steps had to proceed exactly in that order; in other words, sale of the land could not be permitted till a plan was accepted and approved.[27]

In 1966 the city began drawing up plans to deal with the Skid Row/West Madison Street section (designated "Madison-Canal" by the city). According to the initial proposal in March, "of particular concern has been the elimination of the Madison Street Skid Row. . . . Without question . . . [this] represents the single most deleterious influence impeding the redevelopment of the West Central Area." Most of the proposal described existing populations and land use, but there was also a recommendation that the area was particularly suited for office buildings, support services for the central business district, business-related retail establishments, hotels and motels, "and possibly elevator apartments along the Kennedy Expressway."[28]

As part of the preparations, Ronald Vander Kooi, then professor of sociology at the University of Illinois at Chicago Circle, was hired to conduct a study of the area's population and to make recommendations regarding programs. Vander Kooi took another survey of West Madison Street residents, producing another set of statistics. Already well known in the area because of his participant-observer work for his dissertation, Vander Kooi was contacted by one resident who suggested, "Why not build urban centers having modest but reasonable living conditions, adjacent to clearing houses for employment, public health and vocational upgrading?"[29]

Vander Kooi recommended that urban renewal officials approach the elimination of Skid Row, not as "a simple relocation of residents," but as a way of recreating community. This "new community" should include not only housing but restaurants, employment offices, religious institutions, and retail outlets. Local control, however, would be in the hands of the authorities. Drinking outlets would be "controlled" and the entire neighborhood would be "carefully planned and supervised," with a "strong emphasis upon rehabilitation and the routing of individuals through personal counseling, alcoholism programs, vocational training . . . and various agencies back into more normal American communities and activities." The city should build between 100 and 800 units of new housing to replace the estimated 3,100 units that currently existed in the area. These buildings "should be operated with careful supervision and strict adherence to necessary rules." [30]

Because it called for sweeping changes (the creation of an entire new community, rather than relocation on an individual basis), Vander Kooi's proposal was considered extreme. The first city document to consider it was a *Report to the Department of Urban Renewal on the Designation of Slum and Blighted Area Madison-Canal* in May 1967, the same month Vander Kooi presented his work. Most of the report was a statistical analysis of the area, noting that all the residential structures in the area qualified as slum and blighted and that 97 percent of the population consisted of single-person households. There was also the notation that "relocation of the residents of the area will involve a carefully thought out program of residence change and social orientation coordinated by the Department of Urban Renewal." [31]

In October 1968 the Department of Urban Renewal presented its redevelopment plan for the Madison-Canal district. This was a modest document of some half-dozen pages, including maps, that laid out the goals of the project, the area's boundaries, and the new land uses that would be permitted. The stated objective of the plan was "the removal of structurally substandard buildings to allow redevelopment for office, residential, parking, and related uses"; "structural, substandard buildings" included, of course, all multi-unit residential structures in the area. Proposed activities included "acquisition, clearance and disposition for redevelopment uses." [32]

Following release of the plan, the city published in August 1968 an "Invitation to Proposals" to purchase the land. Letters were also mailed to 764 parties. By November 19, 1968, four sealed offers had arrived. On December 5 Department of Urban Renewal Commissioner Lewis Hill announced that the winning bid ($30.25 per square foot) came from the Madison-Canal Development Company. Local newspapers questioned the process as arbitrary and political, especially considering that one of the directors of the winning firm was Charles Swibel, long considered one of the city's paramount wheeler-dealers. Swibel was chairman of the Chicago Housing Authority Board of Commissioners, a position that was not supposed to have been used to personal advantage. The Better Government Association and the *Chicago Sun-Times*, however, accused him of depositing CHA funds in interest-free accounts in a bank that helped him finance other development projects, and of having an expensive burglar alarm installed in his home, free of charge, by a company that received large CHA contracts afterward. In addition, Swibel was president of Marks Company, which held mortgages on various slum properties as well as managing several West Madison Street SROs (in 1975 he was fined $700 in Housing Court for violations in the McCoy Hotel). According to one newspaper account, Swibel's contract with the Madison-Canal Development Company stated that he was to receive $1 million if the bid was accepted, without making any investment in the company or incurring any liability. Swibel was depicted, in other words, as a unethical broker for Chicago's version of Molotch's growth coalition. According to city records, Madison-Canal Development Company had the high bid.[33]

After this action, the city proceeded to follow its urban renewal agenda, acquiring land and demolishing the hotels and other structures along Skid Row. Sixteen SRO facilities with a total of 2,849 units were destroyed. Thousands of residents, of course, were displaced, from some of the last private low-income housing in Chicago.

Nevertheless, for more than a decade, little redevelopment, either commercial or for the Skid Row residents, came as a result of these actions. The federal government temporarily blocked action when it took possession of a key block for a high-rise Social Security facility. As a result, the Department of Urban Renewal could not deliver the packages as described in its proposal, and the Madison-Canal Company rejected the revised contract, retaining only one square block (which they had already purchased.) Eventually this land was taken over to build the Presidential Towers project, described in chapter 9.[34]

Similarly, Vander Kooi's replacement housing projects also floundered. His concept of a "new community" was reduced to a single five-story forty-unit hotel. Lots were acquired and architectural drawings drawn up that included a tavern and retail shops. The foundation was dug. Before construction started, however, the city decided not to go through with the project and filled in the hole. The land was then bought by the National Cash Register Corporation, which owned an office building across the street; the company turned it into a fenced-in parking lot for employees. Although there was some discussion of other plans, in time the notion of replacement housing for Skid Row residents was, in the words of Ron Vander Kooi, "eventually forgotten." [35]

Urban renewal accomplished its goal to eliminate the Skid Row neighborhood. Analysis of census tract data for the twenty years following Bogue's study documents the devastating effects of demolition on the residential community of Skid Row. Table 6-1 compares changes in the number of

TABLE 6-1

The Loss of Skid Row SRO Units, 1960–1980

	1960	1970	1980	% CHANGE 1960–80
WEST MADISON				
Group quarters	6,327	1,901	490	−92
Occupied rental units	6,145	2,050	1,075	−82
Single-room units	4,529	1,627	672	−85
Units lacking plumbing	5,835	958	392	−93
SOUTH STATE				
Group quarters	1,516	891	442	−71
Occupied rental units	1,875	1,789	1,872	0
Single-room units	1,910	1,174	989	−48
Units lacking plumbing	2,822	776	237	−92
NEAR NORTH				
Group quarters	321	459	261	−19
Occupied rental units	2,586	1,278	490	−81
Single-room units	2,572	1,236	403	−84
Units lacking plumbing	2,407	703	126	−95

Source: U.S. Department of Commerce, Bureau of the Census, Census Tract Data for the City of Chicago. West includes tracts 0415, 0416, 0417, 0418, 0419, 0420; North includes 0135; South includes 0514, 0516. The group quarters data for 1970 includes institutional populations; 1960 and 1980 figures do not. This is a proxy measure for cubicle hotels and missions.

people in group quarters (excluding those in institutions like jails, schools, and hospitals), occupied rental units, single-room units, and units without plumbing in the central Skid Row areas studied by Bogue in 1957.

The population in group quarters (a proxy measure of cubicle hotel and mission residents) concentrated in the West Side dropped more than 90 percent in twenty years. The number of single-room units also dropped by 80 percent or more in most cases. The relatively low rate of decline in the South Loop reflects rehabilitation and new construction in the late 1970s. Similar efforts on the North Side explain the relatively stable number of occupied rental units despite the drop in single-room units. The decline in units without adequate plumbing measures the successful implementation of renewal programs that specifically targeted such structures as dilapidated and ready for removal. Most of these were hotels with shared baths and toilets. Although no one indicator captures the SRO hotels precisely, taken together they provide clear evidence of a dramatic wholesale elimination of the single-room housing stock on Skid Row. The loss of rental units displaced the single male population, and with them left the employment agencies, bars, pawnshops, missions, restaurants, barber shops, and other services of Skid Row. Many in the relatively elderly population died and others secured subsidized housing for the elderly. Others moved to rooming houses or SRO hotels in other areas of the city.

Conclusions

By the late 1980s Skid Row in Chicago no longer existed. West Madison Street, which originally gained fame at the turn of the century, no longer provided the poor with shelter, food, clothing, entertainment, or any sense of community. This loss was the result of decades of antagonism from civic and business leaders, legitimated from the 1950s on by social scientists, and incorporated into dramatic change-oriented programs like urban renewal.

Because government policy makers and social scientists, often with the highest and noblest of motives, directed their concern and caring at one small part of the population, their programs did not respond to the needs of the rest of the men who lived on Skid Row. Eliminating SRO hotels and substituting alcoholism treatment and rehabilitation programs may have benefited the hard-core derelicts, but it left everyone else seeking cheap shelter in a tight rental market. The elimination of Skid Row also destroyed a way of life; as Herbert Gans and others noted in *The Urban Villagers*, bulldozers frequently destroyed, not just buildings, but communities. This was true not only in the so-called slums of Boston but also on the West Madison Street in Chicago, where men came to live because they needed the cheap housing and the benefits of an urban downtown environment that included cheap services and proximity to employment.

Instead of framing the homeless of Skid Row using theories of social ecology, disease, subculture, or deviance, we have focused our attention on the relative social autonomy of SRO residents before and during the Skid Row era. We believe that the popular stereotype of Skid Row as the exclusive hangout for socially isolated bums and derelicts reflects a mistaken attachment to a half-truth. The Skid Rows of the 1950s and 1960s did have an extremely high proportion of the dependent poor, as the social problem analysts demonstrated, but we believe this was a temporary condition based on postwar prosperity and an expanding welfare state. Even though the number of dependent poor was high, Skid Row residents were still mainly members of the working (versus dependent) poor, actively creating their own social world despite the considerable obstacles of public rebuke and economic exploitation. These residents still participated in what remained of the diverse assortment of distinctly urban social institutions and conventions that had been organized in an earlier era when the main stems served as residential service centers for a huge migrant work force. Although they possessed little economic, political, and social power, the Skid Row inhabitants were not powerless. We agree with the social order analysts who argued that the residents of Skid Row shared a social world with its own bonds of reciprocity in which the homeless found the social strength necessary to carry on an autonomous life—despite the daily imposition of uncertainty by those who would use or exploit them. However, putting the findings of the analysts in historical perspective reveals that the community of Skid Row was a weaker and more fragmented version of the earlier and more robust social community of the Main Stem. Unlike working-class neighborhoods with married couples and families, many of whose members were able to organize and actively resist the imposition of renewal, Skid Row communities, with an occasional exception,[36] usually lacked the social strength necessary for collective resistance.

7 The SRO Hotel Way of Life

In conducting our historical review of the urban settlements for the single poor in Chicago and cities elsewhere, we emphasized three themes. First, that the residents of the Main Stem and Skid Row pursued independence with determination and vigor, an independence facilitated by the design and provision of SRO hotels. Second, that the pursuit of individual autonomy among those single men at the bottom of the urban labor market was made possible by their use of networks of community social ties binding the dependent and independent members of Skid Row together. Third, that these residential communities declined precipitously in the 1960s, not only because the prosperity of the 1950s and 1960s reduced the number of the single working poor who would live there, but also because urban renewal programs leveled most of the SRO hotels. The residents contributed relatively little to the demise of Skid Row. Using these themes to revise the story of the rise of the Main Stem and the fall of Skid Row provides an important correction to the misleading accounts of Skid Row that gained popularity in the 1950s and 1960s. The accounts, which stressed personal failure, continue to shape public perceptions of the urban homeless today.

We realized, however, that historical revision alone might not prove persuasive to skeptics, who might accuse us of romanticizing the Skid Row community, or argue that although our account may have been true for SRO hotels in the past, the remaining hotels no longer offer the useful physical and social resources they once did. In order to test our beliefs, therefore, we devised a survey that would have the same scope of Bogue's earlier study but would include a sample of residents from all the SRO hotels in the city of Chicago rather than just the few hotels remaining in the original Skid Row area.

Our research is not without important precedents. As we mentioned in chapter 6, social order analysts classified SRO hotel residents using concepts of social community rather than social disaffiliation. Initially, the social order analysts avoided the political implications of their research, but the enormous social costs urban renewal imposed on residents of working-class neighborhoods eventually inspired other research analysts, schooled in the same tradition, to put the community interpretation to political use.

For instance, studies by Marc Fried, Chester Hartman, Jim Ward, and others exposed the way labeling the residents of inner-city neighborhoods as "Skid Row bums" served the political purposes of local developers and officials looking for reasons to displace the low-income residents quickly and cheaply.[1] Forcibly removing working-class citizens from the local community to which they belong, they argued, was a terribly destructive action requiring a great deal more compensation, care, and respect than redevelopment authorities had provided. Documenting the social costs of community destruction and the unfair burdens of forced relocation, these critics helped liberal lobbyists convince legislators to shift the focus of urban renewal from slum clearance to rehabilitation, and to increase relocation benefits to those people and businesses evicted as a direct result of federally funded development projects.[2]

It is in the context of this research that individual SRO hotels became the object of studies conducted by social analysts critical of both the Skid Row stereotype and large-scale redevelopment clearance schemes. For instance, in 1975 analysts at the Western Behavioral Sciences Institute studied a sample of residents from twelve hotels in downtown San Diego, California. Their purpose was to explore whether the nonwelfare poor living in hotels managed to avoid dependency. They found little in the way of social pathology and a great deal of social support among elderly residents.[3] Other studies of SRO hotels came to similar conclusions about the usefulness and value of the SRO hotels as inexpensive living environments contributing to the autonomy of residents.[4] New evidence on the social usefulness of hotels, however, did not inspire widespread revisions of the stereotype developed from the earlier Skid Row studies. Other than the San Diego case, most studies of SRO hotels used ethnographic in-depth analysis of individual hotels, which provided convincing detail about a single hotel but prevented the construction of unbiased inferences to all the hotels in a particular city.[5] Hence, proponents of the Skid Row stereotype could dismiss the findings as valid, but exceptional. Furthermore, some in-depth studies of SRO hotels did not find benign systems of social supports, but instead found environments characterized by social isolation.[6]

We designed our research study in order to test whether the sorts of social communities analysts found for individual hotels would exist for a sample of residents representing all the SRO hotel residents in a single city, Chicago. (See appendix A for details on the way we conducted the census and drew the sample.) We first conducted a census of all the SRO hotels in the city and then randomly selected both hotels and rooms to ensure an unbiased as well as representative sample of residents whom we intended to interview. We stratified the sample by three geographic areas: North Side, Central (Skid Row and peripheral areas), and South Side. In all, we managed to collect 185 interviews with residents from eighteen hotels during the late spring and summer of 1985. Since we undersampled from the North Side and oversampled from the South Side hotels, we weighted the sample to correct for this bias.

The analysis of our survey findings provides a systematic assessment of the empirical foundations for the popular Skid Row stereotype. Our findings contradict the five most common generalizations about "Skid Row bums": that they are deviant, transient, lazy, dependent, and isolated. For example, we found that although the demographic characteristics of SRO residents do differ from the general population, these differences do not make them deviants. The frequent moves of SRO residents can also more accurately be ascribed to displacement than transience. SRO residents are mostly poor, not because they avoid work, but because they earn low wages, cannot find work, or receive inadequate retirement or disability benefits. The social vulnerabilities of SRO residents do not predict their dependence. Despite considerable economic hardship and personal illness among the SRO population as a whole, these difficulties do not accumulate among such vulnerable social groups as blacks, women, and the elderly. Finally, the SRO residents maintain their autonomy not by isolating themselves, but by contributing responsibly to the well-being of others through ongoing reciprocal relationships. We conclude that the stereotype falsely attributes socially deviant or otherwise pathological meanings to the social characteristics and relationships of SRO hotel residents, and thereby hides the distinctive and valuable social benefits of the SRO way of life.

SRO Tenants: Different but Not Deviant

The SRO residents differ significantly from the general city population in age, sex, race, and other demographic characteristics. However, these differences are much smaller than those that marked the social distance between the Skid Row residents and other city residents in the 1950s. The residents of SRO hotels come mainly from the ranks of the working poor and so reflect the social characteristics of this population. Hence, comparisons with the general population offer exaggerated estimates of the size of these differences.

The SRO residents who perhaps come closest to maintaining the way of life associated with the real Skid Row (not the stereotype) are the SRO veterans. These were SRO residents who reported living in another SRO hotel before moving to their present address, hence the title of "veterans." SRO veterans were older and more likely to be white and to have never married than the first-timers. In these respects they more closely resemble the Skid Row population studied by Bogue. The SRO veterans lived mainly in the hotels near downtown (41 percent) and the North Side (56 percent). Barely 3 percent of the black South Side residents had a history of living in SROs.

The SRO hotel population remains overwhelmingly male, and because the residents rent single rooms, the majority live alone. The most surprising finding was that almost one in five shares his tiny living quarters with someone else. The above characteristics more than any others separate this population from the general city population. Alcoholism, the problem that figured so prominently in the Skid Row study by Bogue, appears to be much less pervasive among the SRO residents of the 1980s. Only 14 percent of the SRO residents drank alcohol as frequently as once a day or more, and 37 percent did not drink at all.

Almost 15 percent of the residents suffered from such life-threatening conditions as heart disease, emphysema, cirrhosis of the liver, tuberculosis, cancer, and paralysis due to a stroke. Another 22 percent lived with less serious but still chronically disruptive illnesses like diabetes, high blood pressure, cataracts, arthritis, asthma, or muscular dystrophy. Fewer than 5 percent of the SRO residents reported suffering from mental illness. Overall, 38 percent of the SRO residents endured some form of serious illness at the time of our interview. An additional 3 percent reported chronic minor ailments. The SRO residents reported twice the proportion of serious illness as the adult population nationwide.[7]

The differences between SRO residents and Chicago residents in terms of race, marital status, schooling, and age are much smaller than they were thirty years ago. In part the change reflects the fact that the first-timers in the SRO closely resemble the typical single poor adults of all Chicago while the overall socioeconomic characteristics of the city's residents have fallen in comparison with those of the people in the surrounding suburbs (see table 7-1). The SRO residents' choice of a single room accommodation necessarily places them in a distinct category of single-person households, a category that ironically is becoming increasingly popular among young single professionals pursuing the advantages of urban living by renting small studio apartments near downtown. In certain neighborhoods the influx of professionals has been so great as to pit the SRO residents against the wealthier newcomers in a bidding competition for scarce residential space, including the SRO hotels. The wealthier bidders always win. The SRO residents end up being displaced.

When Push Comes to Shove: Transiency Reconsidered

We found that, contrary to the stereotype of rootless wanderers or transient alcoholics, about one-half of the SRO residents had lived in their present unit for two years or more, and 29 percent had lived there four years or more. The burden of moving, however, was not evenly distributed. Sixty-five percent of the women had lived in their current residence less than two years, compared with only 44 percent of the men. Comparing the young with the overall population, we found that 80 percent of the residents below thirty-five years of age had lived in their current unit less than two

TABLE 7-1

Demographic Profiles of General Population and
SRO Residents in Chicago, 1980

| | | SRO RESIDENTS (%) | | |
CHARACTERISTIC	CITY RESIDENTS (%)	All	Veterans	First-Timers
Live alone	11	81	83	80
Male	48	78	82	75
Black	36	48	32	60*
Never married	35	44	51	39*
< High school diploma	72	79	81	78
55 years & up	30	33	45	25*

Source: U.S. Department of Commerce, Bureau of the Census, 1980 Census
data.

*Chi-square test: probability <.05 that difference between veterans and first-
timers is not random.

years, but that only 48 percent of all residents had changed residences that
recently.

SRO residents do tend to move more frequently than the general population. For instance, among all U.S. households, only 35 percent of the
homeowners and 60 percent of the renters move every five years, as compared with 75 percent of all SRO residents.[8] However, when compared
with other unrelated individuals in midwestern metropolitan areas, the SRO
residents do not differ much in their transience. Overall, 29 percent of unrelated individuals had moved between March 1982 and March 1983 (34.5
percent of those below the poverty line), whereas 37.8 percent of the SRO
residents had moved during the year preceding the interview (summer 1984
to summer 1985). A greater proportion of the SRO residents than unrelated
individuals in the Midwest move, but this difference reflects the peculiar
pressures of hotel life as much as it does the characteristics of the tenants.
SRO residents face far greater displacement pressures than do those individuals renting apartments or houses. When we analyzed each respondent's
housing history, we discovered that moving depended less on initiative and
desire than on pressures of physical, social, and economic circumstance
(see table 7-2).

When we asked respondents why they left their prior residence, 80 percent referred to conditions that pushed them out of their homes. One in five
(23 percent) were evicted mainly because of closure or conversion of the

TABLE 7-2

SRO Residents' Primary Reasons for
Leaving Prior Residence

REASON	%
PUSH	
Building lost, eviction	23.0
Poor physical environment	6.4
Increasing social pressure	31.1
Increasing economic pressure	9.9
Other pressures	10.4
Total	80.8
PULL	
Social independence	11.6
Attractive economic conditions	5.7
Other attractions	1.9
Total	19.2

building. In one instance, a man was forced out because "they condemned the building and turned off the heat." About one in three (31 percent) left for reasons of social pressure, usually either to avoid the dangers of on-going social disputes with household members, local gangs, or landlords, or to accommodate changes in household organization. For instance, one respondent left her residence because her husband died, and an elderly black man complained that he moved because the bigoted landlord would not allow black people to visit.

Overcrowding, divorce, and other social pressures were also mentioned frequently, as in the case of the twenty-nine-year-old black man who moved out because "my sister's new apartment lease only allowed a certain amount of people to live there," or of the man on leave from work who told us that, after separating from his wife, "I wasn't getting an income and I couldn't afford the rent." An elderly black woman complained that she was forced to move away from her daughter because, as she put it, "My daughter was on AFDC and I was on General Assistance, and the Public Aid office told me I had to move because too much money was coming into one place."

Problems with the physical conditions of the prior residence or the pressures of decreasing income and increasing rent together accounted for only about 20 percent of the reasons respondents offered for moving. Rising rent was the most frequently mentioned economic pressure, followed closely by job loss. Environmental complaints included lack of repairs, the presence of vermin, and noise. One woman summed up her reasons for moving: "the management didn't service the building—no cleaning, spraying, painting or repairs were done."

Only one in five of the reasons respondents gave to explain their most recent move reflected a desire to change residence or express a preference. Those few who left without external pressure did so to pursue more advantageous employment (5.7 percent) or to obtain greater autonomy by living on their own (11.6 percent). Comments such as "I just need a place of my own" were frequently made. Although we interpreted these as voluntary choices, the desire for privacy was usually expressed by someone who felt confined living in a household with others. Someone seeking privacy and autonomy is obviously leaving a dwelling where these conditions are lacking and so is responding to the social pressures of shared living arrangements. The remaining 9 percent simply replied that they had left from another city to come to Chicago without specifying what attracted them.

When we call someone a "transient" we usually mean a person whose frequent moves reflect a chosen life-style of constant migration. These residents do not choose to move but move because they are forced to do so. In other words, SRO residents in Chicago face powerful displacement pressures at a level far greater than does the general population, so their frequent moves should not be mistaken for transience.

At the time of our census in 1984, SRO hotels provided about 11,800 units of affordable housing. We knew the spaces were small, but we also measured other characteristics of the room to assess the quality of the space. We utilized a measure of overall room quality with a high score of 11 and a low score of 0. Each room received 3 points for a bath, 2 points for a closet, and 1 point each for the following: sink, heater, window, stove, phone, and television set. We discovered that the hotel rooms with the lowest scores clustered in two cubicle hotels. Rooms in these hotels had an average score of 0.85, whereas the private rooms in the other SRO hotels averaged 9.60. The cubicle hotels in our sample accounted for only 5 percent of the units and 3 percent of the hotels in the city. In contrast, cubicle hotels accounted for almost 85 percent of the 11,943 hotel units and 32 percent of the hotels on Skid Row in 1958.[9]

Most SRO residents actively choose their housing, selecting an SRO not simply as a haven of last resort, but as an urban home. The socially and economically diverse clientele of SROs report a correspondingly complex assortment of reasons to explain why they chose their present residence (see table 7-3). We had expected to find that most tenants would, like the cubicle tenants, claim low rent as the primary reason they chose an SRO residence. Though a plurality did offer economic reasons for their choice (39 percent), only about half of these reported low rents (23 percent). Most of these were the tenants in cubicle hotels. Typical of the reasons offered by these residents was the explanation offered by one elderly man who declared,

TABLE 7-3

SRO Residents' Reasons for
Choosing Present Residence

REASON	%
Economic	
Low rent	23.0
Quality	19.7
Total	42.7
Social	
Live near friends	7.6
Live near relatives	4.2
Referred by friend	11.6
Rented before	6.9
Total	30.3
Other	
Convenient location	14.5
Agency referral	3.7
Ad referral	3.9
No reason given	4.9
Total	27.0

"I can't afford to pay a lot of rent or utility bills." Interestingly, a few of the more prosperous and discriminating residents (4 percent) contend that their present SRO provided better quality shelter than competing hotels; for example, one man stated, "This is better than other hotels. It's cleaner, kept up better, and quieter."

A substantial portion referred to social relationships as the primary reason for choosing their present living arrangements in an SRO. Some wanted to live near friends (7.6 percent) or relatives (4.2 percent), as in the case of a son who moved to his present address because, as he put it, "My father lives across the street and it's convenient to cross and take care of him." Many based their choice on the referral of a trusted friend (11.6 percent). A few mentioned that they had rented in the SRO before or knew the owner (6.9 percent).

The most unexpected finding popped up in the "Other" category. Slightly more than 15 percent chose their hotel accommodation because of its convenient location. Convenience meant various things to people. For instance, one woman specified: "It has a convenient location because church is close by and anything you would need for living you can find in this area."

Another woman defined convenient as "being close to where I work and close to good transportation." Access to employment and services (especially good public transportation) at affordable prices makes SRO living an attractive residential option for low-income renters. This was akin to the situation at the turn of the century when most SRO hotels were built to accommodate low-income workers and transients. Although the present residents are not hoboes, tramps, or bums of years gone by, they nevertheless rely on the accessibility of the hotels to city services and activities just as their predecessors did.

Others admitted that, despite searching, they chose their present SRO hotel because it was the only one with vacancies at the time. One woman lamented, "I had gone to five different places and they were all filled and this was the first one which had a room, so I took it." Fewer than 8 percent gave no reason for their choice.

Finally, only about 4 percent found their present accommodation by referral from a social service agency. At the present time the use of SRO hotels in Chicago as residential placements for social service institutions is not as widespread as in the past or in other cities. This contrasts with common practice in New York or Los Angeles, where SRO hotels are routinely used to house welfare recipients through use of rent vouchers. The hotels included in our sample got their residents from the rental market, not the state.[10]

Poor but Not Lazy

According to the Skid Row stereotype, SRO hotel residents will likely prefer irregular or even criminal employment to a steady job. They will act like bums, seeking free handouts and welfare in order to escape the burdens of work. But do SRO residents actually exhibit an aversion to work and a desire to live off the system? Our evidence disputes this image. The interviews made it clear that residents not only acknowledge the value of work but that economic necessity provides a powerful incentive for them to stay in the labor market as long as possible.

The SRO inhabitants work or pursue work if they can. At the time of our interviews 42 percent had permanent jobs, 23 percent were searching for work, and only 35 percent remained outside the labor market. Furthermore, among those who were neither employed nor searching for work, 24 percent claimed retirement, 55.5 percent permanent disability, and 9.5 percent other conditions as reasons why they did not seek work. Only 11 percent received public aid payments. That leaves a small fraction of people who might fit the stereotype of the shiftless bum, though even in this category most cases could not be described as "shiftless." This group included two single women with children not on aid, a housewife, a student, and a part-time day laborer. Only one person claimed that he wanted to work but just was not able to find it and had given up.

TABLE 7-4

Estimated Annual Incomes of SRO Residents,
by Income Interval and Primary Source

INTERVAL	WAGES		PREVIOUS EARNINGS		UNEARNED AID	
	Mean	N	Mean	N	Mean	N
$3,600	$3,044	4.0	$3,094	12.0	$2,738	30.0
$3,600–$5,199	4,347	8.0	4,370	33.0	4,293	12.0
$5,200–$8,399	6,687	28.0	6,034	15.0	6,062	4.5
$8,400+	15,007	38.5	13,300	4.5	12,819*	7.0
All	$10,275	78.5	$5,078	64.5	$4,759	53.5

Note: Missing observations = 6.

*The high values for this cell are due to the fact that we included the income of a roommate as part of the residents' household income. These were usually spouses. The number values reflect the weights assigned to compensate for sample bias. See appendix A.

The key to independence and autonomy is a secure source of income. The SRO residents who enjoyed full-time employment, as well as those who received Social Security, Supplemental Security Income (SSI) benefits, or pension funds, could rely on the predictability of their checks, even if the amounts were modest. Those who worked part time at low-wage jobs or were unemployed and on public aid faced a more precarious economic condition. These were the dependent poor, most of whom struggled to obtain access to employment and a few of whom sought a more dependable and substantial public source of aid (such as SSI) other than General Assistance (GA) grants.

About 60 percent of the SRO residents enjoy modest economic security that makes independent life in the SRO hotel a viable living arrangement. The remaining 40 percent, however, include those who must routinely face serious economic and hence shelter uncertainty. We calculated the predominant income source for each resident based on the proportion of income from each of three sources: earnings from wages, previous earnings (mainly disability, Social Security, or pension payments), and unearned aid (usually General Assistance). Wage income offered the most secure source of income and hence the greatest freedom from want, whereas reliance on unearned income left recipients at the mercy of their scrutinizing benefactors. Table 7-4 illustrates the magnitude of the differences in income for each source. The employed residents averaged an annual income of $10,275,

TABLE 7-5

Occupational Profiles of SRO and Chicago Residents

	SRO RESIDENTS, LAST PRIOR JOB (1985)	CHICAGO (1980)
Professional/management	6.3%	22.6%
Clerical/sales	9.6	30.1
Crafts/skilled	6.2	10.2
Operative	16.9	16.8
Service	51.7	14.4
Labor	9.4	5.9
Total (*N*)	(182)	(1,235,865)

Source: Census Report on Population (STF-3A), City of Chicago, 1980.

whereas those dependent on unearned entitlements subsisted on an estimated annual income of less than $5,000! (The official poverty line for a
single-person household in 1985 was $5,250.) The residents who rely on
earnings-related entitlement income such as Social Security tended to fall
between the other two groups, although they were much closer to the aid
recipients than to the wage earners. Three out of five SRO residents support
themselves solely on earnings-related income. Almost one in four (24 percent) who are looking for work use General Assistance and food stamps to
make ends meet while they search. Most of the remaining residents receive
disability payments.

The occupational profile of the SRO residents reveals their roots in the
working class (see table 7-5). Only a tiny portion of the residents had
worked as professionals or managers, compared with more than one in five
of the city work force. The residents labored mainly in service occupations
(52 percent) or as operatives (17 percent) and laborers (9 percent). This
again squared with historical analysis, which indicated that most SRO tenants provided low-wage service labor to the city's office and commercial
districts.

Low-status jobs usually meant low-paying and insecure jobs as well.
Less than half of the SRO residents employed at the time of our interview
received medical insurance coverage (42 percent), life insurance (36 percent), workers' compensation (50 percent), or unemployment benefits (51
percent) as part of their employment compensation. In addition, 50 percent
worked on an hourly or daily wage rate, and 26 percent worked part time.
Although the employed residents had on average held their present job for
four and a half years, 43 percent had done so for only one year or less.

Part-time employees earned on the average about $634 per month, compared with $910 for all employed residents and $1,134 for full-time job-holders with benefits. In effect, full-time employees with benefits earned almost twice the monthly income of part-time employees without benefits. But only a tiny portion of the SRO residents enjoyed such jobs. The majority made just about enough to make ends meet, and a substantial minority (40 percent) earned less than the official poverty threshold.

The most substantial source of formal aid for SRO residents comes from the federal and state governments in the form of transfer payments. Thirty-five percent were receiving public assistance from such programs as General Assistance (GA), Supplemental Security Income (SSI), food stamps, Medicaid, and Aid for Dependent Children (AFDC). These residents had managed to reach the safety net of the welfare state. However, their position was precarious, as most were receiving GA benefits that in 1987 provided a maximum of $154 per month. Overall, the 35 percent who got aid received only 17 percent of the total income received by all SRO residents. The relatively small amount of aid, given the high cost of living, made sustained provision of rental housing even in the SRO hotels extremely difficult.

Conditions of economic dependence are far more common among the homeless. A 1985 survey of street and shelter homeless in Chicago conducted by the National Opinion Research Center (NORC) found that 22 percent had received GA, 6 percent AFDC, 6 percent SSI, and 2 percent disability payments, or less than 36 percent overall after controlling for overlap. Although one in three was receiving aid, these recipients were still unable to secure rental shelter in the housing market. Furthermore, the NORC analysts compared actual use to eligibility for GA and AFDC and discovered that almost two out of three of the homeless who were eligible for GA benefits were not getting them.[11] Not only are people on the streets and in shelters falling through the mesh in the public aid safety net for the poor, but even when they manage to grab hold, the benefits are still too little to cover the lowest market rent.

Vulnerable but Not Dependent

Instead of treating the vulnerabilities of SRO residents as direct and unmediated indicators of dependence, we analyzed the relationship between economic status and individual hardship. We expected the distribution of hardship to follow the contours of economic status. Thus, we first analyzed the incidence of economic hardship among SRO residents and then traced its distribution according to the social vulnerabilities associated with being a woman, black, or old. The burdens of different economic hardships among the SRO residents, we argue, do not pile up disproportionately upon the vulnerable, but upon those with the lowest income.

At the time of our interview almost one out of three residents (32 percent) carried a rent burden of greater than 50 percent; 15 percent had been displaced from their prior residence because of economic pressures sometime during the most recent six months, and almost one in ten (9.5 percent) had slept outside or in an emergency shelter at least once in the previous six months. The incidence of hunger was quite high among SRO residents. We asked residents whether there had been any time in the past six months when they had been unable to buy food for themselves; 31 percent answered yes. More than half (51 percent) of those dependent on unearned income from others had found themselves in such a plight.

To measure the cumulative economic hardship among the SRO residents, we assigned the presence of each economic hardship a value of 1, summing these to produce an economic hardship score for each resident. The maximum score was 3. The unfortunate resident who received this score had, during the six months preceding the interview, been displaced from his residence for economic reasons, been forced to sleep outside, and gone without food at least once. Furthermore, the same resident at the time of the interview was paying more than 50 percent of his income in rent.

Economic hardships were evenly distributed by race and age. However, women were more likely to suffer economic hardships than were men. In particular, women carried heavier rent burdens and were subjected to displacement for economic reasons twice as often. However, women endured these economic shelter-related hardships, not out of discrimination, but choice. Women were unwilling to rent poorer quality (and usually less expensive) rooms than were men with equivalent incomes. Furthermore, women residents were far more likely (57 percent) to be sharing their room with a spouse, friend, or close relation than were men (8 percent). An additional roommate translates into a higher rent. If one of the roommates makes little income, this means the higher rent will likely impose a greater rent burden on others in the household. Thus, women endured a greater share of the housing difficulties for economic reasons, not because they were women.

The distribution of economic hardship, predictably, was closely related to source of income. However, women, blacks, and the elderly—frequently discriminated against in the distribution of economic resources—did not endure significantly more economic hardship than did others who were younger, male, or white. Although their resources are meager and the presence of some hardship likely, most SRO residents do not suffer from the cumulative maldistribution of economic hardship because of their social vulnerabilities. The social diversity of the SRO environment helps vulnerable residents avoid the dependence that befalls those who must live in institutional settings that concentrate people with the same vulnerabilities (e.g., nursing homes or high-rise public housing projects).

A better-quality lodging house on the Main Stem, circa 1900.
Note the variety of service establishments in the immediate vicinity.
Chicago Historical Society, ICHI 16930.

A Main Stem lodging house on West Madison Street, including the ever-present
saloon, circa 1910. Chicago Historical Society, by Chas. E. Barker, ICHI 20655.

The McCoy Hotel on Skid Row, 1954. A number of
stores are part of the building. Chicago Historical Society,
by Lil and Al Bloom, ICHI 20658.

Skid Row in 1964. Several lodging houses, including the large Workingmen's
Palace, a cage hotel, are shown. Chicago Historical Society, by Sigmund J. Osty,
ICHI 20656.

The Starr Hotel in the late 1950s, a Skid Row SRO that was destroyed to clear land for Presidential Towers. Chicago Historical Society, by Lil and Al Bloom, ICHI 20654.

West Madison Street looking east in 1963, when Skid Row was still in existence. Several hotels and many stores are visible. The Major Hotel, on the left, is the last remaining SRO on Madison Street, and is slated for demolition when the second construction phase of Presidential Towers begins. This photo contrasts with that of West Madison Street today, on facing page. Chicago Historical Society, by Sigmund J. Osty, ICHI 20657.

West Madison Street today, looking east, with one of the Presidential Towers on the right. Note the contrast to the earlier buildings in photo on facing page. This photo and all following by Robert A. Slayton.

The Mark Twain Hotel, a large endangered SRO in the rapidly gentrifying Near North section.

The Chateau du Roi, a typical South Side hotel in the all-black neighborhood near 47th Street and Martin Luther King Drive, as mentioned in Chapter 3.

The Carling Hotel, an SRO in the Near North section. It survives despite its location near some of the most valuable residential high-rise developments in Chicago.

The former Moreland Hotel, recently taken over by a not-for-profit group that is rehabbing the building while maintaining it as an SRO for low-income tenants. It was renamed the Harold Washington Apartments in memory of the late mayor.

The St. James Hotel, postponing South Loop development pressure by charging rents in excess of $250 a month.

The Wilson Hotel in the Uptown area, one of the last cage hotels left in Chicago.

The Aragon Arms Hotel, one of the better SROs on the North Side today.

A modern Salvation Army shelter on Chicago's North Side, showing the starkness and barrenness of this housing in contrast to the SRO hotels.

Shelter run by the Chicago Christian Industrial League. Like the Salvation Army shelter, this is bleak housing compared to the SROs.

The Norman Hotel, one of the better and larger hotels in the Uptown area. It has been refurbished by a syndicate of private investors put together by a not-for-profit community organization.

The attractive Carter Hotel, surrounded by parking lots and vacant land, a vulnerable target for rehabilitation in the gentrifying South Loop.

Presidential Towers, the major development that transformed West Madison Street, described at length in Chapter 9.

Independence, Not Isolation, as a Way of Life

Perhaps the most serious misconception of the SRO residents places them among the ranks of the disaffiliated. Our research disclosed that most SRO residents possess a variety of social attachments to kin, friends, and neighborhood life. Though the existence of such attachments has been documented in studies like those of Bogue and Bahr, analysts have missed the significance of their own findings in their search for disaffiliation. We take a different tack, arguing that SRO residents belong to communities that not only nurture social identity but help them cope with economic hardship.

We asked residents in our survey to give the names of all the relatives and friends they felt closest to and to indicate which of these they had contacted at least once in the past year. The two lists, with few exceptions, were the same. Residents seldom mentioned close relatives or friends whom they had not contacted during the previous year. Almost as many respondents mentioned relatives (133) as did friends (127). Combined, the personal social networks included 666 close relationships distributed among 85 percent of the respondents. Overall, the average number of ties with both relatives and friends was about four per resident. The size and composition of the social networks varied with the social characteristics of the residents. Women and blacks had much larger networks of close personal relationships (5.02 and 5.21, respectively) than did the elderly (3.58). Relatives predominated in the networks of women and blacks. Only 15 percent of the SRO residents reported having no close personal relationships (see table 7-6).

Although the number of personal social relationships per SRO resident may seem small when compared with the social networks of middle-class households, the figure is close to the average number of social ties (4.93) among working-class respondents also interviewed in a study of three Chicago residential neighborhoods in 1985. The fact that a variety of working-class households had social networks only slightly larger than those among SRO residents suggests that the small networks among SRO residents reflects their class position rather than some sort of disaffiliation.[12]

Besides their personal networks, we also identified the less intimate social ties residents used with others in the SRO hotel and surrounding neighborhood. We constructed an SRO social network index to provide a composite summary of the number of social ties linking each resident to others inhabiting the SRO world. The classification scheme is outlined in appendix C and includes the description of each type of social tie.

About 84 percent of the residents had some SRO network ties. However, more than half of the 375 ties (57 percent) included ongoing contact with hotel staff. These staff ties predominate among those residents having no close personal network but some SRO relations. Eighty percent of the social contacts within these SRO networks were with SRO staff. Clearly,

TABLE 7-6

The Social Affiliations of SRO Residents

TYPE OF SOCIAL TIE	N	%
Both personal and SRO ties	139	75.1
Personal ties only	17	9.2
SRO ties only	27	14.6
Neither SRO nor personal ties	2	1.1
Total	185	

the hotels provided an important social milieu for the SRO residents who had few personal or no close ties. These residents come closest to fitting the social conceptions of the Skid Row isolate featured in earlier studies of Skid Row. However, we are much less willing to call them disaffiliated than were earlier researchers.

Although almost 15 percent of the SRO residents appear to be attached exclusively to the local social world of their SRO (see table 7-6), possessing only a few local social ties does not mean they are isolated and dependent. Many have chosen to live alone and enjoy the autonomy and anonymity of hotel life. Compared with the hardships of illness and poverty, the lack of close social relationships may be a relatively minor problem. In some cases these close relations contribute to the economic and social marginality of SRO residents who use the hotel as a haven from troublesome and even dangerous relations with kin or gangs.

SRO residents proved to be resourceful and capable individuals despite their modest means and considerable hardship. We believe their autonomy was possible in large part because most possessed informal helping networks among relatives and friends, as well as knowledge of formal service providers. The close personal relationships residents enjoy with friends and relatives provide an important social resource. More than three out of four residents with close personal ties claimed that some sort of helping occurred among friends and relatives. On the average, three out of five personal relationships involved some sort of help during the past year.

Despite the frequency of such helping relationships, the SRO residents gave little indication that they were dependent partners. If SRO residents perceived themselves as passive victims or self-centered sociopaths, we expected them to report receiving help much more than they gave or shared it. However, such was not the case. They were primary recipients in only 24 percent of the relations, and major contributors in the remaining 16 percent. Respondents reported giving and getting help equally with other members of their network in 60 percent of the helping relationships. Their preference for reciprocity reflects not only a basic attachment to the cultural value of autonomy but more important, the protection and enhancement of this independence through the social bonds of mutual aid. The autonomy of SRO residents, like those in other social communities, rests on a foundation of security obtained through social interdependence, not social isolation.[13]

The relationships between different helping interactions (e.g., reciprocity) and type of social tie (e.g., kin) among SRO residents resembled the patterns found among residents of diverse working-class households in Chicago. Interviewed at about the same time as part of a different study, these residents lived in apartments or single-family dwellings clustered in three ethnically distinct neighborhoods. For instance, for both samples the proportion of helping network ties with kin was almost identical: 53 percent among SRO residents and 55 percent for neighborhood residents.[14] The residents of SRO hotels possess helping relationships like those of re-spondents from other working-class households. The modest differences indicate the inaccuracy of pinning the label of disaffiliation on SRO residents. Furthermore, these helping networks reflect the presence of a social community whose members utilize complex moral judgments to justify each helping relationship.

Thus, when we asked residents with helping relationships why the particular form of helping interaction had turned out that way, we further discovered a complex set of moral bonds. Most SRO residents, it seems, did not follow a particular moral scheme, applying, for instance, the Golden Rule to all their relationships. Instead, residents based their moral assessments on the kind of relationship that tied them implicitly or explicitly to each person. The moral quality of the helping interaction depended on the type of social relation they shared with each member of their network.

The norms guiding the provision of informal help tended to reflect the social differences between kinship and friendship ties.[15] Most ties with close kin involve duties based implicitly in the social requirements of the particular kinship bond (e.g., "She's my mother, that's why I give more to her") or based on additional considerations of relative strength (e.g., "My brother is older and looks out for me") and need (e.g., "My mother is blind, so I give more to her"). These can be distinguished from the voluntary obligations that characterize the reciprocity of friendships based either on comradeship (e.g., "We found something common. We're friends"), intimacy (e.g., "We love, care, respect, and appreciate each other"), or fair exchange (e.g., "We just take each other places if needed").

The relationship between helping interaction and type of moral reason is analyzed in table 7-7, which sorts the reasons for each helping relationship into two groups: those based on voluntary obligation and those based on the stronger sense of duty. When residents get help from others, they mostly claim that others owe it to them not only out of a sense of prescribed duty (41 percent) but because of the altruistic strength (usually economic) of

TABLE 7-7

SRO Residents' Moral Rationales for Helpful Interaction

	INTERACTION			
REASONS	Gets help (%)	Gives help (%)	Shares help (%)	All (%)
Duty	42	31	29	32
Obligation				
Altruism	27	19	—	10
Need	14	38	4	12
Empathy	15	12	61	42
Fairness	2	1	6	4

the giver (27 percent) as well. Few residents contended that they got help because of their need (14 percent); slightly more residents (15 percent) admitted that they got more help in a relationship because the other valued them as a lover, intimate, or comrade. In contrast, residents reported that they gave help mostly because they felt obliged by the other's need (38 percent), their own relative strength (19 percent), or prescribed duty (31 percent) based on the bonds of kinship. The pattern in these reports by respondents points (whether accurately or inaccurately, we do not know) to a strong desire for autonomy in the context of unbalanced helping relations. Residents who were recipients of help in a relationship claimed that the moral bonds of duty or the voluntary obligation of altruism on the part of prosperous and capable kin entitled them to aid. They seldom mentioned their own need and the dependency associated with it, even though low income and frequent hardship makes such reasons likely. However, when the situation was reversed and residents acted as the primary giver, they claimed that they gave help mainly in response to need and out of their own relative strengths rather than in response to the duties of kinship or the bonds of comradeship. Residents perceive themselves as actors motivated to give out of a sense of responsibility and to receive out of a feeling of solidarity. Thus, the moral sensibilities residents reported dispute claims of disaffiliation, since these are clearly not the sentiments of sociopaths or anomic derelicts.[16]

Reciprocity in helping was based mainly on the voluntary obligations of comradeship and intimacy (61 percent) or contract (6 percent). Clearly, the very meaning of reciprocity in our culture is so closely tied up with the practice of sharing that the connection fits our common sense. Less

obvious are the reciprocal helping relationships based on involuntary duty
(29 percent). Here, residents usually referred to the implicit expectation
of mutual aid associated with kinship bonds. Thus, although reciprocal
aid may not be based exclusively on voluntary obligations (and rarely on
instrumental exchanges common among the helping networks of the middle
class), it does not seem to be based on shared strengths or needs for SRO
residents.

The distribution of different kinds of informal help within the personal
networks of residents is complex, following paths organized by both the
kind of social relationships and type of helping interaction. Thus the significance of the social tie and the nature of the helping interaction shape not
only how informal help is delivered but what kinds are delivered. Unlike
the formal care-giving system with its requirement that recipients be needy,
with care organized in functionally discrete and coherent categories, informal care is relational and complex. SRO residents do not have to demonstrate their eligibility to friends and kin to deserve aid; they receive this
entitlement (or at least claim they do) as part of the moral bonds that make
up the various social relations they inherit, maintain, and create.

Within their personal social networks SRO tenants play active roles,
usually sharing aid, seldom just getting it. Help is also defined on a complex situational basis rather than in limited, carefully defined categories.
The residents justify and interpret their helping relationships in terms that
display moral schemes sensitive to the needs of others, responsive to reciprocal exchanges based in mutual trust, and wary of the stigma and disgrace
of dependency. Though their reasons for sharing help may differ from those
of middle-class service providers, officials, bureaucrats, and the likes, SRO
tenants offer reasons that justify a coherent and generous reciprocity that
enables them to get and give help without sacrificing their often fragile
independence.[17]

Many SRO residents (about 15 percent) had no close personal relation-
ships, and some of those who did got no help from either close friends or
kin. Overall, 36 percent of the tenants had no personal helping network.
Most of these residents, however, were neither isolated nor dependent.
They received aid from others in the SRO hotel. About 70 percent of the
SRO residents without personal helping relationships got help from others
in the SRO hotel at least once during the year preceding the interview.
Although they did not describe close and ongoing relationships with their
helpers, the residents who relied on others in the SRO for aid got help
mainly from friends and SRO staff, usually in the form of referrals to jobs,
shelter, or medical care. (See appendix C for a detailed description of the
kinds and amounts of help, controlling for the presence of close personal
relationships.)

Putting these referrals to good use requires a minimum threshold of independence, so when residents lose their capacity to act autonomously, they

no longer can take this information and put it to good use. They fall outside the boundaries of help within the SRO world. This seems to be happening to some of the poorest and most physically vulnerable SRO residents (about 11 percent of the SRO residents). Since they have no personal helping network, they have no alternative but to turn to the formal care-giving system for help. Thus, when residents become too economically or physically dependent, the SRO social world cannot substitute for the close ties of family and friends or the resources of formal helping institutions. Instead, the SRO network provides an informal linkage between residents and the formal system of jobs and services. We explored therefore the extent to which residents rely on formal services. The most important question was whether those residents who lack any informal helping ties, either personal or SRO based, receive aid from the formal care-giving system.

We found that the most frequently used formal nonprofit services were local hospitals and clinics. Despite the lack of medical insurance, most residents with serious chronic illnesses (93 percent) had used nonprofit hospitals or clinics to obtain health care. About one in three had sought such aid using referrals from friends and relatives; the others relied on their own knowledge and experience in selecting where they went.

Residents were less successful at using the food distribution network that has expanded rapidly since 1982 with federal funding authorized by the Federal Emergency Management Act (FEMA), supplementing donations from churches and philanthropic foundations. Only 60 percent of the hungry SRO residents knew of a place they could go to obtain free groceries or a free meal. Another 15 percent reported that they got most of their clothes free from church and nonprofit charities in order to avoid the expense of purchasing their own.

Aid for those burdened with excessively high rents or recently displaced from their prior residence was virtually nil. However, two out of three of those who had been forced to sleep out sometime during the first six months of 1985 did receive aid, either sleeping in an emergency shelter or receiving an agency referral to the SRO hotel where they resided at the time of the interview.

We prepared a composite measure of residents' use of formal care, mainly from nonprofit institutions, by assigning one point for the receipt of each of the following kinds of aid in 1985—health care, free food, free clothes, and free shelter—and then summing these points for each resident. We used this composite to assess whether those groups of SRO residents who had little or no access to sources of informal help obtained a disproportionate share of the aid from formal sources of help.

SRO veterans and the elderly, two groups who usually possessed the fewest and smallest helping networks, used formal aid far more frequently than did the other SRO residents. Over half (53 percent) of the elderly had used some type of formal aid, compared with only 42 percent of the younger residents. Two out of three of the SRO veterans versus only one out of three (32 percent) first-timers used formal aid. Blacks, who usually possessed large helping networks, relied on formal services significantly less than did nonblacks (37 percent to 64 percent). Thus, poor blacks, despite long-established programs designed to meet their needs, are still not being effectively reached by these social service programs. The SRO veterans and elderly used formal services to substitute for a lack of informal sources of aid. Conversely, blacks relied on aid from their informal networks instead of using formal services, a practice common among the working poor of Chicago, especially among black households.[18]

SRO veterans do not form relations of mutual aid based on close personal ties as do black residents, especially black women. First, the SRO veterans are far less likely to have ties with kin, the social group at the core of most helping networks. In part this reflects the fact that veterans of the SRO way of life are older than first-timers and so have fewer relatives with whom mutual aid can be expected. The largely male SRO veterans also purposely avoid the sorts of social bonds like marriage that would place involuntary and perhaps restrictive obligations on them. When the veterans did report helping networks, these were composed largely of friends, not the inherited ties of kinship. Second, the SRO veterans know how to use the SRO hotel and other formal institutions in the city to meet their needs without relying on personal networks. The use of formal institutions and the weak ties of the SRO world to obtain occasional help from acquaintances and friends reflects an urban style of social life for this segment of the SRO residents.

Conclusions

The residents of SRO hotels do not fit the stereotype of transient and isolated social deviants avoiding work and social responsibility. The vulnerabilities from which these residents suffer are not social, but economic and physical. Their deviance has more to do with the economic weakness their class position imposes on them. If many of the residents are misfits, it is not by design or choice. What marks these single members of the urban working class as a group is residence in an SRO. But the legacy of Skid Row removal and reform—the stereotype of the Skid Row bum—continues to push these residents to the margins of acceptable, normal city life. To the uninformed outsider, residence in an SRO merits the stigma of moral corruption, the taint of illegitimacy.

This morality-play conception of SRO life does not square with the evidence. The tales of deviance and pathology used by middle-class reformers, officials, reporters, and others to repudiate the SRO way of life are little more than misleading metaphors based on exceptional cases. The residents of the SRO hotels in Chicago choose to live there for much the same reasons that the urban middle-class residents are returning to high-density luxury apartment towers near downtown: convenience and security. Unlike their wealthy neighbors, however, SRO residents can neither afford to pay to live among others who match their social standing nor avoid forming social ties that might bind them to their neighbors. The wealthy urbanites purchase security and the trappings of community; the SRO residents must make it. The hotel residents cannot insulate themselves from the dangers of the city, so they collaborate despite their differences to make their world safe.

8 The SRO Hotel: An Urban Outpost

The spatial design of the SRO hotel with its high-rise density of tiny one-room units earned the scorn of housing reformers, planners, and public officials for decades. However, it was not until the mid-1950s that the Chicago housing code was revised, virtually outlawing the SRO hotels. Thus, when Bogue conducted a comprehensive assessment of the SRO hotels on Chicago's Skid Row in the late 1950s, although the vast majority passed inspection with respect to operational standards, most failed to meet the structural standards of the building code. The SRO hotels lacked adequate plumbing (69 percent), sprinkler systems (86.7 percent), and enclosed stairways (54.4 percent) because these physical features were not included in the original construction of the buildings. In contrast, few hotels failed to meet the standards for such operational conditions as heat (1.3 percent), hot water (1.3 percent), pest control (6.3 percent), unblocked fire exits (7 percent), functioning fire escapes (5.1 percent), and the like. The managers and owners did for the most part meet the basic standards of physical maintenance and fire protection, as long as these did not require major structural improvements.[1]

The deteriorating physical appearance of the SRO hotels when combined with the negative assessments of their physical quality by city inspectors, public officials, and professional reformers contributed to the public perception of the SRO hotel as a nasty and dangerous environment unfit for human habitation. The popularity of the hotels among the single poor was therefore interpreted among officials and reformers as a sign of the economic desperation of the Skid Row residents as well as these residents' deviant tolerance for substandard living conditions. Such interpretations made way for the argument that the SRO hotels actually contributed to deviant and pathological life-styles among their impoverished clientele. Few professionals came to the defense of the hotels when urban renewal programs planned and carried out their destruction.[2]

We analyzed the social value and usefulness of the SRO hotels remaining today from the point of view of the residents rather than relying on the preconceptions of middle-class analysts, planners, and officials. The SRO residents did not consider the hotels to be dangerous or oppressive envi-

155

ronments. They expressed considerable satisfaction with those qualities of hotel living that make luxury high-rise buildings attractive to young single professionals, that is to say, convenience and security.

The SRO hotels attract a relatively diverse clientele, thereby avoiding the stratified homogeneity created by the housing market or by the policies of public housing authorities. The structure and organization of the hotels encourage residents to collaborate in ways that produces a characteristically urban, tolerant residential community. The distribution of security, affordability, and informal aid does not depend on the social status or income of SRO residents, but on their common residence in the SRO hotel.

In contrast to homogeneous public housing projects for low-income residents or congregate housing for special populations, the SRO hotels offer a social organization that combines a generous tolerance for social differences with a strictly enforced set of house rules. The social ties among residents do not reflect a community of shared sentiment, but instead an urban sense of public responsibility. Privacy is respected, but residents need not be socially isolated unless they choose to be.

SRO Hotels as a Place to Live

Most residents were pleased with their living arrangements. Forty-four percent claimed that they were very satisfied, and another 48 percent reported that they were somewhat satisfied. Only 16 percent expressed dissatisfaction. We analyzed the reasons residents offered for their satisfaction and dissatisfaction and discovered some dramatic patterns (see table 8-1).

Tenant complaints concentrated on the physical deficiencies of both a single room (12.1 percent) and the quality of the hotel (7.2 percent). By far the most common complaint was the small size of the room. Among other objections, the most poignant came from residents of cubicle hotels. One fifty-five-year-old male suffering from emphyzema feared that "my children may be ashamed of me if I die in a flop." Another man of about the same age but in better health emphasized that the cages offer little privacy. "It's a flophouse—you can't bring visitors. It's not like having an apartment where you can have people over." Most others facing less unpleasant quarters mentioned specific problems they faced at the time of the interview: a leaky sink, the lack of a kitchen or a telephone, an infestation of vermin, noisy neighbors, or other such problems.

The residents of cubicle hotels have significantly lower incomes on average ($5,027) than do residents in other SRO hotels ($7,511). And although the same proportion are employed, more than three out of five cubicle residents work as unskilled operatives or laborers, compared with only 30 percent of the other SRO residents. These are tenants whose economic status places them only one step above people who were forced to sleep outside or in an emergency shelter in 1985. Socially, however, the cubicle tenants

TABLE 8-1

SRO Residents' Overall Satisfaction with the SRO Hotel

REASON	% SATISFIED	% DISSATISFIED
PHYSICAL		
Room quality	4.4	12.1
Hotel services	10.1	1.5
Maintenance, repair	2.9	7.2
ECONOMIC—RENT LEVEL	16.5	2.7
SOCIAL		
Privacy, independence	9.8	1.7
Other tenants	14.1	1.5
Management	11.3	—
Security	12.1	—
LOCATION		
Convenience	20.2	.7
Neighborhood	4.9	1.0
OTHER		
Miscellaneous	7.4	.7
No response	7.3	7.3

Note: The satisfaction percentages were calculated from a content analysis of open-ended questions. Respondents frequently mentioned several items, which required multiple codings per respondent. Thus, the percentages are based on the total number of respondents for each row. "No response" is the same for both satisfaction and dissatisfaction since this refers to people who offered no opinion.

include people different from those who have ended up on the street. They are mainly older white males with a history of SRO living. The few cubicle hotels that remain continue to serve as a haven for the dependent poor, but not for those who match the characteristics of today's homeless; these are the poor who match the single poor who faced the threat of homelessness in the 1950s on Skid Row. Seventy percent of the cubicle hotel residents were veterans of the SRO way of life and had learned to use these scarce hotels as an alternative to homelessness and a foothold in the bottom rung of the private housing market hierarchy.[3]

In contrast, residents rarely mentioned the physical qualities of the SRO when describing their satisfactions. Most emphasized the convenience of the hotel's location, its affordability, and a variety of social benefits including relationships with other tenants, management, security, and privacy. One out of five tenants liked SRO living because of the location of the hotel. Most comments were like those of a white thirty-five-year-old woman who reported that "everything I need for living is near—church, grocery store, the loop, North Michigan Avenue."

Other comments were similar to those offered by a fifty-year-old unskilled operative who pointed out that his SRO hotel "is close to where I work and near good public transportation." A few emphasized the advantages of the surrounding neighborhood. "Compared to other neighborhoods that I know of, things are cheaper," claimed a Greek male in his early fifties. "I eat out a lot and there are a lot of places to eat in the neighborhood. I have epilepsy and can't cook." Thus, what makes SROs satisfactory is not just affordability and the collective facilities, but location as well. Location is important for the poor as well as the middle class and represents a crucial ingredient in the success of the SRO hotels.

Many of the tenants enjoy SRO living because of social ties to other residents (14.1 percent) and managers (11.3 percent). For instance, some respondents, like one middle-aged black woman, referred to a community in which "everyone seems to look out for each other here, and that makes me feel good." In a few cases the ties with owners and managers were quite strong, as in the case of one thirty-six-year-old female tenant who liked her female building manager because "she's real good to me. I've been here so long it feels like home." But most respondents simply referred to the "nice" people and managers who were friendly and predictable and, most important, who proved not to be aggressive or threatening.

The SRO offers many tenants a safe and secure haven in the frequently risky environments of surrounding urban neighborhoods. The social ties of the SRO contribute to the security of tenants. "I feel very secure," replied a thirty-five-year-old woman when asked about the reasons for her satisfaction with the SRO. "The people living here are very nice. They're pleasant, and if something goes wrong, they help." Another tenant, a forty-six-year-old black male, summed up a common experience when he explained that "I feel safe here. There are no break-ins. We are like one happy family."

But references to a sense of community were not universal. Other residents preferred the privacy and independence of the SRO environment (9.8 percent). "No one bothers you and you have your privacy. I like that," said a thirty-eight-year-old black man recovering from surgery. "It's quiet and no one disturbs me," claimed a fifty-eight-year-old cancer victim. The response of a sixty-year-old black man perhaps best captures the essence of these remarks. "Nobody bothers me and I don't bother nobody. That's it!" Although the appreciation for privacy was strong, it did not preclude social ties. Many who mentioned multiple reasons for their satisfaction were like the elderly white male who professed the following list. "People are nice. The rent is reasonable. No one bothers you, and I like talking to the other boys that live here." Privacy and comradeship complement each other in the social world of the SRO hotel.

The affordability of the SRO units was significant mainly to those tenants with low incomes, especially those residing in the cubicle hotels. Like most tenants, residents did not express satisfaction with the rent they had to pay, but those with few resources appreciated the importance of a rent they could afford. Some offered excuses, like the twenty-two-year-old black man who claimed, "This is all I can afford right now." Others were less apologetic. "For the money, its an all-right place to live," declared a fifty-nine-year-old Hispanic male. "It's cheap. I can't afford no forty to fifty dollars a week."

The cubicle hotels offered the cheapest rents of all the hotels in the survey. Whereas the average monthly rent for the entire sample was $199, the cubicle hotel rooms rented on average for half as much, $99. When asked why they had moved to their present hotel, considerably more than half of the cubicle residents gave cheap rent as their reason, compared with barely 17 percent of those living in the better quality SROs. The cubicle hotels provide the first step of rudimentary shelter for single people on the rental housing market ladder. Furthermore, these are the only hotels in which the Illinois General Assistance (GA) grant for poor individuals —$154 a month—could actually pay a month's rent and still leave some money for other expenditures.

Cubicle residents recognize the precariousness of their perch and the serious shelter privation that awaits them should they fall from the security and privacy of their cubicle nest. In expressing his satisfaction with this otherwise dismal housing, one tenant from a cubicle hotel explained, "I like living here. There aren't too many places like this anymore, and if you don't live in a place like this you live in the street." Or as another tenant put it, in more abbreviated fashion, "It beats sitting on the street." The positive evaluations of their hotels by cubicle residents usually reflect their relief at having escaped both the insecurity of the streets and the indignity of the shelters.

Assessing Preferences and Problems

Because residents offered multiple reasons for their satisfaction, we did not know which reasons were the most important to them. Therefore, we also asked residents what they most liked about living in their present SRO hotel (see table 8-2). Tenants most like the social benefits of SRO living (42.8 percent); location (21 percent) and affordability (17.5 percent) follow. The physical features of the single rooms and the hotel proved to be the least preferred aspect of SRO living (31.7 percent).

Perhaps the most important finding was the fact that almost two out of five of the respondents could not name or mention anything that they disliked, compared with only 7.2 percent who had similar difficulty thinking

TABLE 8-2

SRO Residents' Preferences for SRO Accommodations

REASON	MOST LIKED (%)	MOST DISLIKED (%)
PHYSICAL		
Room quality	.8	20.4
Hotel services	3.7	5.9
Maintenance, repair	4.7	5.4
ECONOMIC—rent level	17.5	5.4
SOCIAL		
Privacy, independence	12.9	1.0
Other tenants	13.2	5.9
Management	6.5	4.9
Security	10.2	1.5
LOCATION		
Convenience	20.0	—
Neighborhood	1.0	3.2
OTHER		
Miscellaneous	6.7	4.7
No response	2.7	41.7
	100.0	100.0

Note. The preference questions from which we constructed this table allowed only one choice. Thus, the percentages are based on the total sample of respondents for each column and sum to a hundred.

of something they most liked. Residents do not feel trapped in the hotels; rather, they appear to like and take advantage of those aspects of the hotel that make urban living easier and more efficient: convenience, social contact, and affordability. Most do not like the fact that their rooms are small and cramped, the hotel old and unattractive, but they are willing to overlook the lack of such amenities in return for other benefits. Residents know their economic limitations and have found a niche in the residential marketplace that offers them a valuable tradeoff between convenience or access and living space.

We also asked residents to report their concern with a selection of characteristics that critics depicted as uniquely associated with SRO hotels. The results strongly contradict the image of the SRO as a squalid flophouse. More than three out of every four residents praised the safety (76 percent), quiet (77 percent), privacy (78 percent), and winter warmth (76 percent) of their rooms. The only environmental problems complained about that even approached the conditions of the stereotype were summer heat (34 percent) and roaches (53 percent). In other words, with the exception of the very real problem of infestation, the quality of individual units in SROs in comparison with other forms of low-rent housing seems quite high. Comments such as "I'm comfortable in my room" or "It's my home" were not uncommon.

Residents especially recognized and appreciated the social management of the buildings. Nearly 88 percent of the residents knew the managers or desk clerks personally. These staff people take phone messages, distribute mail, screen visitors, and perform other small but important services for residents. Another 52 percent said they knew the owner, whom three out of four claim they see at least once a month. These social ties between resident and manager provide in most cases a mutually beneficial relationship. For instance, the brother of a hotel owner lives in the hotel and helps out by working there. In his own words, "I have everything at one place and I like it." Another resident praised the desk clerks because "they screen people that come see you and if they don't like them they tell them [the visitors] they can't come in." This link between screening and security plays an important role in making these modest units livable. One respondent was proud of this arrangement and felt that her sister "who lives in an expensive building" enjoys less security than she does, given the protection from unwanted intrusions she enjoys. "No one goes upstairs unless the desk clerk okays it," she explained. Ironically, the respondent's sister pays more rent for an apartment that offers less apparent security than the SRO hotel room.

SRO hotels do not provide simply an inexpensive room for the single working poor, functioning as a sort of private-sector public housing in which affordability becomes the sole criteria of access. The hotels do provide relatively inexpensive shelter, but what is more important, they offer services that enhance the quality of life for those of modest means without requiring the sacrifice of autonomy or independence. For many of the first-time residents the SRO hotel provides a way station, a place to stay until their personal circumstances change and enable them to move to more spacious quarters. Others, for whom expectations of increased economic prosperity or social reunion are improbable, may learn to adopt the social life of veteran SRO users. Initiation into the SRO life-style, however, does not necessarily mean a loss of economic and social resources. As Bogue found among the migrants to Skid Row in the 1950s and as we discovered in the mid-1980s, the newcomers to the SRO world usually come there initially out of necessity, a necessity imposed by a lack of economic and social resources.[4] The SRO environment does not create these pressures, nor does it contribute to them. Instead, the SRO provides an alternative for poor single people, making it possible for them to use their residential space both as a means of recovering lost prosperity and social ties as well as creating a meaningful way of life in the midst of severe social disadvantages and economic uncertainty.

The Social Diversity of the SRO Hotels

Most developers and owners of multifamily residential buildings seek to specialize, attracting residents similar in age, race, income, or—less frequently—sex. Discrimination in the real estate market and the rental market is not only taken as given but promoted as a marketing device to attract small middle- and upper-middle-class households back to the city from the suburbs or outlying city neighborhoods. New high-rise residential buildings, physically cordoned off from the poor who inhabit the older structures nearby, offer specialized living environments for narrow social segments of the growing professional and managerial class. Ironically, these buildings mirror the public housing programs in Chicago, which were also organized on the basis of policies that would separate their residents from nearby neighborhoods, by confining the city's black residents in spatially segregated communities. The result today is hundreds of high-density buildings filled with an almost exclusively dependent population in which female-headed households predominate.

These common social and economic divisions that shape the residential organization of virtually all urban space in Chicago do not seem, however, to fragment the social order of the SRO hotels. As we point out in chapter 7, the social divisions that usually link the uneven distribution of income with the social characteristics of race, sex, and age among members of urban society tend to be less prevalent among SRO hotel residents. The variations that do occur cut across the social inequalities that usually define the boundaries that segregate residential neighborhoods into relatively homogeneous social enclaves. Most of the hotels offer a residential environment that allows for social and economic diversity without the systematic imposition of hierarchical order across different social domains. Perhaps because most are poor or on the threshold of poverty, they cannot use economic strength to entice or even pressure others to do their bidding. The residents share enough different yet overlapping vulnerabilities to make mutual exploitation not only risky, but even dangerous.

The hotels provide an institutional setting that protects privacy by involving residents in the provision and maintenance of social order in the public spaces of the building. Detailed ethnographic studies of individual hotels in other cities have documented the way the social organization of SRO hotels combines a generous tolerance for social difference with a strictly enforced set of house rules. The social ties among residents do not reflect a community of shared sentiment, but an urban sense of public responsibility.

TABLE 8-3

Distribution of Eighteen SRO Hotels,
by Heterogeneity of Residents' Characteristics

HETERO-GENEITY SCORES	SEX	RACE	AGE	INCOME	EMPLOY-MENT	LENGTH OF STAY[a]	VETERAN
High 0.80–1.00	8	6	12	13	12	14	8
0.60–0.79	5	2	5	4	3	3	3
0.40–0.59	1	2	1	—	1	—	3
0.20–0.39	2	—	—	—	2	—	2
Low 0.00–0.19	2	8	—	1	—	1	2

[a]See note in Appendix B for explanation of index values.

Privacy is respected, but residents need not be socially isolated unless they choose to be.[5]

Although we lacked the resources needed to study the relationships within each hotel, we did estimate the degree of social heterogeneity of the respondents in each hotel. To compare a variety of characteristics using a single measure, we used the index of dispersion.[6] This technique provides a straightforward and easy-to-interpret measure of heterogeneity. A value of 0 on the index means that the residents in that hotel all fall within a certain nominal category (e.g., greater than fifty-four years of age), and so for that particular score we could say that the residents of that hotel are similar in age. A value of 1 on the index would mean the opposite, that the residents are evenly distributed among the different age categories (25 percent in each of four categories), in this case, that the residents are heterogeneous in age.

We calculated index scores for three social, two economic, and two SRO characteristics. The scores are listed in appendix B. These scores have been summarized in table 8-3 and illustrate the distribution of the eighteen sample hotels according to the heterogeneity of their resident characteristics. The majority of the hotels possess residents who differ greatly in age, income, employment status (employed, unemployed, or out of the labor market), and length of stay. Despite the relatively small proportion of women overall, most were dispersed among the hotels. Only a few hotels had no women at all. The predominantly male SRO veterans, however, were unevenly distributed. As we noted above, there were few veterans of SRO living in the South Side hotels that scored low on the heterogeneity index. A similar pattern was evident for race as well. Since virtually all residents of the South Side hotels are black, the heterogeneity scores of these hotels are quite low. However, the low scores of the South Side hotels reflect the fact that the overwhelming proportion of residents in these neighborhoods where the hotels are located are black, not that hotel management here is discriminatory. Only three of the hotels on the North Side fall into the homogeneous category (in this case, all white). The other nine exhibit some racial integration.

The unique social environment of the successful SRO depends, we think, on this mix of different kinds of tenants. The emphasis on decent collective services combined with the social bonds of trust formed among residents ties the diverse people together in a community of bounded responsibility. Residents respect the privacy of others and yet share the expectation of mutual cooperation and even aid to promote a secure living environment. Conflicts do emerge between such disparate neighbors as a young day laborer and an elderly retiree, but the established social routine of the hotel —the "house rules"—provides a framework for negotiating settlements and avoiding escalating conflicts.[7]

At the time of our interview residents in one hotel were especially upset by changes in the admission policy for new residents. The management had begun to accept a large number of outpatients from a nearby psychiatric care facility to reduce the hotel vacancy rate and increase cash flow. The residents felt especially threatened, not necessarily by the fear that these people were dangerous (the middle-class response), but by the inexperience and in some cases inability of the former patients to collaborate in the maintenance of the fragile social order of the hotel. The old residents did not believe that these new residents could be trusted to follow the informal house rules on their own. Half the residents in the hotel, when asked to describe anything unusual around the hotel during the past six months, complained that the crazy newcomers were "replacing the old tenants." Since the outpatients were not employed, they tended "to stand around a lot and loiter outside the hotel." Some feared that they gave the impression that there are "just a bunch of crazy folk living here now." The visible and vulnerable tenants attract trouble, and as a result, one old-timer emphasized, "the police end up coming into the hotel to handle problems with the crazy people." The newcomers were mainly dependent and hence vulnerable residents whose dependency, as their numbers increased, threatened to overwhelm the balance of reciprocal exchanges that kept the hotel secure. The old residents felt offended and resentful at the management and the newcomers for imposing the burden of the newcomers' dependency on their social world.

To more accurately assess the relationship between the social diversity of the SRO residents and the security of SRO living, we developed two measures of security for each resident. One measure indicates whether a resident mentioned security or relationships with other tenants as one of the things he or she liked or disliked about SRO living. The other measure is an interval-level score of reported security breakdowns, including one point for each of the following problems: an influx of dependent tenants, disturbances requiring that the police be called, vandalism of the common spaces (e.g., lobby furniture broken), or arson. The security indicator measures the perception of security; the safety indicator measures the actual incidence of security breaches. We analyzed the effect of SRO resident social characteristics on variation in the size of both the safety and security indicators.[8]

If security and safety depend on the social and economic homogeneity of residents, then we expected to find that residents of a certain type, for instance, women, would score consistently low or high on these measures. The perception and experience of security did not vary much with the social and economic characteristics of the residents. In other words, the distribution of security did not depend on particular characteristics, as it so frequently does in the residential environments of the middle class. There were two exceptions. In the case of safety, SRO veterans reported significantly fewer breaches of security in their buildings than did nonveterans. This may reflect either the fact that in the hotels where SRO veterans live there are fewer breakdowns in security or that SRO veterans are less likely to report such breaches as a problem than are nonveterans. We believe the first explanation is consistent with the other evidence on SRO social organization, but we cannot test this inference directly. Residents with a greater burden of economic hardship, but not necessarily lower incomes, were also likely to live in hotels where security breakdowns were more frequent. Since the economic hardship score consists mainly of residents with high rent burdens who may also suffer from recent economic displacement, shelter deprivation, or hunger, the positive relation may indicate rent gouging of new and vulnerable residents by management. Breakdowns in security are frequently accompanied by short-term economic exploitation as owners prepare to abandon their property. Residents have little defense against such systematic practices, when they do occur.

Despite these exceptions, the overall security of residents remains tied to a shared vulnerability within the confines of the SRO regardless of status or means. This shared fate promotes a sense of common defense that encourages residents to follow the house rules. The social mix of the relatively strong and weak protects against the dependency of a homogeneous population of physically or mentally disadvantaged residents. We disagree with authors like Janice Smithers who argue that a shared "consciousness of kind" promotes mutual security. Smithers focused on an exclusively elderly population in a single SRO hotel and, we think mistakenly, ascribed shared vulnerability to the shared demographic characteristic of advanced age. We do not dispute her findings, that the elderly helped contribute to their mutual security, but argue that these efforts were not based so much on similar age as on shared vulnerability to nonresident strangers in the inner-city neighborhood nearby. The combination of shared vulnerability and shared weakness does not promote security; rather, the combination of shared vulnerability and a mix of strong and weak does. In the hotel that Smithers studied the management and local public housing authority provided a twenty-four-hour security guard to discourage intruders. It was the combination of the powerful threat of the guard with the surveillance efforts of the weak residents that made for a secure hotel environment— not the fact that all the residents were old.[9]

Unlike most other forms of residential shelter, SROs offer little private dwelling space. Furthermore, compared with differences in the size and composition among rental units in apartment buildings, the differences among single room units in SRO appear marginal. What counts, as our respondents made quite evident, is the quality of the collective services of the hotel and its location. Hence, we expected to find that rent differentials within SROs would reflect differences in the quality of the individual dwelling rooms less than the different types of rental agreements formed between tenants and landlords. Most important in this respect are the different room rates based on the payment interval. Renting by day or week costs more than renting by the month. In effect, the weekly renter usually pays more for the same amount of space a monthly renter enjoys. In addition, renters who inhabit the same building for a long time tend to avoid rent increases of the magnitude that newcomers face. Their predictability is rewarded with a lower rent.

The mix of short-term and long-term payers produces a symbiotic community within an SRO hotel. The short-term payers are predominantly wage workers, many of whom constantly confront the uncertainty of layoffs or cutbacks. The demands of the labor markets for the working poor undermine efforts to maintain the routine payment of large sums of money such as rent. Although the annual income of some of the better paid workers might allow them to rent their own apartment, renting an SRO room on a daily basis proves not only less expensive but more convenient. The old-timers who rent on a monthly basis tend to receive income from entitlements. These residents enjoy a predictable flow of funds that makes routine rent payment desirable. The incomes of these residents usually fall below those of their employed neighbors. However, because they pay by the month, they usually pay less rent. The predictable flow of funds from the monthly renter reduces the cost of turnover for the management and provides greater social stability, all of which reduces the operating costs of the hotel. The managers return a portion of these savings to the long-term renters in the form of lower rents.

There are of course exceptions among these two types of residents, for instance, poor public-aid recipients who pay an exorbitant portion of their

TABLE 8-4

Mean Values of Residents' Characteristics,
by Rent Payment Interval

CHARACTERISTIC	ALL	WEEKLY	MONTHLY	
Mean annual income ($)	7,073	9,378	5,293	*
Mean age (years)	45.9	40.5	50.5	*
Mean stay (years)	3.0	2.0	3.9	*
Source from Wages (%)	41.0	68.0	32.0	*
Mean rent burden (%)	45.1	47.5	43.2	n.s.
Mean rent ($)	199	248	162	*

Note: We used a T-test of the difference between two sample means. The asterisk denotes statistically significant differences between the two groups' means at the .05 level or less.

income for rent, or relatively wealthy eccentrics whose rent burden (the ratio of rent paid to income) may not even reach the double digit mark. In order to test for these relationships among the SRO residents in our sample, we calculated the differences in source and amount of income, length of stay, rent, age, and rent burden. The mean values are presented in table 8-4.

The weekly rate payers were younger and far more likely to earn their higher incomes from wages than were the monthly rate payers. Two out of three (68 percent) reported wage-based earnings, compared with barely one in three (32 percent) of those renting by the month. However, the weekly rent payers reported a much shorter average stay (a little more than two years) than did the monthly rate payers (an average of almost four years). The weekly rate payers also paid substantially higher rents on the average ($248) than those who paid by the month ($162). However, despite higher incomes and more reliable source of income from wages, the weekly rate payers did not enjoy a substantially lower rent burden.

The differences between the two groups of rate payers supported our expectations. The weekly renters were younger newcomers whose wage earnings provided a higher income than the entitlement income relied upon by most of the old-timers. Most important, the relatively more prosperous newcomers usually paid more rent for their rooms than did the old-timers who paid monthly. Usually, when their incomes increase, people pay a smaller proportion of their total income for rent. Thus, we needed to find out if the relatively more prosperous newcomers who paid by the week paid more for the same kinds of rooms as the old-timers who paid by the month.

If so, this meant that newcomers who paid by the week in the same hotels with monthly rate payers actually subsidized the rents of the old-timers.

To test for a subsidy we had to control for the actual mix of rate payers (weekly and monthly) in the eighteen hotels included in our study. To control for this potential subsidy effect, we divided the hotels into two groups, those with a mix of rate payers (a minimum of three each) and those with a virtually uniform rate payment pattern (predominantly weekly or predominantly monthly). Although all the SRO hotels advertise differential rates, our sampling uncovered de facto specialization. We grouped the hotels by mix because in the uniform rate hotels, weekly rate payers' higher rents could not subsidize the rents of monthly rate payers who did not live in the same hotel.

We compared the rent burden of residents in hotels where tenants reported a mix of weekly and monthly rate payers. Although the rent difference was significant between weekly ($247) and monthly ($155) rate payers, the difference in rent burdens was not. Thus, the weekly ratepayers not only receive a significantly larger income than monthly rate payers, but they pay a higher rent on average as well, regardless of hotel type. However, the weekly rate payers in the mixed-rate hotels carry a greater rent burden than they otherwise would in a hotel where all the residents pay by the week. The higher rents paid by these weekly rate payers in hotels with both weekly and monthly rate payers indirectly contribute to lower rents for the monthly rate payers—if the rooms are not substantially different in quality.

We suspected that much of the difference in rents and even rent burden might hinge on difference in the quality of the individual rooms within the hotels with a mix of payment rates. About 50 percent of the residents in the mixed-rate hotels rented rooms with a private bath. After analyzing our exhaustive inventory of room characteristics, we found that the presence of a private bath was the characteristic that most clearly defined a large difference in room quality meriting more rent.

We knew that tenants renting rooms with baths paid significantly more rent than those renting only a room (see table 8-5). However, when we calculated the difference between the average rent burdens carried by weekly and monthly rate payers, we found that their burden did not vary significantly when controlling for the presence of a bath. In other words, the difference between the rent burden carried by weekly and monthly rent payers was not statistically significant regardless of whether both rented a room with a bath or not. Despite their having higher average incomes, the weekly rate payers did not enjoy a lower rent burden. In effect, the weekly rate payers in hotels with a mix of rate payers appear to pay more than monthly rate payers for the same quality of units.

This difference in rent level combined with no difference in rent burden signifies that the short-term payers subsidize the incomes of the long-term

TABLE 8-5

Average Rent Burdens and Rents in Hotels
with a Mix of Rate Payers

RENT INTERVAL	RENT BURDEN (%)	RENT ($)
Units with Bath		
Monthly	52.7	216
Weekly	66.9 n.s.	299*
Units without Bath		
Monthly	32.2	118
Weekly	40.3 n.s.	150*

*Difference between the two groups' means are significant at .05 level.

payers by enabling the owners to charge lower rents to monthly rate payers. The arrangement works to the benefit of all parties, including the owners of the hotels. Without the mix of tenants, the symbiotic link that helps ensure the quality of collective services might be undermined. If the hotel becomes inhabited exclusively by old-timers, the rent might drop precipitously, necessitating cutbacks in services and perhaps major rehabilitation or conversion. If the hotel becomes exclusively dedicated to short-timers, then the costs of maintaining the predictability and security of the collective services might rise enormously. The economic viability of many SRO hotels is tied, we believe, to successful management of this social balance.

Helping Episodes and the SRO Network

Sharing referrals and other information represents a relatively low-risk form of aid available to virtually anyone who lives in an SRO hotel, regardless of social vulnerabilities and characteristics or the extent of economic hardship. Because the more substantial forms of help provided within personal helping networks rely on bonds of trust established in close relationships to ensure that reciprocity will be respected, aid within personal helping networks will follow the social and economic characteristics of residents, just as it does in such networks elsewhere. However, aid within the SRO networks does not follow the segmented pathways of shared social characteristics, but rather knits together a diverse SRO clientele.

The frequency of SRO helping episodes that residents reported for the year prior to the interview did not vary with resident needs and resources, as did the size of personal helping networks. Using regression models to test for the statistical effects of SRO resident characteristics on the size of the SRO helping episode index, we found that the needs and resources of SRO residents, whether social or economic, predict little of the variation in the size of the SRO helping episode index, regardless of who provides the help. Thus, the distribution of informal aid in the SRO helping network is not organized according to a social and economic hierarchy, but on the basis of shared residence in a hotel. The SRO helping network matches the diverse needs and resources of the residents because it is based on weak ties requiring only very modest contributions. The information and occasional money distributed in the SRO social world forms a latticework of weak ties that help residents take advantage of opportunities or anticipate and avoid privations. The management of the hotel plays a crucial role in maintaining the hotel community, not only by enforcing security measures or controlling the number of vulnerable tenants but by actively supporting and encouraging the provision of informal aid. The withdrawal of such support is usually a prelude to the demise of the hotel.

Conclusions

SRO residents enjoy the benefits of social ties in ways common to other working-class individuals. However, the tenants of the SRO hotel live in a more socially diverse residential environment than do their class peers and in most cases benefit from this diversity. The perceptions of insecurity and reports of social disorder in SRO hotels did not come from any particular strata of the residents. The vulnerable did not feel more threatened, nor did the more prosperous enjoy greater safety. Security was a common good to which each contributed and from which all benefited, although the extent of mutual benefit is not evident.

The mix of rate payers in many hotels put the economic diversity of the residents to good use in a different fashion. The management charges higher rents for weekly renters, anticipating the costs of frequent turnover. This premium is quite substantial, even when controlling for differences in room quality. The owner makes more revenue from the weekly tenants, giving less cause to raise the rent for long-term monthly ratepayers. The weekly rate payers with higher average incomes modestly subsidize the rents of the lower income monthly rate payers. Diversity in this case produces unintended redistribution.

Taken together with the findings in chapter 7, the data in this chapter, we believe, provide substantial evidence of an active and useful community life shared both by residents within the hotels and between individual residents and others outside. Furthermore, this community builds upon and complements the privacy, security, accessibility, and affordability of the SRO hotel units. All of this occurs despite the fact that most of the SRO residents are poor, suffering from a wide variety of physical, social, and economic hardships, and must make do with a tiny room. When contrasted with the standards of middle-class residential standards and social life, the SRO world may appear terribly deficient. However, when compared with living in an overcrowded household, an emergency shelter, or the street, the SRO hotel appears quite attractive.

The residents of SRO hotels offer real-life examples of the social prototype of what urban life has frequently promised but seldom delivered, for those of modest means: trading off space for the convenience, security, and affordability of high-density living. The tenants, drawn mainly from the ranks of the working poor, utilize the convenience, security, and affordability of the SRO hotels to maintain their independence and social standing in the midst of the serious economic obstacles they encounter at the bottom of the occupational hierarchy. Yet, SRO residents live in a socially and economically diverse environment enabling tenants and their hotel managers to maintain a symbiotic relationship of mutual support. SRO hotels not only provide affordable shelter but also make a unique contribution to the diversity of social life in Chicago. In a city infamous for its residential segregation, the remaining SROs stand as outposts of civilization in a city landscape increasingly fragmented into bunkers of uniform prosperity or vulnerable pockets of poverty.

9

The Loss of
SRO Hotels

The SRO hotels provide private and secure dwellings for the single urban poor, as well as a residential community offering unique social and economic benefits. Although the hotels are not subsidized by public funds, they still offer affordable shelter for low-income tenants while earning a modest profit for the owners. These benefits of the SRO hotels, however, continue to be obscured by the Skid Row stereotype. How did such profound mislabeling succeed for so long, and why does it continue in the face of so much evidence discrediting the stereotype?

In part, the widespread acceptance of the Skid Row stereotype can be traced to the fact that the middle-class researchers, officials, and bureaucrats who proposed and used the stereotype did so largely unchallenged. The low social status and geographic segregation of the Skid Row SRO hotel residents created and maintained an enormous social distance between the residents and others up the social class hierarchy. Furthermore, their poverty and vulnerability to relatively unconstrained policing discouraged vocal and organized protest by Skid Row residents in defense of their community. Thus, the stereotypical images of the residents and SRO hotels proposed by middle-class policy makers and caretakers took hold by default.

Even more important than the contribution of social distance was the exceptional economic prosperity enjoyed by the vast majority of urban residents in the 1950s and 1960s. The postwar boom dramatically reduced the number of single poor people, thereby eliminating new recruits for the Skid Row labor markets and the SRO hotels. Among the hundreds of SRO hotels destroyed by urban renewal demolition schemes, some were abandoned and many had high vacancy rates. At best, the SRO hotels were considered obsolete housing for the single poor transient. More frequently, public officials condemned SROs as a form of structural blight, harboring a residual population of vulnerable deviants whose removal and rehabilitation would put an end to the problem of homelessness in the inner city.

In this chapter we examine some instances of resident resistance to public displacement, arguing that such actions challenged the legitimacy of stereotypical portrayals of hotel residents as disaffiliated and transient bums.

172

However, these cases were too few to provide sufficient impetus to change the well-established stereotype. The value of SRO-type housing obtained recognition only after more than half the SRO hotels had been destroyed, and officials in some cities began to recognize the connection between these losses and the increasing number of visibly homeless single people in the early 1980s. And even then, as we show in chapter 10, officials continued to misunderstand the unique value of the SRO hotels, seeking to use them as shelters rather than preserve them as residential communities.

In Chicago, although city government has abandoned wholesale clearance schemes, urban redevelopment continues to destroy SROs in gentrifying neighborhoods, while discriminatory regulations discourage reinvestment in less attractive areas. When combined with increasing economic hardship among the urban poor, these losses go a long way toward explaining the growing numbers of single homeless people in Chicago. We use results from our survey of residents and a survey of homeless people conducted by the National Opinion Research Center (NORC) to illustrate how the previously homeless use the SRO hotels to maintain their grip on security, while those on the streets or in shelters usually remain cut off from this resource.

We argue that the loss of SRO hotels was the major reason why the single poor became visible street people in big cities. The unexpected rise in economic hardship among working-class households in large cities had increased the number of destitute single people, but it was the destruction of thousands of SRO hotel units that left these people with too few affordable rooms to rent. Poverty is a necessary but not sufficient condition to account for homelessness. It is the lack of cheap SRO-type housing that turns urban poverty into homelessness.

Urban Renewal and the SRO Hotel

The thinning ranks of the white single male poor in the 1960s and early 1970s legitimized the urban renewal policies of displacement, dispersal, rehabilitation, and relocation. As fewer young recruits joined the aging working men who had been pushed out of Skid Row either to settle in smaller satellite Skid Rows or be placed in the institutional accommodations of a growing welfare state, the demolition of the hotels appeared to be simply the removal of obsolete substandard housing. But like so many American policy advocates, the promoters of Skid Row removal did not anticipate a significant downswing in the economy, much less the radical restructuring of the economy that in 1987 promised to virtually eliminate unskilled industrial jobs by the year 2000. Hence, only a few low-income housing advocates noted the seriousness of the housing gap created as a side effect of urban renewal.

Similarly, wholesale clearance of inner-city SRO hotels as part of the extensive urban renewal schemes of the 1960s aroused little protest from the general public, who believed that the Skid Row SRO hotels were obsolete and socially undesirable living environments. As we mention in chapter 6, successful protests by residents of working-class neighborhoods did eventually manage to stop some renewal projects; these residents used the political experience gained in these struggles to build new electoral coalitions that challenged the political officials who had supported the urban renewal objectives of the growth coalition.[1] The Skid Row neighborhoods, however, had offered little organized resistance to renewal and so suffered perhaps the most extensive clearance and demolition.

An important exception was the effort by a small coalition of Skid Row hotel residents and middle-class organizers to stave off redevelopment efforts in San Francisco's South of Market neighborhood in the late 1960s. Chester Hartman and his co-authors in Yerba Buena provide a chilling blow-by-blow account of the callous practices adopted by the San Francisco Redevelopment Agency to force uncooperative hotel owners to sell their properties and evict their tenants. After the Redevelopment Agency purchased a hotel, it would remove the experienced management and withhold repairs, thus speeding up the departure of tenants while accelerating the physical deterioration of the building.

> Old-time hotel staff, who performed important and friendly functions in the lives of the old people, were replaced by often insensitive and incompetent clerks and maintenance personnel. . . . Heat and hot water were shut off because of "boiler problems"; lobby doors were kept locked and residents admitted only upon showing identification; linens were unavailable and maid service terminated; hall toilets were locked; comfortable lobby chairs were replaced by benches and camp chairs; mail and messages got lost; rubbish stood uncollected; desk clerks and security guards drank, slept on the job, and were insolent to and on occasions physically abused residents.[2]

A local advocacy organization was formed in response to these deteriorating living conditions. A small group of retired labor leaders and union activists who lived on Skid Row collaborated with a small group of legal aid lawyers to put legal and political pressure on the Redevelopment Agency to provide relocation housing and assistance for residents displaced from the SRO hotels destroyed as a result of renewal efforts. The use of legal pressures proved effective enough to obtain important concessions from the Redevelopment Agency, most notably, 400 units of replacement housing. However, the authors point out that this successful effort relied crucially on the expertise and determination of a small group of dedicated lawyers, as well as the sympathy of a judge.[3] Perhaps more important in the long run was the effect this struggle had on the public perception of the Skid Row population. The Skid Row residents could no longer be so easily dismissed as a socially irresponsible and deviant social population. In fact, the sight of vulnerable old people publicly struggling to retain possession of their hotel rooms became part of a broader national movement to improve the quality of life for poor elderly citizens.

Interest in the value of the SRO hotels expanded in the 1970s as those seeking to improve shelter for the elderly poor began to reassess the merits of single-room living. Ironically, this reassessment came about only after the destruction of thousands of Skid Row hotels units. The stereotypical relationship between undeserving Skid Row residents and their hotel environments was replaced by analysts and advocates focusing on the SRO hotel as a way of meeting the needs of the single elderly (see the introduction to chapter 7). The testimony and papers presented at Senate hearings by a Special Committee on Aging in 1978, for example, document the shift toward a more benign evaluation of the SRO hotels.[4] Local efforts were also undertaken in many cities to identify how much SRO-type housing remained and to assess the magnitude of the losses. Advocates for preservation hoped to use the evidence of decline to create a sense of urgency that might motivate public officials to adopt measures that would protect the SRO housing from further destruction.

Although research efforts got underway in the late 1970s, it was the homeless crisis of the early 1980s that sparked widespread concern about the loss of SRO hotels. Studies conducted in cities all across the United States documented and deplored the loss. New York City lost 30,385 units in 160 buildings between 1975 and 1981, for a decrease of 60 percent overall. In San Francisco 5,723 (17.7 percent) of 32,214 units disappeared between 1975 and 1979. Denver, which had forty-five SRO hotels in 1976, had fewer than seventeen left in 1981.[5] In Seattle the number of SRO units dropped by 15,000 between 1960 and 1981. San Diego lost 1,247 units in thirty hotels between 1976 and 1984 and has only about 3,500 units left.[6] Smaller cities lost hotels as well. Portland eliminated 1,700 units in the 1970s.[7] Cincinnati lost 42 percent of its SRO units during the 1970s and has only fifteen hotels remaining with 875 units.[8]

The Housing Squeeze for the Urban Poor

The rapid loss of SRO hotels during the 1970s was part of a larger process of economic restructuring in urban housing markets, a restructuring that shifted the burden of economic decline onto the shoulders of those least able to escape, young members of the urban working class. Declining incomes and a decreasing supply of low-rent (especially SRO) housing together increased the angle of the incline up which the poor must travel to obtain modest shelter security. As a result, those poor people burdened with social vulnerabilities were more likely to lose their grip and slip down the incline toward homelessness. The mentally ill, physically disabled, blacks, and women, for example, possess characteristics that place them at a disadvantage in both the labor and housing markets. However, although their physical and social vulnerabilities grease the skids, their movement downward comes as a result of a steeper incline rather than any increase in the slipperiness of their soles.

The U.S. unemployment rate rose throughout the 1970s, peaked in 1982 at 9.7 percent, and has dropped off some since then. Furthermore, a restructuring economy has displaced many people from lifelong occupations and left them vulnerable to economic collapse as they engaged in unfamiliar and frequently unsuccessful job searches. A recent study of displaced workers in the United States between 1979 and 1984 found that by 1984 only 60 percent of the whites, 52 percent of the Hispanics, and 42 percent of the blacks among the 5.1 million displacees had been reemployed. For example, in the East North Central Region, which includes the state of Illinois, the impact was even more severe, with barely 50 percent returning to work. Steelworkers, concentrated in the Chicago area, not only encountered a disproportionate share of the job loss, but just 44 percent had found work since their layoffs. This failure to find work reflected the permanent loss of manufacturing jobs. Thus, of those fortunate enough to find full employment, 45 percent worked for lower wages and frequently in different industries and occupations.[9]

The U.S. economy managed to produce more than 21 million jobs between 1973 and 1985, an astounding growth in the employed work force, especially when compared with the sluggish job growth in western European countries at the same time. But the growth in the civilian labor force was even greater, keeping unemployment higher than 7 percent. Furthermore, a higher proportion of the jobs being created in the 1980s offered significantly lower wages than those created in the early 1970s. Between 1973 and 1979, 12 million jobs were created, of which only 20 percent were low wage (less than $7,400 per year in constant 1986 dollars). During the next seven years only 8 million jobs were created, and 44 percent of these were low wage. Though a portion of this decline reflects the impact of the large proportion of young people and women entering the work force since 1973, the downswing is based more on such structural changes as the expansion of part-time employment (30 percent of net job growth between 1979 and 1985).[10] The editors of *Dollars and Sense* note that "the shift of employment out of the high-paying and widely unionized manufacturing sector and into services has boosted the growth of low-wage jobs. Manufacturing has not added any net new jobs to the economy since 1979. Employment growth has been concentrated in services and retail trade—industries with twice the proportion of low-wage jobs as manufacturing."[11]

Not only are workers losing hold of high-wage jobs, but the floor toward which they are falling is slanting downhill as well. Although the nominal minimum wage increased from $2.30 in 1977 to $3.35 in 1981 and then leveled off, the real minimum wage (which converts the 1985 nominal value into constant 1977 dollars to control for increases in the cost of living) had actually declined to $1.88 by 1985. "Some studies indicate that as many as 70 percent of those earning the minimum wage are adults. Almost half of those earning the minimum wage or below are over 25 years old, and one quarter are heads of households." [12]

The economic recovery of 1983–84 did bring more income to the poor overall, but mainly to those whose poverty was tied directly to the downswing in the economy—the temporarily unemployed. The growing ranks of the dependent poor, those who remained outside the labor force, included a rapidly growing proportion of female-headed households and young single individuals (especially black males) whose public aid benefits have not kept pace with the cost of living. Contributing to the increased poverty of female-headed households was the fact that "the real value of AFDC benefits declined by 28 percent between 1970 and 1980." [13] This impact was intensified during the first two years of the Reagan administration when "tighter income eligibility limits and sharper benefit offsets for earnings and other income eliminated 'an estimated 400,000 to 500,000 AFDC families and nearly a million potential food stamp beneficiaries' and greatly reduced benefits to others (Palmer and Sawhill 1984, 13). Between 1979 and 1982, the proportion of all poor children enrolled in AFDC dropped from 72 to 52 percent (Taylor 1986)." [14] The situation was no different for the single poor. The real value of the primary source of aid for nonelderly unrelated individuals, General Assistance (GA) benefits, dropped 30 percent during the 1970s in those states that offered this aid. [15]

This combination of increasing unemployment, declining wage rates, and welfare cutbacks put an end to the almost uninterrupted rise in median family income that accompanied the economic prosperity between 1950 and 1973. Since the 1974 recession, median family income has remained relatively stable, a stability based mainly on a growing proportion of families that have two wage earners. Even more troubling than the lack of income growth at the median is the growing inequality at the extremes. Congressional research analyst Peter Edelman noted in 1985 that "since the beginning of the Reagan administration, the bottom 20 percent of the population has lost 7.6 percent in real disposable income while the top 20 percent of the country has gained 8.7 percent, and that is the first time there has been that kind of movement in the last six decades." [16]

In their study of metropolitan housing markets in the United States between 1973 and 1980, Turner and Struyk identified five major trends: "First, the demographic composition of metropolitan households changed: the share of single individuals and single headed households increased substantially. Second, by the end of the 1970s, the pool of renters had substantially lower purchasing power than the pool of owners did. Third, the costs of generating housing services increased considerably more rapidly than incomes did, particularly for renters. Nevertheless, owner-occupants and investors in rental housing spurred housing production substantially, so that net additions to the residential stock exceeded household growth and there was an excess of vacant for-sale units. On average, households enjoyed increases in the quantity of housing services consumed, but spent an increasingly large share of their incomes on housing as a result." [17]

The first three trends continued into the recessionary years of the early 1980s, twisting the rent squeeze into a tourniquet for the very poor, while new construction came to a virtual standstill and consumers got less in housing services for their dollar.

Liberal economist Anthony Downs, studying the supply of rental housing at an aggregate level for the entire nation, argues that rents during the 1960s and 1970s did not keep pace with the costs of financing, building, and operating rental housing. Investors stayed in the rental market only because they could take advantage of tax shelters, low real interest rates, and anticipated appreciation that produced profits even when net operating income was zero. [18]

As a result, Downs reasons, since 1960 "rapid increases in operating costs and interest rates, plus lagging rents, have wiped out much of the real value of the nation's rental housing inventory" [19] Since the construction of rental housing in the 1970s was stimulated mainly by tax shelters, leveraging, low real interest rates, and anticipated appreciation, rather than net income, the rise in real interest rates in the 1980s was devastating. The increased costs of borrowing reduced both the benefits of leveraging as well as price increases, thus lowering appreciation upon resale. Those rental owners unable to shift their investments have had little option but to raise rents to increase net operating income.

Institutional changes in the organization of capital markets, financial institutions, lending policies, and tax policy in the late 1970s and early 1980s have made investments in rental units increasingly risky while placing a depressing effect on the economic value of the rental housing inventory. In the urban context this has meant little new construction of rental units, encouraging two types of economic responses: gentrification and abandonment. We agree with Peter Marcuse, who claims that these two responses reflect two larger economic shifts restructuring the employment composition of the central city: "the shift from manufacturing to services, from reliance on mid-level skills to automation and de-skilling, on the one hand, which renders redundant large parts of the workforce and reduces lower-income rent-paying ability; and the increasing professionalization and concentration of management and technical function, on the other, which creates additional higher-income demand for housing. . . . Housing adjacent to central business districts reflects these changes. The pull exerted on one group by the changing economy of the central business district (CBD) fits in with the push against another. For the gentrifiers, all roads lead to downtown. For the poor, all roads lead to abandonment." [20]

Similarly, Downs points out in his longitudinal analysis of national rental housing data that between 1974 and 1979 new units added to the rental housing inventory equaled only 60 percent of what he calls "non-new construction," that is, units that had been temporarily lost from the inventory and then restored through rehabilitation and repair. During the same period, new ownership units exceeded "non-new construction" of ownership units by more than five to one. Overall, new construction of rental units was only slightly more than half (55 percent) the number of rental units renewed from the rental housing inventory. Thus, in the late 1970s the supply of new rental units was dwindling greatly, with rehabilitation and repair of renewable units accounting for an increasing share of construction activity in the rental inventory. Investors were selectively reclaiming buildings from the existing rental stock.[21]

In large cities this reclamation of rental housing, as Marcuse argues, occurred in a concentrated fashion. Enjoying fewer means of ensuring their profits (especially the lack of federal subsidies for new low-income rental construction), investors in rental real estate focused on rehabilitating units for middle- and upper-income households who could afford to pay rents at levels high enough to guarantee net operating income. In order to reduce the risk of a decline in economic value, investors, developers, real estate agents, and others whose livelihood was tied to property development in the residential rental sector concentrated investments in locations so that the economic value of their private developments would be mutually reinforcing.

However, the selective geographic concentration of real estate investment in rental rehabilitation for the prosperous occurred in neighborhoods with a relatively good-quality rental stock whose economic value had been depressed by the sorts of economic pressures mentioned above. Geographically concentrated speculation and upgrading acted to displace existing low-income renters from affordable units into more expensive rental housing nearby. Summarizing evidence compiled from sixteen studies analyzing gentrification, Richard LeGates and Chester Hartman argue that the conventional profile of the young, high-status, prosperous professional moving in was largely correct. The displacees, however, were composed of a heterogeneous socioeconomic mix of households coming mainly from racially mixed lower-middle-class neighborhoods, rather than from neighborhoods composed largely of poor minorities.[22] In effect, reinvestment occurs in urban places where there are still substantial economic and social values, and produces land economic pressures that push the low-income old-timers out.

Furthermore, one of the most crucial values for the newcomers is access to the central city. Analyst Dennis Gale, reporting on the results of a relatively large-scale survey of residential gentrification in central cities between 1974 and 1976, pointed out that most gentrifying neighborhoods were located within two miles of the central business district. Although economic factors of low price and potential appreciation were the main reasons gentrifiers offered for purchasing housing in inner-city neighborhoods, the future value of these factors relied heavily on the central location and accessibility of these neighborhoods.[23]

The accumulating evidence, therefore, indicates that market-rate new construction and rental rehabilitation adds little if anything to the stock of low-income housing and, in fact, may decrease it. Though there may be benefits from gentrification, such as an increased property tax base for the city, these rarely filter down to low-income residents, since few if any municipalities have launched major programs to construct low-income housing.

Most urban neighborhoods with concentrations of rental housing do not possess the physical and locational characteristics that make possible the concentrated reinvestment and upgrading associated with gentrification. Many neighborhoods possess large concentrations of aging rental housing inhabited by low-income residents whose landlords, faced with the same economic pressures of landlords elsewhere—but with the added difficulty of exclusively poor tenants, end up providing poorer quality housing for their tenants. Ironically, as these neighborhoods usually possess the largest proportion of households living in substandard units and overcrowded conditions, they also are the locales where rental housing abandonment is greater.

Owners abandon rental properties when the costs (e.g., maintenance, mortgage payments, repairs, utilities, taxes) exceed rent revenues, producing losses that cannot be offset by tax-shelter benefits or future resale appreciation. Worse yet, the process tends to be geographically contagious. Abandoned buildings reduce the land value of surrounding buildings whose owners now have little incentive to reinvest and repair, but plenty of economic reasons to disinvest and defer repairs. Financial institutions, responding to the perceived risk, steer investment away from such places, turning selective disinvestment into a systematic practice.

Thus, the housing squeeze in big cities of the 1980s exhibits a spatial configuration that violates the basic presuppositions of the filtering model that has guided housing policy since the 1940s. Housing constructed for high-income residents in the central city does not seem to be inducing cycles of downward filtering. The gentrification contributes to the elimination of low-rent units and the displacement of low-income residents. Meanwhile, abandonment continues, pushing outward from depopulated neighborhood clusters of virtually uniform poverty. As a result, not only are increasing numbers of low-income renters kept off the housing escalator that many middle- and working-class homeowners traveled in the 1950s and 1960s, but many find they can no longer afford even the cheapest rental housing and so become homeless.

Recent research conducted by the Congressional Research Service analyzed whether there were enough decent vacant units of sufficient size to accommodate overcrowded and poorly housed households in each of forty-eight metropolitan areas for 1982 and 1983. Using distribution simulations matching different size households with available standard quality vacant units by size, the study failed to find a single metropolitan area with an adequate supply of housing—that is, housing that met minimum standards for habitation or avoided overcrowding.[24] Another study by sociologists James Wright and Julie Lam measured changes in the affordability gap between rental household income and gross rent over a four-year period within a sample of central cities. By measuring changes both in the number of units with affordable rents and the number of households below the official poverty line, this study assessed the extent to which rental affordability problems were due mainly to declining incomes of rental households or the loss of low-rent dwellings. The analysis found that a housing gap for low-income urban residents was emerging on both counts. The population of renters below the poverty line had increased 36 percent, while the number of affordable low-rent units had declined 30 percent.[25] Finally, a 1986 study sponsored by the nonprofit Neighborhood Reinvestment Corporation and conducted by urban planner Phillip Clay projected that between 1983 and the year 2003 the number of poor urban households would increase by 44.5 percent, whereas the number of low-rent housing units would decrease by about 30 percent. The report concludes that by the turn of the century about 18.7 million people will be homeless or on the verge of losing their shelter.[26]

These research findings on the rental housing squeeze link the present low-income housing crisis to a combination of declining incomes and a diminishing supply of low-rent housing, both of which place greater housing burdens on poor households. Furthermore, these studies provide convincing evidence that the decline in the availability of adequate low-rent dwelling units plays the central role in the continuation of homelessness among the poor nationwide.

In order to understand how this process works, we turn next to a more detailed treatment of the current reasons for the loss of SRO hotels in Chicago, and the impact this loss is having on homelessness.

Chicago's Shrinking Supply of SRO Hotels

The destruction of SRO hotels appears to have occurred in two phases, reflecting changes in the city of Chicago's urban renewal policy. The first phase corresponds with the land-clearance programs of renewal initiated in the 1960s, but the second phase corresponds more with pressures for gentrification, supported by municipal housing code regulation, enforcement, and rehabilitation. The first phase concentrated on SRO hotels near downtown; the second phase, still underway, has targeted the structures that remain in attractive and accessible locations along the lakefront.

The Skid Row SROs were destroyed mainly as a result of urban renewal programs implemented in earnest in the 1960s. Table 6.1 in chapter 6 illustrates the effectiveness of these land-clearance policies in eliminating the hotels on Skid Row. The number of low-rent SRO hotel units declined 80 percent between 1960 and 1980. But the destruction was not limited to Skid Row. A 1984 survey of the number of SRO hotel units lost in urban renewal areas estimated that 18,000 SRO hotel units had been converted, abandoned, or destroyed between 1973 and 1984, a loss of almost half the units citywide.[27] Besides the rate of loss in Skid Row, the rate of SRO loss in Chicago has been greatest in a cluster of South Side and a few West Side community areas. However, these changes do not reflect the same causes. In many of the South and West Side areas the local conditions of neighborhood decline, disinvestment, and abandonment undermined the viability of the small SROs (the proportionate loss of South Side SROs was great, but the actual number of units lost was small compared with the Loop and North Side). The loss of the SROs paralleled the loss of other forms of low-rent housing in areas where the majority of the population was simply too poor to pay even the lowest market rents, and where disinvestment and abandonment became the de facto policies of accommodation on the part of owners.

In addition, throughout the 1970s residential rents did not increase at nearly the rate of other consumer goods (especially energy costs and the cost of borrowing money). Landlords faced with rapidly rising costs and slowly increasing rents encountered difficulties not only in maintaining a profitable business but in financing improvements or repairs. The robust and excessive conversion of apartments to condominiums in the late 1970s can be explained in part by the relative attraction of the ownership versus the rental market during the late 1970s. The loss of SRO units in the Loop and North Side areas resulted from pressures for conversion and redevelopment, rather than decline and abandonment. While the socioeconomic status of the population in the vicinity of lost South Side SROs declined between 1970 and 1980, the status of those living near the Loop and North Side SROs increased.

The demise of the St. Regis Hotel offers an excellent example of how the economic pressure of private reinvestment and the resulting escalation in land value and property taxes make the cost of private ownership prohibitive. Bob Berry, manager and co-owner of the St. Regis, sold the 112-year-old hotel at the corner of Grand and Clark streets in the prestigious near North neighborhood in 1985. The new owners promptly converted the hotel into commercial offices. According to Berry, the expenses of running the hotel decreased its profitability at the same time as offers to buy the building increased in frequency and amount. Berry claimed that "electricity, gas and water combined ran him close to $9,000 a month in 1984 and his yearly tax bill was $32,000 on the 110 room structure. Both amounts were double what they were five years ago." [28]

A recent study of downtown office-space construction within the Loop and bordering areas revealed that the office space provided in the recent boom between 1979 and 1984 accounted for 30 percent of all downtown office space constructed since the 1871 Chicago fire! In addition, new (luxury) residential construction has increased during the same period by 500 percent.[29] In part, these new developments reflect changes in federal policies that increasingly discourage investment in residential real estate while encouraging investment in nonresidential real estate—in many cases regardless of the demand for new construction. In the summer of 1985 the vacancy rate for commercial office buildings in Chicago was 17.3 percent.[30] These developments also occurred with the assistance of local government loans, tax breaks, and other public subsidies that encourage their downtown location.

Although the currents of the urban land market may eventually erode the foundations of any low-rent housing near the center of the city, most buildings prove to be formidable obstacles to natural erosion except in the most attractive of locations. Thus, even after the demise of federal redevelopment programs, the main currents of redevelopment have not followed the natural and inevitable contours of the marketplace, but have been channeled by the government policies that subsidize private projects on sites that once harbored SROs.

A recent and relevant example of such a subsidized project is a massive two-part residential development known as Presidential Towers. This project rests on the site of the Skid Row urban renewal area described in chapter 6. The first phase of the development included more than 3,000 apartments in four forty-nine-story towers placed atop three stories of office and commercial space covering two city blocks adjacent to the West Side of the Loop. A consortium of developers purchased the land from the city of Chicago in 1980. Most of the former Skid Row land was vacant at the time of purchase, having been cleared of structures more than ten years earlier as part of the Madison-Canal urban renewal project.[31]

The design of Presidential Towers separates the public activities of the towers from the surrounding streets, promising a self-sufficient environment for the residents. With only 200 of its units equipped with two bedrooms, the Towers attract middle-class singles and couples who work in the downtown area and can afford rents that start at $749 per month. As of 1986, the median age of the residents in Presidential Towers was twenty-eight years, the median salary $31,000. Ironically, 83 percent of the residents are single and, like the SRO hotel residents they displaced, trade off private space for convenience and access to the urban activities unique to the central city.

The development of Presidential Towers was the product of Chicago's urban growth coalition. It illustrates how the powers of government at all levels—local, state, and federal—were used to foster development of profitable upper-income housing at the expense of low-income renters. From its inception the Presidential Towers project received enormous public subsidies. First, the city sold the land in 1980 at the 1968 price of $30.25 per square foot, which was set after the land was cleared of its previous uses. Thus, instead of capturing the enormous increases in land value for the city treasury by requiring the developers to pay market prices, officials allowed the developers to collect this substantial speculative windfall. Second, real estate transfer taxes for both the city of Chicago and the state of Illinois were waived, realizing a savings of $20,000 for the developers. Third, the city paid for demolition of the remaining structures (including an SRO hotel) and provided improvements such as sidewalks and street lighting. The combined cost was $1,215,000. Fourth, the city sold $180 million in municipal bonds at 9 percent interest; the developers used this as a short-term construction loan instead of using loans at higher interest from private financial institutions. In addition, the city of Chicago offered the developers a long-term $5.8 million loan at 2 percent interest, using the money the city had earned on the receipts from the large bond sale between the time of the sale and the time it was used to pay for construction. Finally, the developers secured a $158 million mortgage insured by the federal government at 9.5 percent interest, a bargain rate in the early 1980s.

Despite these subsidies of cheap land, low-interest construction loans, and a low-risk fixed-interest mortgage, the developers requested and received from Congress three profitable exemptions. First, the investors and developers were released from paying penalties of $3 million the developers incurred after delaying insignature of the federal mortgage commitment within the standard two-year limit. Second, the investors received permission to use accelerated rather than straight-line depreciation in calculating their tax loss. This enabled the investors to write off the cost of the building at a much faster rate than actual depreciation. These tax savings translated into greater earnings of nearly $7 million for the investors. Third, the developers were allowed to ignore their original commitment to ensure that 20 percent of the units would be rented to low- and moderate-income households. Although Congress had passed the Ullman provision in 1980 requiring developers who used funds from the sale of municipal bonds to set aside 20 percent of the apartments for low- and moderate-income households, the developers of Presidential Towers received a special exemption with the aid of U.S. Representative Daniel Rostenkowski, a longtime Chicago Democrat and chair of the powerful House Ways and Means Committee.

The total amount of public expenses associated with Presidential Towers, including direct expenditures and lost revenues to city, state, and federal governments, has been estimated at over $100 million.

Reshaping the residential landscape of downtown with projects like Presidential Towers required the purposeful collaboration of powerful public officials, investors, and developers to overcome the inertia of earlier developments. Unwilling to bear the risk associated with efforts to overcome the legacy of past investments, private investors relied on public subsidies to virtually eliminate their risk and ensure their profits. Thus, it is inconceivable that the construction of this project would have come about without these millions of dollars of public funds. But when development uses public funds to decide the destiny of SRO hotels, that destiny usually proves fatal to these buildings. Once public officials identify an SRO hotel as an obstacle to redevelopment plans, that hotel's gradual slide into obsolescence turns quickly into a reckless plunge.

Besides siphoning off public resources that might have been better spent for pressing urban needs, the Presidential Towers project required the destruction of an SRO hotel (the Starr Hotel), displacing about three hundred residents. Since the city and the developers used federal funds to support this project, the forced evictions of residential or commercial tenants required a payment of compensation by the local government (using federal funds) to those forced to move. Under the Uniform Relocation Act of 1970, each displaced SRO resident was eligible for up to $4,250 of relocation assistance. Local officials, however, gave the residents a token payment of ten dollars each—regardless of need or eligibility.

The injustice and indignity of this failure to follow even the most modest requirement for public compensation inspired the *Lacko* vs. *City of Chicago* lawsuit, filed in the name of a displaced SRO resident by lawyers from the Chicago Legal Assistance Foundation. The court eventually found the city in violation of federal guidelines (using federal funds to demolish the Starr Hotel and failing to compensate the evicted residents) and required that the city track down, where possible, those displaced and pay the compensation the tenants deserved (as much as $4,250). Additionally, the city was required to prepare a report documenting both the loss of SRO units over the preceding ten years and the housing needs of low-income single households. Although drafts of this report circulated in 1985, no official report has yet been completed outlining a plan of action.

Although the case of Presidential Towers may offer an extreme example of public subsidy for private gain, its process of upscale development and subsequent loss of SRO units is typical. A more common scenario is that unfolding around the Rialto Hotel. Barbara Bratman, a reporter for the *Chicago Tribune*, interviewed several tenants of the Rialto in early 1988. The tenants face certain displacement after the building is demolished in

conjunction with construction of the new Chicago library across the street.
Many of the residents, already displaced from other previously demolished
SRO hotels, expressed frustration mixed with a sense of resignation.[32]

> They speak of the inevitable as just that. "Everybody knows it's coming
> down," said a Rialto resident who identified himself as Edward. . . . Edward
> seemed to sympathize with those who do not want his 10 year home—or him
> —around. "You're gonna build a library, you don't want a building like this
> there," he said.

Discussing the future of the hotel with residents uncovered a skepticism
based on long experience enduring the burdens imposed by others. One
resident claimed the city would simply put a parking lot on the hotel site,
and another complained that it would not even build the library at all. The
deputy commissioner of the Department of Planning could be no more
specific as to the future use for the site than "some kind of retail use."

Although the city officials explained they would provide relocation benefits to any eligible displaced residents, the obsolescence and expendability
of the hotel were never questioned. The residents, however, expressed to
Bratmann considerable satisfaction with their SRO accommodations.

> "It's about as perfect as you can get it," said Charles Martinez. "It ain't a
> bad place for the rent you pay," said Andrew Cantore, who, like Martinez,
> pays $140 a month for his room. "There ain't no bed bugs in this place.
> Maybe a few roaches."

Though hardly the qualities that would fulfill the dreams of housing reformers, the permanance, privacy, and affordability of the Rialto make this
hotel a valuable resource for its tenants, especially since they know all too
well their limited shelter options.

> Martinez once stayed in a shelter for a year, abiding by its strict rules on
> when to arrive for a night's bed. He has been at the Rialto for eight years and
> prefers it vastly. "You go in and out like anybody else," he said. "It should
> be like any place else."

Many SRO hotels located in neighborhoods with less development pressure than those near the central business district still face the obstacles
of public regulations that undermine the economic viability of the hotels.
Our conversations with hotel owners and our discovery of the relative stability of most residents convinced us that for the majority of the tenants,
the SRO serves more as a long-term apartment than a short-term hotel.
The licensing requirement and some building code regulations, however,
consider the SRO buildings exclusively in terms of what is now an obsolete use—short-term transients. In addition, changes in the codes over the
years have introduced higher standards that virtually all SRO hotels vio-
late by reason of age. Though ensuring the safety of tenants is critical, the

strict implementation of these inappropriate standards could in most cases leave the owner with the limited options of conversion or demolition and new construction. Protecting the safety promised tenants would in this case undermine their shelter security.

Ironically, the existence of strict building codes also frequently promotes less safety by generating an atmosphere of profound uncertainty. Since owners may at any time be subject to the strict enforcement of existing rules, this constant threat discourages large and costly investments or repairs because a forced shutdown would mean a loss from both the original and more recent investments. In addition, the strict rules increase the arbitrary discretion of those who enforce them. In other words, since the rules make every SRO unsafe and the city is unwilling to enforce that rule strictly, uneven, idiosyncratic, and perhaps even corrupt enforcement practices may develop. Either side of the paradox yields uncertainty, diminishing the economic predictability associated with the ownership of SROs. Furthermore, the economic uncertainty is compounded when financial institutions treat it as an unacceptable form of risk and so refuse to give loans to the owners of SRO hotels.

SRO hotel owners complained about the difficulty they faced in obtaining loans from financial institutions to pay for major improvements or in obtaining a mortgage. Their difficulty stems from the traditional image of the SRO hotel as a flophouse for poor transients; the hotel is viewed by lenders as a high-risk property. Discussions with owners about operating and maintenance costs, vacancy rates, rental income, and the overall economy of the buildings did indicate that the return on investment (presuming no disinvestment or bleeding on the owners' part) was modest and the risk moderate, compared with other investment opportunities in the real estate market. Most important, however, the SRO hotels are neither losing propositions nor extremely risky investments. Had the SROs economically conformed to their poor social reputation, they would have disappeared decades ago.

Until recently, the social stigma and small rooms of SRO hotels also discouraged federal agencies (mainly the Department of Housing and Urban Development, or HUD) from making low-income SRO tenants eligible for shelter subsidies.[33] In 1985 the secretary of HUD, Samuel Pierce, Jr., reported that his agency would waive restrictions on the use of section 8 rental certificates by individuals. Section 8 certificates, which entitle their holders to a substantial rent subsidy, usually go to eligible families. Despite this favorable decision for low-income SRO tenants, there are reports that HUD officials have not supported policies that benefit SROs. For instance, before localities can seek funds for SROs, local officials must demonstrate that no other low-income housing for individuals is available. The HUD bureaucrats assume that small rooms without baths represent substandard housing and should only be preserved as housing of last resort.[34] In addition, this decision was made at a time when funding for the section 8 program has virtually dried up.

The residents of Chicago SROs, on the contrary, told us they chose SRO living not simply because of the push of affordability but also because of the convenience and security the social management of these buildings make possible (see chapter 8). Many persons without private baths would have preferred to rent rooms with a bath. However, if renting a room with a bath meant paying more rent or losing the services, convenience, and security of the SRO hotel, the additional room was not worth the sacrifice. Housing standards based primarily on measures of physical space do not adequately capture the alternative, valuable social benefits of the SRO residential environment.

SRO hotels are being lost in Chicago, and in other cities, not because they are bad investments—both the evidence from tenants and cost accounting data from landlords dispute this—but because of public policy. Policy at both city and federal levels reflects a view that devalues SRO-type housing, relegating these structures to the bottom of the priority list for preservation. As a result, when public decisions pit the future of an SRO hotel against virtually any competing use, the SRO hotel loses the contest. The consequence, of course, is the unabated loss of affordable housing for the urban single poor, many of whom go without any shelter at all.

SRO Losses and Homelessness in Chicago

Like other industrial cities in the Northeast and Midwest, Chicago absorbed a disproportionate share of the job loss during the two recessions of the early 1980s. In particular, blacks in the Chicago work force were disproportionately employed in the manufacturing industries that suffered some of the highest rates of unemployment. The black community, which already endured twice the rate of unemployment as whites, absorbed even greater economic hardship as a result of the restructuring. In 1983, the first year of recovery from the 1982 recession, the median income for black Chicago households was $14,520, compared with $24,001 for whites. One year later the median income for white households had increased by about $1,000, whereas that of blacks had declined by about the same amount.[35]

In Chicago the economic hardships fueled a surge in the number of GA recipients, from 68,000 in 1981 to about 120,000 in 1983. The benefit levels, however, remained the same, at $154 per month. A study of new GA applicants and recipients in 1984 found that two out of three (67 percent) had turned to welfare only after having lost full-time employment and been unable to secure another job before they ran out of money. Changes in federal welfare policy that restricted eligibility had, it seems, only a modest effect on the increasing number of new GA applicants. Roughly one in ten of the new GA applicants had turned to the welfare of last resort because other sources of benefits had been cut off. The newcomers were mainly young (43.5 percent were less than twenty-four years of age), black (71 percent), and male (68 percent); their primary reason for applying for GA was the difficulty in finding a job (78 percent).[36]

Between 1970 and 1983 the vacancy rate for all rental units in Chicago increased from 6.7 percent to 7.5 percent. Compared with Los Angeles and especially New York City, where rental vacancy rates dipped below 3 percent in the early 1980s, Chicago's rental market was under less strain. But these figures do not adequately depict the market. Although the average rent is lower in Chicago than these places, the consumer benefits do not filter evenly across income levels. Higher income renters have benefited from the high vacancy rates in luxury apartments, whereas low-income renters scramble for a decreasing supply of low-rent units.[37]

A good indicator of the segmented impact is household rent burden, the percentage of annual gross household income paid in rent. HUD has set 30 percent as the maximum allowable rent burden for low-income households participating in rent subsidy programs, increased from 25 percent in 1981 to reduce the benefit levels to subsidy recipients. Households paying more than 30 percent of their income for shelter are carrying an excessive rent burden, according to this standard.

The median rent burden for all Chicago tenant households increased from 21 percent to 30 percent between 1970 and 1983. Whereas only one-fourth of Chicago renters paid more than 35 percent of the annual income for rent in 1970, this proportion had jumped to nearly two of five renter households (39.5 percent) by 1983. This excessive burden was perversely distributed. Households suffering rent burdens greater than 60 percent of their gross income almost doubled during the eight years after 1975, accounting for more than one in five rental households by 1983. An equally disturbing measure of inequality was that in the same year, almost *half* the black renter households (47.8 percent) carried rent burdens of 35 percent or more, with 30 percent paying 60 percent or more of their incomes in rent. Housing affordability is definitely a problem for low-income households, especially those that are black, in Chicago.

The increasing pressure on household shelter budgets became so extreme in part because the growth in income dropped precipitously in the late 1970s. Income and rent increases were evenly matched in the first five years of the decade. However, during the recovery years of 1975 through 1979 median incomes increased 43.6 percent as median rents went up only 30.6 percent. This improvement was swamped by what followed. Between 1979 and 1983 median incomes posted only a 16-percent gain, compared with a median rent increase of almost 42 percent. The gap became so great that many young adults in low-income households could not afford to form separate households, and others who could no longer afford to pay increasing rents moved in with relatives. The result frequently was overcrowding. By 1979 overcrowding (more than one person per room) had declined to less than 7 percent of all renter households. However, after the recession struck, the number of overcrowded households jumped up to almost 8.5 percent—approximately 52,000 Chicago households.

Results of a special telephone survey sampling all Chicago residents in 1985 corroborated the findings from the Annual Housing Survey and offer evidence of the economic hardships low-income households experienced between 1981 and 1983. Almost 13 percent of Chicago renter households missed at least one rent payment during this period, and another 1.2 percent were evicted. Calculated in raw numbers, this comes out to about 81,000 households that had fallen behind in rent, with 7,600 evicted. These hardships fell disproportionately on black, young, low-income households, most of them female-headed households or those of unattached single males.[38]

During the recession years of the early 1980s the number of low-rent units was declining at the same time that the number of low-income households was increasing. Almost half the rental units (46 percent) removed from the Chicago housing stock between 1979 and 1983 had rented for less than $175 per month (the rent a household earning $6,000 would pay by carrying a rent burden of 35 percent). In 1983 only 12 percent of rental households enjoyed rents less than $175. Most of the units lost were abandoned by owners who could no longer afford to profitably maintain the buildings at rents low-income tenants could afford to pay. A 1982 study by the Chicago City Planning Department, for instance, listed 7,000 buildings vacant, 20,000 in need of repair, and 1,000 uninhabitable. Another 65,000 units citywide were considered not worth rehabilitating since the cost of repairs would have exceeded the cost of demolition and replacement. Finally, the study made it clear that the loss of rental units was concentrated in poor neighborhoods with large, poor minority populations.[39]

The shelter hardship of poor households was made even worse by the loss of low-rent units for both single unattached persons and large households whose members were doubling up. Single-room units (units with no bedrooms according to AHS data) were being removed from the market far faster than they were being replaced. Thus, between 1970 and 1983 there was a net reduction of all rental housing of 14 percent, but single units with no bedrooms declined by 45 percent citywide. Compared with other types of low-rent housing, the SROs faced virtual elimination by the year 2000.

The burden of shelter uncertainty was distributed unevenly among SRO hotel residents in 1985. During the six months preceding our interview about 15 percent of the residents had been displaced from their prior residence because of economic pressures, and almost one in ten (9.5 percent) had slept outside or in an emergency shelter at least once. These high rates of displacement and acute shelter deprivation among residents indicate that the SRO hotels provide an important haven for those who have managed to escape the streets. In this respect, the SROs in the 1980s continue to function as they always have for members of the single urban poor.

The SRO residents who had slept outside differed little in marital status, race, or education when compared with the homeless interviewed in the NORC study of Chicago. However, there was one significant difference. None of those SRO residents who had slept out in the 1980s were women, whereas almost one in four of those counted among the homeless in the NORC study was a woman. In effect, this means that women who have suffered serious shelter privation and managed to obtain increased economic security have not used SROs as a place to stay. Whether this is because of the undesirability of SRO accommodations, the rent level, the small number of women who obtain economic security, or other reasons we do not know.[40]

Like other homeless people, the SRO residents who had recently slept outside or in a shelter possessed significantly fewer close relationships with kin than did the other SRO residents. Though only one in four of the other residents reported no close kin relations, nearly one in two of those who had slept out lacked any close ties with relatives. Lacking such kinship ties meant that those who had slept out had little opportunity to seek shelter from relatives in a time of crisis. Research on economic hardship among working-class households in Chicago and elsewhere has documented that people first turn to kin for shelter when they face the prospect of going homeless.[41] Furthermore, besides kin, most poor single people, especially men, have no one else to turn to for shelter. So, for instance, although the residents who had endured the dangers of the street possessed close ties with friends in the same proportion as other SRO residents, these friends were not likely to take them in as roommates.

By the time of our interview the previously shelter-deprived residents had managed to acquire sufficient income to pay rent. However, they enjoyed less economic independence than did other SRO residents. Forty percent remained dependent on unearned transfer payments (mainly GA payments), compared with only 23 percent of the other residents. This condition was especially true for those who had slept out in 1985. Almost 70 percent of these men relied on GA benefits to pay their rent. Although less secure than their SRO neighbors, those SRO residents who had slept outside were considerably better off than those still without shelter. For instance, the average monthly income of the homeless on the street or in shelters in 1985 was $168, compared with $462 for those SRO residents who had previously slept out in the 1980s.[42]

The hierarchy of shelter uncertainty to which the working poor are subject is based on persistent conditions of low economic status intensified by unexpected economic, physical, and social hardships. Residing in an SRO increases the shelter security of those with low incomes, by offering not only affordable rent but control and privacy, a place in which household disputes that lead to sleeping outside are unlikely.

The images used to identify the "new" homeless tend to separate these victims of acute economic hardship from the ranks of those who evidence chronic but less debilitating economic burdens. These images do not simply reflect a social condition but actually shape public expectations, including the expectations of researchers. In Chicago, for instance, the NORC study of the homeless was designed to find, identify, and survey only those people facing the most acute (i.e., day-to-day) shelter uncertainty.

The analysts estimated that within Chicago the number of people sleeping outside or in emergency shelters on an average night was 2,020. These estimates were considerably smaller than the numbers used by local advocates for the homeless, who had previously claimed there were as many as 25,000 homeless in Chicago. The public release of the NORC estimates set off a series of rancorous political debates in which the advocates dismissed the study as politically biased (the state of Illinois had contributed $50,000) and methodologically flawed. Regardless of the methodological criticisms, the narrow focus made sure that only those facing daily shelter uncertainty who ended up on the streets or in emergency shelters would count among the "new" homeless.[43]

Sorting poor people without any place to sleep into a separate group deserving special attention and care has tended to promote the belief that the homeless make up some kind of social type. If such were the case, we would expect to find that the characteristics of the homeless would distinguish them from other members of the poor. The fact is, however, that those coping with daily shelter uncertainty differ little from those across the threshold of minimal shelter security. The social characteristics of Chicago's homeless in the 1980s closely match those of SRO hotel residents. But although the social differences are small, the economic differences are big. The homeless are urban poor people who either cannot afford to rent a room or can no longer share space with relatives and friends.

The poor residents of SROs can be arrayed along a hierarchy of shelter uncertainty from those most secure at the top who rent by the month to those least secure on the bottom who rent from day to day. The greater the shelter uncertainty, the greater the burden of economic hardship. Shelter uncertainty is thus a form of economic hardship among the poor, especially the poor residents of SROs whose households usually include only a single household member. Such shelter uncertainty has always been a hardship for the poor, but its scope and intensity have increased for the poor SRO residents in the past two decades because of the destruction of single-room accommodations and the increasing incidence of poverty among single working-class men and women.

Thus, thirty years ago when Bogue studied the residents of Chicago's Skid Row, the homeless did not stand out as a particularly serious social problem because in 1958 even the most destitute single poor person usually managed to obtain shelter in the cheap and plentiful cubicle hotels or missions of Skid Row, while the more prosperous members of the working poor (wage workers and retirees on Social Security or a pension) rented rooms in the SRO hotels. Street people were primarily derelicts who congregated in Skid Row. The spatial breakup of Skid Row and the demolition of SRO hotels, however, separated the destitute poor from the social and economic means of obtaining cheap shelter and employment. Thus, in the 1980s the economic difference between the independent and dependent members of the single urban poor has widened and been institutionalized, because of the spatial dispersal of the dependent poor who sleep in public places throughout the city or in emergency shelters organized and funded by public or private caretakers. Map 9-1 compares the locations of the permanent shelters for the homeless as of 1987 with the locations of SRO hotels in 1985. The remaining hotels cluster at major intersections along the North-South lakefront public transportation lines, whereas the shelters are scattered within the poorest residential neighborhoods. Emergency shelter beds are concentrated in the impoverished West Side neighborhoods, while hotel rooms are concentrated in the gentrifying lakefront neighborhoods (see Map 9-2).

Table 9-1 compares the social and economic characteristics of SRO residents and shelter residents for both 1958 and 1985. The first two columns compare social and economic differences between the independent poor living in SRO hotels and the dependent poor residing in cubicle hotels and missions on Chicago's Skid Row in 1958. The third and fourth columns compare differences on the same measures for SRO hotel residents and emergency shelter residents in 1985. The table illustrates two important findings: first, that the two segments of the single poor differ little in social composition in either 1958 or 1985, with the exception of race in 1958 and age in 1985; second, that both differ significantly in terms of economic status. The homeless in 1985 were much more likely to be unemployed, possess very little income, and rely on public aid than were the cubicle and mission residents in 1958. Socially, the SRO tenants and the shelter residents are members of the same social class, whether in 1958 or 1985. Economically, however, if we accept as given that obtaining sufficient income to meet the threshold of the cheapest available shelter remains a prerequisite for independence, then it is clear that unlike the cubicle inhabitants in 1958, the shelter residents in 1985 have been unable to cross this economic threshold. The cubicles were horrible physical environments, but they offered a cheap, secure, and private place to stay.

The dependent poor living in the missions and cubicle hotels of Skid Row in the 1950s, like other SRO residents, had access to many social and economic networks (some of which were exploitive and illegitimate) of Skid Row which they could use to increase their incomes, improve their

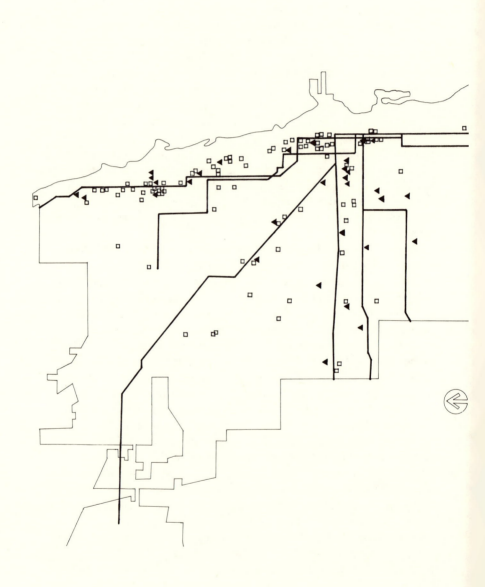

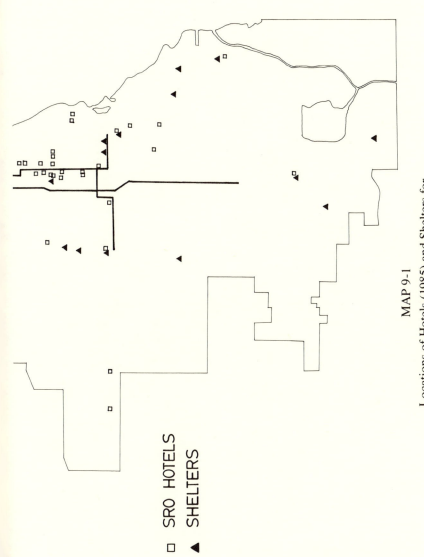

□ SRO HOTELS

▲ SHELTERS

MAP 9-1

Locations of Hotels (1985) and Shelters for
the Homeless (1987) in Chicago

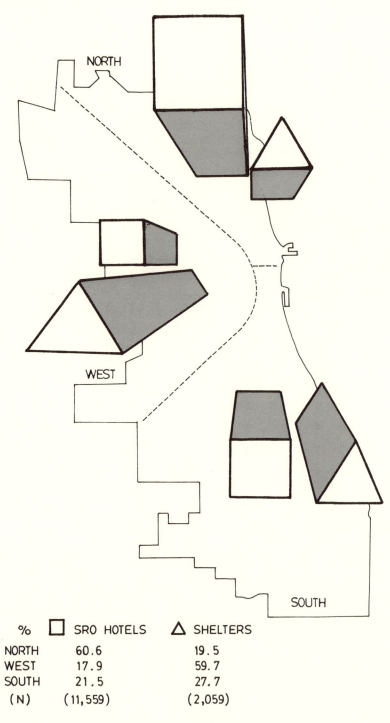

%	□ SRO HOTELS	△ SHELTERS
NORTH	60.6	19.5
WEST	17.9	59.7
SOUTH	21.5	27.7
(N)	(11,559)	(2,059)

MAP 9-2

Proportionate Distribution of Hotel Rooms and Shelter Beds in Chicago

TABLE 9-1

Social and Economic Profiles of SRO and
Shelter Tenants, 1958 and 1985

	1958		1985	
CHARACTERISTIC	SRO (%)	Shelter (%)	SRO (%)	Shelter (%)
Social				
Male	96.0	96.0	77.8	75.5
< 35 yrs.	6.0	14.8	24.9	38.4
> 55 yrs.	52.0	27.1	33.0	19.4
Black	2.0	31.0	48.4	53.0
Single	97.0	99.0	92.8	92.1
< High school diploma	94.0	93.2	79.5	76.5
Economic				
Employed	42.0	42.0	41.0	34.5
< $5000 income	46.5	58.8	47.1	95+
On some aid	44.8	49.0	35.1	54.1
Services	57.2	31.5	32.4	21.6
Laborers	14.3	36.8	9.3	53.5
Transience				
< 1 yr. in Chicago	25.9	39.2	7.0	11.1
Total N	(146)	(112)	(185)	(722)

Note: The 1958 figures were derived from D. E. Mackelman, *The Homeless Man on Skid Road* (Chicago: Tenants Relocation Bureau, 1961). Data in the SRO column reflect the characteristics of the North Clark residents, 71% of whom lived in SRO hotels; data in the shelter column describes those in the South State area who lived in missions (13.7%) or large (300 or more) cubicle hotels (55.7%). Breakdowns by shelter type only were not available. For the 1985 data, the characteristics of the shelter population were obtained from a 1985 study conducted in Chicago by the National Opinion Research Center. The employment rate for this shelter population is somewhat misleading in that only 3% reported that they worked at steady jobs. The 1958 income data was adjusted to reflect 1985 dollars.

economic security, and perhaps eventually afford to rent a single room. The shelter occupants of the 1980s are dispersed, with few ties to a residential community of their own. Unable to rely on their own limited skills and without access to the social institutions of Skid Row SRO hotels, the contemporary homeless can turn only to public and private caretakers for help. The contemporary homeless, therefore, become increasingly dependent on

caretakers from the middle class whose sincere and generous aid undermines the dignity of the homeless, relieving, at best, only their immediate
needs.

Conclusions

Evidence of the spread of poverty, of increasing economic hardship
among the poor, and of the close ties between increasing poverty, the declining supply of low-income housing, and increases in homelessness strongly
point to economic and political causes for the homeless problem. The contemporary homeless come from the ranks of the working class, but they do
so in an urban economy where low-paying service jobs are expanding at
the same time as the availability of inexpensive living accommodations is
contracting. Unlike earlier periods when single white ethnic males carried
the burden of low-paying industrial jobs, the burden has been shifted to
minority youth and women in the expanding service sector of the post-
industrial metropolis. In the 1970s and 1980s the middle-aged and elderly
single poor represent a decreasing proportion of the homeless as the number of young single men and women (many with children) increases. Thus,
the social composition of the contemporary homeless reflects the social
composition of a growing poor population.

We believe the contemporary homeless have become the problem of the
"new" homeless because the dependent poor can no longer settle in the
SRO hotels of Skid Row communities. The loss of thousands of SRO units
has also intensified the social dependence of these growing ranks of the
single working poor. Ironically, the destruction of SROs has continued to
be justified during the 1970s and 1980s by analysts, reporters, caretakers,
developers, and public officials who deplore the lack of affordable housing
and yet dismiss the demolition of SROs as simply the removal of substandard blight. Squeezed out of the rental market by the dual pressures
of declining income and increasing housing costs, and no longer able to
use the resources of the SRO hotels, the homeless rely instead on service
providers, charities, and public institutions for income, benefits, and care.
Meanwhile, the most deprived spend their days on the streets in neighborhoods and public spaces where their poverty, illness, and unkempt physical
appearance make them a public eyesore subject to the gaze and judgment
of the more prosperous passers-by. Their visible vulnerability inspires both
compassion and contempt, creating the moral foundations for the social
problem of the 1980s—the "new" homeless.

10 The "New" Homeless and the Skid Row Stereotype

The story of the SRO hotels and their residents provides an important prelude to a critical reassessment of the problem of the "new" homeless in the 1980s. Misconceptions about Skid Row residents and the SRO hotel way of life have played a central role in framing public debates about the contemporary homeless. Specifically, analysts have mistakenly used the stereotype of the Skid Row bum to provide a blameworthy image of the "old" homeless against which they contrast the moral innocence of the "new" homeless. The salience of this moral contrast between the "old" homeless on skid row and the "new" homeless reflects the intensity of the ideological disputes between liberal Democrats and conservative Republicans as well as disagreements among professional caretakers (advocates and service providers) about the nature and scope of contemporary homelessness. The liberals appear to have won the first round of ideological disputes, with compassion displacing blame as the proper public response to the homeless. The professional service providers appear to be winning the second, as eclectic definitions of the "new" homeless now catalogue and rank the homeless according to individual vulnerabilities, especially mental illness. The combination of moral desert and dependent vulnerability justifies the legislation of liberal politicians funding shelter and services for the homeless, while enabling diverse professional caretakers to take responsibility for treating the particular dependency that matches their expertise.

The homeless poor, when studied in this century, have usually been found to have a disproportionate share of physical illness and social problems as compared with the general population. We do not mean to diminish the significance of the needs those vulnerabilities impose on the poor, but we do mean to criticize those who would identify these needs as the problem and so propose treating the vulnerabilities as its solution. The portrayal of the "new" homeless as a dependent population overwhelmed by personal vulnerabilities has led analysts to focus on individuals, deflecting attention away from explanations attributing the growth in the homeless population to actions taken by powerful social, economic, and political institutions.

199

We believe that analysts of the "new" homeless, instead of contrasting images of these people as deserving victims against the stereotypical images of the undeserving bum on Skid row, should focus on the social continuity between the two groups. The beginning chapters of this book were written to revise misconceptions of the "old" homeless that have obscured the social community of the urban single poor and the value of SRO hotel as a crucial component of the infrastructure that made this community possible. The residents of Skid Row and the SRO hotels were not for the most part disaffiliated bums or immoral derelicts. They were poor single people using the modest resources of the Skid Row community to secure both a living and a modicum of independence. The struggle for autonomy has always been a crucial ingredient of social life among poor SRO hotel residents, whether on the Main Stem of the 1920s, the Skid Row of the 1960s, or the remaining hotel clusters in the 1980s. Thus, the "new" homeless do not differ in moral character from their predecessors. The "new" homeless want to earn a living and protect their independence. What sets the contemporary homeless apart from their predecessors is not their moral integrity or greater vulnerability, but the loss of SRO hotels and the community resources of Skid Row that enabled single poor people to survive the hardships of poverty with their autonomy intact.

The Homeless as a New Social Problem

Since the early 1980s the "new" urban homeless have been subjected to extensive media exposure, research analysis, and a variety of local service programs. Despite many disagreements about the scope of homelessness, reporters, academics, caretakers, and officials all seem to assume that the urban homeless of the 1980s are essentially a new kind of social problem.

Media accounts spotlight the human-interest stories of elderly street people or middle-class families on the skids. Research studies and official reports emphasize that the "new" homelessness on the streets and in shelters is different from that of the Skid Row derelict. The contrast helps analysts ensure that the images and stories they use to represent the "new" homeless to the general public avoid the social stigma long associated with the Skid Row homeless. The typical portrayal of Skid Row homeless holds these men accountable for their privations and so portrays them as undeserving. The plight of the derelicts and deviants on Skid Row may evoke compassion, but it is a compassion tainted with blame. Contemporary assessments of the "new" homeless, with few exceptions, treat them as unfortunate victims who deserve assistance in coping with debilitating circumstances beyond their control. Efforts to respect the moral integrity of the homeless emphasize the differences between Skid Row and contemporary homeless while overlooking important similarities.

Why did homeless people become a national social problem in the early

1980s? Clearly, any historical review of the working poor—especially the transient hoboes and tramps—will uncover extensive periods of homelessness, as is evident from our accounts in earlier chapters. The homeless, like other members of the poor, have always been among us. The fact of homeless people itself, therefore, does not explain why others labeled their plight a new and important social problem deserving public attention and professional care in the 1980s.

The homeless emerged as an important social problem at about the same time reporters and media analysts were documenting the initial effects of the 1981–82 economic recession. We cannot identify a precise threshold at which homelessness moved from the background to the foreground of public attention. We can, however, identify the crucial point that denoted a successful passage—when the homeless became a symbol of incipient social failure on the part of others, whether an uncaring and selfish public, a mean-spirited government administration, or a faltering economy. As human-interest reports expanded from descriptive accounts of personal tragedy and suffering to include speculations about the responsibility of others, the homeless came to represent innocent victims of precipitous downward social mobility. Tales of downward mobility delivered the most powerful symbolic punch, as otherwise innocent and successful families told how they slipped from middle-class security into near-complete destitution through no fault of their own.[1] Despite the exceptional nature of such cases in fact, they proved credible to the public at large.

Initially, conservative officials, analysts, and reporters protested vociferously against this sort of interpretation, arguing that homeless individuals had done something to merit their predicament. Conservatives like Thomas Main argued that the homeless were actually choosing free shelters so as to avoid paying rent. Just as the nineteenth-century Charity Organization Society of New York City had criticized police provision of lodging and church-organized relief as practices promoting indolence and vagrancy among their clientele, so did conservatives contend that public assistance and shelter for the homeless contribute to the loss of moral integrity among those served.[2] However, the conservative defense of the work ethic by blaming the homeless relied on an appeal to a possessive individualism that had been rejected with public acceptance of the New Deal in the 1930s and that was inconsistent with the expectations of citizens grown accustomed to the social entitlements guaranteed by the welfare state. Furthermore, the projection of moral inferiority upon the homeless at the same time as human-interest stories encouraged the public to recognize the homeless as middle-class people who had fallen on hard times placed the conservatives in the position of apparently criticizing members of their middle-class majority as moral failures.

Liberals took advantage of this misplaced ideological attack and successfully transformed the issue into the social problem of the "new" homeless.

They emphasized the dignity and moral respectability of the homeless, blaming their condition on vulnerability rather than their moral character. Tragic stories of the struggle to survive in the face of unexpected and inevitable uncertainties of economic decline emphasized the limitations of poor education, the disadvantage of poverty, and other characteristics of the homeless that frustrated their efforts to make ends meet. Unlike the "old" homeless on Skid Row who allegedly rejected the work ethic and other social responsibilities, the "new" homeless were responsible people unwittingly overcome by a combination of their own vulnerabilities and changing circumstances. Thus, instead of punishment, the "new" homeless needed help to overcome their vulnerabilities. The appropriate response to homelessness was not punitive social control measures, but compassionate caretaking.

The conservative attack and the liberal defense of the "new" homeless produced a national social problem whose actual dimensions were largely unknown in 1982. As conservatives recognized the limited appeal of their portrayals of the homeless, they turned instead to arguments that minimized the scale of the problem. They shifted the debate from the realm of moral deserts to the arena of policy analysis and research.

The threat of punitive fiscal and regulatory measures by conservative federal and local officials in 1982 and 1983 encouraged liberal professional analysts from disparate disciplines to overlook their disciplinary differences and form political coalitions dedicated to a reform agenda for providing more services and shelter for the homeless. These coalitions sponsored local surveys designed to count the homeless and document the reasons homeless people gave for their lack of shelter, which the service providers and advocates were convinced would discredit the moral assessment of the conservatives—that the homeless were undeserving vagrants. Working with modest budgets, researchers used methodological shortcuts that, although they provided relatively accurate profiles of the homeless as deserving victims, produced relatively inflated and therefore unreliable estimates of the number of homeless people.[3] The most dramatic figure was proposed by Hombs and Snyder, who claimed in 1983 that as many as one out of a hundred persons were homeless, or about 2.2 million people nationwide.[4] This figure quickly circulated in popular press accounts, intensifying the ideological debate, as conservatives vehemently disputed the figure while liberals used the large number as evidence of social policy failure on the part of a conservative administration largely indifferent to the problems of the poor. The administration sponsored a study through HUD for the purpose of calculating a reliable estimate of the number of homeless nationwide, their characteristics, and the availability of emergency shelters.[5] Begun in January 1984, the study results were published in May 1984. The authors estimated the number of homeless nationwide at somewhere between 250,000 and 300,000. Liberal legislators, advocates, and service providers criticized the report for purposely minimizing the estimate to meet conservative expectations, and social analysts criticized the methodological shortcuts used by the consultants who conducted the study.[6] As a consequence, instead of reducing controversy, the low-budget HUD study actually contributed to the ongoing dispute.

Ironically, the heat of the ideological dispute with the conservatives encouraged professional caretakers and political organizers to overlook their own ideological differences and focus on their common interest in the homeless as a growing population in need of help. This consensus is typified in research reports that list the causes of homelessness, emphasizing the complexity of the problem and the multiplicity of causes but without assigning primacy or priority to any one. This eclectic analysis justified a shopping list of policies, which would appeal to coalition members from different professional disciplines holding different policy priorities.

The major ideological difference among the liberals emerged between the professionals and other caretakers who argued that the homeless deserve shelter because they are vulnerable and needy, and the political advocates who contended that the homeless possessed a right to shelter as citizens. Although potentially compatible frames of moral reference in theory, the practical implications of each frame of reference for policy tended to produce distinct and increasingly separate political demands: a politics of compassion and a politics of entitlement.

The Politics of Compassion

Once the coalitions succeeded in having the policy dispute over whether or not to aid the homeless framed in the language of physical and social vulnerability rather than the language of individual moral failure, the politics of compassion quickly overcame the punitive moralism of the conservatives, who were forced to retreat. The outcome was broad recognition and acceptance of homelessness as a legitimate social problem deserving attention and treatment.

Professional caretakers and service providers played a crucial role in establishing which characteristics of the homeless count as vulnerabilities contributing to the inability of the homeless to secure permanent shelter. Doctors, social workers, lawyers, counselors, and a variety of paraprofessional service workers acknowledged that a variety of conditions could cause homelessness. However, the politics of compassion favored assigning moral priority to the treatment of those homeless who were most vulnerable. The emphasis on compassion tended to bias the interpretations of research findings about the homeless in ways that confused causal primacy with moral priority, which had an enormous impact on program development. Thus, even though no studies of the homeless could claim to have assessed the relative influence of different conditions that might cause homelessness, studies that found a high incidence of some vulnerability were used by reporters as if that vulnerability were the primary cause of homelessness. The moral priority assigned those homeless who possessed the most visible and debilitating vulnerability, usually mental illness, therefore, led consumers of the research on homelessness to mistakenly assign causal priority to mental illness as well. This relatively widespread practice encouraged the public to identify homelessness with mental illness, not unlike the identification of the Skid Row homeless as disaffiliated derelicts in the 1950s and 1960s. The diagnosis of mental illness among large proportions of the homeless, however, did not go uncontested.

Portraying the homeless as victims of mental illness emphasizes their visibility and vulnerability. Those suffering from mental disabilities offer the most powerful image of vulnerability because their inability to take any effective action to obtain relief on their own behalf is distressingly visible. The mentally ill clearly exhibit signs of dependence that make them legitimate subjects of compassion and care.

The image of dependency attracts public attention because it simultaneously excuses the viewer from empathizing with the homeless person or otherwise recognizing some shared responsibility for his or her plight, and yet enables the viewer to express sympathy and support for public efforts to care for these unfortunate people. The compassion that normally justifies the general public support for public welfare is least ambiguous in those cases where the obvious mental incapacity of the homeless individual excuses any blame while legitimizing the provision of treatment. We need not worry that the mentally ill somehow get a free ride at public expense or otherwise discredit the work ethic.

Psychiatrists and other mental health analysts studying the homeless in the early 1980s used a variety of diagnostic measurements to estimate the incidence of mental illness among different homeless populations. Many found that the incidence of mental illness was quite high. For example, A. Anthony Arce and his colleagues conducted psychiatric examinations of 193 residents temporarily housed in a Philadelphia adult emergency shelter and diagnosed 84.4 percent as mentally ill.[7] Another study of clients from three New York City shelters determined that 75 percent of the 450 homeless people interviewed had a history of psychiatric hospitalization, with more than half apparently suffering from severe schizophrenia.[8] Finally, Ellen Bassuk and her colleagues interviewed 78 guests at a Boston emergency shelter and found "a 90 percent incidence of diagnosable alcoholism and character disorders."[9] Such an overwhelming incidence of mental illness, despite qualifications by the authors, encouraged readers to interpret the homeless problem largely in terms of mental disabilities.

Recent research by David Snow and his colleagues on a sample of 1,000 adult homeless people in Texas, however, has uncovered important empirical qualifications about the scope of mental illness. These researchers found that only 15 percent of the homeless individuals in their sample showed some evidence of mental illness, and only 10 percent had been institutionalized. Although dramatically exceeding the rate of mental illness among the adult population, these estimates were far lower than the more extreme estimates reported by analysts from the medical community.[10]

Similarly, research conducted by Redburn and Buss in 1984 used a statewide sample of homeless people in Ohio. Anticipating a high incidence of mental illness on the basis of the findings of the earlier shelter studies, they were surprised to find that only 10 percent of the homeless could be classified mentally ill using the Psychiatric Status Schedule designed by Robert Spitzer.[11] Finally, the 1985 NORC study of homeless street people and shelter residents in Chicago found that only 23 percent had received psychiatric care in a formal institution, and only 15 percent appeared to have severe levels of mental illness.[12] Statewide and citywide studies using random samples of homeless populations tend to uncover much less mental illness among the homeless than do studies that focus on single shelters. Thus, if the incidence of mental illness is smaller than the early shelter studies indicated, then the role of mental illness as the primary cause of homelessness becomes much less attractive to analysts.

The attribution of cause is further complicated by the questions surrounding the validity of psychiatric assessments of the homeless. For example, in the Ohio study respondents tended to score high on measures of behavioral disturbance, rather than subjective distress or reality-testing disturbance. For example, many of the behavioral measures included items that could reflect an appropriate reaction to homelessness, not pathology. In addition, some of the items on the Psychiatric Epidemiology Research Interview used in the Chicago study exhibited the sort of ambiguity noted by Redburn and Buss in their Ohio study. For instance, a positive answer to the question "Have you ever felt that there were people who wanted to harm or hurt you?" may not indicate irrational fear, but instead a rational assessment of a respondent's predicament. If you consider the fact that interviewers in the Chicago study believed it was necessary that they be accompanied by two off-duty police officers to act as bodyguards, then it is not hard to imagine that homeless people without such protection might reasonably display fear of others on the same streets. Thus, these studies may be overstating the incidence of mental illness among the homeless by improperly classifying normal people as ill.

Large random surveys like those conducted in Ohio and Chicago found a much smaller incidence of mental illness than those studies that interviewed populations in a few emergency shelters. And although the validity of these survey studies might be criticized for using less accurate diagnostic instruments than the intensive examinations conducted in the shelter studies, it is unlikely that the tremendous difference in the estimates could be explained solely by differences in diagnostic technique.

Efforts to explain the incidence of mental illness among the homeless invariably trace the roots of the problem to deinstitutionalization policies undertaken in the 1960s and 1970s. These programs depopulated state mental hospitals without providing adequately funded community-based mental health care facilities to replace the hospitals. Grants from the federal government also enabled state governments to withdraw support for mental institutions while shifting the responsibility of securing shelter and care to clients. Since individual housing allowances were small and the grants for community care facilities modest, those who were released, as well as new victims of mental illness, ended up living in older, high-density, low-rent residential areas near the inner city. Accommodation in rooming houses, congregate facilities, and SRO hotels usually provided insufficient care but also attracted little public attention, as the mentally ill were sequestered in what Michael Dear and Jennifer Wolch call "service dependent ghettos." [13]

On the supply side the operators of group homes or lodging houses find it economical to locate in the inner city where services are concentrated and accessible, and buildings relatively cheap to rehabilitate and rent. On the demand side, besides the mentally ill, the disabled, probationers, parolees, and dependent elderly were increasingly referred to group homes or rooming houses in inner-city locations that combine cheap residential accommodations with a variety of services. For instance, in a followup study of 495 discharged mental patients in 1980, Dear "found that 70 percent were actually discharged to destinations in the care area." [14]

Wolch and Dear report two antagonistic aspects of this geographic concentration of the service-dependent poor. On the positive side they conclude that the inner city provides a variety of services, access to employment, and a choice of inexpensive housing units. These include the sorts of locational advantages that we argued earlier make SRO hotels desirable dwellings for the single working class. But on the negative side Wolch and Dear contend that the quality of the housing is poor, the services frequently unsatisfactory, and social isolation high both within the building and from the surrounding community. For these vulnerable groups, especially the mentally ill, the inner city reinforces the reliance on caretakers. Instead of rural asylums that isolated the mentally ill in the countryside, deinstitutionalization produced "zones of dependence" that isolated the mentally ill within the inner city.

Wolch and Dear contend that the inner-city service zones functioned, albeit inadequately, until the late 1970s when the economic and political pressures for gentrification began to reclaim portions of these inner-city zones for middle-class housing. The same sorts of social and political pressures that had forced the mentally ill to live in the inner city now were used to displace the mentally ill (and other poor and vulnerable residents) from their marginal existence in the zones of dependence. The evidence they provide on Hamilton, Ontario, and San Jose, California, illustrates how the disruption of the inner-city zones of dependence ends up pushing many of the dependent population, especially the mentally ill, onto the street or into emergency shelters.[15]

In Chicago the zone of dependence did not grow up near Skid Row, since deinstitutionalization was occurring at the same time as urban renewal schemes were destroying the cheap SRO hotels on the old Madison Street Main Stem. Instead, the mentally ill moved into the northside Uptown neighborhood. During World War II many of the apartments in Uptown were subdivided to form inexpensive rooming houses for inmigrating war workers. Combined with the considerable concentration of residential hotels and rooming houses already constructed in the first three decades of this century, these new units made the Uptown neighborhood the second most densely populated residential community area in the city by 1950.[16] After the war the more prosperous roomers moved out of the neighborhood, and the vacancy rates soared. This factor combined with the small size of the unit attracted an increasing number of low-income in-migrants from American Indian reservations in the West and from Appalachia in the South, to be followed in the 1960s by waves of Cubans, East Asians, Koreans, and Arabs. Furthermore, during the late 1960s the Skid Row area in Uptown temporarily expanded, absorbing displacees from the dismantling of the Skid Row near downtown. However, despite the waves of immigration and the dramatic changes in social composition these wrought, Uptown still lost population in the 1960s. State mental health officials took advantage of the vacancies and moved thousands of mental patients into the neighborhood. In one year alone the Illinois Department of Mental Health placed more than 7,000 mentally ill individuals in the rooming houses and hotels of this one community area.[17]

However, in the late 1970s the twin pressures of abandonment and gentrification began to put the squeeze on the poor renters in the conveniently located neighborhood. Between 1960 and 1981 Uptown lost more than 4,000 housing units to the demolition of obsolete and abandoned apartment buildings.[18] During the same period Uptown became the location for some 6,000 units of federally subsidized housing,[19] at the same time as speculators began to purchase and rehabilitate apartment buildings as condominiums or upscale rentals. In effect, these economic pressures pushed up rent levels and increased displacement pressures on the dependent populations, whose housing allowances could not keep pace with the rising rents. As a result, as Dear and Wolch found in Hamilton and San Jose, the population of undomiciled mentally ill in Chicago, and especially Uptown, grew throughout the 1970s and early 1980s. Psychiatrists Appleby and Desai estimated that throughout Illinois mental health facilities the number of admissions without an identifiable address increased from less than 500 (1.8 percent) in 1971 to more than 1,000 (5 percent) in 1980. In the same period, at Chicago Read Mental Health Center—the state hospital serving the Chicago area—the percentage of admissions without an identifiable address increased from 5.9 percent to 14.8 percent. The Chicago Read Center admitted about 63 percent of all state mental patients in 1980.[20]

Appleby and Desai argue that these homeless are mainly "urban nomads," whom they describe using terms quite similar to those used by Bahr, Bogue, and the other social problem analysts who studied Skid Row. The "nomads," according to Appleby and Desai, do not respond to outpatient care—refusing the control altogether. At one point Appleby approvingly quotes a psychiatrist who describes the chronic mental patient recidivist as

> the person who never initiates outpatient contacts. He discontinues his medication, believing it to be the source of his problems, citing as evidence his experience of uncomfortable side effects. He spends whatever he received from an income maintenance program in the first few days of the month. . . . He will not live in any kind of residential care because the programs take too much of his income, threaten him with pernicious control over his long disputed autonomy, and deprive him of the protection of social withdrawal allowed him in an isolated hotel room.[21]

This sort of global characterization and categorical diagnosis of the homeless mentally ill overlooks the social and economic pressures eroding the availability and affordability of low-rent housing in the Uptown community—the zone of dependence for the mentally ill—while portraying the homeless mentally ill as so incompetent as to make any future public efforts at improved community-based care appear unrealistic. Thus, as the mentally ill homeless end up sleeping out in other residential neighborhoods or obtaining a bed in an emergency shelter, they become visible symbols of dependence, once again justifying the expansion of caretaking facilities and services.

Unfortunately, portraying the homeless as vulnerable victims—especially emphasizing their visible physical and social handicaps—may relieve the homeless of moral responsibility for their condition, but it also casts them as passive and dependent subjects of care. The homeless, despite their diverse social characteristics, end up being classified as a new kind of dependent population deserving special aid. Although this justifies the intervention of professional caregivers, it creates a social gulf between the homeless and the rest of the population.

Having failed to win broad public support for a politics of social control with respect to the homeless, the federal administration begrudgingly approved funding in 1983 for shelter under FEMA, emphasizing that the funds were simply a temporary allocation to cope with a minor and passing problem. Despite the modest amount ($100 million), these federal funds provided an important supplement to the efforts of local foundations and philanthropies who were the first to provide funds for social services and emergency shelters. When combined with increasing amounts of money from state governments, these federal funds managed to produce a wide range of caretaking facilities for the homeless, even if supply and quality still continued to lag behind demand.

Once the Democrats won control of the Senate after the 1986 elections, however, the deadlock on federal legislation for the homeless was broken. The new Speaker of the House, James Wright (D–Texas), championed a homeless bill as the top legislative priority for 1987. The *Washington Post* quoted him as offering the following rationale. "The comfortable and polite middle-income people have not wanted to focus on this problem. It's natural that you want to turn your head and avert your eyes. . . . But at the very heart of any society that considers itself humane are those who are afflicted. These too are precious children of our land." [22] In his rationale Wright follows the lead of liberal lobbyists who describe the homeless as dependent people (like children) whose vulnerabilities pushed them undeservedly onto the streets. Like the liberals, Wright argues that the visible suffering of the homeless casts shame on those who witness this privation without taking action to remedy it.

In March of 1987 Mitch Snyder, leader of the Community for Creative Non Violence (CCNV), invited federal legislators to join him and several other homeless people for a night's sleep on a Washington, D.C., sidewalk. About a dozen lawmakers and several movie stars slept with Snyder in an act of symbolic solidarity. [23] Conducted while a new homeless bill was under consideration, the sleep-out attracted widespread media coverage. As political theater, the event symbolically united the well known and respected public figures with the homeless. This encouraged viewers and readers to acknowledge the moral worth of the homeless who are not celebrities. It also enabled viewers and readers to vicariously experience the privation of the homeless by identifying with the public figures. The message was both reassuring and inspirational: The public had little reason to fear the homeless as dangerous and selfish miscreants, and it should support actions that would help relieve the burden of the homeless.

Later that spring both houses of Congress passed comprehensive legislation for the homeless, eventually signed into law by President Reagan in July. Although substantial numbers of Republican legislators had opposed the legislation, they never openly attacked the liberal definition of the problem. Afraid that public opinion might turn against them, the critics emphasized the cost of the legislation as they attempted various parliamentary maneuvers to sabotage the bill, all unsuccessfully. The bill authorized more federal funds for the homeless in fiscal year 1987 than had been allocated in total over the previous four years (1983–86), $354 million. [24] Most important, the funds were allocated mainly to provide either emergency shelter (21 percent) or transitional housing and services for special populations—mainly, the mentally ill (69 percent). Only 10 percent was set aside to subsidize the rehabilitation of permanent low-rent SRO housing.

Mobilizing public support through the politics of compassion succeeded with Congress, we believe, because it had already succeeded in cities all across the country, including Chicago. The focus on the vulnerability and weakness of the homeless had successfully justified state and local funding for short-term and relatively inexpensive programs that directly treated and sheltered people suffering the most acute shelter deprivation. But what about long-term solutions? If homelessness does not spring from mental illness, does reinstitutionalization (whether in shelters or new asylums) make sense? What if the roots of homelessness extend beyond the vulnerabilities of the homeless themselves and into social, economic, and political dislocations?

The Politics of Entitlement

Instead of emphasizing the vulnerabilities of the homeless as the rationale for caretaking policies, political advocates for the homeless (although they acknowledged the vulnerability of the homeless) traced the roots of this privation down institutional rather than behavioral paths. They blame government welfare or housing subsidy cutbacks for pushing poor people onto the streets. They tend to identify the homeless as constituents as opposed to clients, thus justifying political organizing for the homeless on the ground of social justice for fellow citizens rather than the individual need of clients. However, since the homeless can exert little collective political pressure on their own, the advocates have ended up utilizing the images of vulnerability to create public support for the care of the homeless. Mitch Snyder's sleep-out offers an obvious example. Paradoxically, using these tactics had increased the provision of services and caretaking facilities without eliciting an acknowledgment of institutional responsibility. The professionals who tend to shy away from the application of political pressure (not only because they are not accustomed, but because the self-interest might become too obvious) end up benefiting as their activities receive additional funding.

The advocates for a right to shelter, and the institutional reforms that implementation of such an entitlement would require, have been much less successful than liberals emphasizing the vulnerability of the homeless have been in shaping the public perception of homelessness as a product of unjust economic arrangements and unfair government policies. The politics of compassion tends to displace the politics of entitlement. Popular support for programs to "solve" the homeless problem are closely tied to the visibility of the most destitute, making compassion the most promising justification for programs with the most immediate (and visible) payoffs, including not only care for the homeless but their removal from sight. Politicians, especially, benefit by supporting such actions because they can claim honor as generous benefactors without risking disfavor in the eyes of the voters. Hence federal laws to aid the homeless have received bipartisan support under a resistant Reagan administration, whereas appropriations for entitlement-based low-income housing programs have been slashed.

The argument that homeless people possess a right to decent shelter lacks popular appeal. If all citizens deserve decent shelter by virtue of their membership in a jurisdiction, then those without decent shelter, the homeless, are victims of injustice. Duty replaces altruism. Emphasizing the rights of the homeless and other poor people to shelter not only places blame on government and politicians for having failed to respect these rights, but on fellow citizens as well. For both ethical and legal reasons, politicians should adopt legislation that will provide adequate and decent low-rent housing for the homeless in order to rectify this injustice, and taxpayers should willingly support these expenditures. Such proposals at present tend to inspire disapproval from politicians and taxpayers, who perceive otherwise normal (i.e., not particularly vulnerable) poor people receiving for free what they have had to pay for—a decent home. In debates about social rights the work ethic reasserts itself with a vengeance. The belief that normal citizens deserve by right only those social benefits they have earned remains a formidable ideological obstacle to the reform efforts of the advocates. As a result, the benefits and virtue of spreading responsibility for the homeless through an expanded welfare state stirs up considerable disagreement—not just between conservatives and liberals but, even more important, among liberals themselves.

The conservative Reagan administration has been quite successful in gutting federal housing programs for low-income people, which at least since 1949 have been justified as entitlements. Between 1981 and 1987, for instance, the number of subsidized housing starts dropped from 144,348 to less than 23,427 per year.[25] Wisely, the administration did not cut the far more costly housing subsidies for the middle- and working-class homeowners (that is, tax deductions for home mortgage interest). Cutting off the poor did not arouse a cry of protest from the general citizenry as has the emergence of the destitute homeless, despite the fact that the Reagan cutbacks contributed to the increasing number of homeless people. The public seems willing to help the visibly dependent and vulnerable, but it stops short of supporting policies that would subsidize housing for the poor. Ironically, the result has meant increased funding for emergency and transitional shelters, whose residents are likely to find it increasingly difficult to leave. Increasing shelter populations are in turn justifying increased expenditures for additional caretakers and services, producing a new type of public, nonprofit welfare bureaucracy.

Attempts to reverse this situation have also floundered, in part, because of homeless people's lack of political muscle. Efforts to organize this population have proven largely ineffective because of the profound uncertainties the homeless face every day. The homeless do lack shelter, but this problem does not necessarily define a common social experience. On the one hand, this means that the group does not identify with the moral or causal assessments of their condition, preferring to treat the lack of a permanent place to stay as another burden that further inhibits their struggle to maintain some individual autonomy. The homeless do not identify themselves as a particular clientele. On the other hand, the lack of any place to stay and settle makes the formation of stable social ties among the homeless extremely difficult. One can imagine prisoners collectively resisting the imposition of more punitive rules or tenants in a public housing project collectively withholding rent to protest poor management practices, but what can the homeless do together that will prompt the provision of permanent shelter?

The advocates of the homeless have adopted both legal strategies to force local governments to acknowledge a right to shelter for their residents and organized strategies to pressure government agencies for adequate and decent shelter—whether legally entitled or not.

In May 1979 Robert Hayes, a lawyer who wanted to help the homeless of New York City obtain shelter, filed a class-action suit on behalf of the homeless against the state and city of New York. Hayes claimed that the state constitution and social service law as well as the New York City Municipal Code all obligated government to provide aid and care for the needy. In December of the same year the state supreme court required the city and state to provide adequate and decent shelter for the homeless. It was not until August of 1981, however, that the litigation regarding the right to shelter was completed.[26]

A current decree laid out the right to shelter for New York City residents, stipulated certain standards of quality for the shelters, and proposed a process for monitoring compliance by the city. The legal victory did force the city to expand its emergency shelter capacity, but compliance was often late and inadequate. Constant legal vigilance was necessary to keep court pressure on the city administration. Furthermore, the city was choosing large shelters in remote locations rather than the smaller scale, community-based shelters originally proposed by the plaintiffs but bargained away in negotiations that led to the consent decree.[27]

Similarly, in Los Angeles, the county Board of Supervisors had taken little action to provide shelter for the growing number of homeless in Los Angeles even as late as 1983. In that year the Legal Aid Foundation of Los Angeles filed suit against the county for failing to provide housing vouchers for applicants requesting General Relief (GR), thus leaving the applicants with no financial means of obtaining shelter for the several days it took to process their applications. The plaintiffs won the suit, only to find that the county was issuing vouchers worth no more than eight dollars—an amount so small that recipients could not find hotels with rates low enough to make the vouchers useful. Another lawsuit obtained an injunction against the use of the eight-dollar voucher. County officials eventually agreed to increase the vouchers to a rate of sixteen dollars per night. Although these two lawsuits were important steps in establishing county responsibility for sheltering the homeless, they also had the perverse effect of increasing monthly hotel rates to levels that exceeded the monthly GR grants.[28]

The legal advocates for the homeless are usually the first to admit the limitations of litigation and argue for political organizing to build support for the implementation of the legal rights they are managing to successfully defend. One organizing approach has been to adopt self-help practices. In those instances where homeless people have managed to collectively provide shelter and food to meet their own needs, the initial organizing efforts and funds came from advocacy organizations or groups committed to helping the homeless help themselves. CCNV in Washington, D.C., under the leadership of its zealous leader Mitch Snyder, utilized a variety of protest tactics, including a dramatic food strike by Snyder, in order to pressure the national government to provide adequate and decent shelter for homeless people. The CCNV shelter staff collaborate with homeless people in conducting the routine operations of the shelter, seeking to create a humane and cooperative community.

In Philadelphia three homeless men, with the help of a few organizational advocates, formed the Committee for Dignity and Fairness for the Homeless, which applied for and received FEMA funds in 1983 to help start and complete plans for a shelter operated by and for the homeless. As of 1984 the committee operated a forty-bed shelter that offers food, counseling, and an open-door policy to anyone regardless of sex, age, or other personal problems or characteristics. One of the organizers, Chris Sprowal, a former union organizer and social worker, went on to found the National Union for the Homeless.[29]

Los Angeles was the site of several short-lived self-help efforts. In December of 1984 the Homeless Organizing Team established a tent city in a vacant site adjacent to the Los Angeles City Hall to shelter between 200 and 300 homeless during the Christmas season. As a result of this action volunteers from the Los Angeles Labor Council agreed to build a temporary wooden shelter. Constructed in less than a week, the Plywood Palace, as it was called, provided beds for 136 homeless people for two years. About three months after Tent City had been vacated, a group of homeless people initiated another less successful outdoor settlement called Justiceville. The organizers pitched their tents in a former playground near the center of Skid Row. Justiceville sheltered about sixty-four homeless people and included portable toilets, a telephone, and a barrel stove. City officials, however, evicted the residents within a week.[30]

One of the most ambitious organizing actions involved the formation of the National Union for the Homeless with the support of some local industrial labor unions. The purpose of the union was to help the homeless put collective pressure on local government for more and better services. In

March of 1986 the National Union of the Homeless, with the support of the Chicago locals for the United Electrical Radio and Machine Workers Union and the Union of Hospital and Health Care Employees, sponsored a founding convention for the Chicago/Gary Area Union of the Homeless. More than 100 homeless people attended the convention, enthusiastically endorsing resolutions blaming corporations and the conservative Reagan administration for their condition. The constitution of the organization states that members should "act collectively" to demand shelter, housing, services, and jobs from government.

There are significant limits however, to this approach. Unlike trade or industrial unions whose members can threaten to withhold their labor and so persuade an employer to engage in collective bargaining, the homeless possess little economic power. A union of homeless people can only act as a political organization utilizing direct protest actions in order to attract public attention, mobilizing support for their goals in ways that threaten government service providers enough so that they provide additional shelter and services to the union members.[31]

One example of the benefits and drawbacks of this method occurred when homeless union members broke into vacant Chicago Housing Authority units in January of 1988 to take possession by squatting. The selection of CHA housing represented a strategic choice. There are thousands of privately owned, abandoned, and vacant units throughout Chicago. Occupying the public housing units rather than private units turned what otherwise might have been perceived as a criminal case of trespass into a political issue of justice. The media covered the break-in as an act of desperation by poor homeless men seeking shelter in public units which, though they needed repairs, still provided heat and protection from the elements.[32] Even though the authority had waiting lists for these units with the names of thousands of people, and the units that were occupied by the homeless men did not meet the CHA occupancy standards, the reports made it seem as though the CHA were at fault. The eviction of the homeless men attracted public sympathy because both the reporters and the public expect a housing authority charged with housing the poor to fulfill this mission. Furthermore, the CHA had been subject to enormous public scrutiny and criticism and had only narrowly avoided a takeover by HUD earlier in the fall. The public had reason to doubt the sincerity of CHA officials who claimed that the homeless could not be housed in public units.

During the two years since its founding, members of the union have conducted rallies to secure voting rights and job training. Before the January CHA break-in members had squatted in a vacant Veterans Administration home. These actions were initiated under the leadership of the union president, Otis Thomas. When asked by a *Chicago Tribune* newspaper reporter whether he understood that the break-ins and squatting were illegal, Thomas replied, "Sure. . . . I'd rather be in jail than freezing to death on the street," Thomas said. "I get three meals a day in jail. I get medical care. I can read there. I can see movies." [33]

This militant resistance depends crucially on the ambivalent response of local authorities unwilling to substitute peacekeeping for caretaking. Social disruption and direct-action tactics by homeless union members take advantage of this ambivalence to obtain material assistance—even if it exposes them to the risks of arrest and incarceration. Arresting poor people because they have illegally occupied vacant public housing units in order to escape the cold undermines the legitimacy of local government caretaking efforts while mobilizing public support for the homeless.

The National Coalition for the Homeless, headquartered in New York City, has taken up the struggle for a right to shelter as its primary mission. In a 1987 briefing paper for presidential candidates, the coalition outlines a three-part national action program to end homelessness: (1) establishing a right to shelter; (2) enforcing existing programs for the homeless; and (3) funding federal housing programs.

All three parts emphasize the provision of housing benefits for the homeless as a matter of entitlement. The chief lobbyist and legal counsel for the coalition, Maria Foscarinis, has made this message clear whenever she speaks to public officials or reporters. Provide emergency shelter and services to cope with the pressing needs of today's homeless, but construct permanent subsidized housing for low-income households if you expect to solve the problem. Unfortunately, although the coalition has successfully lobbied Congress for more emergency shelters, it has met with less success in obtaining approval for far more costly housing subsidy programs.[34]

The Limits of Compassion and Entitlement

Compassionate altruists utilize their resources and expertise to aid the needy but in so doing reproduce the dependence in their clients they hope eventually to remove. The right-to-shelter advocates proclaim equality yet urge entitlement programs that would grant the poor decent housing paid for by working middle- and upper-class taxpayers on the basis solely of a sense of duty. Compassionate caretaking and egalitarian redistribution, therefore, are both nonreciprocal forms of housing allocation and likely to prove unpopular in a public culture committed to individual self-reliance. Conservative as well as populist critics have successfully focused attention on the perverse effects of formal service provision (e.g., the proliferation of categories of need to fit the proliferation of professional specialties) and entitlement programs (e.g., program administration by housing authority bureaucrats). Conservatives offer as an alternative the social contract of reciprocal exchange among independent individuals, best organized, they believe, in the marketplace. Although their criticisms of welfare state program administration have proven popular, their alternatives (e.g., privatization) have not, since people in all strata of society recognize that the market cannot solve all social and economic problems.[35]

Advocates lobbying city, state, and federal legislatures to adopt laws establishing the right to shelter and appropriating funds for low-income housing entitlements should avoid segmenting their proposals into specialized categorical programs that impose restrictive and divisive means-testing criteria. Efforts to mobilize public and legislative support for a legal right to shelter at best provide only a legal weapon advocates can use to pressure local, state, and federal legislatures and administrations for additional low-income housing funds. The amount of funding, the type of programs funded, and, most important, the quality and security of the housing provided require mobilized constituents to ensure compliance. Serious historical problems in the implementation of welfare state entitlement programs in the service of legally sanctioned social rights should give cause for careful reassessment of a rights-based advocacy approach. Winning the legal right to shelter may end up justifying the institutionalization of the homeless in shelters that offer no privacy and no security of possession for residents who must conform to a regimen ordained by their caretakers.[36]

The social isolation of the homeless poor, despite occasional and spirited efforts at resistance, makes collective organizing efforts extremely difficult. Typical are the prospects of self-help. The crucial ingredient for successful self-help efforts among poor people is relatively stable social ties that are established in local settlements that enable kin, friends, and neighbors to pool their limited resources in ways that produce mutual benefits. Accounts of third-world squatter settlements and neighborhood organizing efforts in this country yield ample evidence that local social attachments provide an important motivation for resisting outside interference and providing for one's own.[37] However, it is precisely these sorts of resources that the homeless lack.

Similarly, direct protests, though they may gain sympathy from the general public, pose little threat to urban social order. The local unions of the homeless, for instance, cannot make developers, builders, or landlords agree to engage in bargaining over the production or distribution of decent and affordable housing in the same way as industrial union representatives can use the threat of a strike to pressure their employers to bargain. The homeless are for the most part so poor that they cannot even afford to pay union dues. Thus, any organizing efforts must rely heavily on outside support, paradoxically reducing the autonomy and independence of the members of the homeless union.

Ironically, the greatest organizing potential for the homeless at present comes from their institutionalization. As the homeless become a clientele of emergency and transitional shelters, they may, like other institutional populations of poor people (e.g., public housing residents) organize to place demands on their caretakers not only for improved services and living conditions but even for a share of control in the management of the shelters. The scenario of a large population of shelter residents militantly seeking to control the allocation of beds does not, we believe, represent the sort of outcome that proponents of a right to shelter have in mind.

11 The Limits of Shelterization

Caretakers and advocates for the homeless have prepared comprehensive plans that call for the provision of short-term emergency and transitional shelters combined with long-term low-rent housing. Comprehensive plans for solving the problem of homelessness acknowledge the danger of constructing only shelters to provide for the housing needs of the poor, and they usually propose a three-step program. The first is short-term care in shelters operated by the nonprofit religious and philanthropic organizations (although funded in part with government contributions) designed to meet the pressing needs of people facing day-to-day shelter uncertainty. Next is intermediate care in transitional housing, also operated by nonprofits with the purpose of aiding the homeless to get on their feet and back into the labor and housing markets. Finally, there is long-term shelter in low-rent housing made available to the homeless through government subsidy, enabling the working poor to maintain possession of decent and affordable housing. However, in most places all three steps are not being implemented. Emergency and transitional shelters have been created in response to compassionate appeals, but officials and the public are slow to take up the cause of affordable housing for the poor. This is a critical gap, however, in that arguments for such housing shift the focus from the homeless to the institutions that provide (or fail to provide) housing for low-income households. The first two steps in the plan assume that helping the homeless with shelter, services, counseling, and aid will enable them to reenter the marketplace successfully. Adopting the third step assumes that housing markets do not presently provide sufficient low-rent housing for the poor and that government funds should be used to do so.

The three-tier plan offers the promise of a comprehensive and integrated housing strategy for the homeless. Unfortunately, the implementation of this plan in the context of fiscal retrenchment has tended to produce fragmented rather than integrated outcomes. Shelter schemes have received the bulk of financial support. The plan mistakenly treats short-term shelter provision as if such provision had been undertaken as the first step in a larger effort to provide affordable permanent housing for the poor. In fact, however, the

218

proliferation of shelters reflects the continuation of a relatively unplanned emergency response to the homeless crisis.

The shelter response to the "new" homeless in urban areas usually followed two phases. Service providers and caretakers initially sheltered the homeless in existing SRO-type housing, especially SRO hotels. However, the diminished supply of SRO units soon proved inadequate, and local officials felt compelled to construct temporary and transitional shelters to fill the gap. Shelter providers gained public support for these shelterization policies by taking a compassionate approach to the problem that focused attention and treatment on homeless individuals. Thus, shelterization obtained public acceptance as a legitimate remedy for homelessness before the three-tier plan had even been proposed.

As we argue in this chapter, shelterization offers a poor substitute for the low-rent SRO-type housing it has come to replace, whether it be through the use of hotel vouchers or of shelter beds. For instance, the concentration of the dependent welfare families in SRO hotels designed for single people generates substantial overcrowding, enhances the mutual vulnerability of tenants, visibly publicizes the shame of homelessness, and escalates the cost of care without providing any means welfare families can use to secure independence. This shelterization of the SRO hotels is most poignantly illustrated by stories of welfare families in New York welfare hotels.[1]

The successful provision of emergency shelters has contributed to the shelterization problem as well. The number of shelters in urban areas has expanded rapidly since 1982, to the extent that the facilities now provide a system of specialized temporary accommodations for the homeless. The shelters successfully remove the homeless from the streets while meeting rudimentary human needs and, in so doing, promote the viability of shelterization as an acceptable (if inadequate) solution to the problem of homelessness. Caretakers use the vulnerabilities and pathologies of the homeless street people not only to inspire public concern and support for shelters but to assign the homeless to specialized shelters organized to meet particular needs. To provide professional care efficiently, caretakers concentrate homeless people who share a common weakness or debilitating condition. Paradoxically, sheltering the homeless in this fashion promotes the very dependency that shelter providers hope to help homeless clients overcome. Ultimately, the shelter system does little to reduce either the sources of homelessness or equip the homeless to achieve independence.

The perverse effects of shelterization derive, not from policy failures or inadequate funding, but from the widespread acceptance of shelters as an acceptable solution to homelessness. The moral arguments of liberals, which assert the moral worth of the homeless by emphasizing the vulnerabilities of homeless people, also tend to justify shelters as a legitimate form of treatment, rather than the dismal and demoralizing habitat of last resort they are. Caretakers and advocates, for example, overlook how the punitive caretaking practices needed to maintain order in a dormitory setting with à large number of strangers undermine efforts to offer compassionate counsel and attention. Overcoming the limits of shelterization supported by liberal arguments for compassion and entitlement requires an approach that starts with a recognition of the useful qualities of social life developed among the single urban poor residing in SRO hotels. This requires not only a rejection of the Skid Row stereotype but an acknowledgment of the social benefits of the SRO hotels as community institutions.

The Use of SRO Hotels as Contract Shelters

Most local governments have long relied on some form of contract arrangement with local hotels and motels to provide temporary emergency shelter for homeless people. In prosperous times this policy proves relatively cost effective, as local governments avoid the expense of maintaining public shelters with a large capacity and constant overhead regardless of changing needs. Local officials can marginally increase or decrease the number of service contracts to meet unexpected shifts in demand. However, in periods of significant economic and social hardship the costs of contract care quickly escalate because each new case costs the same to service as the one before; thus, a large increase in the number of needy people quickly exhausts local welfare funds. Officials are pressured into constructing and operating large-scale institutions designed to reduce the cost per person once a certain minimum threshold of inmates is reached.

The recent surge in the number of homeless people, as we argued earlier, was the result of economic hardships imposed on the poor (especially during the 1981–82 recession) and the loss of low-rent SRO-type housing. In cities like New York, Chicago, and Los Angeles the few available emergency shelters filled quickly, and local government relief agencies utilized rent vouchers or chits to house the poor in the least expensive housing available. However, the cities' reliance on the hotels varied. In New York and Los Angeles the use of SRO hotels as shelters was much more extensive than in Chicago. The extraordinary rent inflation in New York apartment units combined with the abandonment, destruction, and conversion of thousands of low-rent apartment units combined to squeeze thousands of people onto the streets. For instance, in 1982 New York City's Human Resources Administration provided housing vouchers for approximately 600 homeless welfare families in three huge SRO hotels. By the winter of 1987 the number of homeless welfare families had increased more than nine times, to include 5,300 families in sixty hotels and ten congregate family shelters. Voucher policy has had the perverse effect of cramming families into single rooms while reimbursing the hotel owners on a per capita basis. The city has ended up paying as much as $3,000 per month to house a four-person household in a single room.

A typical example in New York was the 390-unit Martinique hotel. In 1986 the owners charged $53 per day to shelter a welfare family of four.[2] Assuming a 20-percent vacancy rate, the gross revenue the Martinique's owners received from New York City rent vouchers was more than $6 million. Such enormous potential for profits attracted investors concerned more about cash flow than quality. William Bastone conducted an investigation of the owners of the twenty largest welfare hotels in New York city in 1986 and found that together they charged the city $72 million per year to house 3,300 families, with a third of this business going to only two partnerships. Bastone provided evidence of systematic exploitation and rent-fixing collusion, made possible by a city administration unwilling to crack down and enforce existing housing codes. The Holland Hotel, for instance, had 970 housing code violations in December 1985, the same year the owners grossed more than $6 million in rent voucher revenues.[3]

In Los Angeles the rent vouchers from the county of Los Angeles, unlike those in New York City, were initially so low that recipients could not find hotels willing to accept them. After considerable legal wrangling the county increased the vouchers from eight dollars to sixteen dollars per day, enabling single poor people to rent rooms in the SRO hotels concentrated in downtown Los Angeles. However, like their counterparts in New York, many owners in Los Angeles specialized in renting to public aid clients, taking the predictable cash flow from the surplus of recipients but scrimping on maintenance, management, and repairs. Recipients overwhelmingly were single, with most families targeted for referral to outlying areas.[4] Furthermore, as reporter Andy Furillo discovered in an interview with longtime Skid Row resident Crazy Joe.

"Once the hotel owners signed up with the county and began accepting residents on welfare vouchers," Crazy Joe said, "the winos were out on the street, unable to match the price that the county Department of Public Services was willing to subsidize for a room."

"That destroyed us economically," Joe said. "And after these hotels signed contracts with the county, you'd get rolled in these places quicker than anywhere because the security guards were in on it."[5]

A comparison of the socioeconomic composition of the SRO hotel residents in Los Angeles and New York City with the residents of Chicago SRO residents reveals how shelterization of SRO hotels in New York and Los Angeles has produced a more homogeneous and dependent population. First, and most important, less than one in four of the Chicago tenants were unemployed and searching for work, compared with at least half the tenants in New York (50 percent) and Los Angeles (55 percent). Thus,

TABLE 11-1

SRO Tenant Profiles for Chicago,
New York, and Los Angeles, 1986

CHARACTERISTIC	CHICAGO (%)	NEW YORK (%)	LOS ANGELES (%)
Female	22	45	9
Age			
< 40 years	33	38	45
41–60 years	49	29	40
> 60 years	18	33	15
Marital Status			
Married	7	6	6
Divorced, separated, widowed	49	36	40
Single, never married	44	58	54
Employment Status			
Employed	41	30	21
Unemployed, searching	23	50	55
Out of labor force	36	20	24

Sources: Anthony J. Blackburn, *Single Room Occupancy in New York City* (New York: City of New York Department of Housing Preservation and Development, January 1986); Richard Ropers and Richard Boyer, *Living on the Edge, The Sheltered Homeless: An Empirical Study of Los Angeles' Single Room Occupancy Residents* (Los Angeles, November 1986).

whereas only 27 percent of the Chicago tenants reported using public aid in the prior month, more than 31 percent of the New York and 66 percent of the Los Angeles SRO tenants relied on such aid (see table 11-1). Second, because welfare vouchers in New York City subsidize welfare families rather than singles, the proportion of female residents is much greater in the SRO hotels there. Finally, Chicago residents exhibited considerably more variation in age and marital status than those of either Los Angeles or New York.

The diversity of Chicago's SRO population compared with those in New York and Los Angeles indicates not only a more prosperous clientele, but one less dependent on public caretakers. In both New York and Los Angeles the visibility of the formerly homeless residents as publicly subsidized tenants enduring substandard housing conditions increased the visibility of the SRO hotels, making them the subject of public debate and the object of new housing policies. The SRO hotels in New York have become a public scandal, putting pressure on the mayor and other city officials to improve the SRO housing stock while providing more emergency shelters for families as well as single people. In Los Angeles protests against the dismal conditions in many of the welfare hotels have put pressure on the city Redevelopment Agency to take control of this housing, both to reduce the exploitation but also to preserve and rehabilitate the existing SRO housing stock. However, because the existing supply is woefully inadequate to meet the growing demand, large emergency shelters are being planned and constructed to fill the gap. The misuse of SRO hotels as specialized shelters for welfare clients has placed public pressure on local officials in New York and Los Angeles to acknowledge the danger shelterization poses to both welfare residents and the SRO hotels in which they are housed, and to take actions to remedy the situation. SRO hotels in Chicago, however, have been used less extensively and more discretely by the city Department of Human Services to shelter welfare families, in part because welfare officials have been able to find other sources of low-rent housing for welfare families, and also because the housing squeeze has been less intense in Chicago than in New York or Los Angeles.

The Shelterization of the Homeless

Shelterization has long been the policy of local governments and local nonprofit caretaking institutions for the treatment of destitute homeless people. As we argued in earlier chapters, dormitory shelters run by both private charities and government have long served as the housing of last resort for the poor in the United States. The most generous and extensive use of shelters was undertaken in the depths of the Depression. In the 1930s the federal government supported a shelterization policy that financed the expansion and operation of temporary shelters while legitimizing public responsibility for the shelter of the homeless across the nation. But federal involvement lasted for only two years (1933–35), after which funding reverted to state and local governments. Even with federal support, however, the shelters converted out of warehouses, offices, schools, and cheap hotels were described as little more than "thinly disguised flop houses" by Harry Hopkins, the director of the Federal Emergency Relief Administration.[6] These perverse effects of shelterization became quickly apparent to shelter operators and residents alike (as we mentioned in chapter 4), but these lessons were quickly forgotten.

As the number of homeless people escalated with the onset of the 1981–82 economic recession, local nonprofit and government service providers once again turned to government to provide emergency shelter assistance. However, as we described in chapter 10, the conservative federal administration was slow to respond, placing responsibility almost entirely on local government and private agencies. Many local municipalities, adopting the ideological rhetoric of the conservative administration, initially proposed local ordinances that threatened to incarcerate and punish homeless people as transient vagrants. (These efforts to "warn off" the wandering poor were part of a long tradition of local government efforts to keep the transient outsider from settling within the city in order to live on the local dole.) Such initiatives received widespread national media exposure, which made these communities the center of political demonstrations by homeless people and their advocates. Like the federal officials who were criticized for blaming the homeless, local municipal officials also received public condemnation for lacking compassion.[7]

Most local government officials, however, recognized that the growing population of homeless people consisted mainly of local residents. Unwilling to propose exclusionary policies, they began to expand support for shelters in response to the need and the political pressures from local advocates and service providers seeking more funds. Yet, municipal officials, once they acknowledged the problem, quickly began to lobby for additional federal funding for shelters.[8]

The number of temporary shelters nationwide has increased dramatically (if inadequately) to accommodate the growing number of homeless people in the 1980s. According to the 1984 national survey of shelter providers conducted by HUD, there were about 91,000 beds available for the homeless. However, of these, slightly more than 37,000 had been created since 1980, with half of this increase occurring during the year preceding the interview.[9] (The HUD report excluded shelters for battered women, halfway houses, and other forms of congregate housing for special populations.) Unlike the hundreds of SRO hotels that had been destroyed over the preceding decade, these shelters did not provide relatively permanent private rooms, but dormitories with lockers.

In New York the use of SRO hotels to house families meant that poor single people who had formerly obtained a room in these hotels were left without any place to live. Thus, the number of single street people increased dramatically, and with their appearance came the public demands for more shelters. In January of 1983 New York city sheltered 4,676 men and 636 women in 18 shelter facilities, but four years later the numbers had jumped to 9,000 men and 1,100 women in 28 facilities.[10]

In Chicago the number of emergency beds skyrocketed from approximately 700 beds in November 1982 (none of which were specifically designated for the homeless) to more than 2,000 beds in 1986. This estimate includes the beds in twenty-eight year-round shelters and seventeen seasonal shelters as of 1985.[11] Researchers for NORC who conducted a 1985 survey of the homeless and their shelters argue that this rapid provision of shelter had closed the emergency housing gap for the homeless. Advocates for the homeless disputed these findings, arguing that many continued to be turned away from full shelters and were forced to sleep outside.[12] Public officials, for the most part, supported estimates of the problem that exceeded the NORC estimates. As a result, the level of public funding allocated to support the operation and rehabilitation of shelters increased from $277,000 in 1982 to $6,597,000 in 1987.[13]

Some of the limitations of shelterization as a solution to the homeless problem become evident in an examination of the political disputes that have emerged over the size, quality, and location of shelters. The visibility and vulnerability of homeless street people, combined with the alarming growth in their numbers in the early 1980s, led local officials and caretakers who eventually acknowledged the problem to approve the speedy construction of emergency shelters that could accommodate large numbers of people. Advocates for the homeless, including both organizers and professionals, criticized the poor quality of these huge dormitories and insisted upon the provision of a broader range of services, longer stays, and greater privacy. The advocates urged dispersal of smaller shelters, but neighborhood residents resisted the location of shelters in their locale. What emerged in practice were two tiers of shelters: large dormitory short-term emergency shelters and smaller transitional long-term shelters.

The rationale justifying the provision of a two-tier shelter system combined the concept of vulnerability and the concept of moral desert. The less vulnerable homeless (e.g., single healthy males) are treated as less deserving and so tend to be channeled to temporary shelters, whereas the more vulnerable homeless (e.g., single women with children) are treated as more deserving and thus receive admission to the better quality transitional shelters. The classification of the homeless according to a hierarchy of needs tends to emphasize, however, only those vulnerabilities that caretakers are equipped to remedy. For instance, although most homeless people are unemployed, caretakers rarely treat this condition as a vulnerability by which to prioritize care, despite the fact that a lack of adequate earnings contributes profoundly to the social dependence of the homeless and their inability to rent a dwelling. Caretakers focus on physical handicaps, mental illness, inadequate education, or lack of training as the sorts of vulnerabilities they can help correct and so reduce the effect these have on the homelessness of their clients.

The transitional shelters attempt to create a sort of surrogate community among the homeless residents and staff, but a community that will prepare the clients to reenter both the labor and housing markets without the aid of other social ties. The concentration of a relatively small number of people (ten to twenty-five) with virtually identical needs makes the development of treatment programs and rule enforcement much easier for staff than if the clientele were more diverse. Though it encourages more efficient and humane treatment, such specialization of the shelter community may actually undermine efforts to foster practical autonomy on the part of the clients.

Among the poor, achieving autonomy requires access to diverse social ties among class peers such as kin, friends, and neighbors, for unlike more prosperous members of our society, the poor cannot afford to purchase what they need to lead a private life. As we argued in earlier chapters, the independence of SRO residents is closely tied to mutual helping relationships with kin and friends outside the SRO world, as well as with neighbors and staff within it. These are precisely the sorts of ties that people sleeping in shelters or the streets have usually lost. Caretakers may expect their clients to take responsibility for reestablishing their independence, but since the resources and skills needed to make the transition are provided by the caretakers, these expectations ignore the sorts of community ties that the poor need to "make it" with so little income.

Nancy Kaufman, deputy director of the Massachusetts Governor's Office of Human Resources in Boston in 1984, argued that the key to successfully implementing the three-tier plan was case management/advocacy. "A case manager can mobilize the resources necessary to assist a person out of the crisis and on the road to stabilization. Naturally, the extent of intervention by the case manager depends on the resourcefulness of the client to share the task of finding transitional and/or permanent housing and other necessary services." [14] This approach reflects an orientation shared by staff for shelters as different as the Catholic Charities Parish Shelter Program in Chicago and Jessie's House in a rural community of western Massachusetts. Both subscribe to the same contradictory principles of care: provide a supportive temporary environment while insisting that individual residents learn to become independent. The director of Jessie's House was quite candid when she explained that "the cooperative household is a demanding place to live. Guests must do their share of cooking, cleaning and childcare. They must respect the rights of others. And with the assistance of the housing advocate, they must begin to confront the causes of their homelessness and make progress toward finding a solution to their homelessness." [15]

These organizational features place caretakers in the bind of treating and even creating dependence in the name of independence. Although many of the services provided are valuable to residents, they are no match for serious economic and social obstacles the residents face. Staff members usually acknowledge that their clients face an extraordinarily steep uphill struggle toward individual security but respond by providing more intensely and completely what they are equipped to provide. More caretaking, however, if the climb toward security is too steep, will simply result in backsliding. Most of those successfully aided during their previous bout with homelessness courageously struggle up the precipitous grade only to find themselves slipping down the slope of shelter security once again, and ending up at another shelter. Thus, as the size, quality, and locations of shelters become standard, the limitations that emerge are likely to become permanent institutional features unless we change the present policy of shelterization.

The Problems of Shelter Size

Emergency shelters were constructed in a barracks-like fashion to house as many residents as possible, up to two hundred per facility. In 1984 the average cost of providing overnight shelter nationwide was only nineteen dollars.[16] The scale of these shelters may make them less costly to operate on a per-bed basis, but their spare and temporary accommodations make them the housing of last resort for the most destitute and desperate homeless. More importantly, they offer little privacy or permanence. Hence, these are the least desirable shelters and the ones most likely to possess vacant beds except in times of the most inclement weather. Furthermore, the large scale of the shelters makes them the subject of considerable public controversy. On the one hand, advocates for the homeless protest the lack of privacy and the imposition of strict intake and management procedures by the operators of large shelters. On the other, residential and commercial neighbors vociferously resist the location of such large facilities nearby for various reasons, including fears of diminished property values and safety.

Despite the controversy stirred up by this combination of large scale and poor quality, these emergency shelters have proven to be popular responses to the homeless problem. Most of these shelter facilities are converted from industrial warehouses located in relatively isolated urban locations. A dramatic example is the Charles H. Gay Center for Men on Wards Island east of Manhattan in New York City. This huge center can house 800 men per day at a cost of about seventeen dollars per resident.[17] Staff spend most of their time maintaining social order and providing the most minimal services. Another large emergency shelter is Transition House, located in a converted warehouse in downtown Los Angeles, which can shelter about ninety-five men and thirty-five women. Although it is organized in large dormitories, Transition House allows tenants to stay longer than a single night; also, it does provide counseling and referral services to aid residents in the search for public assistance, jobs, and permanent low-rent housing.[18]

Although most large shelters are unpopular with the homeless and their advocates, they remain the primary source of housing for the homeless in big cities because of their low operating costs. New large-scale shelters recently designed and constructed in Denver, Washington, D.C., and San Diego attempt to improve the quality of the shelter by providing more physical privacy (partitions between beds), greater permanence (weekly stays), and improved services. However, operators make it clear that these improvements, though meant to treat the tenants with greater respect, are also designed to discourage any expectation of permanent settlement. Furthermore, these new facilities are purposely located away from residential neighborhoods where resistance would be strongest. Hence, the spatial exclusion and high visibility of these shelters highlights the social stigma of failure, reinforcing the social distance between the homeless and those further up the shelter hierarchy, not only the middle class but other poor as well.

A new generation of multipurpose large-scale shelters have recently been constructed with physical designs that can accommodate homeless people with various problems and needs while providing space for a variety of social services. These structures demonstrate how aspects of the SRO hotel design are being adapted to limit the negative effects of shelterization. Designer Mark McCormick, for example, in preparing plans for Samaritan House in Denver, "discovered that the requisite open dormitory spaces for single men and women on the ground floor . . . could be based on the design of military barracks to reinforce a sense of order, and to maximize light and ventilation. For the families and teenagers on the third floor, a series of private rooms and a communal lounge were developed based on residential hotel prototypes." [19] Ironically, the designer used the physical organization of the SRO residential hotels, which has historically housed single people, as a model for family housing. The plans relegate single people to a ground-floor barracks. The design incorporates a social hierarchy favoring families over singles into a spatial hierarchy that places families in private rooms above single residents in the downstairs dormitory. The Denver shelter can serve as many as 284 homeless adults, families, and teenage runaways.

Similarly, in Washington, D.C., architect Conrad Levenson prepared plans to convert a vacant three-story office building into shelter for 150 women and 800 men. In effect, the design provides five separate shelters. "Each is treated as a 'village' of clustered sleeping cubicles . . . , rather than as a cot filled barracks, flanked by dining and lounge areas, a warm-up kitchen, and bathrooms. Communal spaces such as 'drop-in centers' for daytime activities, a central kitchen, medical and social services, are contained within the basement." [20] Instead of emulating the military barracks, this design attempts to recapture some of the privacy offered by the cubicle SRO hotels.

Thus, faced with severe cost limitations, the designers of these new shelters end up producing facilities resembling the dormitory municipal lodging houses or the SRO cubicle hotel buildings. The big difference is that today the homeless population is viewed as victims of economic misfortune, not vagrants or bums requiring discipline, and so each design makes room for a variety of medical and social services. Efforts to emulate the diverse SRO social communities, however, offer little more than the spatial juxtaposition of different groups of "clients" sorted into a hierarchy of physical spaces ordered socially according to their vulnerabilities and characteristics. Furthermore, the semblance of community diversity is undermined by the fact that the facility provides only temporary accommodation. Thus, designers and sponsors minimize amenities that would make the shelter so attractive that residents might want to stay on indefinitely.[21]

The Problems of Shelter Quality

The vulnerability and relative weakness of the homeless exposes them to dangers not only on the streets but in the shelters as well. For instance, in April of 1986 the Catherine Street Emergency Shelter in the Lower East Side of Manhattan was closed because of extensive lead poisoning hazards; later in May the Roberto Clemente shelter in the Bronx was shut by state officials for gross violations of the health and fire codes.[22] In Los Angeles the mayor proposed that a temporary urban campground be set aside for the homeless after his plans to forcibly remove the homeless from the streets of Los Angeles met with strong public resistance. The city provided only the most rudimentary infrastructure: tents, portable toilets, and water. The residents nicknamed the camp the Dust Bowl Hilton. Carol Byrne, a reporter for the *Los Angeles Times*, offers the following description of the camp, which housed about six hundred people a night.

> There are no trees and no grass, just dirt and blowing dust. Row after row of small tents squat under striped awnings faded by the sun. Residents lounge about on army cots, some listening to music, some playing cards, but most just sitting. Occasional loud arguments break out. A few children play in the dirt. About 75 live here at any time. Police cars and security guards stand by. New arrivals are patted down for weapons. The camp is cut off from the street by metal mesh fences, hung with laundry.[23]

Because many of the shelter residents were strangers, customary and routine forms of social order in most institutional settings were rare. Furthermore, residents did not expect to settle in the shelter permanently, so there was little incentive to form ongoing social attachments to the place. When combined with the extreme vulnerability of the homeless, these conditions required others to provide security and order. Thus, despite proclamations about humane treatment and sincere efforts to encourage a sense of community, these structural conditions pressured shelter operators into rule enforcement practices more common to correctional facilities.

This paradoxical connection between social care and control is quite common in the organization of shelters. For example, research analysts for NORC found in their comprehensive study of the homeless in Chicago that, although most of the homeless who had used shelters agreed that they provided a decent and clean place to sleep, 47 percent complained about a lack of personal security and another 40 percent resented the lack of personal freedom imposed by shelter regulations. In other words, users overwhelmingly liked the physical facilities but were divided over social issues such as security and privacy.[24]

Utilizing a more in-depth comparative analysis of shelter organization, sociologist Douglas Timmer conducted interviews with shelter providers and clients in a Chicago shelter and a Tampa shelter, focusing on the use and interpretation of shelter rules. He found that the providers in the two shelters attributed the problems of their residents to a culture of homelessness and thus emphasized the enforcement of rules and application of therapeutic methods aimed at modifying resident behavior. Timmer reported cases in which residents were evicted for smoking in their rooms after receiving two warnings or were chastised for leaving crumbs on the floor after dinner. Shelter care treatment, Timmer observed, improved considerably for those who identified with the cultural attitudes of the staff and who demonstrated compliance with the regulations. The assumption that these behavioral and attitudinal changes will later make for more successful job searches and employment success remains a crucial justification for shelters, whose staff claim to nurture independence and not just to "warehouse" the poor.[25]

For the most part, shelter residents go along with the rules, although there are ongoing efforts to resist the regulations. Service staff frequently lament the difficulties of maintaining compliance but realize that reducing the number of rules would require changing the design and purpose of shelters in ways that would increase the risk of danger, reduce the discretion of staff, taint the public legitimacy of the shelter, and ultimately threaten its funding. Public protests by residents about regulatory abuses are infrequent. An unusual example occurred in the fall of 1985 when two young homeless black men attended a general membership meeting of the Chicago Coalition for the Homeless to protest what they claimed was mistreatment. Speaking for his friend, the bolder of the two explained to the assembly how personnel in an emergency shelter had evicted his partner for reading a pornographic magazine before the lights were turned out. Both men briefly argued that they felt that neither the censorship nor sanction were justified and asked the coalition (which includes a number of shelter operators) to intervene. Nothing was done.

The Problems of Shelter Location

In their book *Landscapes of Despair* Michael Dear and Jennifer Wolch argue that the inner city "zones of dependence" that presently house the bulk of such vulnerable populations as the mentally disabled and retarded are being broken up by redevelopment pressures. Displaced from their central city locations and discouraged from moving to other locations by resistant neighbors, the residents find themselves squeezed onto the street.[26] Geographer Andrew Maier offers an account of just such a case in downtown Columbus, Ohio, where local developers thwarted the construction of a new emergency shelter. He uncovers an important paradox at the heart of the disputes over the location of shelters. The downtown site was chosen because it offered accessibility to clients and availability of low-rent space, and it avoided outlying residential neighborhoods. These conditions, however, were no longer sufficient, as they had been in the case of Skid Row. For although the shelters provided the homeless a place to sleep, they offered none of the other services and activities that made Skid Row a community where the single working poor and homeless chose to live night and day. The contemporary homeless no longer had a place to go during the day, and so they ended up congregating in public spaces. Ironically, designers, developers, and investors eager to remake the image of the central city as a secure yet diverse attraction to a middle-class clientele want to exclude the homeless from the public landscape rather than give the homeless access to facilities that will reduce dependence.[27] In Los Angeles, for example, councilman Gilbert Lindsay, whose district includes the downtown area, stalled approval for a proposed emergency shelter in Skid Row because local business owners disapproved.[28] Gentrifiers redeveloping buildings on the Lower East Side of Manhattan opposed more shelters for the homeless in the area around the remnants of the Bowery, concerned that the homeless would ruin the public ambience they hoped their redevelopment efforts would create.[29]

The dispersal of shelters has encountered even stronger political resistance than have efforts to consolidate shelters and services near downtown. Neighborhood activists treat shelters as they would the threat of group homes or public housing projects. Residents claim that the shelters will generate crime, lower surrounding property values, and produce extra traffic, damaging to the social and economic character of their community. In New York City, for instance, Mayor Koch in October of 1986 proposed that twenty shelters for 7,000 homeless people be distributed four in each borough. The plan called for building fifteen shelters with private rooms for at least 100 families, and five dormitory-type adult shelters with at least 200 beds each. Within weeks, opposition by neighborhood residents began to surface. About five months later, in April of 1987, a proposal was made to convert a vacant four-story building into a 100-family shelter in the Midland Beach neighborhood of Staten Island. About 400 residents attended the public hearing, where all but one of the thirty-five speakers opposed the plan. As reporter Sam Vemirek put it, "Neighborhood opposition to city plans is not new. But the battles have taken on a new sense of drama because the issues more often involve the introduction of poor, neglected or dangerous people to stable neighborhoods, not just the construction of buildings, roads or incinerators."[30]

This sort of protest was not the exception but the rule as the city tried to locate shelters in outlying boroughs. The borough president for the Bronx, for instance, rejected the four sites proposed by the Koch administration, arguing that the $172 million be used to rehabilitate abandoned apartment buildings instead. The other borough presidents protested the allotments as well, although in Queens the borough president proposed a larger number of sites, with a maximum of twenty-five families per site. The director for the homeless and SRO housing services of New York, however, complained that such small sites would not be cost effective.[31]

Such cases were not isolated to New York. Similar cases can be found in Chicago. Efforts to open an overnight shelter in the trendy Lincoln Park neighborhood in the spring of 1984 were blocked by the political resistance of a local neighborhood organization. Similarly, reporter Eric Zorn writes about a 1982 incident in Uptown: a church leased space for a wintertime shelter, and "angry leaflets headlined 'The Bums Are Back' appeared in the nearby, more affluent lakefront area, and residents near a previous shelter site in the neighborhood demanded that the homeless enter through an alley door instead of the front door in order to keep up appearances." [32]

Conclusions

The provision of temporary accommodations has usually given the homeless important benefits that they could not have obtained otherwise. The very success of these efforts, however, now threatens to transform short-term shelter facilities into long-term caretaking institutions, as officials and caretakers build full-service shelter facilities that simultaneously segregate and rank the homeless and organize their treatment. Classifying the homeless as a special population marked by peculiar vulnerabilities, however, not only perversely sets them apart from other citizens but relegates them to the inferior status of worthy dependents.

Those who would grant homeless people a legal right to shelter want to avoid the stigma of dependence by expanding state social entitlements to include shelter. These advocates contend that homeless citizens deserve shelter as a matter of right, rather than because of their vulnerability. The association of a right to shelter with the homeless, however, erodes widespread political support for a universal housing entitlement by linking legal right to social need (versus social inequality). The general public continues to perceive the homeless as a population defined by its vulnerabilities, a dependent group of clients, rather than as an independent group of disadvantaged citizens. But if only the most destitute merit shelter aid as a right, then the relatively independent working-class and middle-class taxpayer will not identify with this right as an economic entitlement for their benefit, but as a social benefit for the poor for which working- and middle-class citizens must pay. In practice, this has meant that the egalitarian promise of a rights-based approach ends up providing legal support for a shelter system designed to temporarily service the homeless rather than provide permanent housing. Without broad public support, government will take little initiative to provide decent housing, especially when such housing goes exclusively to the poor. Compassionate shelter providers and advocates of a right to shelter overemphasize either individual vulnerabilities or individual rights in the definition of the problem of homelessness and thereby end up justifying shelterization of needy individuals as an acceptable solution.

In order to overcome the limitations of a shelterization policy, whether based on compassion or on entitlement, it is necessary to consider the problem of homelessness in ways that tie the homeless to the broader population. One example of such an argument stresses the fact that consumers in local housing markets must all face the economic uncertainty of the competitive marketplace. This shared uncertainty, however, can increase or decrease dramatically, not only because of changes in a variety of conditions affecting individuals: health, kinship ties, employment, and the like, but also because of changes in the production and distribution of various types of housing in different places. Posing the problem in this manner removes the stigma that results from the labeling of the homeless as categorically dependent, that is, as pathological or deviant. There are many reasons why poor people cannot afford to pay for adequate shelter, just as young working- or middle-class renters offer reasons for why they cannot afford to purchase a home. Some of these may result from individual vulnerabilities and failures, but the extremely widespread increase in housing affordability problems across class boundaries suggests that the problems mainly originate in the present organization of the housing system itself.

As we argued in chapter 9, the inequalities of the urban housing market, especially as these are reinforced by existing public policies, contribute significantly to the increase of homelessness. Nevertheless, the shelterization policies implemented by local officials and caretakers to cope with the problem mistakenly assume that today's housing market can accommodate a properly trained and provisioned shelter resident. Yet, even if the caretakers successfully prepare their clients for reentry into the mainstream marketplace, the clients will still face the same sorts of market institutions that caused their homelessness in the first place. Thus, reliance on local housing markets as a solution to the problem will prove ineffective.

Instead of treating the dominance of the market as the preferred form of housing allocation and thereby adopting the liberal version of the social contract, which starts with autonomous individuals and ends with an agreement that assigns joint responsibility (whether based on compassion or duty), we prefer to start with a communitarian outlook that begins with our common interdependence and shared vulnerabilities and ends with a social contract that ties the pursuit of individual purposes to a common good. Families, households, neighborhoods, churches, and other social communities of this sort exist outside the boundaries of the marketplace and the state.

The successful SRO hotel communities offer an important lesson about how the vulnerable poor can receive aid without losing their status as citizens and residents in good standing. First, the SRO hotel communities were socially heterogeneous and economically mixed. This diversity meant that residents did not all share the same weaknesses or strengths. Second, although each resident possessed a unique set of problems, the SRO residents as a group shared common vulnerabilities imposed by their residential environment and its location both socially and geographically at the bottom of the urban class hierarchy. This shared fate provided an incentive as well as a social foundation for collaboration that could reduce their common vulnerabilities. Third, the residents overcame the socioeconomic differences that usually keep people apart, partly because of the pressure of shared risk and partly out of the desire to maintain personal autonomy. They accommodated the push of common necessity and the pull of individual desire by conducting and institutionalizing a variety of reciprocal exchanges that were facilitated by the design and management of the SRO hotels.

Pushed to the margins of modern public life and frequently treated as residual social institutions, the ongoing networks of community ties among the SRO residents offer a promising source of social aid that avoids the fragmentation of market competition and the indignity of dependence. We propose a policy framework that builds on this insight, not to replace compassion and entitlement as justifications for policy, but to incorporate a complementary rationale. We conclude that housing for the poor must be provided as part of a universal entitlement designed to reduce the social inequalities imposed by present market practices using community-based approaches.

12 Revising Policies for the Homeless

The homeless are not a new social problem. Efforts to attract public recognition of the "new" homeless as a deserving social group have met with success, but they have misled us into a portrayal of the problem that focuses on the burdens of individual vulnerabilities and the lack of individual rights as the causes of the problem. As a result, government efforts to solve the problem have focused on the provision of temporary shelters and services organized to treat the needs and vulnerabilities of homeless individuals so that these individuals can "once again" become self reliant. Ironically, the programs dutifully following the objectives of pushing clients "up and out" actually contribute to their institutionalization and dependency, increasing the numbers of the poor.

Homeless people confront many problems, and daily uncertainty about shelter clearly ranks among the most burdensome. But obtaining decent and affordable shelter has long been a problem for most of the single urban poor. We have used the history of the SRO hotel and the Skid Rows where they were concentrated to explore how the single urban poor managed to confront the risk of homelessness. Occasional homelessness was part of a community way of life that made use of a range of residential accommodations: mission shelters, cubicle hotels, rooming houses, and SRO hotels with private rooms, all clustered near the central city. When necessary, single poor persons on Skid Row, especially when unemployed, ill, or drunk, could also use the mission shelter or sleep outside. But the identity and way of life of the single poor person was not defined by a lack of shelter. Instead, homelessness was a temporary state; most residents managed to use the social community of Skid Row to obtain sufficient income to eventually rent a cubicle. Thus, the social community of the Main Stem provided a hierarchical social organization which, although shaped by economic exploitation and constrained by the "peacekeeping" practices of the police, offered opportunities for both social reciprocity and social mobility.[1]

We criticized the analysts of Skid Row who emphasized the disaffiliation and vulnerabilities of the local residents because their ideas contributed to the stereotype of the immoral bum, a stereotype that obscured the crucial

235

link between the efforts of the single poor to obtain economic independence and their access to the diverse institutional resources of the Skid Row·
community. It is true that the changing occupational structure and overall
increase in economic prosperity during the 1950s and 1960s did reduce the
number of young in-migrants, prompting analysts to note the "rise" in deviance among what became known as the Skid Row population. However,
the social order and vitality of the urban communities inhabited by hoboes,
tramps, and bums documented by social scientists in the 1920s was overlooked or dismissed in the 1960s and 1970s by social analysts searching for
disaffiliation and anomie. In reality, however, it was not social disaffiliation
that led the single poor to live on Skid Row. The residents chose to live in
the tiny rooms of the SRO hotels and endure the exploitation and danger of
temporary day labor or other low-paying jobs in part as a result of poverty,
but also to obtain a modest independence; this achievement depended on
the services and social ties of the Skid Row community.

The once robust and dynamic community of the Main Stem with its
concentration of SRO hotels and services did not fade away, solely a victim of social and economic obsolescence. Public officials, caretakers, and
social analysts played a significant moral and political role, not only legitimizing the destruction of Skid Row by stereotyping the residents but
also justifying the expansion of institutional facilities to treat the displaced
derelicts. By the early 1980s the SRO-type housing concentrated in Skid
Rows had been almost entirely eliminated; with its destruction came the disruption and dispersal of the Skid Row community. As a result, newcomers
among the urban single poor in the 1980s no longer possess a community
that makes achievement of marginal economic and social independence a
practical possibility.

Nevertheless, our empirical analysis of SRO hotel residents in the 1980s
presents a dramatically different profile of the hotel resident than the stereotype implies. Most of the residents live on earnings-related income, value
their privacy, and enjoy diverse social networks with kin and friends both
inside and outside the hotel. Despite considerable hardship, residents report a wide range of mutual services with others in their network. In fact,
the helping networks of hotel residents are only slightly smaller than the
helping networks of the heads of working-class households living in apartments or houses elsewhere in Chicago. What sets the hotel residents apart
is not disaffiliation, but their status as single-person households who use the
resources of the city rather than immediate family and a private residence
to meet most of their daily needs.

In addition, we found that the combination of heterogeneous residents
and responsible management contributes significantly to the security and
affordability of the hotels. The social diversity of the clientele allows for a
wide range of socioeconomic strengths and weaknesses among the working-
class residents, avoiding the sort of concentrated vulnerabilities that make

many public housing projects or congregate care facilities for the poor such dangerous and uncertain places to live. These types of situations clearly demonstrate that residential segregation perversely consolidates the weaknesses of tenants, while making their strengths redundant. At best, in the well-funded versions, such concentrations can provide certain efficiencies in the provision of specialized services and care for the tenants. Wealthy condominium owners in a high-rise tower, for example, with similar social needs and characteristics will pay substantial fees to ensure their collective security with twenty-four-hour guards. In contrast, poor tenants must usually rely on an outside party to pay for their collective services, a party usually constrained by regulation and funding to keep these services at a level that falls below existing demand. Hence, high-density housing for poor residents with similar problems generates serious social problems not so much because of the density itself, but because of the concentration of households with similar vulnerabilities and inadequate collective services.

Revising the historical account of the Chicago homeless provides, we believe, an important challenge for analysts, caretakers, and officials who have unwittingly accepted the stereotype of the "old" homeless and so too easily accepted the validity of recent characterizations of the "new" homeless. What sets the contemporary homeless apart from the homeless in earlier decades is their visibility, the absence of a supportive community, and hence, their susceptibility to institutionalization. Thus, the roots of the contemporary problem should not be traced to the behavior of individual homeless people, but to those actions that have led to the increase in the numbers of urban homeless and to the destruction of the SRO hotels and the surrounding neighborhood facilities that catered to the single poor.

As we argued in chapter 9, a restructuring economy combined with cutbacks in public welfare benefits in the early 1980s shifted the worst economic hardships accompanying the recession of those years onto the working poor. Social Security, Medicare, and unemployment insurance, despite their many limitations, did insulate otherwise vulnerable segments of the working and middle classes from the trauma of destitution. The growing numbers of poor people were not so fortunate. They received fewer welfare benefits as well because of cutbacks in AFDC, food stamps, and child nutritional programs. The problems of unemployment, underemployment, and inadequate welfare benefits have tended to accumulate in the 1980s for those at the bottom of the class hierarchy, weakening their economic security and increasing their susceptibility to homelessness. Ultimately, fundamental changes in the domestic economy as well as welfare programs are needed to remedy the inequalities that make poverty a persistent and deplorable condition in a society with the resources capable of putting an end to it. Many analysts have already proposed a variety of policies for reducing and even eliminating poverty in the United States. We refer the readers to some of these authors and turn our attention to what we take to be the crucial reason for the emergence of the "new" homeless, the loss of affordable housing, especially SRO-type units.[2]

As we have argued throughout this book, the emergence and success of the SRO hotels was their ability to protect individual privacy and security by turning the interdependence of poor residents into a community asset. The location and spatial organization of the hotels minimized private space (without eliminating it altogether), while maximizing the advantages of accessibility to urban public spaces. We bemoan the wholesale destruction of Skid Rows because the combination of affordable single room hotels and diverse services balanced self-reliance and social dependence in a mixed community of the working and unemployed poor. It is precisely this sort of mix that specialized shelter programs or targeted national entitlement programs simply cannot reproduce.

We believe that local public officials, professional caregivers, shelter operators, and advocates for the homeless might benefit by paying closer attention to the ways that the SRO hotels contribute to a community of limited accountability among single poor people. At a minimum, the preservation of the remaining SRO-type housing represents a better strategy than the three-tiered plan discussed in chapter 11. The sequential implementation of each tier has placed priority on the provision of emergency and transitional shelters rather than on the construction of permanent low-rent housing. Preservation prevents the loss of permanent low-rent SRO units while reducing the number of displacees who would end up on the streets or in emergency shelters. In other words, saving SROs can work immediately and effectively to deal with the most important need, that of affordable, secure and private housing. Under the three-tier plan, however, the bulk of the resources has gone to the least effective solution—shelters, and little has been done to implement the third stage. Successful efforts to save SRO hotels requires coming to grips with the political and economic pressures that have either legitimized or encouraged the destruction of SRO hotels, including: redevelopment policies, unfavorable building codes, unavailable financing, and the Skid Row stereotype. Several case studies follow that illustrate what New York, Los Angeles, Chicago, and Portland, Oregon, have done to remove the obstacles to SRO preservation.

New York City

The abuses of the welfare hotel voucher arrangements in New York City, combined with the increasing numbers of street people, enabled advocates for the homeless to successfully pressure the mayor to provide additional emergency shelters. As we mentioned in chapter 11, these shelter facilities have aroused considerable community protest, but plans for construction and rehabilitation are still going forward. Less impressive are the city's efforts to protect and improve the remaining SRO hotels.

Sociologist Phillip Kasinitz argued in 1983 that most SRO hotels were concentrated on the Upper West Side and Midtown areas of Manhattan and were therefore subject to intense conversion pressures exerted by the surrounding gentrification. The demolition and conversion of SRO hotels increased enormously with extension of the J-51 tax exemption and abatement program to include SROs in 1975. The J-51 program was established in 1956 to provide tax incentives for developers to upgrade deteriorating structures, especially warehouses and factories, into middle-income rental housing. However, by the mid-1970s developers used J-51 to subsidize the conversion of low-rent residential housing into luxury apartments or co-ops. By 1981 nearly 30 percent of the 298 low-rent SRO hotels in New York City (charging less than fifty dollars per week in 1975) had been closed or renovated.[3]

The loss of so much low-rent housing caused alarm among West Side religious and community leaders, who called for a moratorium on tax abatements for SRO conversions in February of 1981. The mayor, responding to the pressure, supported an amendment of the J-51 program reducing the tax abatement available from conversions for SRO hotels south of 96th Street in Manhattan, and another city law was enacted that extended the J-51 tax benefits to owners who wanted to improve their hotels and were willing to maintain affordable rents.[4] Although helpful, these regulatory reforms only slowed conversion. Since the 1960s it has been city policy to reduce the inventory of single-room housing by effectively discouraging any new construction or conversions that would produce additional single-room housing. Combined with the decline of federal housing assistance, this policy contributed to the enormous gap between the housing needs of low-income residents and the supply of low-rent housing. The problem had become so acute that by 1985 the mayor and City Council imposed an eighteen-month moratorium on conversion, alteration, and demolition. Admitting that the loss of SRO housing was contributing to the growing number of homeless people, the City Council commissioned a study of the "best means of making available single-room occupancy dwelling units and other housing for low-income persons."[5] The final report, completed in January of 1986, proposed policies that would use the regulatory authority of the city to retain existing SRO units and encourage the development of new ones. The City Council a year later passed a law authorizing a five-year moratorium that included provisions allowing owners to convert or demolish an SRO through a buy-out scheme. By making a payment of between $35,000 and $45,000 to the Single Room Housing Occupancy Housing Development Fund, created by the Commission of Housing Preservation and Development, the owner would provide funds for replacing the low-income units that the conversion action removes. Owners who attempt to simply warehouse their buildings by removing them from the market altogether are subject to severe penalties, as are those owners who harrass tenants in an effort to pressure them to leave. Regulatory measures have not been implemented with much vigor and have been bogged down in litigation.[6]

More successful have been the few projects financed with a combination of funds from state-sponsored programs like the Special Needs Housing Demonstration Program, federal section 8 funds, Community Development Block Grant funds, and other private sources. The state demonstration program started in 1982 was a one-time $4-million appropriation to provide funding for the acquisition and rehabilitation of single-room dwelling accommodations throughout the state of New York. One exemplary New York City project, the Heights, received funds from this program to provide SRO housing.

In 1982 Ellen Baxter, a research associate for the Community Service Society who had written about the problems of the homeless, decided to take direct action to provide more permanent affordable housing. She located a vacant SRO with the help of the Department of Housing Preservation and Development and began to gather together the homeless and poor from the neighborhood to form a tenants' association called the Committee for the Heights-Inwood Homeless. Seeking a diverse resident population, Baxter realized the critical importance of establishing a sense of mutual responsibility early on. "The association was practice for us," said Baxter in an interview with reporter Maria Laurino, "to see if the stronger tenants would put up with the weaker ones."[7] The fifty-five-unit project was in 1986 the only nonprofit SRO hotel that served a diversity of homeless individuals rather than a specialized clientele of chronically vulnerable homeless.

The exceptional nature of the project reflects the extraordinary complexity of the financing that made it possible. In addition to $283,000 from the state Special Needs Housing fund, Baxter managed to acquire a $366,000 loan at 1 percent interest from the city, another loan of $366,000 from the Community Preservation Corporation (a consortium of banks) at 14.5 percent interest, and $300,000 in equity capital from a group of seven wealthy investors who profit from the tax-shelter benefits. Finally, Baxter secured some of the last section 8 moderate rehabilitation funds, enabling her to subsidize tenant rents for fifteen years. Although an excellent example of the feasibility and viability of recapturing SRO housing in danger of abandonment, the sort of community that Baxter recovered through the rehabilitation of an SRO remains an exceptional case rather than a model for emulation. The lack of funds and the difficulty in obtaining what is available makes widespread duplication of projects like this unlikely.[8]

Although the city-commissioned report called for an expanded role for nonprofit ownership and management of the SRO housing stock, the city has not made serious efforts to fund the acquisition and rehabilitation of SRO hotels. This is not surprising, given the fact that the city already possesses thousands of units of low-income housing abandoned by the owners that, with some notable exceptions, remain for the most part poorly maintained and managed.

Los Angeles

Like urban renewal programs undertaken in other cities, Los Angeles redevelopment programs destroyed thousands of units of low-rent housing, which were replaced by high-rise commercial office towers in the 1960s and 1970s. As late as 1976 a Blue Ribbon Citizens Committee appointed by the mayor and City Council identified Skid Row as still the primary obstacle to downtown revitalization. They acknowledged, however, that earlier developments had not eliminated the social conditions of blight, but merely dispersed the poor downtown residents into neighboring areas. Thus, instead of persisting in the implementation of a de facto dispersal policy, the city government in conjunction with the Los Angeles Community Redevelopment Agency (CRA) initiated a revised downtown redevelopment plan that emphasized concentration and containment of the remaining Skid Row residential areas with their SRO hotels.[9]

CRA officials recognized the social costs of dispersal, especially the environmental effects of Skid Row residents' mingling with the patrons and employees in the newly landscaped public thoroughfares surrounding the commercial office towers built with urban renewal subsidies. The following policies guided redevelopment practice in the 1970s and 1980s:

1. Facilitate the peaceful co-existence of the Skid Row community and industrial businesses in the area.
2. Do not disperse Skid Row residents to other areas except as they choose to leave and/or reach a level of self sufficiency permitting their departure.
3. Make living conditions safe and humane for those who prefer to or must remain within the Skid Row area. More specifically this means providing public toilets, water fountains, structurally safe dwellings and landscaped open spaces so that residents will have little reason to use such facilities in the commercial areas of downtown.
4. Minimize the impact of Skid Row on the rest of downtown by reducing its physical size and scattered nature, while locating new facilities to the east of the present concentration to discourage the spread of Skid Row into the new commercial development area to the west.

In order to implement these objectives, the CRA captured the property tax revenues generated from the tremendous appreciation in property value that followed the construction of the new high-rise commercial office towers to the west. State enabling legislation had authorized government agencies, such as redevelopment authorities, to finance improvements such as land writedowns, demolition expenses, and infrastructure improvements in a designated district using tax increment financing. This tax mechanism enables the agency, rather than the city government, to appropriate the property tax revenue levied against the difference between the value of vacant parcels before development and their value after construction is complete. The agency continues to receive this tax revenue until the bonds are paid off. These large value increments produced substantial revenue for the CRA, $50 million of which the agency used to implement its Skid Row redevelopment policies.[10]

The CRA created two nonprofit community development organizations to implement its redevelopment plans, the Skid Row Development Corporation (SRDC) in 1978 and the SRO Housing Corporation in 1983. Both of these were officially independent agencies with boards composed of government officials, downtown businesspeople, service providers, and a few residents; however, the operating budgets of both organizations were financed mainly by CRA funds. During its first seven years of operation the SRDC established two shelters for the homeless and four economic development ventures, including two buildings rehabilitated to house light industrial businesses, a labor-intensive recycling project, and a sidewalk cleanup service. Industries leasing space from SRDC had, as a condition of the lease, to hire between 10 percent and 30 percent of their employees from the Skid Row neighborhood.[11] Research conducted in the late 1970s taught the SRDC staff that only about 30 percent of Skid Row residents were alcoholic. "Most people were in Skid Row out of sheer poverty and were willing to work if they could find a job for their very limited skills. Thus, creating job opportunities and helping residents take advantage of them became the number one priority." [12]

In 1983 more than two-thirds of the sixty SRO hotels with about 6,400 units in the Skid Row redevelopment area were in need of substantial rehabilitation and repair in order to comply with the city seismic safety ordinance. The CRA formed the SRO Housing Corporation, a nonprofit development corporation, to make it possible to acquire and rehabilitate up to three thousand SRO units, and still manage and maintain them as low-rent housing.[13] In its first year of operation the SRO Housing Corporation acquired three hotels totaling 520 units and began renovations; in its second year it acquired six more hotels with an additional 348 units and completed renovation of the sixty-unit Florence hotel. Most important, the staff of the SRO Housing Corporation has adopted a policy of purchasing and renovating the housing in clusters. Not only are they improving the quality of the dwellings and ensuring that the structures comply with the city earthquake safety and fire ordinances, but most important, as they explain in their annual report:

> When each hotel in our system is renovated, SRO housing will be able to offer a range of special needs housing opportunities plus a hierarchy of housing choices to the general Skid Row population. Our large hotels such as the Russ (290 units) and Panama (230 units) will continue to serve the homeless indigents and will serve as entry points into the system.[14]

Andy Raubeson, the executive director of the SRO Housing Corporation, stirred up controversy among local activists by setting aside half of the 610 units the agency managed in 1986 for voucher tenants referred from Los Angeles County's Department of Public Social Services. The critics argued that the SRO Corporation should provide permanent housing and not temporary shelters. Raubeson claimed that he understood the criticism, admitting, along with the chairman of the SRO Housing Corporation board, that it would be easier to manage the hotels without the voucher tenants. However, Raubeson pointed out that the efforts to build a community must be balanced against the needs of the homeless.[15]

Chairman Wood defended Raubeson's somewhat unorthodox style of management by telling a story about Raubeson's methods as a community builder.

> He did a spaghetti dinner for the tenants at the Florence. Somebody donated a case of tomato paste so Andy then buys spaghetti and he's in that new kitchen down there at the Florence and makes dinner for the tenants. This is what he does best. His whole purpose there is to weld his tenants together and make them feel part of the family and part of the community.[16]

Though the Los Angeles strategy of conserve and contain does little to dispel the stereotype of the Skid Row derelicts in the flophouses, the implementation of the strategy has produced projects that build upon the strengths of the Skid Row community. Instead of using the strict safety and fire ordinances to justify the destruction of SRO hotels, the CRA utilizes funds from a housing trust fund to finance the necessary improvements, while shifting ownership from the for-profit to the nonprofit sector as a way of reducing the risk of rent gouging and speculation. The redevelopment agency has used its powers to tame the perverse effects of regulation and subsidize the costs of rehabilitation so as to keep future rents affordable to low-income singles.

Chicago

Although still possessing a substantial supply of SRO hotels, the city of Chicago has done little to protect this diminishing community housing resource. Zoning regulations and building codes continue to place unrealistic requirements on the owners, discouraging serious rehabilitation efforts. Redevelopment policies remain insensitive to the residential and social benefits of the SROs. Organized demonstrations and lobbying by several citywide advocacy organizations, including the Chicago Coalition for the Homeless, in the mid-1980s did manage to persuade some city officials that SRO hotels were a valuable source of low-income housing. In 1986 an Advisory Committee on SRO Housing supported by the City of Chicago Housing Department recommended creation of a city SRO preservation office that would identify, monitor, and advocate the protection of the dwindling SRO housing stock. The proposal failed to attract much support from city officials. Most housing and planning officials gave SRO hotels a low priority, convinced that the buildings were simply flophouses undeserving of public support.

In one instance, however, public demonstrations at the newly constructed Presidential Towers successfully publicized the fact that the next phase of construction would destroy another SRO hotel, the Expressway Towers. The city, anxious to avoid any more bad publicity, agreed to contribute $18 million to the City Housing Trust Fund over a forty-year period; this amount derived from the refinancing of the municipal bonds used to subsidize the construction of Presidential Towers.

The most immediate and productive preservation efforts, however, have been undertaken by local community development corporations. For instance, a number of North Side organizations—including the North Side Federal Credit Union, Uptown Hull House, the Salvation Army, and Sarah's Circle—supported the formation of the Lakefront SRO Corporation. This local nonprofit organization provided social services to the residents of the Moreland Hotel, while another local development corporation, Voice of the People, took over receivership and management of the abandoned Moreland. A full-time social worker, Sarah Stein, serves as an ombudsman and advocate for the fifty-five tenants of the hotel. A reporter commented that "her long term goal is to build community spirit among the hotel residents so they care about each other and about what happens there." [17]

In the Woodlawn neighborhood the Covenant Development Corporation acquired and rehabilitated a thirty-five-unit hotel using both public and private funds. More than half the former low-income residents plan to return to their rooms after renovations are completed in the spring of 1988. Local nonprofit development corporations like Covenant have begun to realize the value of the SRO hotels as unique housing environments. Thus, even before completing the renovations on the first hotel project, the Covenant community organization took responsibility for managing another seventy-unit SRO placed in receivership by the housing court.[18]

Local nonprofit community organizations have also served as conduits directing neighborhood reinvestment loans into SRO hotel renovations. For instance, the Organization of the North East (ONE) helped private developers obtain low-interest loans through the neighborhood lending program of the First National Bank of Chicago. The developers received the interest subsidy in return for an agreement to maintain the mix of moderate- and low-income tenants in the 154-unit Norman Hotel.[19] This willingness to collaborate with private developers has been promoted by the efforts of the energetic chair of the Chicago Single Room Operators' Association, Eric Rubenstein.

Rubenstein managed to secure a loan from a private suburban bank to finance the rehabilitation and purchase of the ninety-two-unit Aragon Arms

Hotel in 1984. Persistence and determination enabled him to endure more than sixty rejections in his pursuit of funds. Collaborating with other SRO owners interested in erasing the stereotypical image of the hotel slumlord, Rubenstein joined the efforts of low-income housing advocates to promote the hotels as a valuable source of housing for low- and moderate-income people. Several owners, like those of the Norman Hotel, have received modest financial subsidies to install storm windows, purchase new boilers, replace roofs, and make other basic renovations that improve the quality of the stock without threatening its conversion. The interest subsidies have enabled these social entrepreneurs to keep rents low even after the repairs are completed.[20]

The successful political efforts of community-based development organizations to pressure and persuade financial institutions to lend money in low-income city neighborhoods, combined with joint lobbying efforts that include responsible hotel owners, have begun to rupture the institutional barriers excluding SRO hotels from conventional and subsidized mortgages in Chicago. As reporter Pat King discovered, "banks have come to see SRO funding as more than charity. Citicorp Savings of Illinois holds mortgages on several SRO's. Thomas Gallagher, a senior lending officer at the bank, describes them as respectable, if not hugely profitable, investments. . . . And the bank sees fewer slumlords—the kind who 'pocket the cash and forget to report it to the IRS'—and more professional businessmen with detailed financial statements." [21]

Portland

The scope and intensity of both the loss of SRO hotels and the homeless problem in Portland cannot compare with such difficulties in cities like New York, Los Angeles, and Chicago. But Portland merits attention in this review because of the way local officials, organizers, and residents collaborated, not only to preserve SRO hotels but to preserve and enhance an inner-city community that deserves widespread public recognition and respect.

The initiative to preserve SRO housing started with the efforts of a store owner located in the Estate Hotel who in 1977 purchased the building to protect her store and improve the building for low-income rentals. A local bank provided a mortgage, while the Portland Development Commission (the local urban renewal agency) arranged for a low-interest rehabilitation loan in return for which the owner agreed to keep rents affordable to low-income renters. The successful rehabilitation of the 159 units in this building led to the formation of the Burnside Consortium by local merchants, organizers, and residents interested in protecting their inner-city neighborhood with its 1,500 SRO units.

The consortium started out using grants from the city of Portland's federal Community Development Block Grant (CDBG) funds to subsidize maintenance and repair services for eight SRO hotels with 408 units whose owners might otherwise have avoided or postponed the expense of keeping their buildings in decent condition. The opportunity to engage in serious rehabilitation efforts, however, came as a result of lobbying efforts that eventually convinced legislators to support SRO housing: "In 1980, Oregon's Congressional delegation, led by Congressman Les AuCoin, persuaded HUD to permit Section 8 housing assistance to be permitted in SRO's. This breakthrough allowed Portland to participate in a HUD SRO Demonstration and special allocation of Section 8 that produced the rehabilitation of 247 SRO units in four hotels: the Jefferson West (50), Fairfield Hotel (81), Butte Hotel (38), and the Biltmore (70)." The Butte and Biltmore were managed by the consortium (later renamed Central City Concern), which had by 1986 also rehabilitated the Beaver (59 units) and Estate (160 units) with the assistance of tax-increment funds from the Portland Development Commission. The commission used funds generated from the Downtown South Waterfront Urban Renewal Area to create a hotel acquisition program, just as the CRA had done in Los Angeles.[22]

The city planning bureau and the Portland Development Commission proposed and implemented a variety of policies that used the regulatory and financial powers of local government to enhance the economic survival of the SRO hotels in the inner city. For instance, in addition to the hotel acquisition program, the Portland Development Corporation had used federal Housing and Community Development funds to provide low-interest rehabilitation loans of 3 percent or less to the owners of fourteen SRO hotels with 866 SRO units. In addition, the city of Portland offered ten-year property tax abatements for the added value of the improvements to a hotel structure resulting from rehabilitation, if the owner agreed to keep the rents affordable to low-income renters. On the regulatory side, the city adopted zoning provisions that reduced the building density in the Burnside neighborhood, establishing a mixed-use commercial residential area that would discourage commercial speculation common to downtown neighborhoods. As a last resort, the city also adopted a demolition delay ordinance that requires those seeking a permit to demolish large residential structures like SRO hotels to wait forty-five days while the Portland Development Commission investigates the feasibility of keeping the structure in residential use for low- and moderate-income residents. A finding of feasibility can delay issuance of the permit up to 105 additional days, during which time the city can seek to acquire the building through condemnation proceedings. In effect, this ordinance enables the city to pressure the owners of SRO hotels to consider other options besides demolition.[23]

Crucial to the success of these collaborative efforts was the perception by public officials, bureaucrats, owners, and advocates that the hotel renovations were a contribution to a community rather than just improvements to the low-income housing stock. Efforts to revise the public misconception of the Skid Row stereotype had begun in the 1970s, as newcomers discovered the vitality and diversity of the neighborhood. In 1979 the local historical society funded a pictorial essay on the Burnside community. A portion of the authors' introduction captures the essence of the revised understanding of the Skid Row community:

> Outsiders have been typically unaware of Burnside as a community. Because most only come to visit—to eat, sleep, shop, drink, or be entertained—they see the area through eyes clouded by their own transiency. With vision limited to the surface meaning of street scenes, visitors have been most impressed by the neighborhood's seamy side. Alcohol, drugs, sex, and poverty have formed images leading to the stereotype of Skid Row.
>
> The pictures and words in the book are to break that stereotype. Specifically, there are two goals. The first is to show Burnside as a full-fledged neighborhood instead of one narrowly based upon rejects and misfits. The second is to show that even indigents—the winos, bums, prostitutes, and pushers undeniably there—are part of a genuine community. That is not to glorify their lives, but merely to point out that destitution does not rob them of human concerns.[24]

The Burnside neighborhood activists initiated a hobo parade in 1981 to provide a local celebration that would attract the public to the neighborhood in order "to bridge the gap between those who have and those who have not, and to reach those people who, because of their lifestyle find it difficult to identify with the needs of the homeless." The organizers of these parades made every effort to use the festive and playful elements of the parade to represent to outsiders the humanity of the homeless and the values they share with the broader public. The theme for the 1986 parade, for instance, was "The Homeless: Liberty Belongs to Us All." Supporters defended the parade against critics who claimed the event shamefully glamorized the poverty of the homeless. Activist Erika Greene explained that she and her colleagues did not pity the homeless. "Rather, we respect those people, who, through no direct fault of their own, have found a great deal of misfortune and are handling it to the best of their abilities." [25]

Thus, unlike Los Angeles, the public agencies in Portland did not use their regulatory and financial authority to contain and concentrate the redevelopment of Skid Row as an undesirable but inevitable consequence of downtown renewal. City officials adopted a more inclusive approach that recognized the importance of protecting the geographic integrity of the Burnside neighborhood, but without reproducing its social marginality. In this respect Portland is unique among large cities in the United States.

Policies for Protecting and Promoting the SRO

There are several important and useful policy lessons one can draw from these local efforts to protect and rehabilitate SRO hotels. First, the stereotypical image of the SRO hotels must be publicly repudiated. Local officials, planners, caretakers, owners, and lenders must recognize the legitimacy and value of the SRO hotels as community institutions in order to adequately discourage their conversion into welfare hotels or destruction as substandard housing.

For example, in Los Angeles, where the city spent millions of dollars on SROs, preservation was shaped out of a public desire for segregation and containment, not a commitment to community preservation. In fact, the Los Angeles case is an example of a policy that combines the frequently competing ideological interests at social control, compassionate care, and redistributive entitlement. The spatial containment element insulates the new commercial businesses and upper-class residents from the Skid Row residents, while the redevelopment agency redistributes a portion of the public funds generated by taxing these upscale developments in order to improve the Skid Row hotels. Furthermore, these improvements include not only acquisition and rehabilitation costs, but the design and dedication of certain hotels as special-needs housing for people suffering from serious vulnerabilities such as alcoholism, drug addiction, and mental illness.

The Los Angeles Skid Row redevelopment project remains a politically unstable compromise, however, because it is still essentially a policy of separate and unequal. Ironically, the leaders of the Skid Row Development Corporation and the SRO Housing Corporation recognize the precarious nature of their enterprises as they frantically struggle to promote the benefits of diversity in place—the concentration of SRO hotels, shelters, service facilities, and other support institutions near the center of a revitalizing city that poor single people can use to keep their modest independence intact. The issue is whether they can acquire enough SRO hotels and businesses as independent nonprofits to become financially self-sufficient before the Community Redevelopment Agency eventually cuts off the flow of funds.

Portland offers the most exemplary case of SRO preservation precisely because public agencies collaborated with neighborhood organizations and SRO owners to protect the integrity of the low-income residential community of the single poor near downtown. Recognition of the SRO hotels as a community resource able to harness the interdependence among hotel residents to the desire for individual independence provides an important foundation for successful long-term preservation efforts.

The first step in preserving the existing SRO hotels must be taken by local government, usually the municipality and redevelopment agency, to change policies that encourage the destruction and loss of SRO hotels. At a minimum, SRO hotels within existing or planned redevelopment areas should be given a privileged status. Priority should be given to their preservation and rehabilitation as affordable low-income housing. If SROs are threatened with destruction or conversion, affordable replacement housing and relocation assistance must be allocated to the residents. Replacing the successful residential hotels of the single working poor with commercial office space or luxury high rises for upper-income tenants may promise short-term revenue gains for the city but actually guarantees long-term social costs as the displacees turn to social service agencies and the growing shelter system for care. Furthermore, the tax revenues generated by downtown development may be more than offset by the rising social costs of displacement.

Cities as diverse as New York, San Diego, and Seattle have all adopted ordinances penalizing owners of low-rent SRO hotels who convert or destroy their buildings. The ordinances were usually preceded by adoption of a temporary moratorium on conversion or demolition of SRO hotels, during which time the city inventoried the existing SRO housing stock and designed a new ordinance. The purpose of the SRO preservation ordinance is to outlaw conversion or demolition in SRO hotels covered by the ordinance unless a permit by the city is awarded. Permits usually require the owner to provide either replacement housing or pay a fee equivalent to the replacement cost of such housing into a city fund dedicated to the construction of low-income housing. Furthermore, the ordinance usually guarantees occupancy in the replacement units and ensures that the displaced receive adequate relocation assistance.[26]

New York appears to have enacted the stiffest penalties for unauthorized demolition at $150,000 per unit and the highest per-unit buy-out fees of $45,000 per unit.[27] In contrast, San Diego requires that the developer contribute a fee equal to only 50 percent of the replacement cost of the hotel rooms demolished (about $7,500 in 1987).[28] In Seattle the City Council adopted an ordinance to discourage warehousing of SRO hotels by owners. On the negative side, the ordinance threatens civil penalties and potential public receivership; on the positive side, the ordinance offers moderate rehabilitation subsidies of up to $2,000 per unit to encourage landlords to rent habitable units to low-income tenants.[29]

The regulations governing SRO hotels were developed when SROs served a transient clientele and functioned largely as commercial hotels. However, today, SROs function more as a residential hybrid that combines aspects of hotel and apartment organization, a hybrid that does not fit existing codes. Stoves are a good example of such misclassification. The existing code in Chicago requires that for every two rooms with a stove there must also be one bathroom. If the building does not conform, the owner must either add baths or remove stoves. Adding baths becomes prohibitively expensive given the original design of the building, whereas eliminating stoves means discouraging the sort of long-term tenants that make up the majority of SRO residents. Portland officials led the way in lobbying HUD to amend regulations that made the subsidized rehabilitation of SRO hotels both difficult and expensive. However, many cities have not made similar adjustments to their local housing and building codes, and thus continue to discourage reinvestment and repair by private hotel owners.

Existing housing and building codes should be amended to accommodate the existing residential function served by SRO housing. In Chicago, for instance, SROs receive many more inspections each year than do apartments. The city's fire department may visit as many as six times per year, and the health department may send inspectors as often as four times per year. Frequent inspection, however, whether punitive or benign, does not necessarily provide more effective enforcement of regulations, especially when improvements and repairs are costly. In this respect, Seattle offers a useful model. The city combined punitive sanctions with incentives to encourage successful preservation of SRO hotels. Their experience shows that enforcement is much more effective when tied to the financial assistance needed to rectify the problems uncovered by inspection.

Instead of offering tax abatements for new commercial developments, local governments should consider offering property tax abatements to the owners of SRO hotels who agree to rehabilitate their buildings and retain a significant portion of low-income tenants during the term of the abatement. Portland, for instance, used these abatements to reduce the cost pressures on owners and help ensure the preservation of low-rent housing. The short-term loss of revenues to the city and county were quite modest, while the benefits of protecting vulnerable low-income housing and preventing displacement were quite large.

Although regulatory reform will inspire political resistance and legal challenge from segments of the development community, the adoption of such reforms formally acknowledges the public value and legitimacy of SRO-type housing. Ultimately, regulations alone will prove a limited strategy unless combined with access to financing. But the combination of a positive public image and regulatory protections will go a long way toward improving the economic viability of existing SRO hotels and so improve their attractiveness to lenders.

SRO hotel owners have long had difficulty obtaining funds from private or public sources, whether long-term mortgages or short-term improvement loans. The image of the hotels as social and economic liabilities has contributed to a perception of financial risk that is largely undeserved. But as public agencies at the federal, state, and local levels increase their financial involvement in the rehabilitation of SRO hotels as valuable sources of low-income housing, this perception is likely to change. Once eligible for federal Community Development Block Grant funds or section 8 subsidies, state housing finance interest subsidies, or local government housing trust fund loans, many vulnerable SRO hotels will not only survive but demonstrate their economic value to private lenders as well.

Although public financing frequently offers generous subsidies, it also may threaten the socioeconomic mix of hotel residents that makes for successful community life in the SRO hotels. If the public agency, in return for the subsidy, requires that the hotel be populated by a relatively homogeneous population of vulnerable poor people, then the hotel is in danger of becoming a welfare institution. Mixing public subsidy with conventional financing, however, will enable the hotels to maintain the socioeconomic mix of tenants. Using public funds to leverage conventional financing seems especially attractive. The housing benefits per dollar of subsidy are greater since the per-unit costs of rehabilitating SRO rooms are lower than they are for larger multiple-room units. The subsidy enables owners to reduce their costs and make repairs without raising rents to levels that exceed what those in the market for hotel rooms can afford to pay. The mix of tenants enables the owners to make sufficient profit to stay in the business and reduce the risk for lenders. This has happened in San Diego, where a developer has constructed a new SRO hotel using a mix of public and private financing. The construction of the 207-room Baltic Hotel was made possible by a $2.2 million loan from the Bank of San Diego, a $500,000 loan from the city at 3 percent interest, and $700,000 equity by investors. Opened in 1987, the hotel offers rooms for rent at $220 per month.[30]

The preservation of SRO hotels has usually been initiated and sustained by the political and technical efforts of nonprofit organizations. The economic independence and territorial loyalty provided by local nonprofit development corporations has proven an important resource in what successful prevention efforts have occurred so far. Nonprofit development corporations, removed from the profit incentive and tied to promoting the welfare of a particular locale, offer a flexible vehicle that can not only help curb land speculation and social exploitation but provide a tolerant institutional receptacle for the diversity of the inner city. One can imagine nonprofit development corporations, once they have reached relative financial autonomy, using for-profit development firms to engage in the rehabilitation and construction of residential and commercial buildings for an upscale clientele. The parent nonprofit would utilize the profits from these firms to finance improvements in the SRO housing stock, thereby tapping directly into the speculative appreciation that would otherwise go to developers who do not reinvest their profits in low-income housing. Instead of relying on the redevelopment agency to redistribute a small portion of the public revenues generated by rising economic values of downtown property, the local nonprofits could capture the bulk of the profits to subsidize the maintenance and expansion of the SRO housing on Skid Row.

According to journalists Neal Pierce and Carol Steinbach, commissioned by the Ford Foundation to report on the status of community development corporations (CDCs) across America, these CDCs (generously estimated to number 3,000) have, since the cutbacks in federal housing construction funds, become the principal suppliers of low-income housing. The researchers attribute the successful growth of these local nonprofit organizations to "the qualities of our society that so impressed Alexis de Tocqueville in the 1830s: our penchant for innovative civic association, our belief that individuals can bring about change, our openness to risk taking and to bridging lines of class, ideology and party." When they characterize the spread of CDCs as a kind of "corrective capitalism," however, Pierce and Steinbach go too far. We agree that the local nonprofits draw on a uniquely American cultural tradition, but this is not the tradition associated with the culture of the capitalist entrepreneur, that is, the possessive individualism that embraces economic competition as a means to accumulate wealth, concentrate political power, and secure social position. Instead, authentic local development corporations draw on a tradition that the autonomy of individuals derives from their participation in collective efforts to overcome uncertainties imposed by shared vulnerabilities. These are the sorts of communities we found on Skid Row and the SRO hotels. Thus, we are skeptical that CDCs can correct the class divisions and socioeconomic inequalities so central to capitalist accumulation, especially in urban areas, unless they are closely tied to the social resources of a diverse and tolerant local community. Only when they function to mobilize and unify the diverse strengths of a locale can community development corporations contribute to the formation of economic alternatives in the interstices of the existing system.[31]

Planner-architect Jacquie Leavitt and sociologist Susan Saegart studied groups of tenants in New York City who had formed nonprofit organizations in order to purchase and repair their buildings after the landlord had abandoned them. Leavitt and Saegart explained how these socially and economically vulnerable households formed what they called "community households" to provide for their individual housing needs by collaborating in the management of their building. These community households reduced the uncertainty imposed by the common threat of displacement "by drawing on the sociable collaboration of kinship and friendship ties, the reciprocity of mutual aid, as well as emotional attachments to dwelling and its setting." The authors compared the effectiveness of these community households using private versus cooperative forms of ownership and management; they found that the co-ops were more successful than other organizational forms. The co-op structure of shared ownership built upon and in turn strengthened the community bonds that already tied the residents together. Thus, the nonprofit nature of the co-op protects the members against the pressures of the land market while encouraging individual gains through shared investment rather than individual benefit at community expense.[32]

There are important limits to a community-based approach to the preservation of SRO hotels and the provision of low-income housing. Even if local preservation efforts in cities like Portland, Los Angeles, Chicago, and New York were to save all the SRO housing that remains, the supply would still fall short of the demand. Furthermore, the relatively small scale of community-based developments may avoid the perverse effects of bureaucratic administration that accompanies large-scale programs, but it also limits the impact these organizations can make. Recognizing the fact that the causes for the demolition of low-income housing like the SROs, as well as the political and economic barriers to its provision, remain closely linked to corporate and government institutions outside the local community may keep advocates from unrealistically expecting too much of local CDCs.[33]

Nevertheless, the importance of local community development efforts, we believe, is not mainly due to the scale of their impacts, but rather to the quality of their innovations. What frequently appears insignificant measured against a quantitative scale can, because of its unique treatment of a difficult problem, offer an important practical alternative.

Thus, new national housing policies have usually been adapted from programs tried and tested on a smaller scale in one locale. The National Low Income Housing Information Service has in fact drafted a legislative proposal for a national community-based housing supply program that would use the "community-based, non-profit housing delivery systems to create a long lasting supply of affordable low income housing."[34] Additionally, low-income housing eligibility standards should be expanded to explicitly include single persons, a group that has (with the exception of the elderly) been excluded from national housing programs.[35]

Toward Community

The difference between those facing daily shelter uncertainty and those with housing security is not, we believe, based on vulnerabilities such as alcohol addiction or mental illness, but on the social and economic advantages our class standing allows us. We believe that the distance between the middle and lower classes has begun to shrink dramatically; middle-class households now experience the problem as an inability to afford owning a home, just as homelessness has increased dramatically. What we share across class lines is increasing shelter uncertainty, not increasing physical vulnerability.

The middle classes have long been the primary beneficiaries of federal tax policies that subsidize homeownership. However, as ownership costs increase and fewer young households can afford to buy, there may be increasing support for direct housing subsidy programs that are more inclusive.[36] Universal versus targeted entitlement programs go a long way toward overcoming the public resentment and political resistence to aid for the dependent poor.[37]

Thus, solving the problem of the homeless does not require that we despair at the complexity of the many causes of the problem or the variety of homeless people. The solutions are not necessarily new or difficult to conceive, just difficult to implement. We especially want to discourage institutionalization and sanctification of homeless people as a new kind of special social problem group. We hope that caretakers of all affiliations, by exploring the working-class roots of the single homeless, might reconsider their preconceptions about the "new" homeless and beware the perverse social effects that an expanded shelter care system portends.

We adopted a community-based approach because we think it represents a crucial but missing link, not only in framing national debates about homelessness but in shaping the national housing policy agenda as well. For too long the policy implications of a communitarian argument have been dismissed as either a mean-spirited provincialism or a utopian fantasy of egalitarian solidarity. We have told the story of the Skid Row community and the social world of the SRO hotels in such detail precisely to avoid simpleminded ideological categorization. Instead, we would argue that what our cities cannot afford is more of the same—the same policies and programs, both private and public—that have lead to the grim tradeoff between life on the streets or life in a shelter. It is in this context, therefore, that we urge public officials, developers, planners, caretakers, and housing advocates to learn from the lessons of hotel life that the independence of the single poor can survive not only the imposition of control but also the dependence of compassionate care and the bureaucratic allocation of public benefits, if those subjected to these interventions remain tied to a social community. We must protect and promote these urban communities of the working poor not simply to avoid the perverse effects of doing good but to foster provision of affordable housing for the poor that contributes to the diversity and hence the viability of city life.

APPENDIX A
Research Method

Studies of SRO hotels and their residents rarely combine a census of hotels with the analysis of their residents. Usually, researchers focus on the detailed characteristics of residents in a single hotel[1] or conduct a census of the SRO housing stock while including a few demographic characteristics of the residents.[2] We attempted to capture the detail of the first approach and combine it with the scope offered by the second. Although we sacrificed much of the detail of ethnographic research, we were still able to analyze the social ties of SRO residents.

We undertook this study to determine whether our positive experience with SRO residents, hotel managers, and the SRO environment in our roles as advocates for preserving and building low-income housing in Chicago merely reflected our personal contact with exceptional cases or an accurate assessment of social life in all SRO hotels. Thus, we adopted the sampling methods of social science to control for our own bias and then asked questions we hoped would provide answers that both supported our experience of the social and economic viability of SRO hotels and undermined the validity of the Skid Row stereotype held by our critics. We made every effort to design our research to respect the rules of fair and open inquiry. We had others who did not necessarily share our values review the survey to help us avoid asking leading questions, and trained professionals conducted the face-to-face interviews for us.

Our research was divided into two phases. In Phase One we conducted a comprehensive census of Chicago SRO hotels in 1984. During Phase Two we interviewed face-to-face 185 residents selected from samples of SROs in three areas of the city.

Phase One: The Census of SRO Hotels

We began the first phase of the project in August by consulting the yellow pages, the Illinois Hotel and Motel Tax List, the Department of Inspectional Services' list of annually inspected buildings, the Fire Department's list of annual inspections, and a list provided by the Board of Elections. Hotels listed on the advertising brochures of the Chicago Chamber of Commerce were eliminated from the original master list, as these were the high-priced luxury and tourist hotels that fell outside the universe of low-rent SRO hotels we wanted to identify. The names of the remaining hotels were then cross-checked to eliminate duplications. The final master list included 350 potential SRO hotel names and addresses.

We conducted a phone survey in September 1984 to identify which buildings on the master list actually fit our definition as SROs. Speaking to the manager or desk clerk, we asked if the hotel offered a twenty-four-hour desk clerk, a switchboard service for residents, units with shared bath, units with kitchenettes. Besides these characteristics, we asked about the number of rooms and the rate structure, including daily, weekly, and monthly rent, where appropriate. We used these criteria to identify which of the 350 hotels on our master list would be classified as SROs. At a minimum, a hotel had to offer either a twenty-four-hour desk or switchboard service at no extra charge. This working definition eliminated apartment hotels and other nontraditional SRO hotels. The final population included 115 SRO hotels inside the city of Chicago.

Geographically the hotels tended to concentrate in clusters along the Chicago Transit Authority train lines, especially the north-south line along the lakefront. Virtually every hotel possessed a desk clerk (99 percent) and a switchboard service (89 percent). Slightly more than half (52 percent) rented rooms with shared baths, and about a third (33 percent) provided rooms with kitchenettes.

Phase Two: Interviewing SRO Residents

Since we lacked the resources to conduct a census of SRO residents, we decided to do the next best procedure, interview a sample of SRO residents. Our census had identified 11,822 single-room units, which together made up the population we intended to sample. We divided the SROs into three groups based on geographic clusterings: North (including Uptown, Edgewater, Lakeview, and Lincoln Park), Central (near West Side, near North Side, and Loop), and South (Grand Boulevard, Hyde Park) (see appendix B). We randomly selected five hotels from the cluster on the North, seven from the Central cluster, and six from the southern cluster.

Only one manager refused us entry on the North Side and none in the Central area, but we were less fortunate on the South Side. The managers of the hotels initially drawn from our sample refused to allow any interviewing to be conducted. Unable to gain permission to interview over the phone, several interviewers visited these and others on an additional list of randomly selected hotels to explain in person the purpose of the study. Two interviewers familiar with the area were able to establish rapport with the managers or owners of six hotels whose residents eventually were interviewed. We suspect that the hotels whose managers refused us entry may have been harboring residents whose characteristics varied significantly in some cases from those of the residents interviewed. We made every effort to reduce selection bias, but the high refusal rate meant that some bias in our South Side sample was unavoidable.

The staff of the Survey Research Laboratory at the University of Illinois at Chicago helped us pretest a method for selecting interviewees in March and April of 1985. Two hotels in the Loop chosen for their disparate size (one was small, the other large) were approached by the research director for participation in the selection procedures and survey. Once the managers and owners agreed to allow the interviews to take place, rooms were randomly selected from each hotel, and each tenant was notified by letter of the upcoming interview. The letter explained the purpose of the study and offered respondents a fee of five dollars for their time.

The letters proved useful, but the pretest made evident that the collaboration of the desk clerks and managers was crucial. Many tenants agreed to participate only after receiving the reassurance of the hotel staff. In effect, the screening that SRO hotel clerks and managers conduct to ensure residents' privacy and safety applied to interviewers as well as to anyone else. Before we completed even a single interview, we learned about the significant social control exercised among staff and residents to maintain a high level of security and privacy.

Survey Research Lab interviewers attempted to contact the tenants originally selected. If after three different visits they were unable to complete an interview, the interviewers visited another randomly assigned unit in the same building. This process continued until a quota of interviews was attained. Larger quotas (10–16) were set for the large hotels and smaller quotas (7–10) for the small hotels; the total was limited, however, to a maximum of 185. This was all we could afford to pay for.

In cases where the respondent refused to be interviewed or was unable to complete the interview, the interviewer visited another randomly assigned unit in the same building. The results of the field work are summarized in table A-1. Six interviewers conducted 185 interviews out of 262 personal contacts (499 actual visits) in a six-week period. Given the uncertainty we confronted at the beginning of the project, we believe that the field work carried out by the Survey Research Lab was quite good. The overall refusal rate was slightly less than 10 percent. SRL staff verified all field procedures, edited each completed survey, and validated 15 percent of the interviews completed by each interviewer.

Table A-2 illustrates how closely our sample reflected the actual distribution of hotel units in the three geographic clusters. In effect, we slightly oversampled (25 percent) the South Side units, in part because we wanted to be certain we gathered enough cases to make quantitative analysis meaningful. The North Side sample (31 percent) fell below our original quota because of a last-minute defection by an otherwise cooperative hotel man-

TABLE A-1

Final Disposition of Randomly Selected Interview Candidates

| | | | REASONS FOR NO SURVEY INTERVIEW | | | | |
HOTEL	COMPLETED SURVEYS	NO SURVEY	Refuse	Incomplete	Vacant	Over 3 visits	Other
1	10	6	1	—	—	4	1
2	5	20	2	—	—	18	—
3	14	5	1	—	—	4	—
4	9	15	4	3	—	3	5
5	14	11	1	4	1	—	5
6	14	—	—	—	—	—	—
7	16	17	5	2	1	9	—
11	9	16	6	4	2	3	1
12	12	1	—	—	—	1	—
13	11	4	—	—	—	2	2
14	10	15	6	2	1	6	—
15	14	12	2	—	—	10	—
21	8	6	1	—	1	3	1
22	10	4	2	—	1	1	—
23	7	8	—	1	—	7	—
24	10	3	2	—	—	1	—
25	5	6	1	—	4	1	—
26	7	7	—	—	—	6	1

TABLE A-2

Distribution of Sampled Units by Geographic Cluster

CLUSTER	TOTAL SRO UNITS	SRO UNITS SAMPLED	COMPLETED SURVEYS
Central	4,824	104	56
North	4,406	156	82
South	1,258	81	47
Total (N)	10,488[a]	341	185

[a]The units in outlying hotels (N = 1,334) were excluded from the sample, so the results of this report may not reflect characteristics of respondents in these hotels.

TABLE A-3

Sample Weighting Scheme

LOACTION	EXPECTED SAMPLE *N*	ACTUAL SAMPLE *N*	WEIGHT EXPECT/ACTUAL
Central	85	56	1.5
North	78	82	1.0
South	22	47	.5
Total	185	185	3.0

Note: Weights were rounded off.

ager. We believe the sample to be representative but with a slight overrepresentation of the South Side SRO residents and a slight underrepresentation of the North Side SRO residents.

In order to compensate for this sampling bias, we increased the relative values of those respondents we had undersampled from the North Side by 50 percent while reducing the South Side respondent values by 50 percent. Each Central area respondent represents 1.5 times its actual value; each South Side respondent is worth .5 times its value. The sample weights are listed in table A-3.

The research director prepared the survey itself, using the advice of the oversight committee and consultants. The final survey (after pretest) included 120 open- and closed-ended questions. The survey gathered information on resident housing preferences, housing history, employment history, income, hardship, health, neighborhood services, social networks, demographic characteristics, as well as resident reports on the conditions of the SRO they inhabited at the time of the interview. The surveys took 75 minutes on average to administer.

APPENDIX B
Index of Heterogeneity for Select Variables, by Hotel

HOTEL	FEMALE	BLACK	AGE	SRO VETERAN	INCOME	EMPLOY-MENT STATUS	LENGTH OF STAY
Central							
1	.93	1.00	.86	.18	.96	.64	.96
2	.61	.95	.75	.96	.96	.96	.75
3	.97	.00	.88	.26	.18	.26	.91
4	.58	.84	.85	.90	.96	.98	.99
5	.97	.91	.69	.92	.67	.26	.76
6	.00	.00	.80	.67	.80	.49	.88
7	.33	.94	.57	.86	.98	.98	.93
North							
11	1.00	.69	.95	.89	.92	.98	.95
12	.71	.75	.83	1.00	.89	.75	.96
13	.75	.99	.97	.79	.84	.99	.86
14	.52	.00	.99	.96	.98	1.00	.83
15	.00	.48	.96	.97	.99	.98	.92
South							
21	.55	.44	.75	.43	.83	.94	.91
22	.00	.00	.88	.00	.77	.80	.91
23	.83	.00	.82	.48	.73	.97	.76
24	.00	.00	.93	.36	.89	.96	.93
25	.62	.00	.75	.61	.84	.96	.96
26	.71	.00	.76	.48	.77	.93	.00
All	.69	.99	.99	.96	.99	.97	.99

Note: The formula for the index: $D = k \ (N^2 - f^2)/N^2 \ (k-1)$ where k=number of categories, f = frequency in each category, N=number of observations in hotel. Gene Lutz, *Understanding Social Statistics* (New York, 1983), p. 107. The index scores are particularly sensitive to the interval values used to define the categories. For the measures age, income, and length of stay we defined the interval values on the basis of even distribution of all respondents into three categories of equal size. Hence, the dispersion scores for all observations (respondents) for these measures are extremely high, reflecting the fact that we set the intervals so as to maximize the even dispersion of respondents. In the case of nominal measures like sex, race, and employment status we used the actual distribution among all residents. Hence, the dispersion scores for these measures are much lower, reflecting the fact that women, blacks, and the employed make up a minority of all respondents.

APPENDIX C
Defining Social Life in the SRO Hotel

We used multiple items from the survey form to construct a measure of the social relationships associated with life in the SRO hotel and its surrounding neighborhood. The classification scheme is outlined in table C-1, which lists each question and the value assigned for a yes response to each item. Each yes response was considered an indication of a unique social tie. The values were summed to provide a global measure of the SRO network. We expected to find that residents who denied close relations with kin and friends would still enjoy social ties with others nearby.

The SRO network index is a conservative measure of the scope of SRO social ties. That is, the index probably understates the number of local social ties residents actually possess. Most of the items in the SRO network index reflect preference ratings of residents for affiliation over other economic (e.g., cheap) and material (e.g., good quality) values. The SRO network index indicates that social ties were valued highly by SRO residents compared with other competing choices. The relationship with the SRO owners and staff represents an important exception. The contacts between residents and staff frequently involve a mix of companionship and business. Consequently, residents did not usually describe their relationships with staff as friendships, but many residents clearly valued their ties with hotel staff in ways that were not strictly instrumental or economic. Only a handful disliked the management.

The SRO Network Index may include members from a resident's personal network. The two measures are not exclusive. The SRO index, however, indicates the extent to which the social ties of a resident are related to the social world of the SRO. For instance, a resident who decided to live in the present SRO because another tenant who lived there was a friend may also have identified this same friend as a member of his or her personal network. Most important, the index also measures the extent of social ties for those residents who claimed they had no close relationships with kin or friends.

Throughout the survey we asked residents about specific problems they had recently faced in finding shelter, employment, clothing, food, and health care services and about whom they turned to for referrals and from

TABLE C-1
SRO Network Index Composition

	SCORE

I. SRO HOTEL SOCIABILITY INDEX

1. Decided to live in this hotel to be with friends/relatives — 1.00
2. Thing liked most about living in this hotel is other tenants.
   a. First Choice — 1.00
   b. Second Choice — .66
   c. Third Choice — .33
3. Thing disliked most about living in this hotel is other tenants.
   a. First Choice — −1.00
   b. Second Choice — −.66
   c. Third Choice — −.33
4. Usually watch TV in friend's room at hotel — 1.00
5. Usually drink in a friend's room — 1.00

II. SRO NEIGHBORHOOD SOCIABILITY INDEX

1. Go to local bar mainly to meet friends there — 1.00
2. Go to local cafe mainly to meet friends there — 1.00
3. Go to local restaurant mainly to meet friends there — 1.00
4. Go to local church mainly to meet friends/relatives there — 1.00
5. Thing liked most about living in this hotel is the neighborhood.
   a. First Choice — 1.00
   b. Second Choice — .66
   c. Third Choice — .33
6. Thing disliked most about living in this hotel is the neighborhood.
   a. First Choice — −1.00
   b. Second Choice — −.66
   c. Third Choice — −.33

III. SRO STAFF SOCIABILITY INDEX

1. Know the regular desk clerks and managers — 1.00
2. Contact with the owner of the building weekly or more — 1.00
3. The thing liked most about living in the hotel is the management.
   a. First Choice — 1.00
   b. Second Choice — .66
   c. Third Choice — .33
4. The thing disliked most about living in the hotel is the management.
   a. First Choice — −1.00
   b. Second Choice — −.66
   c. Third Choice — −.33

TABLE C-2

Frequency of Helping Episodes, by Kind and Source

| | SOURCE OF HELP | | | | |
TYPE OF HELP	Friends	Relatives	Both	SRO staff	Total
Referrals					
To present employer	23.5	—	—	—	23.5
To prior employer	60.5	8.0	—	—	68.5
To present SRO hotel	20.5	—	—	—	20.5
To doctor/dentist	1.0	41.5	—	24.5	67.0
To place with free meals	—	—	37.0	—	37.0
To place with free food	—	—	14.0	—	14.0
To place with free clothes	—	—	10.0	—	10.0
Actual Help					
Loaned/gave money	—	—	39.0	—	39.0
Cashes check	—	—	—	43.0	43.0
Total	105.5	49.5	100.0	67.5	322.5

whom they got aid. To indicate the extent of help each respondent received from all these sources, we assigned a value of 1 to each positive (plus sign) response a respondent made to these questions. This helping index provided an episodic rather than a relational indicator of help.

Most of the episodes consisted of informal referrals to formal service providers. Table C-2 lists the number of episodes for each kind and source of such help. The row totals in column five indicate that employment referrals were mentioned most frequently (92). Such frequent referrals also number among the most valuable since securing employment creates an enormous lift in the standard of living of a poor single person. Referral to health care providers (67) was the second most frequent type of helping episode reported. Uninformed about the availability and relative merits of various providers, about one in three residents turned to relatives or SRO staff for advice about where to go. Many fewer residents received money (39) when they found themselves without adequate funds. Yet, those who could do so enjoyed a substantial benefit.

The remainder of the helping episodes include a smattering of referrals to places where residents could obtain free meals (37), food (14), or clothes (10). The hotels offer check-cashing services for residents (43) in order to ensure timely payment of the rent, but the effect is to provide vulnerable

TABLE C-3

Helping Episodes Between Residents with/without
Personal Helping Networks, by Kind and Source of Help

TYPE OF HELP	SOURCE OF HELP (%)				
	Friend	Relative	Both	SRO	All
Referral to:					
Present employer	66/34	0	—	—	66/34
Prior employer	66/34	69/31	—	—	66/34
Present SRO	68/32	—	—	—	68/32
Doctor	100/—	86/14	—	67/33	79/21
Place with free meals	—	—	82/18	—	82/18
Place with free food	—	—	50/50	—	50/50
Place with free clothes	—	—	85/15	—	85/15
Actual					
Loans/gifts	—	—	92/08	—	92/08
Check cashing	—	—	—	63/37	63/37
All	86/34	83/17	82/18	64/36	73/27

Note: The value to the left of the slash (/) is the percentage of residents with personal networks reporting an episode in that cell. The value to the right is the percentage of residents with no personal helping network reporting an episode of help in the same cell.

residents with a convenient and relatively risk-free method of getting cash. Finally, about 10 percent of the residents claimed that they found their present SRO hotel room through the advice of others who had lived there (20.5). Altogether, these episodes compose a wide range of referrals that 78 percent of the residents used at least once.

Table C-3 compares the relative frequency of residents with and without personal helping relations for each type of episode of help identified in table C-1. Given that the distribution of those with helping networks to those without was 64 percent to 36 percent overall, this same split can be used as a standard for interpreting the splits in each cell. Thus, residents with helping networks who receive more than 64 percent of the help in a cell obtain a proportionally greater share than those residents without helping networks. In most cases a difference of at least plus or minus 15 percent is needed to yield a statistically significant difference.

NOTES

Chapter 1

1. Eric Zorn, "No Place Called Home," *Chicago Tribune*, Sept. 30, 1984.
2. William Breakey and Pamela Fischer, "Down and Out in the Land of Plenty," *Johns Hopkins Magazine*, June 1985, pp. 18–19.
3. Ibid., p. 18.

Chapter 2

1. Stephan Thernstrom, *The Other Bostonians* (Cambridge, Mass., 1973).
2. Robert Slayton, *Back of the Yards* (Chicago, 1986), pp. 90–91; Kenneth Allsop, *Hard Travellin'* (London, 1967), p. 89.
3. Slayton, *Back of the Yards*, p. 11.
4. Samuel Wallace, *Skid Row as a Way of Life* (Totawa, N.J., 1965), p. 19; Chicago Municipal Markets Commission, *Report to the Mayor and Aldermen* (Chicago, 1914), pp. 45–46; Tenants Relocation Bureau, *The Homeless Man on Skid Row* (Chicago, 1961), p. 5; Donald Bogue, *Skid Row in American Cities* (Chicago, 1963), pp. 236–37; Allsop, *Hard Travellin'*, p. 147; Nels Anderson, *The Hobo* (Chicago, 1923), pp. 110–11; John Schneider, "Tramping Workers," in Eric Monkkonen, ed., *Walking to Work* (Lincoln, Nebr., 1984), p. 227; Alice Solenberger, *One Thousand Homeless Men* (Chicago, 1911), p. 214.
5. Harvey Zorbaugh, *The Gold Coast and the Slum* (Chicago, 1929), p. 70; Evelyn Wilson, "Chicago Families in Furnished Rooms" (Ph.D. dissertation, University of Chicago, 1929), pp. 188–22; Grace Abbott, *The Tenements of Chicago* (Chicago, 1936), pp. 321–23.
6. Zorbaugh, *Gold Coast*, p. 73; Albert Wolfe, *The Lodging House Problem in Boston* (Boston, 1906), pp. 46–47.
7. "Landladies I Have Known," *Independent*, Dec. 1, 1910; pp. 1197, 1199.
8. Wolfe, *Lodging House Problem*, pp. 5, 47.
9. *Chicago City Directory*, 1885–1915; Joanne Meyerowitz, "Women Adrift" (unpublished MS. provided by the author), pp. 178–79; Zorbaugh, *Gold Coast*, p. 70; Harvey Zorbaugh, "The Dweller in Furnished Rooms," in *Papers and Proceedings of the Twentieth Annual Meeting of the American Sociological Society* 20 (1925): 85–86; *The Rooming House and Hotel Guide*, October 1926: 8, 10.
10. Meyerowitz, "Women Adrift," p. 179.
11. Paul Groth, "Forbidden Housing" (Ph.D. dissertation, University of California at Berkeley, 1983), p. 75.
12. Albert Wolfe, "The Problem of the Roomer," *Charities and the Commons*, Nov. 2, 1907, p. 959; Wolfe, *Lodging House Problem*, p. 72; Kenneth Jackson, *The Crabgrass Frontier* (New York, 1985), pp. 88, 104.

13. Zorbaugh, *Gold Coast*, p. 69; Ann Trotter, *Housing of Non-Family Women in Chicago* (Chicago, 1921), p. 5; Joanne Meyerowitz, "Holding Their Own" (Ph.D. dissertation, Stanford University, 1983), pp. 164–65; Wilson, "Chicago Families," p. 24; Groth, "Forbidden Housing," pp. 109–10; Wolfe, "The Problem of the Roomer," p. 958.

14. Sam Bass Warner, Jr., *The Private City* (Philadelphia, 1968), p. 4; James Borchert, *Alley Life in Washington* (Urbana, Ill., 1980), p. 23.

15. Groth, "Forbidden Housing," p. 201; Eleanor Woods, "Social Betterment in a Lodging District," *Charities and the Commons*, Nov. 2, 1907, p. 962; Wolfe, *Lodging House Problem*, pp. 38, 52–57; Meyerowitz, "Women Adrift", p. 186.

16. *The Rooming House and Hotel Guide*, Oct. 1926, p. 33.

17. Groth, "Forbidden Housing," pp. 201–202; Alice Fox and Edith Hadley, "Chelsea House," *Charities and the Commons*, Aug. 22, 1908, p. 611; Wolfe, "The Problem of the Roomer," p. 961.

18. Groth, "Forbidden Housing," p. 201; Wolfe, "The Problem of the Roomer," p. 961.

19. Groth, "Forbidden Housing," p. 201; Wolfe, *Lodging House Problem*, p. 65.

20. Zorbaugh, *Gold Coast*, p. 74; Groth, "Forbidden Housing," p. 202; Wolfe, *Lodging House Problem*, p. 64; Fox and Hadley, "Chelsea House," p. 611.

21. Zorbaugh, *Gold Coast*, pp. 70–72; Robert Woods, "The Myriad Tenantry of Furnished Rooms," *Charities and the Commons*, Nov. 2, 1907, p. 956; Wolfe, *Lodging House Problem*, p. 88; Meyerowitz, "Women Adrift", pp. 23, 255; "Working Women in Large Cities," in U.S. Commissioner of Labor, *Fourth Annual Report*, p. 183; Lynn Weiner, "Sisters of the Road," in Monkkonen, ed., *Walking to Work*, p. 180; Meyerowitz, "Holding Their Own," pp. 23–27.

22. Meyerowitz, "Holding Their Own," pp. 40–43.

23. Trotter, *Housing of Women*, pp. 6–12; Groth, "Forbidden Housing," p. 76; Meyerowitz, "Women Adrift", pp. 70, 72, 172; Wolfe, *Lodging House Problem*, pp. 35, 36.

24. "The Menace of the Boarding House," *Literary Digest*, Oct. 28, 1916, p. 87.

25. Wolfe, *Lodging House Problem*, p. 138; Meyerowitz, "Women Adrift," p. 73.

26. Trotter, *Housing of Women*, p. 11; Meyerowitz, "Holding Their Own," pp. 106–107, 111–13; Meyerowitz, "Women Adrift", p. 174.

27. Harriet Fayes, "Housing of Single Women," *Municipal Affairs* 3 (March 1899): 99; "Furnished Lodgings," *Living Age*, May 7, 1904, p. 381; "Franklin Square House," *Charities and the Commons*, May 3, 1902, p. 427; Mary Ford, "The Case of the Working Girl," *Critic*, Aug. 1906, p. 122.

28. Gunther Barth, *City People* (New York, 1980), pp. 3, 16.

29. Meyerowitz, "Women Adrift," p. 42; Barth, *City People*, p. 13.

30. Meyerowitz, "Women Adrift," pp. 42–43.

31. Groth, "Forbidden Housing," pp. 207–208, 477; Meyerowitz, "Women Adrift," p. 182.

32. Wolfe, *Lodging House Problem*, pp. 141, 143, 151, 159; Meyerowitz, "Women Adrift," pp. 43, 256–58.

33. Meyerowitz, "Women Adrift," p. 40.

34. Wolfe, *Lodging House Problem*, p. 27.

35. Ibid., p. 109; "The Experiences of a Boarding-House Keeper," *American Magazine*, Nov. 1922, p. 134.

36. Allan Spear, *Black Chicago* (Chicago, 1967), p. 12; Meyerowitz, "Holding Their Own," p. 42; Trotter, *Housing of Women*, p. 26.

37. Wilson, "Chicago Families," pp. 43–47, 57–65; John Schneider, "Tramping Workers," in Monkkonen, ed., *Walking to Work*, pp. 214–15; W. E. B. Du Bois, *The Philadelphia Negro* (Millwood, N.Y., 1973), p. 292.

38. St. Clair Drake and Horace Cayton, *Black Metropolis* (New York, 1945), p. 576.

39. Ibid., p. 572.

40. Thomas Philpott, *The Slum and the Ghetto* (New York, 1978), pp. 303–304; "A Negro Girl and a Y.W.C.A.," *Survey*, July 15, 1926, p. 464.

Chapter 3

1. Jesse Dees, Jr., *Flophouse* (Francestown, N.H.), p. xxv.

2. John Schneider, "Tramping Workers," in Eric Monkkonen, ed., *Walking to Work* (Lincoln, Nebr., 1984), pp. 224, 226–27; Kenneth Allsop, *Hard Travellin'* (London, 1967), pp. 168–71; Nels Anderson, *The Hobo* (Chicago, 1923), pp. 14–15; Edith Abbott, *The Tenements of Chicago* (Chicago, 1936), pp. 322–23; W. P. England, "The Lodging House," *Survey*, Dec. 2, 1911, p. 1314.

3. Thomas Philpott, *The Slum and the Ghetto* (New York, 1978), p. 100; Anderson, *Hobo*, pp. 8, 263; Paul Groth, "Forbidden Housing" (Ph.D. dissertation, University of California at Berkeley, 1983), p. 187.

4. W. E. B. Du Bois, *The Philadelphia Negro* (Millwood, N.Y., 1973), p. 271.

5. James Borchert, *Alley Life in Washington* (Urbana, Ill., 1980), pp. 108, 126; Du Bois, *Philadelphia Negro*, pp. 231–32.

6. John Schneider, "Skid Row as an Urban Neighborhood," in Jon Erickson and Charles Wilhelm, eds., *Housing the Homeless* (New Brunswick, N.J., 1986), p. 173; Harvey Zorbaugh, *The Gold Coast and the Slum* (Chicago, 1929), pp. 105, 116; Groth, "Forbidden Housing," p. 314; Anderson, *Hobo*, pp. 33–35; James M. Cain, "Dead Man," in Bill Pronzini, ed., *Midnight Specials* (New York, 1977), p. 109.

7. Zorbaugh, *Gold Coast*, pp. 105, 106, 108, 124, 125; Meyerowitz, "Holding Their Own" (Ph.D. dissertation, Stanford University, 1983), pp. 168–69; Schneider, "Skid Row," p. 172; Groth, "Forbidden Housing," p. 318; Anderson, *Hobo*, pp. 33–39, 184, 264.

8. Anderson, *Hobo*, p. 36; Samuel Wilson, *Chicago and Its Cess-Pools of Infamy* (Chicago, 1909), pp. 67–76; W. R. Patterson, "Pawnbroking in Europe and the United States," *Bulletin of the Department of Labor* 21 (Mar. 1899): 256–79; Frank Beck, *Hobohemia* (Rindge, N.H., 1956), p. 16.

9. Roger Bruns, *The Damndest Radical* (Urbana, Ill., 1987), pp. 1–2, 26–47, 202–14, 246–48, 269–71; Anderson, *Hobo*, pp. 8–10, 171, 183–84, 228–29, 237–39.

10. Robert Slayton, *Back of the Yards* (Chicago, 1986), pp. 124–25.

11. Meyerowitz, "Holding Their Own," p. 108; Schneider, "Tramping Workers," pp. 214–16; Anderson, *Hobo*, pp. xiv, 150–51.

12. Municipal Markets Commission, "Report to the Mayor and Aldermen" (Chicago, 1914), pp. 44–45; Zorbaugh, *Gold Coast*, p. 7.

13. Kenneth Kusmer, "The Underclass in Historical Perspective" (paper presented at the Conference on Being Homeless in New York, Museum of the City of New York, Jan. 27–28, 1987), pp. 5–7.

14. Schneider, "Tramping Workers," pp. 213, 216; Eric Monkkonen, "Afterword," in Monkkonen, ed., *Walking to Work*, p. 238; Alice Solenberger, *One Thousand Homeless Men* (New York, 1911), pp. 39–40, 241.

15. Eric Monkkonen, "Regional Dimensions of Tramping," in Monkkonen, ed., *Walking to Work*, p. 204; Schneider, "Tramping Workers," pp. 214–15.

16. Allsop, *Hard Travellin'*, p. ix.

17. Solenberger, *Homeless Men*, p. 135; Beck, *Hobohemia*, p. 76.

18. Anderson, *Hobo*, p. 93.

19. Dees, *Flophouse*, p. xix.

20. Monkkonen, "Introduction," and Monkkonen, "Regional Tramping," pp. 5, 208.

21. Anderson, *Hobo*, p. 90.

22. Ibid., pp. 94–95.

23. Ibid., p. 41.

24. Solenberger, *Homeless Men*, pp. 164–65.

25. Josiah Flynt, *Tramping with Tramps* (New York, 1901), p. 124.

26. Anderson, *Hobo*, p. 100.

27. Ibid., pp. 100–101; Willard Motley, *Let No Man Write My Epitaph* (New York, 1958), p. 75.

28. Flynt, *Tramps*, pp. 128–34.

29. Ibid., p. 119.

30. Ibid., pp. 114–19. See also the engraving of beer tramps on p. 119 of Wilson, *Chicago Cess-Pools*.

31. Dees, *Flophouse*, p. xxiv.

32. Kusmer, "Underclass in Historical Perspective," p. 11; Solenberger, *Homeless Men*, pp. 2, 139; Allsop, *Hard Travellin'*, pp. 105, 108; *Final Report of the Commission on Industrial Relations*, quoted in Anderson, *Hobo*, pp. 61–62, 64.

33. Joseph Kirkland, "Among the Poor of Chicago," *Scribner's*, July 1892, p. 12.

34. Alexander Irvine, "A Bunk-House and Some Bunk-House Men," *McClure's*, Aug. 1908, p. 462; Bruns, *Damndest Radical*, p. 29; Wilson, *Chicago Cess-Pools*, pp. 118–121.

35. Anderson, *Hobo*, pp. xx–xxi.

36. Samuel Wallace, *Skid Row as a Way of Life* (Totawa, N.J., 1965), p. 17; Solenberger, *Homeless Men*, p. 314; Albert Wolfe, *The Lodging House Problem in Boston* (Boston, 1906), p. 1; Jacob Riis, *How the Other Half Lives* (New York, 1971 edition), p. 69.

37. Anderson, *Hobo*, p. 29; Groth, "Forbidden Housing," pp. 181–82.

38. Solenberger, *Homeless Men*, pp. 318–19; John Bogue, *Chicago's Cheap Lodging Houses* (Chicago, 1899), p. 5; Philpott, *Slum and the Ghetto*, p. 97; W. P. England, "The Lodging House and their Lodgers," *Survey*, Dec. 2, 1911, p. 1315; Riis, *Other Half*, p. 70; Groth, "Forbidden Housing," p. 87.

39. Solenberger, *Homeless Men*, p. 318; Norman Hayner, "The Hotel" (Ph.D. dissertation, University of Chicago), p. 48; Flynt, *Tramps*, p. 123; Groth, "Forbidden Housing," p. 87.

40. Solenberger, *Homeless Men*, pp. 318–20; "Fifty Cheap Lodging Houses," in Chicago Department of Public Welfare, *First Semi-Annual Report*, March 1915, pp. 66, 68, 70; Anderson, *Hobo*, p. 132.

41. Bogue, *Lodging Houses*, p. 4; Paul Kennaday, "New York's Hundred Lodging Houses," *Charities*, Feb. 18, 1905, p. 488; "Fifty Cheap Lodging Houses," p. 70; Flynt, *Tramps*, p. 123; England, "The Lodging House," p. 1315.

42. Anderson, *Hobo*, p. 132; Solenberger, *Homeless Men*, p. 317; England, "The Lodging House," pp. 1313, 1315; "Fifty Cheap Lodging Houses," pp. 70, 72.

43. Solenberger, *Homeless Men*, pp. 322–25; England, "Lodging Houses," pp. 1313, 1315; "Fifty Cheap Lodging Houses," p. 72; T. Alexander Hyde, "A Paying Philanthropy: The Mills Hotel," *Arena*, July 1898, p. 84.

44. Solenberger, *Homeless Men*, pp. 320–22; "Fifty Cheap Lodging Houses," pp. 72–73.

45. See, for example, Clifford Shaw, *The Jack-Roller* (Chicago, 1930).

46. Solenberger, *Homeless Men*, pp. 315–17; Bogue, *Lodging Houses*, p. 4; Philpott, *Slum and the Ghetto*, p. 97; Irvine, "Bunk-House," p. 455; William Stead, *If Christ Came to Chicago* (Chicago, 1894), p. 162; Riis, *Other Half*, p. 74.

47. Kennaday, "New York's Hundred Lodging Houses," p. 487; Stephen Crane, "An Experiment in Misery," in Fredson Bowles, ed., *Stephen Crane* (Charlottesville, Va., 1973), pp. 287, 288; Riis, *Other Half*, p. 74.

48. Philpott, *Slum and the Ghetto*, p. 97; Riis, *Other Half*, p. 74; Groth, "Forbidden Housing," pp. 88–89; England, "The Lodging House," p. 1316; Anderson, *Hobo*, pp. 31–33.

49. Riis, *Other Half*, pp. 62, 64, 72; Anderson, *Hobo*, p. 27; Schneider, "Tramping Workers," p. 225; Flynt, *Tramps*, p. 120.

50. Anderson, *Hobo*, pp. 10–13; Riis, *Other Half*, p. 64; Arnold Rose, "Living Arrangements of Unattached Persons," *American Sociological Review* 12 (Aug. 1947): 433.

51. Solenberger, *Homeless Men*, p. 318.

52. Patricia Cooper, "The 'Traveling Fraternity': Union Cigar Makers and Geographic Mobility, 1900–1919," in Eric Monkkonen, ed., *Walking to Work*, pp. 122, 124; Tenants Relocation Bureau, *The Homeless Man on Skid Row* (Chicago, 1961), p. 5; "Lodging House Reform," *Charities and the Commons*, Mar. 23, 1907, p. 1118.

53. Stead, *If Christ Came*, pp. 27–29.

54. Ibid., pp. 29–30.

55. Alvan Sanborn, "A Study of Beggars and Their Lodgings," *Forum*, Apr. 1895, p. 207; Riis, *Other Half*, p. 72; Schneider, "Tramping Workers," p. 221; *Chicago Tribune*, Dec. 12, 1899; Stead, *If Christ Came*, p. 29; Eric Monkkonen, *The Police in Urban America* (New York, 1981), p. 87.

56. James Mullenbach, "The Sifting Process and the Unemployed," *Proceedings of the National Conference of Charities and Corrections* (1916), p. 193; Stead, *If Christ Came*, pp. 19–22; Monkkonen, *Police*, pp. 89–99.

57. Monkkonen, *Police*, pp. 94–96.

58. Dees, *Flophouse*, p. 40; Philpott, *Slum and the Ghetto*, p. 99; Anderson, *Hobo*, pp. 260–61; Edwin Sutherland and Harvey Locke, *Twenty Thousand Homeless Men* (Chicago, 1936), p. 186.

59. Elizabeth Hughes, "Five Hundred Lodgers of the City," in City of Chicago, Department of Public Welfare, *Annual Report* (1926), pp. 10, 11, 14.

60. Philpott, *Slum and the Ghetto*, p. 99; Dees, *Flophouse*, p. 41; Bruns, *Damndest Radical*, p. 31; Kusmer, "Underclass in Historical Perspective," pp. 20–21.

61. William Whiting, "A Dead Letter Office for Misdirected Men," *Survey*, Nov. 27, 1915, p. 208; Anderson, *Hobo*, p. 261.

62. Kusmer, "Underclass in Historical Perspective," pp. 20–21; Philpott, *Slum and the Ghetto*, p. 99; Dees, *Flophouse*, pp. 42–43; Sutherland and Locke, *Homeless Men*, p. 188.

63. Dees, *Flophouse*, p. 43; "The Municipal Wood Yard," City of Chicago, *Bulletin of the Department of Public Welfare*, Sept. 1916, pp. 13–15; Raymond Robins, "What Constitutes a Model Municipal Lodging House," *Proceedings of the National Conference of Charities and Corrections* (1904), p. 163.

64. Philpott, *Slum and the Ghetto*, pp. 99–100; Anderson, *Hobo*, pp. 260–61; Dees, *Flophouse*, pp. 42–43; "Municipal Wood Yard," pp. 14–15, 21; Sutherland and Locke, *Homeless Men*, p. 188.

65. "An Interesting Scientific Experiment," *Scientific American*, Nov. 6, 1897, p. 291; "Model Lodging Houses for New York," *Review of Reviews*, Jan. 1897, pp. 59–61; Hyde, "Paying Philanthropy," pp. 78–81; John Thomas, "Workingmen's Hotels," *Municipal Affairs* 3 (March 1899): 85–90; *Chicago Tribune*, Dec. 12, 1899; Philpott, *Slum and the Ghetto*, pp. 97–99.

66. "A Place for Men on the City's Threshold," *Survey*, June 17, 1916, p. 303; "Chicago's Memorial Hotel for the Unemployed," *Literary Digest*, Jan. 31, 1914, p. 121; "Decent Lodgings for Poor Men," *Independent*, Sept. 11, 1913, p. 638; Anderson, *Hobo*, p. 28.

67. Schneider, "Tramping Workers," p. 222; Bogue, *Lodging Houses*, p. 6; Groth, "Forbidden Housing," pp. 91–92; Chicago Christian Industrial League, *Remaking Men and Materials* (Chicago, n.d.); Hayner, "Hotel," p. 51; Travelers Aid Society Papers, Access 73–17, box 27, folder 1; box 3, folder 3, University of Illinois—Chicago.

68. Bruns, *Damndest Radical*, p. 145; Wilson, *Chicago Cess-Pools*, p. 135; Kirkland, "Among the Poor," p. 10; Anderson, *Hobo*, p. 54; Joseph Speed, "A Study of Beggars and Their Lodgings," *Forum*, Apr. 1895, pp. 206–207; Stead, *If Christ Came*, pp. 26–27.

69. Kusmer, "Underclass in Historical Perspective," pp. 24–25; Schneider, "Tramping Workers," pp. 222–23; "The Salvation Army," in *Proceedings of the National Conference of Charities and Corrections* (1906), pp. 504–13.

70. Anderson, *Hobo*, pp. 31, 103, 197; Speed, "Study of Beggars," p. 206; Ronald Miller, *The Demolition of Skid Row* (Lexington, Mass., 1982), p. 5.

71. James Rooney, "Organizational Success through Program Failure: Skid Row Rescue Missions," *Social Forces* 58 (Mar. 1980): 904–24; Beck, *Hobohemia*, pp. 20, 21.

72. Frances Bjorkman, "The New Anti-Vagrancy Campaign," *American Review of Reviews*, Feb. 1908, p. 208; Anderson, *Hobo*, p. 251.

Chapter 4

1. Nels Anderson, *The Hobo* (Chicago, 1923), pp. xix, 9–11; Eric Monkkonen, "Introduction," in Monkkonen, ed., *Walking to Work* (Lincoln, Nebr., 1984), p. 7; Nels Anderson, *Men on the Move* (Chicago, 1940), pp. 2, 38; Kenneth Allsop, *Hard Travellin'* (London, 1967), p. 45.

2. Roger Bruns, *The Damndest Radical* (Urbana, Ill., 1987), p. 26; John Schneider, "Skid Row as an Urban Neighborhood," in Jon Erickson and Charles Wilhelm, eds., *Housing the Homeless* (New Brunswick, N.J., 1986), p. 174; Kenneth Kusmer, "The Underclass in Historical Perspective" (paper presented at the Conference on Being Homeless in New York, Museum of the City of New York, Jan. 27–28, 1987), p. 12.

3. Kenneth Jackson, *The Crabgrass Frontier* (New York, 1985), p. 220.

4. Anthony Jackson, *A Place Called Home* (Cambridge, 1976), p. 157.

5. Steven Diner, *A City and its Universities* (Chapel Hill, N.C., 1980), p. 64.

6. Ibid., pp. 65–66.

7. Quoted in ibid., p. 6.

8. Quoted in ibid., pp. 17–18.

9. Ibid., pp. 28–32, 198–99; Robert Faris, *Chicago Sociology* (San Francisco, 1967), pp. 12, 52.

10. Diner, *City and its Universities*, pp. 121–22, 124–29, 136; Louise Rowe, *A General Report of the Department of Public Welfare* (Chicago, 1915), p. 3.

11. Diner, *City and its Universities*, pp. 32, 132.

12. Ibid., p. 10.

13. Ibid., p. 57.

14. Alice Solenberger, *One Thousand Homeless Men* (Chicago, 1911), p. vii; Kathleen McCarthy, *Noblesse Oblige* (Chicago, 1982), pp. 114–15; Anthony Travis, "The Impulse toward the Welfare State" (Ph.D. dissertation, Michigan State University, 1971), pp. 96–97.

15. Two of the leading studies on this are Robert Wiebe, *The Search for Order* (New York, 1967), and Burton Bledstein, *The Culture of Professionalism* (New York, 1976).

16. Roy Lubove, *The Professional Altruist* (New York, 1965), pp. 20, 47, 122.

17. Ibid., pp. 139–44; McCarthy, *Noblesse Oblige*, pp. 136–37; Diner, *City and its Universities*, pp. 46–47.

18. Diner, *City and its Universities*, p. 46.

19. Lubove, *Professional Altruist*, pp. 220–21.

20. Diner, *City and its Universities*, pp. 122–23.

21. Robert DeForest, "A Brief History of the Housing Movement in America," *The Annals of the American Academy of Political and Social Science* 51 (Jan. 1914): 8; Alice Higgins, "Comparative Advantages of Municipal and C.O.S. Lodging Houses," *Proceedings of the National Conference of Charities and Corrections* (1904), p. 151; Robert Hunter, *Tenement Conditions in Chicago* (Chicago, 1901), p. 161.

22. Edith Abbott, *The Tenements of Chicago* (Chicago, 1936), pp. 34–54; Hunter, *Tenement Conditions*, p. 343.

23. Abbott, *Tenements*, pp. 58–61; Hunter, *Tenement Conditions*, p. 343; Thomas

Philpott, *The Slum and the Ghetto* (New York, 1978), pp. 92–93; Lawrence Veiller, "Housing Conditions and Tenement Laws in Leading American Cities," in Robert DeForest and Lawrence Veiller, eds., *The Tenement House Problem* (New York, 1903), pp. 131–32.

24. *Chicago Tribune*, Dec. 12, 1899.

25. "Fifty Cheap Lodging Houses," in Chicago Department of Public Welfare, *First Semi-Annual Report* (Mar. 1915), pp. 66–73; Frances Bjorkman, "The New Anti-Vagrancy Campaign," *American Review of Reviews*, Feb. 1908, pp. 208–209.

26. Robert Park, "The City as a Social Laboratory," in Ralph Turner, ed., *Robert E. Park on Social Control and Collective Behavior* (Chicago, 1967), p. 9; Ernest Burgess, "The Ecological Approach," in Robert Park, Ernest Burgess, and Roderick McKenzie, *The City* (Chicago, 1967 ed.), p. 73; Ernest Burgess, "Urban Areas," in T. V. Smith and Leonard White, eds., *Chicago: An Experiment in Social Science Research* (Chicago, 1958), p. 113; Ernest Burgess, "The Growth of the City," in Park, Burgess, and McKenzie, *The City*, p. 57.

27. Bruns, *Damndest Radical*, p. 35; Paul Groth, "Forbidden Housing" (Ph.D. dissertation, University of California at Berkeley, 1983), p. 191; W. P. England, "The Lodging House and Their Lodgers," *Survey*, Dec. 2, 1911, p. 1317; John Schneider, "The Police on Skid Row: Historical Perspectives" (paper presented at the Annual Meeting of the American Society of Criminology, Atlanta, Ga., Oct. 29, 1986), p. 3; Eric Monkkonen, "Regional Dimensions of Tramping," in Monkkonen, ed., *Walking to Work*, p. 207; Kusmer, "Underclass in Historical Perspective," p. 4; William Stead, *If Christ Came to Chicago* (Chicago, 1894), p. 24; Bjorkman, "Anti-Vagrancy Campaign," p. 206; Michael Davis, "Forced to Tramp: The Perspective of the Labor Press," in Monkkonen, ed., *Walking to Work*, p. 142; Faris, *Chicago Sociology*, p. 86.

28. Raymond Mohl, *The New City* (Arlington Heights, Ill., 1984), pp. 178–79; Sam Bass Warner, Jr., *The Urban Wilderness* (New York, 1972), p. 104; Roy Lubove, "The Roots of Urban Planning," in Allen Wakstein, ed., *The Urbanization of America* (New York, 1970), pp. 323–24; Jackson, *Crabgrass Frontier*, pp. 241–42; Catherine Bauer, "Good Neighborhoods," *Annals of the American Academy of Political and Social Science* 242 (Nov. 1945): 105, 106–107.

29. Tenants Relocation Bureau, *The Homeless Man on Skid Row* (Chicago, 1961), p. 6; Ronald Miller, *The Demolition of Skid Row* (Lexington, Mass., 1982), p. 21; Robert Wilson, *Community Planning for Homeless Men and Boys* (New York, 1931); Joan Krouse, *The Homeless Transient in the Great Depression* (Albany, N.Y., 1986), p. 70.

30. Groth, "Forbidden Housing," p. 231; Abbott, *Tenements*, pp. 70–71.

31. Jesse Dees, Jr., *Flophouse* (Francestown, N.H., 1948), p. 55; Edwin Sutherland and Harvey Locke, *Twenty Thousand Homeless Men* (Chicago, 1936), pp. 191–95.

32. Anderson, *Men on the Move*, pp. 59–60, 62, 65, 105–107, 114; Weiner, "Sisters of the Road," in Monkkonen, ed., *Walking to Work*, pp. 184–85; Kathryn Close, "Women Alone," *Survey*, Sept. 1938, p. 281.

33. Anderson, *Men on the Move*, p. 77.

34. Ibid., pp. 81–83, 93, 239; Sutherland and Locke, *Homeless Men*, pp. 17, 35, 37, 39, 50–62; Chicago Relief Commission, *Unattached Non-Resident Men* (1939), p. 29.

35. Illinois Emergency Relief Commission, *First Annual Report* (1935), p. 75.

36. Anderson, *Men on the Move*, pp. 69, 301–303; Schneider, "Skid Row," p. 175.

37. Anderson, *Men on the Move*, pp. 69, 303–307; C. M. Bookman, "The Federal Transient Program," *Survey* (April 1935), pp. 104–105.

38. Anderson, *Men on the Move*, pp. 303–307; Arnold Rose, "Interest in the Living Arrangements of the Urban Unattached," *American Journal of Sociology* 53 (May 1948): 490–91.

39. Dees, *Flophouse*, pp. 135–40.

40. Ibid., p. 68; Sutherland and Locke, *Homeless Men*, pp. 195–96; Frank Glick, *The Illinois Emergency Relief Commission* (Chicago, 1940), p. 62 (hereafter cited as *IERC*).

41. Glick, *IERC*, pp. vii, 30; Krouse, *Homeless Transient*, p. 86.

42. Glick, *IERC*, p. 83.

43. Dees, *Flophouse*, pp. 68–71; David Scheyer, "Flop-House," *Nation*, Aug. 22, 1934, p. 217.

44. Dees, *Flophouse*, pp. 73–74.

45. Ibid., p. 76; Scheyer, "Flop-House," p. 217.

46. Dees, *Flophouse*, pp. 69, 77, 95, 105, 112; Sutherland and Locke, *Homeless Men*, p. 8.

47. Dees, *Flophouse*, pp. 78, 79, 80, 97, 103–104; Krouse, *Homeless Transient*, p. 73.

48. Sutherland and Locke, *Homeless Men*, pp. 6, 106; Scheyer, "Flop-House," pp. 216–17; Dees, *Flophouse*, p. 101.

49. Dees, *Flophouse*, pp. 69, 71, 85, 86.

50. Sutherland and Locke, *Homeless Men*, p. 21; Chicago Relief Commission, *Unattached Men*, p. 29; Bookman, "Transient Program," p. 104; Krouse, *Homeless Transient*, p. 188.

51. Quoted in Glick, *IERC*, pp. 138–40.

52. Chicago Relief Commission, *Unattached Men*, p. 30.

53. Sutherland and Locke, *Homeless Men*, pp. 144–49; Dees, *Flophouse*, p. 126.

54. Sutherland and Locke, *Homeless Men*, pp. 9, 10, 13, 14, 145, 147–48, 151, 153–54; Dees, *Flophouse*, p. 88.

55. Dees, *Flophouse*, p. 134.

56. Sutherland and Locke, *Homeless Men*, pp. 52–62, 147–48; Chicago Relief Commission, *Unattached Men*, p. 29.

57. Sutherland and Locke, *Homeless Men*, pp. 68, 86.

58. Scheyer, "Flop-House," p. 218; Sutherland and Locke, *Homeless Men*, p. 204.

59. Judith Trolander, *Settlement Houses and the Great Depression* (Detroit, 1975), p. 122. On reformers and the destruction of low-income housing, see Philpott, *Slum and the Ghetto*.

60. Bruns, *Damndest Radical*, p. 267.

61. Diner, *City and its Universities*, p. 119.

Chapter 5

1. Wallace Turner, "On the First Skid Row, Clash Over Efforts To Help," *New York Times*, Dec. 2, 1986; Ronald Vander Kooi, "The Main Stem: Skid Row Revisited," *Society*, Sept./Oct. 1973, p. 65; Paul Groth, "Forbidden Housing" (Ph.D. dissertation, University of California at Berkeley, 1983), p. 187; Ronald Miller, *The Demolition of Skid Row* (Lexington, Mass., 1982), p. 2.

2. James Rooney, "Societal Forces and the Unattached Male," in Howard Bahr, ed., *Disaffiliated Man* (Toronto, 1980), p. 19; Barrett Lee, "The Disappearance of Skid Row," *Urban Affairs Quarterly* 16 (Sept. 1980): 97.

3. Samuel Wallace, *Skid Row as a Way of Life* (Totowa, N.J., 1965), p. 23.

4. Margaret Chandler, "The Social Organization of Workers in a Rooming House Area" (Ph.D. dissertation, University of Chicago, 1948), pp. 8, 12–15, 54, 143.

5. Patricia Bronte, *Vittles and Vice* (Chicago, 1952), pp. 147–48.

6. Joanne Meyerowitz, "Women Adrift" (unpublished MS provided by the author), p. 256; Bronte, *Vittles*, pp. 146–47; Norman Hayner, "The Hotel" (Ph.D. dissertation, University of Chicago, 1923), pp. 44–46; Joanne Meyerowitz, "Holding Their Own" (Ph.D. dissertation, Stanford University, 1983), pp. 168–69.

7. William McSheehy, *Skid Row* (Cambridge, Mass., 1979), pp. 13–15; Tenants Relocation Bureau, *The Homeless Man on Skid Row* (Chicago, 1961), p. 6; Howard Bain, "A Sociological Analysis of the Chicago Skid-Row Lifeway" (M.A. thesis, University of Chicago, 1950), pp. xx–xxi; Donald Bogue, *Skid Row in American Cities* (Chicago, 1963), pp. 79–80.

8. Howard Bahr and Theodore Caplow, *Old Men Drunk and Sober* (New York, 1973), pp. 16, 46–49; Wallace, *Skid Row*, p. 22.

9. Bogue, *Skid Row*, p. 17.

10. McSheehy, *Skid Row*, p. 97.

11. Bogue, *Skid Row*, pp. 14, 15, 100; Tenants Relocation Bureau, *Homeless Man*, p. 31.

12. Bogue, *Skid Row*, pp. 15, 176–77; Tenants Relocation Bureau, *Homeless Man*, p. 29; Wallace, *Skid Row*, pp. 82–83; Leonard Blumberg, Thomas Shipley, and Stephen Barsky, *Liquor and Poverty* (New Brunswick, N.J., 1978), pp. 146–47; Kenan Heise, *They Speak for Themselves* (Chicago, 1965), pp. 96–97; Bain, "Sociological Analysis," pp. 111–18.

13. Bogue, *Skid Row*, pp. 6, 15, 182; Tenants Relocation Bureau, *Homeless Man*, p. 15.

14. Bogue, *Skid Row*, pp. 6, 104, 184; Tenants Relocation Bureau, *Homeless Man*, pp. 34–35; Sara Harris, *Skid Row, U.S.A.* (Garden City, N.Y., 1956), pp. 91, 102.

15. Tenants Relocation Bureau, *Homeless Man*, pp. 17, 38; Bogue, *Skid Row*, pp. 15, 238; Ronald Vander Kooi, "Skid Rowers: Their Alienation and Involvement in Community and Society" (Ph.D. dissertation, Michigan State University, 1966), pp. 153–54; Bahr and Caplow, *Old Men*, p. 14.

16. Willard Motley, *Let No Man Write My Epitaph* (New York, 1958), pp. 55–56; Bogue, *Skid Row*, p. 91; Tenants Relocation Bureau, *Homeless Man*, p. 15; Vander Kooi, "Skid Rowers," p. 102; Bain, "Sociological Analysis," pp. 33–37; John

Schneider, "Skid Row as an Urban Neighborhood, 1880–1960," in Jon Erickson and Charles Wilhelm, eds., *Housing the Homeless* (New Brunswick, N.J., 1986), p. 178.

17. Tenants Relocation Bureau, *Homeless Man*, pp. 15, 101; Bogue, *Skid Row*, p. 108; Bain, "Sociological Analysis," pp. 39–46.

18. Bogue, *Skid Row*, pp. 6, 106–107, 256–70; Bain, "Sociological Analysis," pp. 45, 92; Vander Kooi, "Skid Rowers," p. 139; Howard Bahr, *Skid Row* (New York, 1973), pp. 168–69.

19. Tenants Relocation Bureau, *Homeless Man*, pp. 18–20, 17–18, 34, 101; Bogue, *Skid Row*, pp. 90–93.

20. Harris, *Skid Row*, p. 19; Vander Kooi, "Skid Rowers," pp. 219–20. For material on the role of bars in working-class neighborhoods, see Perry Duis, *The Saloon* (Urbana, Ill., 1983), and Robert Slayton, *Back of the Yards* (Chicago, 1986), pp. 99–104.

21. Bahr, *Skid Row*, p. 103; Bogue, *Skid Row*, p. 170.

22. Vander Kooi, "Skid Rowers," pp. 2, 180; Wallace, *Skid Row*, pp. 157–58; Bogue, *Skid Row*, p. 398.

23. Harris, *Skid Row*, p. 79.

24. Pat Nash, *The Methodology of the Study of Bowery Lodging Houses* (New York, 1964), pp. 18, 29–34; James Spradley, *You Owe Yourself a Drunk* (Boston, 1970), p. 191.

25. Willard Motley, *Knock on Any Door* (New York, 1947), pp. 129–30; Harris, *Skid Row*, pp. 22–24.

26. Vander Kooi, "Skid Rowers," p. 211.

27. Tenants Relocation Bureau, *Homeless Man*, p. 95; Bogue, *Skid Row*, pp. 82–84.

28. Bogue, *Skid Row*, pp. 83–84; Tenants Relocation Bureau, *Homeless Man*, pp. 11–14, 97; McSheehy, *Skid Row*, pp. 37–38.

29. McSheehy, *Skid Row*, pp. 37–40, 126–27; Wallace, *Skid Row*, p. 39; Vander Kooi, "Skid Rowers," pp. 34–35; Bahr, *Skid Row*, pp. 123–27; Blumberg, Shipley, and Shandler, *Skid Row* (Philadelphia, 1973), pp. 77–79.

30. Bain, "Sociological Analysis," p. 109; Tenants Relocation Bureau, *Homeless Man*, p. 8; Bogue, *Skid Row*, pp. 262, 410.

31. Bogue, *Skid Row*, pp. 446–48; Tenants Relocation Bureau, *Homeless Man*, pp. 57, 95.

32. Bogue, *Skid Row*, p. 191; Chicago Christian Industrial League, *Fifty Years* (Chicago, 1959); Bain, "Sociological Analysis," p. 133; Kenneth Allsop, *Hard Travellin'* (London, 1967), p. 201; Blumberg, Shipley, and Shandler, *Skid Row*, p. 89; McSheehy, *Skid Row*, pp. 17–33.

33. Wallace, *Skid Row*, pp. 82–83; McSheehy, *Skid Row*, pp. 47–56; Vander Kooi, "Skid Rowers," p. 205; Bogue, *Skid Row*, pp. 55, 489–90; Heise, *They Speak*, pp. 91–92.

34. Vander Kooi, "Skid Rowers," p. 156; Bain, "Sociological Analysis," p. 137; McSheehy, *Skid Row*, pp. 73–75; Bahr, *Skid Row*, pp. 144–47.

35. Motley, *Door*, pp. 131, 140; McSheehy, *Skid Row*, pp. 77; Bahr, *Skid Row*, p. 149; Wallace, *Skid Row*, p. 118.

36. Bogue, *Skid Row*, pp. 409–18.

37. Ibid., p. 434; Vander Kooi, "Skid Rowers," p. 39.

38. Hyman Feldman, "What We Can Do About Skid Row," *Today's Health*, Dec. 1957, p. 19; Vander Kooi, "Skid Rowers," pp. 38, 163; Bain, "Sociological Analysis," p. 94.

39. Wallace, *Skid Row*, p. 92; Bahr and Caplow, *Old Men*, p. 16; Bahr, *Skid Row*, p. 228.

40. John Schneider, "The Police on Skid Row: Historical Perspectives" (paper presented at the American Society of Criminology, Atlanta, Ga., Oct. 29, 1986, pp. 10–11.

41. Spradley, *You Owe Yourself a Drunk*, pp. 118, 256; Jerome Ellison, "The Shame of Skid Row," *Saturday Evening Post*, Dec. 20, 1952, p. 13; Motley, *Door*, p. 174.

Chapter 6

1. Donald Bogue, *Skid Row in American Cities* (Chicago: Community and Family Study Center, University of Chicago, 1963); Howard Bahr, *Skid Row: An Introduction to Disaffiliation* (New York, 1973); Leonard Blumberg, Thomas Shipley, and Stephen Barsky, *Liquor and Poverty: Skid Row as a Human Condition* (New Brunswick, N.J., 1978).

2. Samuel Wallace, "The Road to Skid Row," *Social Problems* 16 (1967): 92–105; James Spradley, *You Owe Yourself a Drunk* (Boston, 1970); William McSheehy, *Skid Row* (Cambridge, Mass., 1979); Ronald Vander Kooi, "Skid Rowers: Their Alienation and Involvement in Community and Society" (Ph.D. dissertation, Michigan State University, 1966); James Rooney, "Group Processes Among Skid Row Winos," *Quarterly Journal of Studies on Alcohol* 22 (Sept. 1961): 444–60.

3. McSheehy, *Skid Row*; Jacquelyn Wiseman, *Stations of the Lost: The Treatment of Skid Row Alcoholics* (Englewood Cliffs, N.J., 1970).

4. Vander Kooi, "Skid Rowers," p. 96.

5. Howard Bahr and Theodore Caplow, *Old Men Drunk and Sober* (New York, 1973), p. 10.

6. Ibid., p. 13; Bogue, *Skid Row*, pp. vii, 476–77; Tenants Relocation Bureau, *The Homeless Man on Skid Row* (Chicago, 1961), p. 1.

7. "American Cities Must Get Rid of Their 'Skid Rows,' " *Saturday Evening Post*, Feb. 21, 1959, p. 10; William Slocum, "Skid Row U.S.A.," *Colliers*, Aug. 27, 1949, pp. 25–26, 40–41; James O'Gara, "Chicago's Misery Mile," *Commonweal*, Sept. 30, 1949, pp. 598–600; John Schneider, "Skid Row as an Urban Neighborhood," in Jon Erickson and Charles Wilhelm, eds., *Housing the Homeless* (New Brunswick, N.J.), p. 179; Howard Bain, "A Sociological Analysis of the Chicago Skid-Row Lifeway" (M.A. thesis, University of Chicago, 1950), p. 4; William Gleason, *The Liquid Cross of Skid Row* (Milwaukee, 1966), p. 137.

8. Samuel Wallace, *Skid Row as a Way of Life* (Totowa, N.J., 1965), pp. 181, 188; Ronald Miller, *The Demolition of Skid Row* (Lexington, Mass., 1982), p. 49.

9. Miller, *Demolition*, p. 25; Blumberg, Shipley, and Chandler, *Skid Row* (Philadelphia, 1973), p. 209.

10. Theodore Caplow, "Transiency as a Cultural Pattern," *American Sociological Review* 5 (Oct. 1940): 739; Theodore Wallace, *A General Report on the Problem*

of Relocating the Population of the Lower Loop Redevelopment Area (Minneapolis: Minneapolis Housing and Redevelopment Authority, 1958).

11. Bahr and Caplow, *Old Men*, pp. 5–6.

12. Ibid., p. 59.

13. Ibid., p. 62.

14. See in particular the classic ecological text, Robert Park, Ernest Burgess, and Robert McKenzie, *The City* (Chicago, 1925). Recent critics include Michael Smith, *The City and Social Theory* (New York, 1979); Manuell Castells, "Is There an Urban Sociology," in Christopher Pickvance, ed., *Urban Sociology: Critical Essays* (New York, 1977), pp. 33–59.

15. Mark Gottdiener, *The Social Production of Space* (Austin, Tex., 1985), p. 31.

16. Ibid., p. 33.

17. John Mollenkopf, *The Contested City* (Princeton, N.J., 1983), pp. 32–46.

18. Harvey Molotch, "The City as Growth Machine: Toward a Political Economy of Place," *American Journal of Sociology* 82 (1976): 309–30.

19. Robert Dahl, *Who Governs?* (New Haven, Conn., 1961); G. William Domhoff, *Who Really Rules?* (Santa Monica, Calif., 1978).

20. Peter Marcuse, "Housing Policy and the Myth of the Benevolent State," in Rachel Bratt, Chester Hartman, and Ann Meyerson, eds., *Critical Perspectives on Housing* (Philadelphia, 1986), p. 353; "Survey Reveals Widespread Agreement on Slum Clearance Needs," *American City*, Apr. 1948, p. 5; Miller, *Demolition*, p. 15.

21. Leonard Blumberg, Thomas Shipley, and Stephen Barsky, *Liquor and Poverty* (New Brunswick, N.J., 1978), pp. 87–99.

22. William Slayton, "Report on Urban Renewal," in Jewel Bellush and Murray Hausknecht, eds., *Urban Renewal: People, Planning and Politics* (Garden City, N.Y., 1967), pp. 381–85.

23. Martin Anderson, "The Federal Bulldozer," in Bellush and Hausknecht, eds., *Urban Renewal*, p. 391; Charles Abrams, "Slums, Housing, and Urban Renewal," in Allen Wakstein, ed., *The Urbanization of America* (Boston, 1970), p. 8; Herbert Gans, "The Failure of Urban Renewal," *Commentary*, Apr. 1965, pp. 29–31.

24. Mollenkopf, *Contested City*, pp. 180–212.

25. Miller, *Demolition*, pp. 87–88; "Illinois Cities and Villages Get Added Housing Aid and Powers," *American City*, Aug. 1945, p. 97; Devereux Bowly, Jr., *The Poorhouse* (Carbondale, Ill., 1978), p. 61.

26. "Businessmen and the Slums," *Fortune*, Dec. 1953, p. 101.

27. McSheehy, *Skid Row*, p. 90; Chicago Department of Urban Renewal, *Madison-Canal: Proposal for Renewal* (Mar. 1966), p. 11.

28. Urban Renewal, *Madison-Canal*, pp. 1, 5–6.

29. Ronald Vander Kooi, *Relocating West Madison Street "Skid Row" Residents: A Study of the Problem, With Recommendations* (May 1967), p. 30.

30. Ibid., pp. 2, 31.

31. Chicago Department of Urban Renewal, *Report to the Department of Urban Renewal on the Designation of Slum and Blighted Area Madison-Canal* (May 1967).

32. Chicago Department of Urban Renewal, *Redevelopment Plan for Slum and Blighted Area Development: Project Madison-Canal* (Oct. 1967).

33. Chicago Department of Urban Renewal, *Staff Report on Offers to Purchase*

Land in Slum and Blighted Area Redevelopment Project Madison-Canal (Dec. 5, 1968); Bowly, *Poorhouse*, p. 132; McSheehy, *Skid Row*, pp. 91–92.

34. Arthur Lyons, *When Everything Works and Nothing Is Right* (Chicago, 1986), pp. 9–10.

35. McSheehy, *Skid Row*, pp. 91–92; telephone interview with Ronald Vander Kooi, Sept. 4, 1987.

36. Chester Hartman, *Yerba Buena* (San Francisco, 1974), pp. 92–119.

Chapter 7

1. Marc Fried, "Grieving for a Lost Home," in Leonard S. Duhl, ed., *The Urban Condition* (New York, 1963), pp. 151–71; Chester Hartman, *Yerba Buena* (San Francisco, 1974); James Ward, *The Street Is Their Home: The Hobo's Manifesto* (Melbourne, 1979).

2. U.S. Department of Housing and Urban Development, Office of Policy Development and Research, *Displacement Report* (Washington, D.C., Feb. 1979); Richard LeGates and Chester Hartman, "Displacement," *Clearing House Review* 15 (July 1981): 207–49; Richard LeGates and Chester Hartman, "The Anatomy of Displacement in the United States," in Neil Smith and Peter Williams, eds., *Gentrification of the City* (Boston, 1986), pp. 178–203.

3. Rosemary Erickson and Kevin Eckert, "The Elderly Poor in Downtown San Diego Hotels," *Gerontologist* 17 (1979): 440–446.

4. Harvey Siegel, *Outposts of the Forgotten* (Edison, N.J., 1978).

5. Janice Smithers, *Determined Survivors* (New Brunswick, N.J., 1985).

6. Janice Stephens, *Loners, Lovers and Losers: Elderly Tenants in a Slum Hotel* (Seattle, 1976).

7. A 1982 national survey found only 18 percent of United States adults claimed fair or poor health status. See Peter Rossi, Gene Fisher, and Georgianna Willis, *The Condition of the Homeless in Chicago* (Chicago: National Opinion Research Center, 1986), p. 104.

8. Larry Bourne, *The Geography of Housing* (New York, 1980), pp. 134–35; U.S. Department of Commerce, Bureau of the Census, *Geographical Mobility: March 1983 to March 1984*, in no. 407, Current Population Reports Population Characteristics, Series P-20 (Washington D.C., 1986), p. 117.

9. Donald Bogue, *Skid Row in American Cities* (Chicago, 1963), p. 142.

10. See ibid., pp. 410, 428–29; Siegal, *Outposts*, pp. 7–20, provides a brief summary of the controversy surrounding the use of SRO hotels exclusively for public welfare clients in New York City in the late 1960s and early 1970s. Unlike hotels on Skid Row, these hotels were dispersed in middle-class neighborhoods, stimulating considerable protest from the neighbors. The problem has expanded, causing enormous fiscal drain as hotel rates have been raised to keep pace with the extraordinary inflation of housing prices in Manhattan during the 1980s. In Los Angeles the hotels near Skid Row provide shelter for public welfare recipients who use vouchers from the county welfare department. Richard Ropers and Richard Boyer, *Living on Edge, The Sheltered Homeless: An Empirical Study of Los Angeles Single Room Occupancy Residents* (Los Angeles: UCLA School of Public Health, 1986).

11. Rossi, Fisher, and Willis, *The Condition of the Homeless*, pp. 95–100.

12. Claude Fischer, *To Dwell Among Friends* (Chicago, 1982), pp. 130–131, 252–253; George Hemmens et al., *Changing Needs and Social Services in Three Chicago Communities*, vol. 4 of *Hardship and Support Systems in Chicago* (Chicago, 1986).

13. Kevin Eckert, "The Unseen Community," *Aging* 129 (1979): 28–35; Kevin Eckert, "The Social Ecology of SRO Living," *Generations* 3 (Winter 1979): 22–23; Rosemary Erickson and Kevin Eckert, "The Elderly Poor in Downtown San Diego Hotels," *Gerontologist* 17 (1979): 440–46; Jay Sokolovsky et al., "Personal Networks of Ex-Mental Patients in a Manhattan SRO," *Human Organization* 37 (1978): 9; Siegal, *Outposts*, pp. 173–97.

14. Hemmens et al., *Changing Needs*, pp. 69–70.

15. Allan Graham, *A Sociology of Friendship and Kinship* (London, 1979); Fischer, *To Dwell Among Friends*, pp. 125–38.

16. Smithers, *Determined Survivors*, pp. 105–32; Karen Jonas and Edward Wellin, "Dependency and Reciprocity: Home Health Aid in an Elderly Population," in Christine Fry, ed., *Aging in Culture and Society* (New York, 1980), pp. 217–38; Nancy Sheehan, "Informal Support Among the Elderly in Public Senior Housing," *Gerontologist* 26 (1986): 171–75; Maria Teski, *Living Together: An Ethnography of a Retirement Hotel* (Washington, D.C., 1979), pp. 151–52.

17. The theoretical foundations for balanced reciprocity can be traced in sociology to George Homans, "Social Behavior as Exchange," *American Journal of Sociology* 62 (1958): 597–606; also Peter Blau, *Exchange and Power* (New York, 1964). The theoretical idea of generalized exchange was used by anthropologist Marshal Sahlins and applied by Larrisa Lomnitz, *Networks and Marginality* (New York, 1977), pp. 187–92.

18. Hemmens et al., *Changing Needs*, pp. 63–87.

Chapter 8

1. D. E. Mackelman, *The Homeless Man on Skid Row* (Chicago, 1961), pp. 96–98.

2. One important exception was Catherine Bower and Davis McEntire, *Relocation Study, Single Male Population, Sacramento's West End* (Sacramento: Sacramento Redevelopment Agency, 1953). The authors acknowledge the economic importance of the residents to the region and discuss options for relocating the entire community into new SRO-type quarters well served by the cluster of Skid Row services. In Chicago, many of the proposals of Ronald Vander Kooi were based on a recognition of the Skid Row community. See chapter 6.

3. The socioeconomic differences between the residents in the private rooms in two cubicle hotels and those in the sixteen hotels with private rooms are as follows (the first value for each characteristic is that of the cubicle hotel residents): *Social characteristics*—black: 6% and 57%; female: 0% and 27%; SRO veteran: 70% and 34%; average age: 52.3 years and 44.6 years; average stay at SRO: 2.3 years and 3.2 years; average income: $5,027 and $7,511; employed: 40% and 41%; laborer or operative: 63% and 30%. *Network characteristics*—average number all ties: 4.3 and 7.0; average SRO network size: 1.6 and 2.4; average personal helping network

size: 0.8 and 2.4; average size of SRO helping index: 1.3 and 1.6. *Rent*—average
rent payment: $99 and $220; average rent burden: 29% and 48%.

4. Donald Bogue, *Skid Row in American Cities* (Chicago, 1963), pp. 305–14.

5. Our interpretation contrasts somewhat with that offered by Janice Smithers in
her *Determined Survivors: Community Life among the Urban Elderly* (New Brunswick, N.J., 1985). Smithers argues that social ties in the SRO hotel she studied
led to mutual assistance because of a shared "conciousness of kind" among elderly
residents (p. 110). We utilize the broader concept of shared vulnerability.

6. Gene Lutz, *Understanding Social Statistics* (New York, 1983), pp. 107–109.

7. Smithers, *Determined Survivors*, pp. 107–113; Carl Cohen and Jay Sokolov-
sky, "Social Engagement versus Isolation: The Case of the Aged in SRO Hotels,"
Gerontologist 20 (1980): 36–44; Jay Sokolovsky, Carl Cohen, Dirk Berger, and
Josephine Geiger, "Personal Networks of Ex-Mental Patients in a Manhattan SRO
Hotel," *Human Organization* 37 (1978): 5–15; Janice Stephens, *Loners, Lovers and
Losers: Elderly Tenants in a Slum Hotel* (Seattle, 1976).

8. The regression models are given below. Significant effects show up as a
relatively high positive or negative coefficient value. (High in this case would mean
statistically significant.) The models take into account the independent effect of each
variable on the dependent variable (measures of security and safety in this case),
while simultaneously controlling for the effects of all the other independent variables
as well. Statistically significant coefficients are those marked with an asterisk (*)
or a plus sign ($^+$). Only those variables with such a sign provide reliable estimates
of the relationship between each independent variable and the dependent variable.
Although coefficient values are calculated for the other variables in each model,
these values when submitted to statistical test fall outside the limits of acceptable
error. The more social, economic, and hardship variables that produce a significant
effect on the dependent variable, the less likely it is that security or safety is not
related to the particular characteristics of residents. If, however, safety and security
hinge on the diversity rather than homogeneity of resident characteristics, as we
expected, then there should be few if any significant effects due to the independent
variables in the two models. The effects of select resident characteristics on the size
of security and safety scores are given below. The first regression coefficient for
each characteristic is for security; the second, for safety. The standard errors are
enclosed in parentheses. Levels of statistical significance are noted by * p < .01 and
$^+$ p < .05. Intercept: .244 (.325) and .208 (.180); woman: .257 (.224) and .154
(.136); black: .069 (.181) and .030 (.114); elderly: .296 (.167) and −.036 (.113);
SRO veteran: .168 (.201) and −.273 (.116)+; income: −.0000005 (.0000181) and
.000009 (.000012); economic hardship: −.027 (.119) and .232 (.074)*; personal
hardship: −.102 (.029) and .032 (.085); room score: .030 (.029) and −.00005
(.0174). R^2 = .075 (security) and .10$^+$ (safety).

9. Smithers, *Determined Survivors*, pp. 135–53; J. Gubrium, "Victimization in
Old Age," *Crime and Delinquency* 20 (1974): 245–50; Helene Lopata, "Support
Systems of Elderly Urbanites: Chicago of the 1970's," *Gerontologist* 5 (1975):
35–41.

Chapter 9

1. John Mollenkopf, *The Contested City* (Princeton, N.J., 1983), pp. 180–212.

2. Chester Hartman et al., *Yerba Buena: Land Grab and Community Resistance in San Francisco* (San Francisco, 1974), p. 105.

3. Ibid., p. 210.

4. U.S. Senate, Special Committee on Aging, *Single Room Occupancy: A Need for National Concern*, 95th Cong., 2nd sess. (Washington, D.C., 1978).

5. Paul Bradford, "Rehabilitating Residential Hotels," in the National Trust for Historic Preservation *Information Sheet* 31 (Washington, D.C., 1981), p. 3.

6. San Diego Housing Commission, *San Diego's Downtown Hotels:* SRO *Study* (San Diego, 1985), p. 4.

7. Phillip Kasinitz, "Gentrification and Homelessness: The Single Room Occupant and Inner City Revival," *Urban and Social Change Review* 17 (1984): 12.

8. David Varady, "Conserving Single Room Occupancy Housing: A Cincinnati Case Study," *Urban Resources* 2 (1985): 39.

9. Paul Flaim and Ellen Sehgal, "Displaced Workers of 1979–1983: How Well Have They Fared?" *Monthly Labor Review* 108 (June 1985): 3–16.

10. "New Age, Low Wage," *Dollars and Sense* 125 (April 1987): 12–13.

11. Ibid., p. 13.

12. "The Falling Minimum Wage," *Dollars and Sense* 117 (June 1986): 19. See also Isaac Shapiro, *No Escape: The Minimum Wage and Poverty* (Washington, D.C.,: Center on Budget Policy Priorities, 1987).

13. Kim Hopper and Jill Hamberg, "Making of America's Homeless: From Skid Row to New Poor, 1945–1984," in Rachel Bratt, Chester Hartman, and Ann Meyerson, eds., *Critical Perspectives on Housing* (Philadelphia, 1986), p. 20.

14. John Palmer and Isabel Sawhill, *The Reagan Record* (Cambridge, Mass.: 1984); and Paul Taylor, "The Coming Conflict as We Soak the Young to Enrich the Old," *Washington Post*, Jan. 5, 1986; both cited in F. Stevens Redburn and Terry Buss, *Responding to America's Homeless* (New York, 1986), p. 68.

15. Hopper and Hamberg, "Making of America's Homeless," p. 20.

16. Interview quote in Timothy McNulty, "New Approaches to Poverty Alter Conscience of Nation," *Chicago Tribune*, Mar. 17, 1985. See also Stephen Rose, *Social Stratification in the United States* (Baltimore, Md., 1983); U.S. Department of Commerce, Bureau of the Census, *Money Income and Poverty Status of Families and Persons in the United States* (Washington, D.C., 1985).

17. Austin Turner and Raymond Struyk, *Urban Housing in the 1980s: Markets and Policies* (Washington, D.C., 1984), p. 20.

18. Anthony Downs, *Rental Housing in the 1980s* (Washington, D.C., 1983), pp. 32–38.

19. Ibid., p. 107.

20. Peter Marcuse, "Abandonment, Gentrification, and Displacement: The Linkages in New York City," in Neil Smith and Peter Williams, eds., *Gentrification of the City* (Boston, 1986).

21. Downs, *Rental Housing*, p. 83.

22. Richard LeGates and Chester Hartman, "The Anatomy of Displacement in the United States," in Smith and Williams, eds., *Gentrification*, p. 198.

23. Dennis Gale, *Neighborhood Revitalization and the Postindustrial City* (Lexington, Mass., 1984), p. 13.

24. Grace Milgram and Robert Berry, "Existing Housing Resources vs. Need," *Congressional Research Service Report for Congress* No. 87-81 (Washington, D.C., Jan. 30, 1987), p. 8.

25. James Wright and Julie Lam, "Homelessness and the Low-Income Housing Supply," *Social Policy* 17 (Spring 1987): 51.

26. Michel McQueen, "Low Income Housing Demand to Reach Crisis Level in Near Future; Study Says," *Wall Street Journal*, June 3, 1987.

27. Chicago City Planning Department, *Report on Chicago's Low Income Single Renters* (Chicago, 1985), p. 35.

28. Eric Zorn, "Headaches and Heartaches: The St. Regis Checks Out," *Chicago Tribune*, Jan. 16, 1985.

29. Mary Ludgin and Louis Masotti, *Downtown Development in Chicago: 1979– 1984* (Evanston, Ill., 1985).

30. *New York Times*, Oct. 21, 1985.

31. All material on Presidential Towers comes from Arthur Lyons, *When Everything Works, and Nothing is Right* (Chicago, 1986), pp. 11–19.

32. All material on the Rialto comes from Barbara Bratman, "City Plan Threatens to Shut Book on Residential Hotel," *Chicago Tribune*, Jan. 5, 1988.

33. Lincoln, "Single Room Residential Hotels Must Be Preserved as Low-Income Housing Alternative," *Journal of Housing* 37 (1980): 383–86.

34. William Fulton, "A Room of One's Own," *Planning Magazine*, Sept. 1985, p. 15.

35. Fay Cook et al., *Stability and Change in Economic Hardship: Chicago 1983– 1985*, vol. 2 of *Hardship and Support Systems in Chicago* (Chicago: Center for Urban Affairs and Policy Research, Northwestern University, 1986), p. 6.

36. Matthew Stagner and Harold Richman, *General Assistance in Chicago: Finding of a Survey of New Recipients* (Chicago: National Opinion Research Center, University of Chicago, 1984): 24–25.

37. The figures for Chicago in the next several pages were calculated from tables in U.S. Department of Commerce, Bureau of the Census, *Housing Characteristics for Selected Metropolitan Areas: Chicago*, in *Current Housing Reports, Annual Housing Survey: 1983*, U.S. Department of Housing and Urban Development, Sponsor (Washington, D.C., 1985).

38. Cook et al., *Stability and Change*, p. 19.

39. *Chicago Tribune*, Oct. 3, 1984.

40. Peter Rossi, Gene Fisher, and Georgianna Willis, *The Condition of the Homeless in Chicago* (Chicago: National Opinion Research Center, 1986).

41. Stagner and Richman, *General Assistance in Chicago*.

42. Rossi, Fisher, and Willis, *The Condition of the Homeless*, p. 83.

43. Although there is merit to some of the criticisms of the NORC study by the advocates, most were neither fair nor correct. This is because the critics attacked what was the greatest strength of the report—its reliability and accuracy. The researchers spent hundreds of thousands of dollars to refine a sampling and survey technique to find and survey homeless people on the street and in shelters. Given their high standards of reliability, they did rather well. However, they made a mistake at the outset by limiting their focus to those confronting daily shelter uncer-

tainty. Why didn't the analysts argue for a more inclusive definition? Why didn't the advocates emphasize a broader definition as well?

We think they remained committed to the narrow focus for political reasons. Officials, reporters, caretakers, and the general public largely shared the perception of the new homeless as a dependent and needy subgroup deserving compassionate attention and aid. Focusing on the destitute, the "truly" homeless, meant focusing on those facing daily shelter uncertainty. Including others who were not so desperate and dependent seemed less pressing because, within this policy framework of compassion, priority should be given those with the greatest need. The researchers dutifully accepted these presuppositions in their research design. Pushing for a more inclusive focus would possibly have challenged these presuppositions and raised moral and policy questions about the purpose of the research. Perhaps the researchers considered these questions outside their legitimate roles. Nevertheless, the researchers did recognize this problem but side-stepped the issue by claiming insufficient resources. As for the advocates, on the face of it one would expect them to have directed their criticism mainly at the narrow focus of the survey, the point at which the study was weakest. The advocates, like the researchers, recognized that public and legislative support for helping the homeless was tied to feelings of compassion for the destitute homeless. A more inclusive definition, if publicly promoted, could threaten to undermine existing public support. Middle-class donors will aid the destitute homeless but reconsider when the homeless include poor people in rooming houses or public housing.

Chapter 10

1. See stories in *Newsweek*, Dec. 27, 1982; *U.S. News and World Report*, Jan. 7, 1983; *Washington Post*, Apr. 4, 1987.

2. Thomas Main, "The Homeless of New York," in Jon Erickson and Charles Wilhelm, eds., *Housing the Homeless* (Rutgers, N.J., 1986), pp. 99–104; S. Anna Kondratas, "A Strategy for Helping America's Homeless," *Heritage Foundation Background* no. 431 (May 1985).

3. Charles Hoch, "Homeless in the United States," *Housing Studies* 1 (Fall 1986): 234–35.

4. Mary Ellen Hombs and Mitch Snyder, *Homelessness in America: One Year Later* (Washington, D.C., 1983).

5. U.S. Department of Housing and Urban Development, *A Report to the Secretary on the Homeless and Emergency Shelters* (Washington, D.C., 1984).

6. U.S. Congress, House Committee on Backing, Finance and Urban Affairs, Subcommittee on Housing and Community Development, *HUD Report on the Homeless* (Washington, D.C., May 24, 1984).

7. A. Anthony Arce et al., "A Psychiatric Profile of Street People Admitted to an Emergency Shelter," *Hospital and Community Psychiatry* 34 (Sept. 1983): 814–15.

8. Frank Lipton, Albert Sabatini, and Steven Katz, "Down and Out in the City: The Homeless Mentally Ill," *Hospital and Community Psychiatry* 34 (Sept. 1983): 819.

9. Ellen Bassuk, "The Homeless Problem," *Scientific American* 25 (July 1984): 42.

10. David Snow et al., "The Myth of Pervasive Mental Illness Among the Homeless," *Social Problems* 33 (June 1986): 413–15.

11. F. Stevens Redburn and Terry Buss, *Responding to America's Homeless: Public Policy Alternatives* (New York, 1986), p. 85.

12. Peter Rossi, Gene Fisher, and Georgianna Willis, *The Condition of the Homeless in Chicago* (Chicago: National Opinion Research Center, 1985), pp. 112–24.

13. Michael Dear and Jennifer Wolch, *Landscapes of Despair, From Deinstitutionalization to Homelessness* (Princeton, N.J., 1987), pp. 8–26.

14. Ibid., p. 137.

15. Ibid., pp. 139–68.

16. Ed Marciniak, *Reversing Urban Decline* (Chicago, 1981), p. 19.

17. Ibid., p. 23.

18. Ibid., p. 25.

19. Ibid., p. 113.

20. Lawrence Appelby and Prakash Desai, "Documenting the Relationship Between Homelessness and Psychiatric Hospitalization," *Hospital and Community Psychiatry* 36 (July 1985): 733.

21. Lawrence Appelby, Nancy Slagg, and Prakash Desai, "The Urban Nomad: A Psychiatric Problem," *Current Psychiatric Therapies* 21 (1982): 255.

22. "Speaker Pledges Aid for Homeless," *Washington Post*, Jan. 17, 1987.

23. "A Night on the Grates," *Washington Post*, Mar. 9, 1987.

24. Illinois State Support Center, Summary of the Stewart B. McKinney Homeless Assistance Act H.R. 558, The Homeless Appropriations Bill, H.R. 1827 (Chicago, Sept. 9, 1987).

25. Low Income Housing Information Service, "Special Memorandum, The 1988 Low Income Housing Budget" (Washington, D.C., Apr. 1987), p. 7.

26. Kim Hopper and Stuart Cox, "Litigation in Advocacy for the Homeless: The Case of New York City," *Development: Seeds of Change* 2 (1982): 58.

27. Ibid., p. 60.

28. School of Architecture and Urban Planning, "Housing the Homeless in Los Angeles County: A Guide to Action," Class Project in Human Environment Relations (University of California—Los Angeles, 1985), pp. 98–99.

29. U.S. Department of Health and Human Services, *Helping the Homeless: A Resource Guide* (Washington, D.C., Summer 1984), p. 77.

30. Allan Heskin, "Los Angeles: Innovative Local Approaches," in Richard Bingham, Roy Green, and Sammis White, eds., *The Homeless in Contemporary Society*, (Newbury Park, Calif., 1987), pp. 179–80.

31. Constitution of the Chicago/Gary Area Union of the Homeless, Presented at the Founding Convention, United Electrical Radio and Machine Workers of America Union Hall, Chicago, March 8, 1986.

32. "Open Up CHA, Homeless Demand," *Chicago Tribune*, Jan. 6, 1988.

33. Ibid.

34. National Coalition for the Homeless, "Homelessness in the United States: Background and Federal Response" (New York, Sept. 1987).

35. See especially Charles Murray, *Losing Ground: American Social Policy, 1950–1980* (New York, 1984), and Richard Mergan, *Disabling America: The "Rights Industry" in Our Time* (New York, 1984).

36. Patricia Sexton, "The Life of the Homeless," in Erickson and Wilhelm, eds., *Housing the Homeless* pp. 77–78.

37. Perhaps the single best source analyzing this literature is Martin Bulmer, *Neighbors: The Work of Philip Abrams* (Cambridge, Mass., 1986). See also Peggy Wireman, *Urban Neighborhoods, Networks, and Families* (Lexington, Mass., 1984); Gerald Suttles, *The Social Construction of Communities* (Chicago, 1972); and Leland Burns, "Third World Solutions to the Homelessness Problem," in Bingham, Green, and White, eds., *Homeless in Contemporary Society*, pp. 231–48.

Chapter 11

1. Jonathan Kozol, *Rachel and Her Children* (New York, 1988).

2. New York Department of Social Services, *Annual Report to the Governor and the Legislature* (Albany, N.Y., Feb. 1987), p. 11.

3. William Bastone, "Who Owns the Welfare Hotels?" *Village Voice*, Apr. 8, 1986, p. 25.

4. Kathleen Hendrix, "Group Vows to Relocate Skid Row Families," *Los Angeles Times*, Dec. 23, 1983.

5. Andy Furillo, "Skid Row Unfit Even for Winos," *Los Angeles Herald Examiner*, Oct. 13, 1985.

6. Joan Crouse, *The Homeless Transient in the Great Depression: New York State, 1929–1941* (Albany, N.Y., 1986), p. 124.

7. See for instance John Lee, "Harrassing the Homeless," *Time*, Mar. 11, 1985, p. 68.

8. United States Conference of Mayors, *Homelessness in America's Cities: Ten Case Studies* (Washington, D.C., 1984).

9. U.S. Department of Housing and Urban Development, *A Report to the Secretary on the Homeless and Emergency Shelters* (Washington, D.C., 1984), p. 34.

10. Suzanne Daley, "City Homeless Reach a Peak in Population," *New York Times*, Jan. 10, 1987; N.Y. Department of Human Services, *Annual Report*, p. i.

11. Chicago Community Trust, "Chicago's Homeless: Who Should Shelter Them?" *Trust Inc.*, Nov. 18, 1982, p. 11; Chicago Coalition for the Homeless, *Shelter Directory* (Chicago, 1985).

12. Peter Rossi, Gene Fisher, and Georgianna Willis, *The Condition of the Homeless of Chicago* (Chicago: National Opinion Research Center, 1986), p. 133.

13. Chicago Coalition for the Homeless, "Emergency Shelter Dollars by Year and Funding Sources" (Chicago, 1988, mimeo).

14. Nancy Kaufman, "Homelessness: A Comprehensive Policy Approach," *Journal of Urban and Social Change Review* 17 (Winter 1984): 23.

15. U.S. Department of Health and Human Services, *Helping the Homeless: A Resource Guide* (Washington, D.C., 1984), p. 92.

16. HUD, *Report to the Secretary*, p. 42.

17. DHHS, *Helping the Homeless*, pp. 74–76.

18. Ibid., p. 84.

19. Deborah Dietsch, "Shelter from the Storm," *Architectural Record* 174 (June 1986): 140.

20. Ibid., p. 142.

21. Ibid., p. 136.

22. *New York Times*, Apr. 18 and May 9, 1986.

23. *Los Angeles Times*, Aug. 9, 1987.

24. Rossi, Fisher, and Willis, *Condition of the Homeless*, p. 136.

25. Douglas Timmer, "Homelessness as Deviance: The Ideology of the Shelter" (paper presented at Midwest Sociological Society Meetings, Chicago, Apr. 1987).

26. Michael Dear and Jennifer Wolch, *Landscapes of Despair* (Princeton, N.J., 1987), pp. 197–99.

27. Andrew Maier, "The Homeless and the Post-Industrial City," *Political Geography Quarterly* 5 (Oct. 1986): 357–63.

28. *Los Angeles Times*, Sept. 21, 1987.

29. *New York Times*, Nov. 11, 1987.

30. Ibid., Nov. 22, 1987.

31. Ibid., Jan. 30, 1987.

32. Eric Zorn, "What's Being Done to Help the Homeless," *Chicago Tribune*, Oct. 4, 1984.

Chapter 12

1. Earnest Bittner, "The Police on Skid Row: A Study of Peace Keeping," *American Sociological Review* 32 (1967): 699–715.

2. See, for instance, Michael Harrington, *The New American Poverty* (New York, 1984); H. Ginsburg, *Full Employment and Public Policy: The United States and Sweden* (Lexington, Mass., 1983); S. M. Miller and Donald Tomaskovic-Devey, *Recapitalizing America: Alternative to the Corporate Distortion of National Policy* (Boston, 1983); Neil Gilbert, *Capitalism and the Welfare State* (New Haven, 1983).

3. Phillip Kasinitz, "Gentrification and Homelessness: The Single Room Occupant and Inner City Revival," *Urban and Social Change Review* (1983): 12.

4. Bradford, Paul, "Rehabilitating Residential Hotels," in *Information: National Trust for Historic Preservation* (Washington, D.C., 1981), p. 13.

5. Anthony Blackburn, *Single Room Occupancy in New York City* (New York: Department of Housing Preservation and Development, Jan. 1986), pp. 1–6, 7.

6. Cindy McKee, "Conversion Moratorium for Hotel Residents," *Shelterforce* 10 (July/Aug. 1987): 19.

7. Maria Laurino, "Better Homes and Guardians," *Village Voice*, Apr. 8, 1986.

8. Saul Friedman, "Partners' Investing Covers Homeless," *New York Newsday*, Jan. 5, 1986.

9. Los Angeles Community Redevelopment Agency, *Public Policy in Central City East: 1974–1985* (Los Angeles, Dec. 1985), p. 1.

10. Los Angeles Community Redevelopment Agency, *Inventory of Homeless Housing and Special Needs Programs* (Los Angeles, Apr. 1986).

11. U.S. Department of Housing and Urban Development, Office of Policy Development and Research, *Official U.S. Special Merit Award Projects Monographs* (Washington, D.C., 1987), pp. 84–91.

12. Dina Klugman Cramer, "Skid Row Redevelopment Plan Considers the Needs of L.A.'s Homeless, Indigent," *Western City*, Sept. 1983, p. 5.

13. SRO Housing Corporation, *Annual Report* (Los Angeles, 1986), p. 3.

14. Ibid.

15. Gary Abrams, "Reweaver of L.A.'s Skid Row Safety Net," *Los Angeles Times*, Nov. 6, 1986.

16. Ibid.

17. Jess Carlos, "Out of Isolation: Unique Social Service Agency Helps SRO Tenants," *Uptown News*, Sept. 16–17, 1986.

18. Danny Kadden and Alan Goldberg, "Shelter for the Poor: 'SRO's Can Work,' " *The Neighborhood Works* 2 (Mar./Apr. 1988): 16.

19. Steve Kerch, "Norman Hotel Commitment Sets Pace for Low Rent Rehabs," *Chicago Tribune*, Aug. 16, 1987.

20. Jane Heron, "Single Room Occupancy Hotels Take Step Up," *Chicago Sun Times*, Apr. 15, 1988.

21. Patricia King, "Help for the Homeless," *Newsweek*, Apr. 11, 1988, p. 59.

22. Housing Section, Bureau of Planning, City of Portland, *Status Report on Low-Income Housing in Downtown Portland* (Portland, Ore., Mar. 1986), p. 6.

23. Ibid., pp. 10–12.

24. Kathleen Ryan and Mark Beach, *Burnside: A Community* (Portland, Ore., 1979), p. 3.

25. Burnside Community Council, *The Homeless Times* 1 (Summer 1986): 10.

26. Francis Werner and David Bryson, "A Guide to the Preservation and Maintenance of Single Room Occupancy (SRO) Housing," *Clearing House Review*, May 1982, p. 11.

27. McKee, "Conversion Moratorium," p. 19.

28. City of San Diego, Residential Hotel Regulations, Municipal Code, Division 19, Section 101.1909, adopted Nov. 16, 1987.

29. Dan Pearlman, "Preservation of Housing in Downtown Seattle," *Housing Law Bulletin* (Mar./Apr. 1987): 33.

30. King, "Help for the Homeless," p. 59.

31. Neal Pierce and Carol Steinbach, *Corrective Capitalism: The Rise of America's Community Development Corporations* (New York: Ford Foundation, 1987), pp. 8–9.

32. Jacqueline Leavitt and Susan Saegart, "The Community Household: Responding to Housing Abandonment in New York City," *Journal of the American Planning Association* 53 (Fall 1988, forthcoming).

33. Rachel Bratt, "Community Based Housing Programs: Overview, Assessment, and Agenda for the Future," *Journal of Planning Education and Research* 5 (Spring 1986): 170.

34. Low Income Housing Information Service, *Low Income Housing Roundup* 108 (May 1987).

35. Carroll Kowal, "Housing Needs of Single Persons," *Journal of Housing* 6 (1976): 277–81.

36. See, for instance, the proposals by Robert Kuttner, *The Life of the Party* (New York, 1987).

37. See, for instance, the proposals in David Schwartz, Richard Ferlauto, and Daniel Hoffman, *A New Housing Policy for America* (Philadelphia, 1988), pp. 273–79.

Appendix A

1. See for instance: Joan Shapiro, "Single Room Occupancy: Community of the Alone," *Social Work* 11 (1966): 24–33; Janice Stephens, *Loners, Lovers and Losers: Elderly Tenants in a Slum Hotel* (Seattle, 1976); Harvey Siegal, *Outposts of the Forgotten: New York City's Welfare Hotels and Single Occupancy Tenements* (Edison, N.J., 1977); Janice Smithers, *Determined Survivors* (New Brunswick, N.J., 1985).

2. These usually included local surveys of hotels like the following: San Francisco Community Design Center, *A Survey of Residential Hotels in San Francisco as a Source of Low Rent Housing* (San Francisco, 1976); New York City Office of Crisis Intervention, *The Diminishing Resource: Lower-Priced Hotels in New York City* (New York: Human Resources Administration, 1979); Skid Row Development Corporation, *Preliminary Results of the Skid Row Hotel Survey* (Los Angeles, 1980).

INDEX

Abbott, Grace, 67, 69, 77
Aid to Families with Dependent
    Children (AFDC), 129, 135, 177,
    237
Alcoholism: and the homeless, 204;
    Skid Row residents and, 4–5, 45,
    93, 98–100, 108–10, 122, 127
Allsop, Kenneth, 12, 63
Anderson, Nels, 35, 46, 48, 51, 63
Appleby, Lawrence, 207–8
Autonomy: of lodging house resi-
    dents, 44–46, 52–53; maintenance
    of, 9, 110; of the poor, 7–9, 124,
    226; and privacy, 130; of rooming
    house residents, 21–24; of Skid
    Row residents, 100–101, 102; and
    social community, 124, 126; of
    SRO residents, 148, 150–51, 234;
    struggle for, 200

Bahr, Howard, 92, 99, 109, 111–12,
    147, 208
Baltimore, 4; Pratt Street in, 29
Barnett, Ida-Wells, 25
Barth, Gunther, 22
Bassuk, Ellen, 204
Bastone, William, 221
Bauer, Catherine, 73, 281n
Baxter, Ellen, 240
Beck, Frank, 59
Beggars. See Bums
Berry, Bob, 182
Bird, Frederick, 109
Blackburn, Anthony J., 222
Blacks: in lodging houses, 29–32, 38;
    in rooming houses, 24–26; on Skid
    Row, 97–98, 102; in SRO hotels,
    136, 147, 153, 164
Blaine, Anita McCormick, 67–68
Blumberg, Leonard, 110, 116
Boarding houses, 14–15, 16
Bogue, Donald, 92, 94–95, 103,
    109–10, 124, 126–27, 147, 155,
    161, 192, 208

Borchert, James, 17, 32
Boston, 11, 18–19, 21, 48–49, 54,
    58, 69, 117, 122; Scollay Square
    in, 29
Boyer, Richard, 222
Bratman, Barbara, 185
Breaky, William, 4
Breckenridge, Sophonisba, 67–68
Bruns, Roger, 72
Building codes, 69, 101, 155, 186,
    238, 243; enforcement of, 84;
    history of, 69–70; reform of, 249–
    50. See also Urban renewal, code
    enforcement and
Bums, 38, 41–44, 96, 125–26, 132,
    236
Burgess, Ernest, 66–67, 70
Buss, Terry F., 205
Byrne, Carol, 229

Cafeterias. See Lodging houses, and
    nearby services; Rooming houses,
    and nearby services; Skid Row,
    services in
Cage hotels, photo, 138. See also
    Cubicle hotels; Lodging houses,
    physical description of
Cain, James M., 33
Capital markets, 178
Caplow, Theodore, 92, 109, 111–12
Caretakers, of the homeless, 5, 197,
    202, 215, 218, 225–26; profes-
    sional, 203
Cayton, Horace, 25
Central Business District (CBD),
    178, 186. See also Inner city
Charitable hotels, 21–22, 26, 57
Charity Organization Society of New
    York City, 201
Chicago: Chicago Christian Industrial
    League, 58, 74, 103; and Chicago
    School Sociologists, 112–13; and
    Coalition for the Homeless, 230,
    243; and Gary Area Union for the

291